PATERNOSTER THEOLOGICAL MONOGRAPHS

Barth and Dostoevsky

A Study of the Influence of the Russian Writer
Fyodor Mikhailovich Dostoevsky on the Development
of the Swiss Theologian Karl Barth, 1915-1922

PATERNOSTER THEOLOGICAL MONOGRAPHS

A full listing of all titles in this series and Paternoster Biblical Monographs will be found at the close of this book.

Karl Barth (left) and Eduard Thurneysen at the Bergli, Summer 1920

PATERNOSTER THEOLOGICAL MONOGRAPHS

Barth and Dostoevsky

A Study of the Influence of the Russian Writer
Fyodor Mikhailovich Dostoevsky on the Development
of the Swiss Theologian Karl Barth, 1915-1922

P.H. Brazier

Foreword by Stephen R. Holmes

WIPF & STOCK · Eugene, Oregon

Wipf and Stock Publishers
199 W 8th Ave, Suite 3
Eugene, OR 97401

Barth and Dostoevsky
A Study of the Influence of the Russian Writer Fyodor Mikhailovich Dostoevsky
on the Development of the Swiss Theologian Karl Barth, 1915-1922
By Brazier, P. H.
Copyright©2007 Paternoster
ISBN 13: 978-1-55635-868-5
Publication date 2/20/2008

This Edition Published by Wipf and Stock Publishers by arrangement with Paternoster

PATERNOSTER THEOLOGICAL MONOGRAPHS

Series Preface

In the West the churches may be declining, but theology—serious, academic (mostly doctoral level) and mainstream orthodox in evaluative commitment—shows no sign of withering on the vine. This series of *Paternoster Theological Monographs* extends the expertise of the Press especially to first-time authors whose work stands broadly within the parameters created by fidelity to Scripture and has satisfied the critical scrutiny of respected assessors in the academy. Such theology may come in several distinct intellectual disciplines—historical, dogmatic, pastoral, apologetic, missional, aesthetic and no doubt others also. The series will be particularly hospitable to promising constructive theology within an evangelical frame, for it is of this that the church's need seems to be greatest. Quality writing will be published across the confessions—Anabaptist, Episcopalian, Reformed, Arminian and Orthodox—across the ages—patristic, medieval, reformation, modern and counter-modern—and across the continents. The aim of the series is theology written in the twofold conviction that the church needs theology and theology needs the church—which in reality means theology done for the glory of God.

Series Editors

David F. Wright, Emeritus Professor of Patristic and Reformed Christianity, University of Edinburgh, Scotland, UK

Trevor A. Hart, Head of School and Principal of St Mary's College School of Divinity, University of St Andrews, Scotland, UK

Anthony N.S. Lane, Professor of Historical Theology and Director of Research, London School of Theology, UK

Anthony C. Thiselton, Emeritus Professor of Christian Theology, University of Nottingham, Research Professor in Christian Theology, University College Chester, and Canon Theologian of Leicester Cathedral and Southwell Minster, UK

Kevin J. Vanhoozer, Research Professor of Systematic Theology, Trinity Evangelical Divinity School, Deerfield, Illinois, USA

For Hilary

Contents

Tables and Graphics	xv
Foreword by Stephen R. Holmes	xvii
Acknowledgements	xxi
Introduction	1
Barth on Dostoevsky	1
Why No Dostoevsky?	2
Aims and Objectives	2
Romans	3
Liberal and Atheist?	3

PART ONE
REVOLUTIONARY THEOLOGY IN THE MAKING

Chapter One: Wendung und Retraktation	7
Karl Barth and Eduard Thurneysen	7
Barth's Theological Development	8
Comrade Barth and War	10
Wendung und Retraktation	14
Hermann Kutter	16
Barth and Thurneysen's Theological Agenda: 'The Problem'	17
Chapter Two: The Apophatic Barth - God's Aseity	19
Kriegszeit und Gottesreich	19
Apophatic Language and Concepts	22
Dialectic and a Critique of Religion in the Service of the Gospel	25

PART TWO
KARL BARTH - SCHULD UND SÜHNE

Chapter Three: Sonya and Raskolnikov-
a Dialectic of Sin and Grace   31
    Crime and Punishment   31
    Trespass and Reparation   32
    Atheism   33
    Dialectic in Dostoevsky's Doctrine of God   35
    Dostoevsky - Judgement and Intellectual Sins   39
    'The Idea'   40

Chapter Four: Die Gerechtigkeit Gottes   47
    Wilfulness   47
    eritis sicut deus - The Tower of Babel   47
    Barth and The Tower of Babel   49
    Dostoevsky and The Tower of Babel   53
    Conscience and the Critical Realism of God   58
    Conscience as Liberal Piety ?   59
    Graceful Sin - Sinful Grace   60
    Luther and Calvin   62

Chapter Five: Barth on the Influence of Dostoevsky   65
    Der römische Katholizismus als Frage an die
       protestantische Kirche (1928)   65
    Barth and Rome   66
    Sin, Grace and Dostoevsky   68
    Grace, Forgiveness and Redemption - Christian Soteriology   71
    Barth's Theological Education - Neo-Protestant Liberalism   73
    Barth on the Influence of Dostoevsky   73
    Von Balthasar's Understanding   76

Chapter Six: Barth and Thurneysen's Theological Agenda: 'The Solution' — 79
Reading: Barth and Paul - Thurneysen and Dostoevsky — 79
Dostoevsky and the Russian New Testament — 81
Die neue Welt in der Bibel — 84
The Early Influence of Dostoevsky on Barth: Interim Conclusion — 86

PART THREE
THURNEYSEN AND BARTH - THEOLOGY, MINISTRY AND PASTORAL CARE

Chapter Seven: Eduard Thurneysen — 91
Eduard Thurneysen (1888-1974) — 91
Works - Ministerial — 94
Works - Theological — 95

Chapter Eight: Pastoral Theology — 99
Die Lehre von der Seelsorge — 99
Sin and the Human Condition before God — 102

Chapter Nine: *Dostojewski* — 107
What is Humanity? — 107
Dostoevsky's Men and Women — 108
Dostoevsky's Perspective — 110
Ivan Karamazov, The Grand Inquisitor, and the Devil — 112
Knowledge of God — 113
Summary of Thurneysen's *Dostojewski* — 114

Chapter Ten: Influences on Thurneysen and Barth's Understanding of Dostoevsky — 117
Thurneysen and Barth's Understanding of Dostoevsky — 117
Influences on Thurneysen: Herman Hesse — 118
Influences on Thurneysen: Stefan Zweig, Karl Nötzel
    Akim Lwowitsch Wolynski and Jeremias Gotthelf — 119
Dostoevsky - 'this Russian' — 122
Russian Orthodoxy and Eastern Platonism ? — 123

Chapter Eleven: Theological Existentialism   **129**
   Religion as the Result of the Fall   130
   Feuerbach and Dostoevsky   133
   God-Humanity   136

PART FOUR
DOSTOEVSKY AND *RÖMERBRIEF 2*

Chapter Twelve: Barth and *Der Römerbrief*   **141**
   Barth-Thurneysen: The Period of The Rewriting of
      Der Römerbrief   141
   Correspondence 1919-1923   141
   Römerbrief 1 (1916-18, Published 1919)   149
   Römerbrief 2 (1920-21, Published 1922)   154
   Der Christ in der Gesellschaft (1919)   155

Chapter Thirteen: Kierkegaard and Dostoevsky   **159**
   Influences on the Rewriting of *Römerbrief 2*   159
   Kierkegaard or Dostoevsky   161
   Infinite Qualitative Distinction   162
   Dialectic and an Interpretation of the New Testament   164
   A Criticism of Religion in the Service of the Gospel   166
   The Nature of the Influence of Kierkegaard and Dostoevsky   168

Chapter Fourteen: Dostoevsky and *Römerbrief 2*   **171**
   The Nature of the Evidence   171
   The Content and Spread of the References to Dostoevsky
      and Others in *Römerbrief 2*: Sources Secular and Ecclesial   171
   Göttingen - a Reformed position   178

Chapter Fifteen: Theological Anthropology   **181**
   Theological Anthropology: The Human Condition and the
      Nature of the Relationship of Sin and Grace between
      Humanity and God   181
   Theological Anthropology in *Römerbrief 2*   181
   The Human Condition before God   182

Chapter Sixteen: A Criticism of Church-Religion — 187

A Criticism of Church-Religion: The Grand Inquisitor,
  Roman Catholicism, Socialism and Atheism — 187
The Brothers Karamazov, Ivan Karamazov and
  The Legend of The Grand Inquisitor — 188
The Influence of Ivan Karamazov on Barth and Thurneysen — 189
Hebrew Religion and the Church seen as Synonymous — 192
Dialectic of Faith-Religion and Theism-Atheism — 193
Criticism of the Pseudo-Religious Archetype of a
  Socialist-Communist Revolutionary — 195

Chapter Seventeen: The Paradox of Christlikeness — 197

The Paradox of Christlikeness: The Parables of Jesus
  and the Characters of Dostoevsky — 197
Myshkin and Alyosha - Christlike Archetypes — 199

Conclusion — 203

The Marginalizing of Kierkegaard and Dostoevsky — 203
Influence or Illustration ? — 203
An Understanding/Doctrine of Sin and Grace ? — 204
Conclusion - Barth and Dostoevsky — 207

Bibliography — 209

1. Karl Barth: Works — 210
2. Eduard Thurneysen: Works — 217
3. Karl Barth and Eduard Thurneysen: Joint Works — 222
4. Fyodor Mikhailovich Dostoevsky: Works — 223
5. General Sources — 229

Index — 233

1. Index of Names — 233
2. Index of Subjects — 236

Tables and Graphics

Frontispiece
Karl Barth (left) and Eduard Thurneysen at the Bergli, Summer 1920

Figure 1
Dostoevsky's Theological Anthropology   44

Figure 2
'The Idea' - Dostoevsky, Nietzsche, Thurneysen and Barth   45

Figure 3
Barth and Thurneysen - The Tower of Babel   57

Figure 4
Thurneysen's Use of Dostoevsky - References   137

Figure 5
A Religion-Atheism Dialectic   166

Figure 6
The Content and Spread of the References to Dostoevsky and Others
in *Römerbrief 2* - Sources Secular and Ecclesial   173

Figure 7
Dostoevsky and *Römerbrief 2*   175

Figure 8
Römerbrief 2 Dostoevsky and Theological Anthropology - Evidence   181

Figure 9
Römerbrief 2 Dostoevsky and a Criticism of Church-Religion - Evidence   187

Figure 10
Römerbrief 2 Dostoevsky and the Paradox of Christlikeness - Evidence   197

Foreword

The book you have before you might surprise you; it surprised me as I watched it gradually come into focus. I had thought, not unreasonably, that the data concerning Karl Barth's movement from his disenchantment with the liberal theology of his early education to his mature position had all been gathered. There was no doubt room for new interpretation of the data on this point or that, but new evidence was unlikely to appear. The admirable scholarship of Bruce McCormack's *Karl Barth's Critically Realistic Dialectical Theology: Its Genesis and Development* seemed to represent the high-water mark.[1] The story has been told often enough, but perhaps a brief rehearsal is in order here.

Karl Barth had studied theology in many of the leading universities of Germany whilst training for the pastorate. He came under the instruction of two of the great intellects of the later period of German liberal theology, Wilhelm Herrmann (in Marburg) and Adolf Harnack (later created von Harnack) (in Berlin). There he learnt a sophisticated theology, built on neo-Kantian philosophy and an understanding of intellectual history, not unconnected to Hegelianism, to which Harnack himself was perhaps the greatest single contributor. Whilst the crude Hegelian history of an earlier generation, postulating Christianity as the result of a collision between a Jewish 'thesis' and a Hellenistic 'antithesis', had been discarded, the overarching notion of a direction and a progression within history, and the concept of Hellenistic ideas as something alien to, and distorting of, the original message of Jesus of Nazareth remained key (as indeed it still does in some circles). Herrmann, meanwhile, was part of a developing theology that assumed a broadly Kantian critique of what had once been orthodoxy (whether Lutheran, Reformed, or Roman Catholic), and attempted reconstruction along lines first indicated by Schleiermacher. At the heart of the critique was a simple refusal to believe that a particular historical person or event could be of decisive and universal significance, and so a re-visioning of Jesus of Nazareth as the exemplar and

---

[1] Bruce McCormack, *Karl Barth's Critically Realistic Dialectical Theology: Its Genesis and Development 1909-1936* (Oxford: Oxford University Press, Clarendon Paperbacks, 1995).

teacher of an ideal to which we could and should all aspire, and towards which (combining with the historical assumptions) the world, led of course by civilized Europe, was pressing.

After a brief time in Geneva, Barth's first solo pastorate was in a small and basically industrial town in the Aargau, called Safenwil. He went basically believing what he had been taught; he served there for ten years, during which time he lost confidence in all he had learnt (as he was to put it, in 'an entire world of theological exegesis, ethics, dogmatics, and preaching...'[2] And, with his old college friend Eduard Thurneysen, he set about searching for sources that might point a way to reconstruction.

Barth recalls, apparently with some amusement, his surprise at the source he and Thurneysen finally found adequate: the Scriptures. As is well known, he set himself to reading Paul's letter to the Romans, and noting what he found there. Published, these notes on *Der Römerbrief* were a sensation, and catapulted Barth into the theological controversy and celebrity that he enjoyed or endured for the rest of his life. It is well enough known also that the first edition of *Der Römerbrief* is not the most exegetically tight commentary ever written (today I suppose it could be seen as a pioneering example of reader-response criticism...). It is, however, a trumpeting of certain new theological conclusions with quite astonishing insistence and power. But whence these conclusions? This is the question to which this study makes a contribution.

In telling his own story of that crucial decade, Barth makes much of the influence of experiencing the realities of pastoral work, of looking for a theology that would speak meaningfully to his people. Swiss social democracy, and its Christian expression by Hermann Kutter and then the Blumhardts, father and son, was important to Barth for a while for precisely such reasons. Again, the influence of seeing his former teachers' support for the war policy of the Kaiser was later recalled to be shattering by Barth. More positively, an encounter with the philosophy of Kierkegaard offered a first glimpse of what reconstruction might look like, and the writings of Overbeck helped to put flesh on it—as I say, the story is familiar enough, and told magisterially by Bruce McCormack.

So when Paul Brazier began his doctorate with me in this area, I expected little more than a conversation with, and perhaps some footnotes to, McCormack. Over the next two years, however, Paul convinced me that there was new data concerning this period, and extraordinarily interesting data too. There was a source for Barth's restless questionings and nascent ideas that had gone all-but unremarked, which turned out to be rather decisive. Despite Barth's own (repeated) acknowledgement of a debt, the work of Fyodor Dostoevsky, the great Russian novelist, had been ignored almost completely as an influence on Barth's developing thought, and yet influence it was - and

---

[2] Karl Barth, *The Theology of Schleiermacher Lectures at Göttingen Winter Semester 1923-4* (Edinburgh: T&T Clark, 1982), p. 265.

serious and important influence as well.

That story is Paul's to tell in the body of the book. He traces, with careful attention to detail and admirable clarity, the various textual indications that Dostoevsky was indeed important to Barth, and what may be deduced from them. He locates the importance of the influence historically and theologically, indicating not just when Barth was influenced, but also which ideas were being derived from the novelist's writings. I feel confident in saying that the evidence considered is displayed here exhaustively: unless there are as-yet-undiscovered manuscripts that add more, Paul Brazier has given us a complete account of the data on this question.

The excellence of the study, however, does not lie in its exhaustiveness. The handling of the data is careful, judicious and deft. Paul Brazier does not just give us compelling evidence that Barth was influenced by Dostoevsky; he gives us a convincing account of the precise nature of the influence, of how it was transmitted, when it arrived, and at what point Barth left it behind. Paul is careful not to overstate his conclusions, or to claim more than the evidence allows. He acknowledges candidly and openly that this was not the major reading in Barth's life. He is appropriately reticent, indicating with some exactness what may be proved from his data, and pointing towards what might be assumed, without ever claiming more than the data allows.

What difference, finally, does this study make? It adds to our knowledge of the development of Barth's theology, unquestionably. Not just through identifying the influence of Dostoevsky, but through a timely reminder that Barth and Thurneysen were working together, and that Thurneysen took the lead as often as Barth did in those early years (as an aside, if Paul's work leads others to pick up with renewed interest Thurneysen's book on Dostoevsky, that would be no bad thing). Perhaps the work also helps, if help is needed, to recapture Dostoevsky as a profound, and profoundly Christian, novelist, whose writings should be of more interest to theologians than they have so far been.

Stephen R. Holmes
St Andrews
March 2007

Acknowledgements

This study is derived from my doctoral work at King's College London. My gratitude goes first to my supervisor Dr. Stephen R. Holmes, and to Dr Murray Rae who took over after the unexpected death of Prof. Colin E. Gunton. Originally my research was to have been on Barth's use of apophatic language and theological concepts, however, it was Stephen Holmes who noted how Dostoevsky's name kept cropping up and suggested I took a term (a half semester) to see if I could pin down the influence of this Russian writer - provided it was more than the obvious illustrative use which the Barthian scholarly tradition acknowledged. My gratitude as well goes to Prof. Oliver Davis also of King's and to the other research students and post-doctoral researchers of the Research Institute in Systematic Theology at King's to whom much of the research was first presented in academic papers.

My thanks go to Dr Iain Taylor, a fellow researcher at King's. Where no translation of the German material was available I have either translated passages myself or I commissioned a translation from Iain: for example, the essay by Friedrich Gogarten on Karl Barth's *Die christliche Dogmatik im Entwurf*. Substantial sections of the first edition of *Der Römerbrief*, also letters and extracts from correspondence between Barth and Thurneysen were translated by Iain, some by myself. My thanks go to Patrick Madigan S.J. for proof-reading the final text for me; my gratitude also go to Derek Brower for advising on and verifying my Russian.

The photograph on the cover and the frontispiece of Barth and Thurneysen is courtesy of the Special Collections, Princeton Theological Seminary Libraries on behalf of the Karl Barth Stiftung of Basel, Switzerland.

Paul Brazier
May 2007

'Very truly, I tell you,
unless a grain of wheat falls into the earth
and dies, it remains just a single grain;
but if it dies, it bears much fruit.'
John 12:24

quoted by Dostoevsky after the title page
of Братья Карамазовы,
(*Bratia Karamazovy - The Brothers Karamazov*)

INTRODUCTION

Barth on Dostoevsky

In the late 1940s the Swiss theologian Karl Barth visited Germany, a country that he had been expelled from by the Nazis almost a generation earlier. It was at this time, in 1946, that he presented the now famous *Dogmatik im Grundriß* in the ruins of the once beautiful and palatial Kurfursten Schloss in Bonn.[1] In 1947 Barth conducted a lecture tour that culminated in a visit to Berlin at the beginning of August. Moving on to Dresden he met lay representatives of various churches. After presenting a lecture to an audience of over three and a half thousand he attended a reception where he gave an after-dinner speech on the Russian writer Fyodor Mikhailovich Dostoevsky (1821-1881), in particular this novelist's understanding of humanity. The topic of this speech was of interest to a Soviet army officer at the reception who proceeded to discuss Barth's presentation of Dostoevsky's theological anthropology with him. Unfortunately no record exists of this, we may surmise, heated discussion - though Barth recalls in a letter to his wife and family on 13 August 1947 that 'I said that the Red Army now had an opportunity to show this humanity to Germany.'[2] Why did he choose Dostoevsky as a topic for this after-dinner speech? Was this a one-off idea? Or was this novelist's ideas and theology more than a mere passing interest to Barth? The answer is yes, Barth had been interested in this Russian since 1915, and Dostoevsky's ideas had pressed, to a greater or lesser degree, on Barth at the time of his move away from nineteenth-century Liberal neo-Protestant theology.

---

[1] Karl Barth, *Dogmatik im Grundriß* (München: Christian Kaiser Verlag, 1947).
[2] Eberhard Busch, *Karl Barths Lebenslauf: nach seinem Briefen und autobiographischen Texten* (München: Christian Kaiser Verlag, 1975), pp. 359-360; ET: Eberhard Busch, *Karl Barth His Life from Letters and Autobiographical Texts* (trans. John Bowden; London: SCM Press, 1976), p. 346. Busch is quoting from letters to his family (13 August 1947) to H. Obendiek (15 August 1947) and to L. Dennenberg (27 March 1959), 'There followed a two-day visit to Dresden, where the Mayor, Martin Richter, showed Barth the "exceptional devastation of the city". After his lecture on The Church to an audience of three and a half thousand, at a reception he sat next to a Soviet officer "whose interest I caught by my after-dinner speech on Dostoyevsky and his attractive humanity".'

Why No Dostoevsky ?

During his lifetime Barth acknowledged that as with the Danish philosopher Søren Kierkegaard the theological ideas of Dostoevsky had influenced him as a young pastor/minister, also that he began to move on and distance himself from these heady existential influences as his mature work developed. Both T. F. Torrance and Hans Urs von Balthasar - two post-war theologians who worked with Barth - acknowledged Dostoevsky as an influence on the formation of Barth's theological ideas;[3] however, after Barth's death in 1968 the Barthian scholarly tradition gradually marginalizes and then denies the place of Dostoevsky as one amongst a range of influences on the young Barth.[4] This study in effect redresses the balance.

Aims and Objectives

The primary aim of this work is to demonstrate that exposure to the writings and thereby the theology of the Russian writer Fyodor Mikhailovich Dostoevsky affected the development of the theology of Karl Barth. The secondary aim is to demonstrate that the theological beliefs of Dostoevsky exerted an influence on a key element of the redevelopment of Barth's theology: his understanding of sin and grace. This influence can be traced specifically to the period 1915-16. There is also a further influence exerted around the years 1918-21, when Barth used Dostoevsky illustratively. The objective of this work is to investigate the nature of the influence of Dostoevsky on Barth: the primary objective will be an investigation into Barth's understanding of the nature of the relationship of sin and grace between humanity and God, which hinges upon a particular understanding of theological anthropology - Barth explicitly assigns this to the influence of Dostoevsky and is evidenced in Barth's correspondence and some of his early lectures. The secondary objective will be an investigation into references by Barth to Dostoevsky in specific addresses he gave and the second edition of his

---

[3] See T.F. Torrance, *Karl Barth: An Introduction to his Early Theology 1910-1931* (Edinburgh: T&T Clark, 1962); and Hans Urs von Balthasar, *Karl Barth, Darstellung und Deutung seiner Theologie* (Köln: Verlag Jakob Hegner, 1951); ET: Hans Urs von Balthasar, *The Theology of Karl Barth - Exposition and Interpretation* (trans. Edward T. Oates, S.J.; San Francisco: Ignatius Press, Communio Books, 1991). All subsequent references are to this English edition and not the John Drury translation from 1971.

[4] A full discursive analysis of what the Barthian scholarly tradition has written on the influence or otherwise of Dostoevsky on Barth is to be found in the doctoral work, on which this study is based: P.H. Brazier, '"Die Freiheit in der Gefangenschaft Gottes", The Nature and Content of the Influence of Dostoevsky on Karl Barth 1915 to 1922' (PhD thesis, King's College London, 2005). See chp. 1 section 1.2 'A Review of Scholarship on Barth's Development' sub-sections a. 'Why no Dostoevsky?' and b. 'Der Krisis in der Offenbarung', pp. 46-56 and 56-59.

Introduction

commentary on Romans - *Der Römerbrief* - though in this instance Dostoevsky is amongst a panoply of writers, artists and philosophers, also theologians, church historians and pastors that Barth used illustratively; specific attention will be paid to Eduard Thurneysen's theological studies of Dostoevsky's writings. The tertiary objective will be to investigate the general influence of Dostoevsky that permeates Barth's writings in the period 1915 to 1922. Therefore the thesis underpinning this study is that the works and thereby the theological beliefs of Dostoevsky exerted an influence on Barth from 1915. Furthermore this influence is also discernable in *Römerbrief 2*. This work takes the conclusions of Bruce McCormack as a given and as a base line. Nothing in this work contradicts his - merely fills the gaps. This work is therefore an attempt to systematically identify, quantify and explicate the influence and use of Dostoevsky on and by Barth.[5]

Romans

Barth's commentary on the apostle Paul's Epistle to the Romans - *Der Römerbrief* - is crucial in understanding this influence: the first edition (written between the summer of 1916 and August 1918, and published in the summer of 1919) is hereafter referred to as *Römerbrief 1*; the rewriting of *Der Römerbrief* as the second edition (written between October 1920 and September 1921, and published in September 1922) is hereafter referred to as *Römerbrief 2*.[6] The title *Der Römerbrief* will be used when referring to both first and second editions, or subsequent editions of Barth's commentary on Paul's Epistle to the Romans.

Liberal and Atheist ?

The influence of Dostoevsky is set against the background of Barth's reaction against his liberal heritage. Liberal/liberalism whether with an initial capital or not is often seen as a contentious and problematic word - often it appears to generate an emotional response, may be considered pejorative and may also be invoked in an equally subjective manner. In this work the word liberal/liberalism is used strictly in the context of nineteenth-century German Liberal Protestantism (often referred to by Barth and Thurneysen as neo-

---

[5] Barth's development against which the influence of Dostoevsky is to be demonstrated is adequately presented by McCormack, *Karl Barth's Critically Realistic Dialectical Theology*, and Busch, *Karl Barths Lebenslauf, Nach seinem Briefen und autobiographischen Texten* (ET: Busch, *Karl Barth His Life from Letters and Autobiographical Texts*), it is these two scholars' work that provides the backdrop and context for demonstrating the influence of Dostoevsky.

[6] Karl Barth, *Der Römerbrief* (Erste Fassung; Zürich: Theologischer Verlag Zürich, 1985 [1919]). Karl Barth, *Der Römerbrief* (Zweite Fassung; Zürich: Theologischer Verlag Zürich, 1999 [1922]); ET: Karl Barth, *The Epistle to the Romans* (trans. Edwyn Hoskyns; Oxford: Oxford University Press, 1933).

Protestantism). Therefore a distinction needs to be drawn between this Liberal neo-Protestantism as a theological movement and what is often euphemistically called a liberal perspective in Christian theology: embedded in the work of Kant and Schleiermacher, epitomized for Barth by the theology of Albrecht Ritschl and the work of his teachers at Marburg (Wilhelm Herrmann and Adolf von Harnack - often referred to as Marburg neo-Kantianism), Liberal neo-Protestantism is what Barth works against, having been an avid advocate in his student days and in his first ministry in Geneva.[7] As such Liberal Protestantism claimed freedom not only from traditional dogmas and creeds but also in the analysis of and value accorded to Scripture; such theology was to a large degree formulated in the light of advances in the natural sciences and philosophy.[8] Both Wilhelm Herrmann and Adolf von Harnack taught Barth, and it is vital to remember that whenever Barth wrote or spoke of liberalism in his early work it was in the context of nineteenth-century Liberal neo-Protestantism and not the liberal perspective in Christian theology (though to be fair he did have much to say on this in his mature work). Therefore the use of the term liberal in this book is derived from Barth's use of the term, rooted in Liberal neo-Protestantism, a theological movement of the nineteenth and early twentieth century against which he was, to a degree, reacting.[9] Having been an avid supporter of Western European liberalism in his heady youth, the Russian novelist Dostoevsky also reacted against what he had seen and read of this liberalism, both theological and socio-political. Barth's use of the term liberal(ism) is therefore in the same context as Dostoevsky's. The term atheist can likewise generate as much confusion in theological circles as does liberal. Barth, Thurneysen and Dostoevsky use the term with qualified respect. Indeed in Dostoevsky's work such a term when applied to carefully constructed characters can appear at times contradictory. In many cases Dostoevsky successfully presented confused characters that did not know their own minds or beliefs, thereby illustrating the inherent contradictions in self-proclamations of atheism/theism. In this book the term atheist/atheism is used entirely in the context that Barth, Thurneysen and Dostoevsky used it, as with liberal(ism). The paradoxical nature of these terms stands as part of the emerging theology of Barth and will become clear when we examine the use of these terms in his work, and also that of Dostoevsky.

---

[7] See Simon Fisher, *Revelatory Positivism? Barth's Earliest Theology and the Marburg School* (Oxford: Oxford University Press, 1988).
[8] See Bernard Reardon (ed.), *Liberal Protestantism* (London: Adam and Charles Black, 1968).
[9] See George Rupp, *Culture-Protestantism: German Liberal Theology at the Turn of the Twentieth-Century* (American Academy of Religion Studies in Religion 15; Missoula: Scholars Press, 1977). See also, Karl Barth, *Die protestantische Theologie im 19 Jahrhundert* (Zürich: Theologie Verlag Zürich, 1947).

PART ONE
REVOLUTIONARY THEOLOGY IN THE MAKING*

*'Do you really think that your so-called religion
has any value at all?'*

Karl Barth, 'Predigte 4 May 1913', *Predigten 1913*, p. 216.

* This part title is taken from the title of a volume of Barth and Thurneysen's correspondence translated by James D. Smart *Revolutionary Theology in the Making* (1959)

CHAPTER 1

Wendung und Retraktation

Karl Barth and Eduard Thurneysen

Installed as pastor in the village of Leutwil in the Aargau region of Switzerland on 1 June 1913, the twenty-four year old theology graduate and Reformed Church Minister Eduard Thurneysen was thereby ministering in the valley next-door to Safenwil where the young Karl Barth had been likewise installed as pastor when he was twenty-four years old two years earlier. Karl and Eduard had initially met while they were theological students in 1906 and then again in Marburg in 1909[1]. Safenwil was a small but highly industrialized town; Barth in the two years prior to Thurneysen's arrival had become highly politicized - something of a Marxist pastor. In socio-cultural and political terms, Safenwil was comparable with how much larger industrial towns and cities had been a century earlier in Britain: the workers lived lives of abject poverty, working long hours in highly dangerous conditions for those who controlled industry, wealth, and hence the labour of the working classes. This ruling class feared revolution; yet they were blind to the political tensions building up which would explode into conflict within a year: the First World War. During the war this political *status quo* would come crashing down, therefore this period is the waning of the great nineteenth-century progressive European liberal-idealistic illusion. An illusion rooted intellectually and culturally in the early nineteenth-century into which Barth and Thurneysen had been educated, and now served culturally and sociologically as ministers. Barth and Thurneysen would travel between their respective valleys, walking or cycling, to meet and to discuss the theological problems that lay behind the difficulties of ministry. There was no telephone in either pastor's house so postcards and letters sufficed. This became a mammoth correspondence of over a thousand items throughout their lives. Although most of this correspondence was in Barth's hand, the exchange was, however, very much of an equal nature. Barth wrote, on reflection, that it would be wrong to suppose that he was the one who provided the stimulus and that Thurneysen was the one on the receiving end.[2] With regard to their

---

[1] Busch, *Karl Barths Lebenslauf*, p. 85/ET: p. 73.
[2] Karl Barth, 'Lebendige Vergangenheit', in Karl Barth (ed.), *Gottesdienst-Menschendienst: Eduard Thurneysen zum 70 Geburtstag am 10 July 1958* (Zollikon-Zürich: Evangelischer Verlag AG, 1958), p. 13.

theological heritage and education they were both even at this time '...saying "no" in a great many directions.'[3] This friendship and conversation with Thurneysen is very important in that it brought Barth back into theological reading and reflection when his study as such had been dominated by factory acts and labour laws in the two years before Thurneysen's arrival. Writing in the late 1950s, Barth commented that without the arrival and influence of Thurneysen he might well have ended up as a trade-union representative or a local socialist councillor.[4] It is this same Eduard Thurneysen that introduces Barth to the writings and theological reflections of the Russian Fyodor Mikhailovich Dostoevsky in the summer of 1915.

Karl Barth had left full-time theological education in 1909 a believer in his theological heritage rooted as it was in nineteenth-century German Liberal neo-Protestantism, derived in part from the theologian Friedrich Schleiermacher and the philosopher Georg Hegel. This was mediated to Barth by his teacher Wilhelm Herrmann. Thirteen years later Barth had in his own way overturned much of this theological tradition in favour of what to a younger generation was being called dialektische Theologie, characterized by a theology of *Krisis*. In addition Barth was by then teaching as Professor of Reformed Dogmatics at the university in Göttingen. Between the completion of his full-time studies and taking up the appointment at Göttingen his thinking changed considerably - subject to the influence of various writers and artists, philosophers and theologians, church historians and pastors, also political events, revolutions and the catastrophe of a world war.

Barth's Theological Development

Marburg was the end of Barth's theological studies (somewhere that Barth had wanted to go, much against his father's wishes) where he absorbed the liberalism of Wilhelm Herrmann (derived from nineteenth-century German Liberal neo-Protestantism). Wilhelm Herrmann (1846-1922), professor of systematic theology at Marburg from 1879, was a follower of Kant in philosophical terms and a follower of Ritschl in theological terms. Herrmann insisted that what should be observed and taught about Jesus of Nazareth were those facts that would act upon humanity - for example, the man's moral teaching but not the story of the Virginal Conception or the Resurrection. Furthermore Herrmann proposed that there might have been other aspects of the man Jesus of Nazareth that were considered relevant and of value by the apostles but these ideas/conclusions were not of importance to late nineteenth- and early twentieth-century humanity. Essentially he held to a Ritschlian Christology but went further - he excluded both the mysticism of personal religious experience and the metaphysical speculation that underpinned any

---

[3] Busch, *Karl Barths Lebenslauf*, p. 84/ET: p. 74.
[4] Barth, 'Lebendige Vergangenheit', p. 13.

1. Wendung und Retraktation

intellectual reasoning about ultimate reality. Any value to the historical Jesus was therefore in the man's moral teaching for humanity.[5] Barth's earliest published papers/articles dealt with the relationship between his theological studies and what he encountered initially as assistant pastor to the German-speaking Church in Geneva, for example, 'Moderne Theologie und Reichgottesarbeit' ('Modern Theology and Work for the Kingdom of God')[6] and 'Der Glaube und die Geschichte' ('Faith and History'),[7] where Barth is aware that individuality characterizes modern theology. This results in irreconcilable tensions between the reality of ministry and the academic world of Marburg and Heidelburg as he calls it. Barth writes, 'It is much more difficult to change over/to go over, from the college halls of Marburg or Heidelberg to the activity of the pulpit, or the patient bed'; Barth explains that this is so because 'the nature of modern theology is religious individualism'.[8] In qualifying, Barth highlights two factors - religious individualism and historical relativism. This is the result of his theological education and forms the base from which he progresses, eventually.

It is in Barth's early talks and addresses to various organisations along with published articles that we can find examples of a growing dissatisfaction with Herrmannian liberalism. Broadly speaking Barth's theological development in the post student years (1909 on) through to when he takes up the appointment as Professor of Reformed Theology at Göttingen (1921) moves from the Herrmannian liberalism he was exposed to at Marburg through a dissatisfaction and disillusion with the theology of his teachers (particularly noticeable at the outbreak of the First World War), through the origins of his use of various forms of dialectic to the first edition of his commentary on Paul's Epistle to the Romans, then onto the second edition where dialectic is used, by and large, as prophecy (or as McCormack refers to it - consistent eschatology[9]), through to the period of his appointment at Göttingen as honorary Professor of Reformed Theology in October 1921. During this period - 1911 to 1921 - we find Barth using what can broadly be termed apophatic theological concepts and themes as he undertakes the task of redefining his theology - not only in terms of content

---

[5] Wilhelm Herrmann, *The Communion of the Christian with God* (Philadelphia: Fortress Press, 1971).

[6] Karl Barth, 'Moderne Theologie und Reichgottesarbeit', *Zeitschrift für Theologie und Kirche* XIX (1909), pp. 317-321.

[7] Lecture delivered to the German Pastors' Conference of Western Switzerland in Neuenberg, 5 October 1910: Karl Barth, 'Der Glaube und die Geschichte', *Schweizerische Theologie Zeitschrift* 29 (1912), pp. 1-18 and 65-95.

[8] Barth, 'Moderne Theologie und Reichgottesarbeit', p. 317.

[9] The reference here is to McCormack's categorization of the period of Barth's rediscovery of Scripture (which forms the basis of *Römerbrief 1*) as process eschatology; the subsequent period (the rewriting as *Römerbrief 2* through to his time at Göttingen) is categorized as consistent eschatology. See McCormack, *Karl Barth's Critically Realistic Dialectical Theology*, pp. 129-203 and 207-323.

but also methodology. Before he can rebuild he must knock down - these years are therefore characterized by a theology of demolition. Apophatic concepts and themes are used in many ways to deny the entire basis of the Herrmannian Liberalism that characterized his theological thinking in the years following the completion of his theological studies at Marburg. But this process takes time - effectively, in its initial stage, from the time of his arrival in Safenwil through to the completion of *Römerbrief 2* in September 1921.

Comrade Barth and War

Barth initially served as assistant in a parish in Geneva (1909-1911). Safenwil (1911-1921) was his first full ministry. The conditions of the parish and congregation focused his concerns on the paucity of his theological heritage. The parish at Safenwil was industrial, small scale that is, but had not experienced the reforming zeal of socialist/trade union activists who would have challenged the poverty and atrocious working conditions and the use of child labour. Workers and bosses/managers worshipped side-by-side on Sunday but were divided during the week - strikes, lock-outs, poor wages and working conditions, industrial strife and so forth.

> It was not so much the Socialism that influenced him but the incapacity of a liberal gospel, or a liberal form of preaching, to actually speak to this situation. You see, when you have got people fundamentally at loggerheads, preaching the religious life does not help much, at least that is what he came to feel. It is no good telling people to be religious when there are more serious problems dominating their lives. [10]

There was a tension between two poles - his theological training and his social and political experience. 'He claims, however, even before 1910, "Even in my inner being I was a stranger to a bourgeois world of Ritschl and his pupils."' [11]

In the context of the class war that fractured Safenwil Barth took sides with the workers, with the poor and oppressed, and became known as the 'Red Pastor' and 'Comrade Barth'.[12] It is important to see this against the background of the abortive revolution in Russia of the year 1912. In addition there were fears amongst Western Europe's ruling classes of a wave of revolutions. Bolshevism had been building its power base for a number of years in several European cities and in Paris workers' communes were challenging the government of the day. As Germany was increasing its military capacity under Kaiser Wilhelm II the old Austro-Hungarian Empire, almost feudal in outlook, was collapsing in on itself.

---

[10] Colin E. Gunton, *The Barth Lectures* (ed. P.H. Brazier; London: T&T Clark, Continuum, 2007), p. 23.
[11] Gunton, *The Barth Lectures*, p. 23.
[12] See Busch, *Karl Barths Lebenslauf*, pp. 72-84 /ET: pp. 60-72.

1. Wendung und Retraktation

Barth became involved in the world of politics and workers disputes' almost from the first day of his arrival in Safenwil. All of this led Barth into the world of Swiss Religious Socialism and the influence of theologians, pastors and local politicians of a socialist persuasion. The world of Swiss Religious Socialism had spawned the Social Democratic Party in 1906. The two key figures in this movement and the party were Hermann Kutter and Leonhard Ragaz. Barth actually delivered an address to the Safenwil Workers' Association on 17 December 1911 - 'Jesus Christus und die soziale Bewegung' ('Jesus Christ and the Movement for Social Justice')[13] - in which, in his naivety, he asserted that: 'Jesus is the movement for social justice and the movement for social justice is Jesus in the present'.[14] Within this period of influence is the genesis of Barth's criticism of religion and the church - triggered by the failure of a liberal theology/ecclesiology to address the problems of the workers he met with on a daily basis. In addition Leonhard Ragaz was highly critical of the Church as an institution - or more pertinently, he was anti-individualism and anti-church because of its perceived failure to care for the poor. In this address to the Safenwil Workers' Association Barth strove to emphasize the separation between Jesus Christ and the church - 'The Church is not Jesus and Jesus is not the Church.'[15] Barth was critical of the way the church had overlooked the poor and had, he believed, hidden away in private bourgeois piety - 'The Church has often performed her service badly.'[16] However, as war loomed he became not only disenchanted with the theological liberalism he had been schooled in but he was also becoming increasingly disenchanted with politics. 'The world had fallen apart but he did not find contentment with the world as the Socialist revolution saw it.'[17] However, this did not prevent him joining The Social Democratic Party in 1915, hoping to influence it for the better from inside, but his theological interests had moved on.

Through his involvement in religious socialism Barth fell under the influence of the Blumhardts, initially as part of the radical Christian socialism of Kutter and Ragaz. Barth through his knowledge of and respect for the Blumhardts and their work was further exposed to the influence of left-wing politics - Christoph Friedrich Blumhardt followed the highly unusual path for a church minister of becoming a Social Democrat MP. Christoph's father, Johann Christoph Blumhardt, was unusual for a nineteenth-century minister in that he

---

[13] Karl Barth 'Jesus Christus und die soziale Bewegung', address to the Safenwil Workers' Association on 17 December 1911, initially published in *Der Freie Aargauer, Offizielles Organ der Arbeiterpartei des Kantons Aargau*, 6.153-156 (23, 26, 28 and 30 December 1911); ET: George Hunsinger (ed.), *Karl Barth and Radical Politics* (Philadelphia: The Westminster Press, 1976), pp. 19-37.
[14] Barth, 'Jesus Christus und die soziale Bewegung', ET: Hunsinger, p. 19.
[15] Barth, 'Jesus Christus und die soziale Bewegung', ET: Hunsinger, p. 22.
[16] Barth, 'Jesus Christus und die soziale Bewegung', ET: Hunsinger, p. 23.
[17] Gunton, *The Barth Lectures*, p. 24.

did believe in the possibility of miracles, of divine intervention, he found miracles happening amongst the people he was ministering to. These were not isolated incidents and he began to realize that there was a strong eschatological element to Christianity - the future breaking into the present - despite liberal and scientific scepticism such eschatological breaking-in was not confined to the New Testament era. This impressed Barth and led him to regard the elder Blumhardt as an eschatological prophet.

An important lecture from our perspective was given by Barth to the Pastors' Association in the Aargau Canton on 19 May 1913: 'Der Glaube an den persönlichen Gott' ('Belief in a Personal God').[18] Although the lecture opens with a discourse on personality, Barth then attempts to show how this is applicable to God: the central question underlying the lecture is how to relate the concepts of 'personality' and the 'absolute' (that is, in terms of the absoluteness of God). What is important here are ideas towards a doctrine of God, even though he still asserts the importance of religious experience. Although Barth is maintaining a position in accordance with Wilhelm Herrmann and cannot avoid stressing the importance of the individual there are certain key changes: God is affirmed as both Spirit and personal Lord, exalted on high yet experienced as a loving Father. To Barth this is a paradox, even a dialectical paradox - there is a tension here, he states, that even religious experience cannot resolve. Therefore the only way of approaching God is dialectically, affirming in God what appears irreconcilable: that God is both personally related to humanity and yet is also the impersonal power represented in the Kingdom of God. God is beyond comprehension by human epistemic methods or categories - no 'system' can grasp God. Barth begins to assert mystery, paradox and dialectical tension as the only method in which to undertake theological discourse. For example, 'Religion lives just in this tension ... Whoever attempts to dissolve this tension ... empties and makes poverty-stricken the religious concept of God.'[19] Therefore any doctrine of God must give equal weight to both 'personality' and 'transcendence' - both must be predicates. Barth further attempts to deal with the relationship between 'personality' and 'absoluteness': 'When we pray to him (God) we stand therewith in a relationship of I and Thou (von Ich und Du).'[20] When Barth asserts that this relationship is as with 'I and Thou' it is important to remember that he is acknowledging God as the subject. What is fundamental to this is the realization that God is absolute in the negative sense of being free from limit, boundary and constraint - God's *aseity* is especially seen in his freedom from time and space. This Lordship transcends time so that God is neither constrained inside nor outside of space-time: 'The abolition of space and time

---

[18] Karl Barth, 'Der Glaube an den persönlichen Gott', *Zeischrift für Theologie und Kirche* XXIV (1914), pp. 21-32 and 65-95.
[19] Barth, 'Der Glaube an den persönlichen Gott', p. 69.
[20] Barth, 'Der Glaube an den persönlichen Gott', p. 67.

1. Wendung und Retraktation

is to be seen as at the same time Lordship over it.'[21] What value is there theologically in what Barth is saying? Bruce McCormack:

> The importance of this lecture from the point of view of the question of Barth's development ... (is) that it demonstrates an early affinity on Barth's part for dialectical thinking. And secondly it betrays a hint of the kind of analogical thinking which would later be referred to by Barth as the *analogia fidei*...[22]

The outbreak of the First World War was a significant event in Barth's theological development. Many years afterwards Barth was to write,

> Was it - this has played a decisive role for me personally - precisely the failure of the ethics of the modern theology of the time, with the outbreak of the First World War, which caused us to grow puzzled also about its exegesis, its treatment of history, and its dogmatics?[23]

Within a few weeks of the outbreak of the war a political manifesto was published by leading German academics and intellectuals supporting the Kaiser's position and claiming the war was justified. Barth commented after the event how in early August ninety-three German intellectuals attempted to impress German public opinion by proclaiming support for the war policy of Kaiser Wilhelm II. Barth was horrified to discover many of his theological teachers whom he had respected were amongst the signatories. He concluded that he could no longer subscribe to their ethics or their understanding of the Bible and of history:[24] 'He (Schleiermacher) was unmasked; in a decisive way all the theology expressed in the manifesto and everything that followed it (even in *Die Christliche Welt*) proved to be founded and governed by him'.[25] This is *Krisis*. Barth refused to support the understanding that God could be enlisted to support Germany's sabre-rattling. Furthermore he regarded both sides as wrong - that the war was the result of sin on both sides. To attempt to enlist God was to identify God with the wholly sinful necessities of the moment, further that the Germans were not 'God's proxies' and God could not

---

[21] Barth, 'Der Glaube an den persönlichen Gott', p. 72.
[22] McCormack, *Karl Barth's Critically Realistic Dialectical Theology*, p. 104.
[23] A lecture delivered at the meeting of the Swiss Reformed Ministers' Association in Aarau, 25 September 1956: Karl Barth, 'Die Menschlichkeit Gottes', in Karl Barth, *Die Menschlichkeit Gottes* (Zollikon-Zurich: Evangelischer Verlag AG, 1956), pp. 6-7; ET: Karl Barth, 'The Humanity of God', in Karl Barth, *The Humanity of God* (trans. John Newton Thomas; Louisville, KY: Westminster John Knox Press, 1960), pp. 40-41.
[24] See an address delivered at the meeting of the *Goethegsellschaft* in Hanover, 8 January 1957: Karl Barth, 'Evangelische Theologie im 19 Jahrhundert', in Karl Barth, *Evangelische Theologie im 19 Jahrhundert* (Zollikon-Zurich: Evangelischer Verlag AG, 1956), p. 14.
[25] Karl Barth, 'Nachwort', in Karl Barth, *Schleiermacher-Auswahl* (Siebenstern Taschenbuch 113-14; München: Siebenstern Taschenbuch Verlag, 1968), p. 293.

be '...drawn into the matter in this way'.[26] With the catastrophe of the First World War the stability, pride and security of Liberal Protestant German society and culture broke down completely. The Great War represented a fragmentation - a disappearance of all of the old certainties about the bourgeois social order in Germany (and for that matter the Victorian Middle Class 'Christian' ethic in Britain and the strict hierarchical social order in Edwardian times).

The First World War is one of many factors that has a profound effect on Barth's emerging doctrine of God - or more pertinently the doctrine of a wholly other (ganz andere), different, transcendent God beyond even the supernatural, so totally different and at odds in many ways to the understanding of God in history that had been prevalent in Germano-Swiss theology prior to the outbreak of war.

Wendung und Retraktation

Barth referred to the momentous and tumultuous changes that his beliefs went through during his time in Safenwil as his *Wendung* and then later, his *Retraktation*. Barth wrote of a *Wendung* - yes, a change of direction but 'eine Wendung um 180°, eine unerwartete/entscheidende Wendung' (a 180° turn, an unexpected/decisive turn of events), 'eine Wendung zum Besseren' (a turn for the better);[27] this decisive, diametric change of heart and mind, a sea change (totale Veränderung), was so complete that there was no going back. Even in his mature work Barth continued to reappraise these changes - not to pull back, to change his mind, to return to the liberalism of his theological training, but to ensure the cogency and permanence of this sea change. Barth referred to this revision/reaffirmation as his *Retraktation*: a term derived from the Latin *retractatio*. This occurred throughout the period of his mature work, but is especially applicable to comments/assertions he and Thurneysen made in published works in the late 1940s and the 1950s. However, the term *Retraktation* applies equally to the period of diametric change, the *Wendung*, during his time in Safenwil and centring on 1915-16. Barth is almost certainly using the term with Augustine's *Retractationes* in mind.[28]

Barth's *Wendung* is his development away from the nineteenth-century Liberal neo-Protestant heritage that had been at the heart of his theological formation - and specifically the Herrmannian liberalism from his student days.

---

[26] Barth, 'Nachwort', pp. 293-294. See also McCormack, *Karl Barth's Critically Realistic Dialectical Theology,* pp. 111-116.
[27] Barth, 'Die Menschlichkeit Gottes', p. 6/ET: pp. 40-41.
[28] See Augustine, *Sancti Aurelii Augustini Retractationum libri II* (ed. Almut Mutzenbecher Turnholti: Brepols, 1984), and A. Traupé, 'Saint Augustine', in Johannes Quasten and Angelo Di Berardino (eds.), *Patrology: The Golden Age of Latin Patristic Literature vol. 4* (Westminster, MD: Christian Classics, 1986), pp. 342-360, in particular p. 355.

This is more than a change of theological emphasis or a shift in theological allegiance; furthermore it covers a number of years in terms of development - it is a wholesale reorientation, a methodological shift so that once the change has been accomplished there is no going back. If so, why? - because Barth wanted to assert the irreversible permanence of his conversion/change of heart from the years 1915-16, with all the implications asserted for Christian doctrine. Writing in the 1950s Barth commented:

> Were we right or wrong? We were certainly right! Why? Let one read the doctrine of Tröltsch, and Stephan! Let one read also the dogmatics of Lüdemann, in its way so solid, or even that of Seeburg! If all that wasn't a blind alley! Beyond doubt what was then in order was not some kind of further shifting around within the complex of inherited questions, as this was finally attempted by Wobbermin, Schaeder and Otto, but rather a *radikale Wendung*. The ship was threatening to run aground; the moment was at hand to turn the rudder an angle of exactly 180°. And in view of what is to be said later, let it immediately be stated: that which is gone does not return. Therefore there never could be a question of denying or reversing that change. It was however later on and it is today a question of '*Retraktation*'.[29] (Barth's emphasis)

For Barth: 'A genuine "*Retraktation*" in no way involves a subsequent retreat, but rather a new beginning and attack in which what previously has been said is to be said more than ever, but now even better.' Barth continued, 'If that which we then thought we had discovered and brought forth', commenting on the changes centred on the years 1915-16, 'was no last word but one requiring "*Retraktation*"' (revision, improvement, reassertion to a degree) 'it was nonetheless a true word.'[30] If one looks closely at the multitudinous influences on Barth in the period 1911 to 1921 as evident from his sermons, addresses and correspondence, there is a constant reappraisal (as with the influence and use of Dostoevsky and Kierkegaard, or Overbeck, or Platonic concepts), a constant reconsideration - a *Retraktation* even at this early stage in his work. Barth discovers, absorbs, is influenced, he critically assesses, however he soon reconsiders and reassesses; then he distances himself and his theology from the influence, to a degree, and moves on. Influences come thick and fast: this is *Wendung und Retraktation*, according to Barth's usage. Barth asserted that the decisive change of this period in Safenwil must stand, this true word must stand, cannot be bypassed and that it constituted the presupposition of what must then in his mature work be considered the humanity of God - God's turn to us, God for us. The foundation, the decisive turn for Barth in 1915 was, as we shall see, the realization that 'God is God', from which flows his mature work focussing on the turn of this *deus absconditus* to and for humanity: the *deus dixit*.

---

[29] Barth, 'Die Menschlichkeit Gottes', pp. 6-7/ET: pp. 41-42.
[30] Barth, 'Die Menschlichkeit Gottes', p. 7/ET: p. 42.

Hermann Kutter

Writing in 1927 to Rudolf Bultmann, Karl Barth commented on the crucial period of change in his theological thinking that started with his arrival in the village of Safenwil that '...partly under the influence of the message of Kutter and Ragaz, which was then at its peak, the social question and the social movement became urgently important to me.'[31] Barth continued to explain that he was touched by the real problems of life. Instead of reading and studying theology and ecclesiology to complement his ministry he was spending hours pouring over and studying, '...factory acts, safety laws, and trade unionism, and my attention was claimed by violent local and cantonal struggles on behalf of the workers.'[32] However, the impact of the war was also causing a profound disillusionment with his involvement with socialism. Barth commented:

> ...(the war) brought concretely to light two aberrations: first in the teaching of my theological mentors in Germany, who seemed to me to be hopelessly compromised by their submission to the ideology of war; and second in socialism. I had credulously enough expected socialism, more than I had the Christian church, to avoid the ideology of war, but to my horror I saw it doing the very opposite in every land.[33]

In 1913 Thurneysen, shortly after he arrived in Leutwil, had personally introduced Barth to the giant of Swiss Religious Socialism - Hermann Kutter (1863-1931) - who was fifty-years old at the time. Kutter, pastor of the Neumünster Zürich from 1898 to 1926, rated conformity to the will of God over mere piety. In his work *Sie Müssen! - Ein offenes Wort an die christliche Gesellschaft (They Must! - An Open Word to Christian Society)*,[34] he asserted that the Bible affirms a living God who liberates humanity from sin to a new life, therefore we should, like Jesus, be aware of the God-given imperative (müssen) to love. Kutter regarded Jesus' teaching as apocalyptic, therefore the true follower of Jesus must be active, even allowing for the fact that s/he may be an atheist. In 1906 Kutter had founded the Swiss religious-socialist movement.

In discussions with Kutter Barth learned to speak the word 'God' with reverence, to emphasize the separateness, the distance, the otherness of God,

---

[31] See Karl Barth, 'Autobiographische Skizzen Karl Barths aus den Fakultätsalben der Evangelical Theologie Fakultät in Münster (1927)', in Karl Barth, *Karl Barth-Rudolf Bultmann Briefwechsel 1922-1966* (Zürich: Theologischer Verlag Zürich, 1971), pp. 301-312; ET: Karl Barth, 'Autobiographic sketches of Karl Barth from the faculty album of the Evangelical theology Faculty in Münster (1927)', in *Karl Barth-Rudolf Bultmann Letters 1922-1966* (trans. and ed. G.W. Bromiley; Edinburgh: T&T Clark, 1971), pp.150-158. Quotation is from p. 306/ET: p. 154.
[32] Barth, 'Autobiographische Skizzen', p. 306/ET: p. 154.
[33] Barth, 'Autobiographische Skizzen', pp. 306-307/ET: pp. 154-155.
[34] Hermann Kutter, *Sie Müssen - ein offenes Wort an die christliche Gesellschaft* (Berlin: H. Walther Verlagsbuchhandlung, 1904).

which was implicit in the much used phrase, 'The Kingdom of God' - the implication being that this world was not, that we were a long way from God and that we should earnestly strive to bring about 'The Kingdom of God'. Barth also learned from Kutter that God might use all the forces and agencies in this world to try to force the church to see the error of its ways when it did not serve the Gospel. A criticism of religion was not simply implied here in conversation with Kutter - it was explicit. Eberhard Busch quoting from an interview between Barth and Fischer-Barnicol, notes the impact this meeting had:

> From Kutter I simply learnt to speak the great word 'God' seriously, responsibly and with a sense of its importance. When he preached, and indeed in private conversation, he could impress on one that this was a deadly serious matter, which could not be taken lightly. And it was this prophetic thinker and preacher... who at that time, with a force unrivalled by any of his contemporaries, represented the insight that the sphere of God's power really is greater than the sphere of the church and that from time to time it has pleased God, and still pleases him, to warn and to comfort his church through the figures and the events of secular world history.[35]

Kutter taught Barth that the world is the world - but that God is God. These meetings/discussions are of crucial importance in the development of Barth's critique of religion. This is a critique that is to be built on this doctrinal separateness, this distinctiveness of God - a God above all human gods who is wholly other and cannot be domesticated in or contained by religion. The understanding that the transcendent God might actually correct, cajole, even humiliate *His* Church was new to the bourgeois liberal humanism of German neo-Protestantism; it was also new to Barth. But it was not new to Dostoevsky.

Barth and Thurneysen's Theological Agenda: 'The Problem'

A central factor underlying the importance of the influence of Thurneysen is that he acts as a catalyst on Barth. Indeed they both generate ideas in each other. Together a problem crystallized in their minds, together they could identify a deep theological difficulty. At the heart of 'The Problem' was their theological heritage - this prompted the question, what is the way forward? The way forward had to be theological: ministry was rooted in ecclesiology and ecclesiology was doctrinal, so the problems they had encountered in ministry could only be solved theologically and not politically. Eberhard Busch notes how the religious socialists (primarily Kutter and Ragaz) had helped him clarify his theological search but he began to keep his distance more and more from them - socialism was not, for Barth, the onset of the Kingdom of God.[36]

---

[35] Busch, *Karl Barths Lebenslauf*, p. 88/ET: p. 76. Busch is quoting from an interview between Barth and H. Fischer-Barnicol from 1964, and from Barth, 'Nachwort', p. 293.
[36] Busch, *Karl Barths Lebenslauf*, pp. 80-90/ET: p. 78.

Revisiting Marburg with Thurneysen, then travelling on to Bad Boll to meet with Christoph Blumhardt, in the spring of 1915 only sharpened 'The Problem', particularly as they were visiting wartime Germany. The impact of the war was pressing in more and more on Barth's mind.

It is this position that in part leads to Barth's disillusionment with the heritage of nineteenth-century Liberal neo-Protestantism. Despite his conservative upbringing (in terms of morality) and his liberal theological education (essentially doctrinally), he was well aware of the inherent problems. Barth had been working on a Schleiermachian type theology; however, he did inherit a strong Christocentric input from Harnack amongst other influences. Indeed he learned from Herrmann, his teacher at Marburg, the importance of the centrality of Jesus Christ. Immediacy had been the key word for Schleiermacher; he believed that all had an unhindered, immediate perception of God - a direct, intuitive grasp of God. However, Christologically it is not possible to come into direct contact with God: Christ mediates. However, in addition to this Christological tension he was confronted in his ministry with the question, how do you teach people to value the pietistic religious life when the world is tearing itself to pieces in a world war and the political *status quo* is collapsing around you? The heart of 'The Problem' was therefore not political or sociological but theological - more pertinently Christological. This is summarized neatly by Colin Gunton:

> He learned from Herrmann the importance of the centrality of Jesus Christ. However, this position was inherently unstable - there was a tension in both the position of Herrmann and Harnack. The tension is that you cannot have the Schleiermachian immediacy and a strongly Christocentric position. If God is immediately perceivable by all people of all religions then you do not need Christ. If you adopt the position of Schleiermacher, who would talk of the white heat of the soul communing with God, then the mediator is not needed. Either God is transcendent and redemption/revelation comes through Christ, or Christ is redundant and all can know God immediately - fallenness does not enter the question. Herrmann wanted both; and Barth again always being the intellectual came to realize that you could not have your cake and eat it in that respect. Either you had religion, which was this immediate relation to God, or your relation to God was mediated by Jesus Christ and that was a different thing.[37]

Christologically it is not possible to come into direct contact with God: Christ mediates.[38] Barth became progressively disillusioned with his teachers, in part because the two positions appeared incompatible. Why? - because their teaching '...didn't rise to the ethical challenges of the day, of the twentieth century.'[39]

---

[37] Gunton, *The Barth Lectures*, p. 21.
[38] See Colin E. Gunton, 'One Mediator - the Man Jesus Christ', *Pro Ecclesia* 11.2 (2002), pp. 146-158.
[39] Gunton, *The Barth Lectures*, p. 18.

CHAPTER 2

The Apophatic Barth - God's Aseity

At the heart of Barth's *Wendung und Retraktation* is an emergent, redefined doctrine of God. Broadly speaking we see Barth's doctrine of God developing away from the Schleiermachian immediacy and the Hegelian metaphysics, which tied God to religious experience and world history - the events of the First World War had exposed the fault lines in this doctrine. Here we have the genesis of Barth's concern for God's *aseity* - God's right, so to speak, to be God, independent from all that humanity imposed on God in theological definitions and religious projections.[1] Many scholars see the year 1915 as the year of a new starting point for Barth, for instance, Spieckermann[2] and McCormack. McCormack categorizes this new starting point as *critically realistic* in the sense that '...God is now seen as a reality complete and whole in itself apart from and prior to the knowing activity of human individuals'; God, for Barth, was no longer to be seen in the terms of nineteenth-century liberal theology, that is, '...in contrast to the idealistic tendency of the Ritschlian School to treat God as a postulated source of the moral ought.'[3]

Kriegszeit und Gottesreich [4]

We find Barth's realization of the utter independence of God from all theological definitions and religious projections encapsulated in an address given in Basel in November of 1915. This address encapsulates the new starting

---

[1] There is only space here to examine Barth's apophatism briefly, this has been dealt with in more depth elsewhere. See P.H. Brazier 'Barth's First Commentary on Romans (1919) - An Exercise in Apophatic Theology?', *International Journal of Systematic Theology* 6.4 (2004), pp. 387-403.

[2] Ingrid Spieckermann, *Gotteskenntnis: Ein Beitrag zur Grundfrage der neun Theologie Karl Barths* (München: Christian Kaiser Verlag, 1985).

[3] McCormack, *Karl Barth's Critically Realistic Dialectical Theology*, p. 129.

[4] Karl Barth, 'Kriegszeit und Gottesreich', an unpublished lecture given in Basle, Switzerland, 15 November 1915. All but the first 12 of 31 pages survive in the Karl Barth archive in Basle. Large parts of the text are presented in Herbert Anzinger, *Glaube und kommunikative Praxis* (München: Christian Kaiser Verlag, 1991). See chp. 3, 'Die Nötigung Zur Grundlagenrevision', sub-section 3.2.2, 'Die Problematik des ethischen Idealismus', p. 117; quotations from 'Kriegszeit und Gottesreich', pp. 120-22. I am grateful here to Bruce McCormack for pointing me to this lecture.

point for this emerging doctrine of God, it illustrates in particular God's sovereignty, *aseity* and autonomy from the theology of his teachers: 'Kriegszeit und Gottesreich' ('Wartime and the Kingdom of God'). This address identifies the ground of Barth's new starting point and the foundation in many ways of his mature work. In 'Kriegszeit und Gottesreich' Barth commented that: 'Welt bleibt Welt ... Daß Gott Gott ist' ('world remains world, but God is God').[5] Herbert Anzinger wrote, quoting Barth's comments (presenting some fragments from the surviving pages of this lecture, discovered in the Barth archive) that we must: 'recognize that God is God, God as he is recognized in the life and word of Jesus, that he is, from the ground up, from reason, something utterly different to all else...'[6]. What we find here in 'Kriegszeit und Gottesreich' is Barth's early use of *negation* in relation to speaking about God; further, we find the use of *Ursprung* (derived from the influence, as we shall see later, of his brother, Heinrich Barth) as well as the emphasis on the wholly otherness of God. Barth:

> What concern to us is the God who was introduced to us once as the highest idea of ethics? The 'Father in heaven', to whom Jesus points us is no Ideality, which lives from its opposition (antithesis?) no formal, unreal magnitude (entity?), that finally also belongs in this world, no idea of justice or love rivalling the ideas of ethics, but rather the reality, out of which our entire world has fallen. That God is our creator and origin in the other, for us, entirely new world, this would be the only positive thing that we can say. All our other speaking of God is a stammering, or it must if it should count seriously, exist in pure negation.[7]

Therefore - from a human perspective - is not all our God-talk a faltering stumble, a stammering, which can only be taken seriously if it is characterized by negation? But not the negation of Buddhist apophatism - for Barth is still asserting that God is. Barth is in effect making space for the *deus dixit* - the self-revelation of the *deus absconditus* in Christ Jesus. For example, when writing *Römerbrief 1* (started within a year of 'Kriegszeit und Gottesreich') he wrote that this negation leads 'not into a mystical vacuum and not into a Buddhist nirvana,' because we must walk in this new life, this new relationship

---

[5] Barth, 'Kriegszeit und Gottesreich', p. 120.
[6] 'Daß Gott Gott ist, Gott so wie er im Leben und Wort Jesu zu erkennen ist, daß er etwas von Grund aus Anderes ist als Alles Andre', Barth, 'Kriegszeit und Gottesreich', p. 120.
[7] The full text is: 'Was soll uns der Gott, der uns einst als die höchste Idee der Ethik vorgestellt worden ist? Der Vater im Himmel, auf den er (sc. Jesus) uns hinweist, ist keine Idealität, die von ihrem Gegensatz lebt, keine formale unreale Groß, die schließlich auch wieder in die Welt hineingehört, keine Idee der Gerechtigkeit oder der Liebe im Wetteifer der Ideen der Ethik, sondern die Wirklichkeit, aus der unse ganze Welt herausgefallen ist. Daß Gott unser Schöpfer und Ursprung in der andern für uns ganz neuen Welt ist, sei das einzige Positive..., das wir sagen können. All unser sonstiges Reden von Gott ist ein Stammeln, oder es muß, wenn es ernst gelten soll, in lauter Negationen bestehen.' Barth, 'Kriegszeit und Gottesreich', pp. 121-122.

2. The Apophatic Barth - God's Aseity

with the unknowable God.[8] Furthermore Barth sees this distance, this separation between the world and God in terms of *diastasis* - a relationship whereby two entities stand over against each other with no possibility of a synthesis (certainly not into a higher form of being in the Hegelian sense). Barth is making a conscious effort to distance himself from idealistic theology and religion. Indeed, this realization of the utter *diastasis* between God and this world was in part learned from the discussions Barth had held with Hermann Kutter - as cited above. It has been noted, that Barth is attempting to think from the standpoint of God himself, as evidenced from a phrase he borrows from Hermann Kutter used in *Römerbrief 1*, 'thinking from or out of God.'[9]

Let us look a little more closely at Barth's comment from 'Kriegszeit und Gottesreich' that 'etwas von Grund aus Anderes ist als Alles Ander.' This is a difficult statement to comprehend yet it contains what is arguably at the heart of Barth's new starting point: translating this in a manner which is quite close to the German in both vocabulary and syntax renders, '(that God is) something other beyond ground(s), beyond reason(s), other as all': therefore, God is from the ground-up, from reason, something utterly different to all else. The key is perhaps in Barth's use of *Grund*, which is inevitably the language of foundational grounding/reasons;[10] Barth wanted to avoid anthropomorphising God, or encompassing God in spatial-temporal language, yet he also wanted to avoid reducing God to an abstract (Hegelian) idea. Thus he asserts that God is something, yet no particular thing; God is no mere ethical ideal, but the reality (again a problematic word for Barth at this time) of God is to be seen utterly unlike anything we can conceive of or know. But, Barth, ever being the Kantian, does not deny reason in how we may know of God: he is reluctant to say that God is beyond reason(s). Or is he? - do we translate *Grund* as *reasons* or *grounds* or *fundamental basics*? Is God beyond our concepts of reason, beyond the grounds of our thought systems, philosophies and theologies? Or is Barth being intentionally paradoxical and dialectically ambiguous here? At this point in his *Wendung und Retraktation* Barth was struggling with words to try to express the inexpressible, further that any idiomatic language inevitably brought God down to earth and packaged in such a way as to make God manageable, malleable, harmless, containable (something he rails against in *Römerbrief 1*). This is about human epistemic limitation and the inadequacy of language: linguistic negation through its apophatism asserts God's *aseity* and utter otherness in being. The most Barth will accept at this point (1915) is the

---

[8] Barth, *Römerbrief 1*, p. 215, on Romans 6:1–14.
[9] '...ein Denken von Gott aus...', Barth, *Römerbrief 1*, p. 71. See also McCormack, *Karl Barth's Critically Realistic Dialectical Theology*, pp. 129-130.
[10] The Oxford Duden German-English dictionary shows the diverse, but interrelated meanings to the noun *Grund*: *basic fundamentals* or *reasons*; *grounds* or *foundations*; *deep down/basically*; *arguments for*; *bases* or *basis*; *apparent reason*: *Oxford Duden German Dictionary* (Oxford: Oxford University Press, 1999).

assertion of God as 'ganz andere' (entirely other).[11]

Apophatic Language and Concepts

As Barth proceeded to untangle his theological thinking from the immediacy of nineteenth-century German Liberal neo-Protestantism he developed further this idea of God as wholly other. Friedrich Gogarten, writing in 1929 on the reception of Barth's *Die christliche Dogmatik im Entwurf* of 1927 commented about the importance of this.[12] Gogarten accepted Barth's assertion of the starting point for all questions in theology - namely the *deus dixit*: that is, God's speaking through Jesus Christ, God's self-revelation. However, Gogarten pointed out that this was built on another starting point from ten to fifteen years earlier - God as *wholly other*, God existing in a realm by Himself beyond and independent of creation or the human he had become in Jesus Christ. For God to reveal himself implies hiddenness, otherness from the start. Gogarten asserted that it was this *God-in-Isolation* that was Barth's actual, almost secret, starting point, the *as-yet-unrevealed-God*; God's being in itself/himself and for itself/himself (in sich).[13] The origins of this concept are in the period 1914-16. Gogarten wrote:

> If one thinks this way, is one not speaking at one time of God in and for Himself isolated from (the hu)man, and at another time of (the hu)man in and for humanity isolated from God?[14]

Gogarten describes this distinction as 'God in Himself' as compared to 'God for us'.[15] This concept is essentially negative in that it asserts that God is so other, different, distinct that we can know nothing of our own accord, save the speculation that God exists - Gott ist.

Therefore if we examine Barth's lectures, addresses and articles in this crucial period of 1914-1918 - including the writing of *Römerbrief 1* (Summer

---

[11] In the context of the way in which Barth used language to negate at this time and how it reflects his changing beliefs, see John Webster, ' "On the Frontiers of what is Observable": Barth's *Römerbrief* and Negative Theology', *Downside Review* 105 (July 1987), pp. 169-180. Concerning Barth's apophatism, see Rico Sneller, 'Crisis in our Speaking about God: Derrida and Barth's Epistle to the Romans', in Isle N. Bulhof, and Laurens ten Kate (eds.), *Flight of the Gods - Philosophical Perspectives on Negative Theology* (New York: Fordham University Press, 2000), and Mary Ann Stenger, 'Ultimacy in relation to Affirmation and Negation: Buddhist and Christian perspectives', *Dialogue and Alliance* 5 (1991), pp. 55-67.

[12] Karl Barth, *Die Christliche Dogmatik im Entwurf - Erste Band Die Lehre vom Worte Gottes, Prolegomena zur christlichen Dogmatik 1927* (Gesamtausgabe 14; Zürich: Theologischer Verlag Zürich, 1982).

[13] Friedrich Gogarten, 'Karl Barths Dogmatik', in *Theologische Rundschau* 1 (1929, new series), pp. 60-80.

[14] Gogarten, 'Karl Barths Dogmatik', p. 72.

[15] '...ebensowenig ist dann "Gott an sich" Gott, sondern nur "Gott für uns" ', Gogarten, 'Karl Barths Dogmatik', p. 78.

1916 to August 1918) - we find several uses of negative theological language and concepts which are then carried through into *Römerbrief 2* (written October 1920-September 1921 but with a different dialectical character and emphasis than in the first edition). How does Barth use such negation in language and theological concept? -

First, we can see negation used in relation to the knowledge of God and the doctrine of God. It is used for ensuring the distinctness, the wholly otherness of God beyond all human knowledge and understanding, beyond human categorisation as an object or thing. God is not a thing in itself (Ding in sich [16]) not a metaphysical essence alongside other essences, not a second something, an-other, but the eternal, the transcendent, the pure *Ursprung* (origin)[17] of everything that is. However to say that God is *no thing* (i.e. *no particular thing, as such*) is not the same as saying God is *nothing* (*nothing at all*). Within this context, for example, Barth uses the term *diastasis* (long before he discovered it also in the work of Kierkegaard) to express this critical distinction between God and this world - 'Welt bleibt Welt, das Gott Gott ist'.

Second, we can see the use of Negation as a refutation of the validity of natural theology, that is, the efforts made by men and women to define God, even invent gods, and attribute divine characteristics, without recourse to divine revelation. However, it is important to remember that during the period following the publication of *Römerbrief 1* Barth is still developing his scepticism of natural theology and it takes the form of a simple denial. This refutation does not have the theological explication that was to characterize his mature work.

Third, there is the critical assumption that the Churches and historical Christianity, human religiosity and piety (at best this is an organized religious response to the historical event of the incarnation and resurrection, at worst this is no more than religious projection) will always be subject to criticism and assessment - from the perspective of the Gospel. Such a critique is negative because it looks critically, pessimistically, destructively on the religious efforts of humanity. All may not have served the Gospel as they should have. Underlying this criticism is a belief in the *aseity*, sovereignty and independence of God from humanity and human history. God in Christ is the final arbiter of whether human religion is acceptable or not, and on what terms, if any.

Fourth, we can see the emergence in the early lectures and addresses of a respect, under certain circumstances, for negation as atheism-atheism as a negation, a paradox. This is seen as the clearing away of all human conceptions and preconceptions, and especially projections. For example, Barth knew only too well that atheists might often have a better grasp of the truth of God than Christians immersed in religious culture (he was to observe this in the

---

[16] Barth, *Römerbrief 2*, pp. 29-30/ET: pp. 51-53.
[17] A term derived from Barth's brother Heinrich.

characters of Dostoevsky's novels). And of course Dostoevsky, Barth and Thurneysen saw varying degrees and forms of atheism/atheists with varying degrees and characteristics of negation, dialectic and paradox.

Fifth and finally, there is negation in relation to the Christian life. Barth, like the apostle Paul also uses negation, as a characteristic of the Christian life (especially seen in both editions of *Der Römerbrief*). For example, to deny oneself and take up Christ's cross is a negation; Barth (like Dostoevsky) emphasizes in *Römerbrief 2* how love is defined in the negative in 1 Corinthians 13 (for example, *love is not...* , etc.). There is also the denial of this life as a paradoxical negation.[18] These ideas were also contained in Thurneysen's book on Dostoevsky:

> This love is astonishingly negative and passive, different from all that we are otherwise accustomed to regard as love. Only in the great negations of 1 Corinthians 13 could it be adequately described: love does not envy; love does not vaunt itself, it is not puffed up, does not behave itself unseemly, seeks not her own, is not easily provoked, thinks no evil.[19]

How does Barth present this negative theology in his early addresses and lectures? In two ways - the language used, which we have examined, and the theological concepts that emerge from the language.[20] In terms of the language the primary terms are: *N/negativ* (*negative*), *Negation* (*negation*); the secondary terms are *P/paradox* (*paradox/paradoxical*), *Paradoxon* (*paradox - philosophical and rhetorical*), *Paradoxie* (*paradoxicalness*), *Dialektik* (*dialectic*), *dialektisch* (*dialectical*) *P/positiv* (*positive*), *unwissentlich* (*unknowingly, unknowability*), *Rätsel* (*mystery, enigma*); the terms *V/verneinungen* (denials) *Verneinungenswort* (negative word) *Verneinungsfall*

---

[18] For example, 2 Corinthians 6:8b-10 and Matthew 10:39.

[19] Eduard Thurneysen, *Dostojewski* (München: Christian Kaiser Verlag, 1921), p. 65; ET: Eduard Thurneysen, *Dostoevsky - A Theological Study* (trans. Keith R. Crim; London: Epworth Press, 1964) p. 71. Thurneysen is referring to 1 Corinthians 13:4b-5.

[20] The root, etymologically, of many German and English terms in this field will be found in the Greek from the intertestamental period and the sixth century (Pseudo-Dionysius), for example, ἀπόφασις (*a denial, negation*); also ἄγνωστος (*unknown* - used by Paul in his Areopagus speech, Acts 17:23a and 23b), also ἀγνωσία (*ignorance, no knowledge, lack of spiritual perception*) and ἄγνοια (*ignorance, unawareness*), also μυστήριον (*secret, mystery - of something formerly unknown but now revealed*); in addition Barth's use of *unwissentlich* is similar to ἀκαταληψία/ἀκατάληπτος (*incomprehensibility*) - he uses the Greek term much later in Karl Barth, *The Church Dogmatics* (14 vols; eds. G.W. Bromiley and T.F. Torrance; Edinburgh: T&T Clark, 1936-77), see II/1, *The Doctrine of God*, §. 27, 'The Limits to the Knowledge of God', pp. 179-256. There are similarities in the use of negative theological concepts and terms by Barth and the use of these Greek terms in the New Testament. However, it is important to remember that *N/negative* (German) and *Negation* (English) are not necessarily a direct translation of ἀπόφασις.

(answer in the negative)²¹ are also used but primarily by Thurneysen (and Barth) in the context of their work on Dostoevsky. In terms of concepts many of these ideas can be traced to 1914/5 and are presented in the lectures/addresses simply as ideas, then used more explicitly in both editions of *Der Römerbrief,* and are only spelt out in so many words in Barth's mature work. For example: *Visibility-Invisibility; Knowability-Unknowability; Negative-Positive; Veiling-Unveiling; Revelation-Hiddenness; Paradoxicalness-Logicality; Yes-No* (Barth assertion of God's *'Yes'* to our *'No',* and *'No'* to our *'Yes'*): a dialectical disjunction between pairs of antinomies, characterized by *diastasis.* This method continues into Barth's writing and rewriting of *Der Römerbrief* and into his mature work - in particular the use of *Visibility-Invisibility, Knowability-Unknowability, Veiling-Unveiling* in *The Church Dogmatics.*²² However, it is in *Römerbrief I* that he makes the most explicit use of negation, but also much of the work is infused with such dialectical negation.

Dialectic and a Critique of Religion in the Service of the Gospel

From the perspective of the influence of Dostoevsky there are two components of this negation that we can look at in more detail: the *denkform* of dialectic and a critique of religion. We have seen some evidence of Barth's use of dialectic already, likewise his negative criticism of religion. The moment Barth began to express doubts about the theology he had been schooled in, a criticism of religion was inevitable. It is false to drive an hermetic distinction between doctrine and ecclesial life - the ecclesial basis of any church or ministry is the result, primarily, of the doctrine espoused by its priestly caste/ruling elite. This is as true with nineteenth-century German Liberal neo-Protestantism as with Rome. McCormack has noted that the reception of religious socialism in the late nineteenth-century and early years of the twentieth century did not happen in Lutheran Germany but did in Switzerland. This rejection, in Germany, was in part caused by the close ties between the bourgeois (bürgerlich) values of Protestantism and the innate conservatism of the Lutheran Church.²³

The moment Barth saw doubts in the way he had been prepared, doctrinally, for ministering to the congregation in Safenwil (the elderly, the sick, the poverty-stricken workers, the wealthy factory owners and managers) then he is starting to criticize religion. What is of fundamental importance, and cannot be stressed enough, is that this is a criticism of Protestant and Reformed religion

---

²¹ *Oxford Duden German Dictionary.*
²² Barth, *Church Dogmatics,* see II/1, *The Doctrine of God,* chp. V, 'The Knowledge of God', §§. 25, 26 and 27, pp. 3-61, 63-178 and 179-256 (in particular, pp. 189-204 on the hiddenness of God and the *terminus ad quo / terminus ad quem* in relation to our knowledge of God).
²³ McCormack, *Karl Barth's Critically Realistic Dialectical Theology,* p. 81.

generally, the Lutheran Church (with its doctrine of German Liberal neo-Protestantism) specifically. In all cases it is a critique in the service of the Gospel: Barth is looking at the church he is part of, looking at the way it ministers, the doctrinal basis of that ministry and criticising in the light of his understanding of the Christian Gospel. It is this disquiet which in part led him to become involved with the religious socialism of Ragaz and Kutter. And it is important to remember that Leonhard Ragaz was highly critical of the Church as an institution - or more pertinently, he was anti-church because of its perceived failure to care for the poor. Further, Ragaz was critical of the way that the German bourgeois elite had defined morality and ethics according to its own agenda, and hidden in the pietistic world of middle class respectability.[24] This influence is the genesis of Barth's own criticism of religion in the service of the Gospel. Initially Barth sees the solution ecclesially and politically - hence his involvement with the religious socialists. However, it is important to remember that Barth did not hold political office nor was he a card-carrying Marxist. Barth, in part through the influence of Leonhard Ragaz, saw the way forward as religious: that is, the spiritual renewal of men and women into a new people - this new creation would then work towards a just social order.[25] These ideas worked through into Barth's weekly sermons to his parishioners. Divine judgement is a theme that occurs in his sermons from 1912-14, but also this criticism of religion. Barth's teacher, Wilhelm Herrmann, held to no criticism of religion - the Lutheran Church was, after all is said and done, an ample spokesperson for the liberalism of his doctrine. Herrmann's religion was primarily individualistic - the individual was encouraged to see how God was working in his/her life. Questions of sin and guilt did not play much of a role in this ecclesial doctrine.[26] Herrmann's attitude and approach to religion was wholly *positive*. Barth's attitude and approach to religion was becoming *negative*, critical, dismissive, destructive. Therefore his critique of religion was an element in his use of apophatic theological concepts. Barth's sermon for 4th May 1913 was based on Amos 5:21-4, and he echoed the prophet's criticism of religion: justice and righteousness were the measure of good religion, and without a commitment to action on behalf of such a cause then religion is no more than dreadful lies.[27] If we do not act for justice, spoke Barth, then a chasm

---

[24] See Leonhardt Ragaz, *Du Sollst - Grundzüge einer sittlichen Weltanschauung* (Leipzig: Waetzel, 1904). Note, the initial, *Du Sollst* (*You Should - Fundamentals of a Moral Worldview*) could be seen as *Thou Shalt*, giving the allusion of a divine command. Ragaz reiterates much of this in the periodical, *Neue Wege* (*New Way*) that he co-founded for the Religious-Socialist movement.

[25] See Andreas Lindt, *Leonhardt Ragaz : Eine Studie zur Geschichte und Theologie des Religiösen Sozialismus* (Zollikon-Zurich: Evangelischer Verlag AG, 1957).

[26] See McCormack, *Karl Barth's Critically Realistic Dialectical Theology*, pp. 31-67.

[27] Karl Barth, *Predigten 1913* (Gesamtausgabe 8; Zürich: Theologischer Verlag Zürich, 1994), p. 217.

opens up between God and us.[28] For Barth, love and truth should be the measure of Christian people and if his congregation answered that they did practise some acts of charity he had already got his answer ready - he criticized the wider sickness within society that exploited children in factories, that failed to speak out about alcoholism, commenting that the little acts of charity were insufficient and that religion masked people from seeing the need for justice, mercy and righteousness. In preaching he commented, 'Do you really think that your so-called religion has any value at all?'[29]

Barth was unmoved and unrepentant when members of his congregation criticized him for speaking out - their argument was that they were employing him. Barth's answer was, of course, that he was answerable to God and God alone. Several years later Barth acknowledged how he had been aligning himself with Amos' cause. In 'Das Wort Gottes als Aufgabe der Theologie' ('The Word of God and the Task of Ministry', 1922)[30] Barth explained that the justification for this approach lay in the theological heritage of Kierkegaard and Dostoevsky, also reformers such as Luther and Calvin. Furthermore, such a heritage stretched back to the great Hebrew prophets like Jeremiah and Amos; and of course in the early Church, Paul.[31] Barth explained that in Jeremiah and Amos we perceive a negativity towards religion, a negativity that is in opposition to priests and Kings, religious festivals and Temple sacrifice. This negativity is carried through to the Gospels in the sayings of Jesus and into the epistles of Paul, then on to Luther's attack on Medieval piety and religious works. Kierkegaard's attack on Christianity *per se* (the domestication of God) and Dostoevsky's dialectical criticism of religion (because of a hunger for God in ordinary people) is because religion is seen as having failed to serve God and place people in a right relation with/to God. A criticism of religion is, therefore, a form of apophatic theology - precisely because the critic is being negative about religion from the perspective of the Gospel. Barth was therefore regarding religion dialectically: it is both the highest and most important enterprise of humanity, yet its failure implies its abolition before the Gospel.

This criticism (of religion) and the solution (ironically, also in what may be considered religion) is seen existentially in the suffering and marginalization of the poor and as such the solution is characterized by praxis (in the form of

---

[28] Barth, *Predigten 1913*, p. 213.
[29] Barth, *Predigten 1913*, p. 216.
[30] An address given to the meeting of Freunde der christlichen Welt (Friends of the Christian World) on the Elgersburg, October 1922, Karl Barth, 'Das Wort Gottes als Aufgabe der Theologie', in Karl Barth, *Das Wort Gottes und die Theologie* (München: Christian Kaiser Verlag, 1924), pp. 156-178; ET: Karl Barth, 'The Word of God and the Task of Ministry', in Karl Barth, *The Word of God and the Word of Man* (trans. Douglas Horton; London: Hodder and Stoughton, 1928), pp. 183-217.
[31] These comments, and those following, summarize Barth's position with regard to Luther and Calvin, Jeremiah and Paul, Kierkegaard etc., as set out in Barth, 'Das Wort Gottes als Aufgabe der Theologie', pp. 164-65/ET: pp. 195-196.

religious socialism). But this still left the doctrinal basis of, for instance, the Lutheran Church untouched. Liberal neo-Protestant theology must be changed. Writing late in life Barth commented that even before 1910 he had been unfamiliar in his innermost being to the bourgeois (bürgerlich) world of Ritschl and his pupils. In terms of his doctrinal thinking there is the important emergence of the use of dialectic. In terms of the *Denkform* of dialectic, we have seen in 'Der Glaube an den persönlichen Gott' how Barth asserted that the use of mystery, paradox and dialectic was the only method to account for and allow the apparently contradictory *diastasis* between the transcendence of God and the immediacy of religious experience to stand. This use of dialectic is essentially from the influence of his younger brother Heinrich who completed his doctoral studies in philosophy in 1913.[32] The precise nature and content of the influence of Heinrich (including the philosophical influence of Immanuel Kant) will be examined later in the context of *Römerbrief 2* when we look at Kierkegaard. A proto-form of this *Denkform* of dialectic also occurred, as we have seen, in 'Kriegszeit und Gottesreich' where Barth opened up the distance, *diastasis*, between the world/humanity and God: 'Welt ist Welt, daß Gott Gott ist'.

These two ideas of (i) the Denkform of dialectic, and (ii) a criticism of religion, are important because they are in part found in Barth's reading of Dostoevsky. Their origin in Barth's thinking is during this period of 1911-15, the early years in Safenwil as we have seen above. However, these two ideas are influenced and changed by Barth's reading of Dostoevsky from August 1915; then by Barth's reading of Kierkegaard from 1919; but most substantially by the posthumously published writings of Franz Overbeck from 1920.

---

[32] Heinrich ('Heiner') Barth (1890-1965), was educated and trained in philosophy at the University of Berne where he completed his PhD: Heinrich Barth, 'Descartes Begründung der Erkenntnis' (PhD thesis, University of Berne, 1913).

PART TWO
KARL BARTH-
SCHULD UND SÜHNE

'Is it not shameful that we needed to have this truth retold to us by the Russian Dostoevsky? If we have refused to hear it from our Reformers who really understood it better than Dostoevsky, are we then still Protestants?'

Karl Barth, 'Der römische Katholizismus als Frage an die protestantische Kirche', in *Die Theoligie und die Kirche*, pp. 356-7

CHAPTER 3

Sonya and Raskolnikov - a Dialectic of Sin and Grace

Crime and Punishment

Writing to Thurneysen on 18 August 1915, Barth commented, 'Yesterday I spent the entire day reading Dostoevsky's Crime and Punishment - I wanted to become completely wise about this Russian'[1]. Why is this relevant? A central idea in the theology underpinning the novels of Dostoevsky is this *diastasis* between world and God. The characters in his novels do not sit cosily in religious piety, mistaking (as Dostoevsky saw it) their own self-love for an experience of God, but are broken and fallen sinners, wretched in the irrational nihilism of their depravity. Change happens: after an existential decision to turn, to alter the way of thinking that has brought them to the state they find themselves in, they live different 'resurrected' lives, but they are still human, still mortal, still fallen though reformed, and the world is still the world and God is still God - transcendent and other.

The central character in *Crime and Punishment* is a young bourgeois student, an intellectual, originally from the country that having dropped out of university is living in a squalid garret in the poorest district of St Petersburg: Rodion Romanovich Raskolnikov. He believes that there are some human beings who have the right to transcend law and custom so as to establish new laws and customs - Napoleon being an example, or so he claims (in the story he has even published an article in a law journal proposing his theory). Therefore he conceives the design of murdering an elderly pawnbroker (Alena Ivanova) not primarily to steal from her but to rid the world of what he regards is a louse! But it all goes wrong - having bludgeoned the pawnbroker to death with an axe he is caught by the early return of her younger sister (Lizaveta). He is forced to kill the sister in the same way so as to cover his crime. But the righteousness of God presses in on him. His conscience will not allow him to settle, it convicts

---

[1] 'Gestern las ich den ganzen Tag Dostojewski "Schuld und Sühne"; ich wollte ich würde ganz klug aus diesen Russen', Barth to Thurneysen, 18 August 1915, in Karl Barth and Eduard Thurneysen, *Karl Barth-Eduard Thurneysen, Briefwechsel Band I 1913-1921* (Gesamtausgabe Bearbeitet und herausgegeben von Eduard Thurneysen; Zürich: Theologischer Verlag Zürich, 1973), pp. 71-72. Note the emphatic emphasis in the German never translated into English - '*ganz Klug*', wholly, whole, very, entirely wise!

him of the depravity and awfulness of his crime. He is plagued by hallucination and guilt-ridden nightmares for weeks after the murders. Salvation comes in the form of a young prostitute - Sofya Semyonovna Marmeladova (Sonya) - not a nice Christian from the *petit bourgeoisie* in St Petersburg. Sonya is responsible for bringing in an income to feed and clothe her consumptive stepmother and stepbrothers and stepsister, her father having lost his job with the civil service through drinking. It is the pressure and witness of Sonya the seventeen-year-old prostitute - on one occasion through her reading the story of the raising of Lazarus to him from St John's Gospel - that contributes to a cataclysmic change in Raskolnikov's thinking. He admits his guilt, publicly, confesses to the authorities and takes his punishment: exile to a Siberian prison camp. Sonya follows and waits for him to serve his sentence: this, for Dostoevsky, is resurrection as it is woven into the heart of existence.

Trespass and Reparation

Crime and Punishment is about sin and guilt, about human fallenness, about the nihilism resulting from bad decisions. The Russian title of the book is Преступление и наказание (*Prestuplenie i nakazanie*). Преступление (*Prestuplenie*) means literally, a *stepping over, a transgression*, therefore it relates to the English verb to *transgress* - or, more pertinently, *to trespass*. Наказание (*Nakazanie*) relates to the English noun *reparation* (or verb, if there is one - *to reparate*).[2] The work is therefore about humanity when it oversteps the limits imposed not just by convention and human law, but rationality and, ultimately, God's law. Modern German translations of Преступление и наказание (*Prestuplenie i nakazanie*) are often entitled, *Verbrechen und Strafe* (*das Verbrechen,* crime; *die Strafe,* punishment, penalty). Older translations (from the time of the First World War) used the title *Schuld und Sühne* (*die Schuld* can be used for guilt, trespass; *die Sühn,* atonement, expiation). But in modern day German the phrase *Schuld und Sühne* is now taken to mean *crime and punishment*. This is in part because the phrase Преступление и наказание (*Prestuplenie i nakazanie*) has been taken over by many world languages to mean *crime and punishment* - Dostoevsky has to a large extent given this phrase to the world! But we must remember that in the original Russian and in the German translation that Barth and Thurneysen read in 1915 the wording had these strong connotations of sin and transgression; trespass and atonement; guilt, expiation and reparation - with obvious theological associations. It is also important to remember that the name Dostoevsky gave to this anti-hero was significant: раскольник (*raskolnik*) means literally a schismatic in Russian (from раскол - *raskol* - schism, primarily, then dissent, the root verb being

---

[2] The verb наказат (*nakazat*), from which is derived the noun *nakazanie*, can under certain circumstances be used for, *to order,* or *to instruct,* as well as relating to *punishment* and *reparation*: does not Sonya effectively instructs Raskolnikov?

3. Sonya and Raskolnikov - a Dialectic of Sin and Grace

расколоть - *raskolot* - to split). Why is Raskolnikov a schismatic - because he separates humanity from God, his actions split, rent, humanity from God. Dostoevsky knew that to his Russian readers a schismatic was one representing a small group who had broken away from the Russian Orthodox Church - for example, the Раскольники (*Raskolniki*) who were members of a sect of old believers who broke away in the seventeenth-century. But what Dostoevsky was saying was that this man, this murderer and intellectual is prepared to 'sacrifice fellow human beings on the altar of theoretical premises and his own satanic pretensions to moral freedom' furthermore that this is 'startlingly modern and by now distressingly familiar'[3] and is in many ways representative of the history of Western civilization in the twentieth-century, and as such represents the schism brought about by the Fall of humanity away from God through original sin.

Atheism

Is Raskolnikov an atheist? Dostoevsky presents characters that are full of contradictions with regard to beliefs, ethics. The question arises, which god does someone not believe in, or which god does another profess. For both Barth (at this time in his development) and Dostoevsky atheists may have a better grasp of the one true God as revealed, than polite respectable Christians; likewise both question whether pious Christian religion really did proclaim the Gospel of God's forgiveness through Christ's redemption. These are polemical points. The term atheist/atheism is likewise contentious. It is important to remember that this cautious respect/value for atheism served in distancing him from his theological and ecclesial heritage.

In *The Idiot* Dostoevsky has Rogozhin ask Prince Myshkin explicitly, 'But I've long wanted to ask you something, Lev Nikolaich - do you believe in God or not?'[4] Myshkin answers obliquely almost in a parable with four stories: the first is about an encounter on a train where Myshkin fell into conversation with a stranger who was bright, clever, kind and considerate but claimed to be an atheist - 'He doesn't believe in God, and he talked a good deal about it, but all the while it appeared to me that he was speaking outside the subject'. There was a clear dichotomy between what the man was and his belief system. Myshkin then contrasts this with the story of two great friends who were respectably poor but comfortable-

...(one of them) was by no means a thief ... but this silver watch and chain so

---

[3] William J. Leatherbarrow, 'Introduction', in Fyodor Mikhailovich Dostoevsky, *Crime and Punishment* (trans. Richard Pevear and Larissa Volokhonsky; London: Everyman's Library, 1993), p. xxvi. Much of this analysis of the title of *Crime and Punishment* is derived from Leatherbarrow's work.

[4] Fyodor Mikhailovich Dostoevsky, *The Idiot* (trans. Richard Pevear and Larissa Volokhonsky; London: Everyman's Library, 1993), p. 218.

fascinated him that he could not restrain himself. He took a knife, and when his friend turned his back, he came up softly behind, raised his eyes to heaven, crossed himself, and saying earnestly - "God forgive me, for Christ's sake!" he cut his friend's throat like a sheep, and took the watch.

Hence we have the relative value of religious belief. Simply declaring belief in God is not enough, likewise denial of God's existence is not irrefutably damning (particularly as it raises the question of which particular god a person does or does not believe in). Holiness/sanctification is what is important - the remaining two parables/stories qualify this. The third is about an old drunken soldier who cons Myshkin into buying what he claims is a solid silver cross on a chain but is really only cheap tin. Myshkin buys it, laments that the old soldier has probably gone off to drink the proceeds but comments, 'I thought, "I will wait awhile before I condemn this Judas. Only God knows what may be hidden in the hearts of drunkards."' The fourth story defines Myshkin's answer:

> ... I came across a poor woman, carrying a child - a baby of some six weeks old. ...the baby was smiling up at her, for the first time in its life... while I watched the woman she suddenly crossed herself, oh, so devoutly! What is it, my good woman I asked her... Exactly as is a mother's joy when her baby smiles for the first time into her eyes, so is God's joy when one of His children turns and prays to Him for the first time, with all his heart! ...such a deep, refined, truly religious thought it was - a thought in which the whole essence of Christianity was expressed in one flash - that is, the recognition of God as our Father, and of God's joy in people as His own children, which is the chief idea of Christ.

So for Myshkin, joy and love are the touchstone of true religion. In recounting the stories Myshkin has told Rogozhin of his implicit belief in God, yet Myshkin cannot assert from cognitive thought in the way Rogozhin expects, he does not express verbally a concept/idea that in effect owns to knowledge of God yet his life exudes holiness. Dostoevsky is saying that simple declarations of belief (partisan allegiance to this god or that) are secondary. Serving the will of God is of primary importance. This marginalizes human assertions, human religious pride and shifts the focus onto God. This is taken further with the story of Marie,[5] another parable, which further pushes this dialectic between simple partisan declarations of religious belief on the one hand and faith on the other. Marie is the victim of religious prejudice and self-righteous moralising by the local minister[6] and his congregation when, unmarried, she falls pregnant, and dies as an outcast, an untouchable having been forced into the role of the village idiot, yet she exudes love, holiness and forgiveness to all - reminiscent of a martyr or saint from the early church.

---

[5] Dostoevsky, *The Idiot*, pt. 1 chp. 6, pp. 67-76
[6] The parable/story is based in Switzerland and the significance of a critical portrait of a nineteenth-century pious Reformed minister would not have been lost on Barth and Thurneysen.

Is Raskolnikov an atheist? It is difficult to say - his belief system can be interpreted as such but more pertinently it is characterized by rebellion. The more he rebels, the more he denies the love of God by his actions, the more he then dissolves into the nightmarish *surd*-like[7] nihilism of sin, the irrationality that flows from his belief system. For example, Raskolnikov affirms the existence of God in answer to Porfiry's questions (the investigating officer), yet earlier he derides Sonya's faith, the existence of her God and the way this God has left her and her family in poverty and illness. Ivan Karamazov (*The Brothers Karamazov*) by contrast goes through what can be identified as various phases and types of so-called atheism, his theologoumena being characterized by rebellion against God more than logical atheism (the divine object of his fury being at times realistic, at others non-realistic): the full implications of this will be discussed in chapter sixteen. However, for Barth, Thurneysen and Dostoevsky there is some value in atheism - it may not always lead to destruction and fragmentation. The first story Myshkin recounts was of a man who professed atheism but was honest and righteous in his heart and yearned for what the Christian should. There are elements here of *The Parable of the Two Sons* (Matthew 21:28-32) - one son says to his father he will not work in the vineyard, but does; the second son says he will, but does not. The parable is about obedience to the will of God - the first son does the will of the Father (n.b. Matthew 7:21). The paradox of atheism and rebellion will come up again when we examine 'The Idea' for Dostoevsky.

Dialectic in Dostoevsky's Doctrine of God

Dostoevsky's work is heavily dialectical. For example, central in his work is the antinomy between the doctrine of a loving and merciful God and the reality of a bleak, cruel life characterized by suffering - all other dialectics in Dostoevsky's work flow from this central dialectical antinomy. There is an implied separation, distinction, even disjuncture between God and life as experienced by humanity. In his days as a 'European liberal' (as he referred to his student days in St Petersburg),[8] he read the German theologian Feuerbach and took on board an atheistic theory of religion. In many ways his entire writing career after Siberia is about coming to terms with how to justify faith in God in the light of Feuerbach. The only way Dostoevsky could claim faith in God was by stressing God's transcendence and otherness - beyond the world of

---

[7] *Surd*-like: *surd*, a Latin translation of the Greek ἄλογος - primarily without speech or word, however, also without reason, irrational. Theologically this is Raskolnikov's irrational nihilistic contradiction of the Word of God in Christ through his behaviour and beliefs.

[8] Fyodor Mikhailovich Dostoevsky, *The Diary of a Writer* (trans. and annotated Boris Brasol; 2 vols; New York: Charles Scribner's Sons, 1949). See vol. II, August 1880, chp. 3, '1 Concerning One Most Important Matter', p. 984.

Feuerbachian religion, peopled by projected gods or idols. But there are two important factors:

First, Jesus Christ - the God-man: Dostoevsky used The Gospel of John as evidence of Christ's divinity. Boyce Gibson noted how Dostoevsky seemed to ground God in Christ and had difficulty conceiving or knowing of God as transcendent such was the importance, existentially, of the immanent to him.[9] At times Dostoevsky so believed in Jesus Christ as God that he lost any understanding or idea of God's transcendence - the Father in heaven. Dostoevsky therefore accepted the transcendence of God axiomatically whilst grounding the knowability of God in Christ.

Second, Russian Orthodox Mysticism: Russian Orthodox beliefs never attempted to close this distance in the way that it was closed, relatively, by theologians and philosophers in nineteenth century Liberal neo-Protestantism and in the theology of Schleiermacher; furthermore Orthodox epistemology stated that we mere humans could not know God but any encounter with the Holy Spirit would be perturbing, puzzling and certainly not conforming to the cognitive and epistemological expectations of humanity. Further, any mystical experience must be measured against, validated by sacred scripture. This was Dostoevsky's standpoint also.

Dostoevsky therefore saw the first person of the Trinity as wholly transcendent and other. Dostoevsky took his theological beliefs from the Russian New Testament and later in life from staying in Russian Orthodoxy monasteries. This distinction of his is not just grounded in the separateness and independence of creation from God but is the result primarily of the Fall. Humanity is lost, fallen, separate, distant from God - humanity must turn and make a decision to live for God and not for themselves. As Thurneysen notes in his work on Dostoevsky,

> The question of God is the question of all his works: God, the root of all life, and the basis of the world, which gives everything its basis, but also its abrogation, its torment, its 'dis-ease,' the enigmatically unreal in all that is real, the unearthly, toward which all that is earthly aspires. The dialectic of this paradoxical truth is the dialectic of all Dostoevsky's men and women. They all have God as their goal, they are all moved and driven by him from the beginning on. They press toward him in the insatiability of their longing for life, in the search for final answers, and yet no step leads over from man, for how would God still be God if man could become god?[10]

Despite this unbridgeable gulf, humanity can through an act of directing the will, turn to God and know God. This is then the doctrine of God in *Crime and Punishment* contrasted as it is with the doctrine of the man-god (Raskolnikov). Despite this dialectical disjuncture it is fair to consider Dostoevsky's doctrine

---

[9] Alexander Boyce Gibson, *The Religion of Dostoevsky* (London: SCM Press, 1973), p. 166.
[10] Thurneysen, *Dostojewski*, p. 37/ET: pp. 42-43.

of God as Trinitarian. There is the distance, the unbridgeable gulf, between humanity and the Father (caused by the Fall, original sin), with the Father only known through the Son; the Holy Spirit moving in, convicting people, reordering them to the Father's will for their salvation through the Son. For example, in his Russian New Testament Dostoevsky had heavily annotated John's Gospel. Within John's Gospel there are the passages annotated/underlined relating to how the Father is in the Son and how those who know the Son know the Father -'Jesus said to him, "I am the way, and the truth, and the life. *No one comes to the Father except through me. If you know me, you will know my Father also.* From now on you do know him and have seen him"' [11] (this passage is marked 'N.B.' in the margin with verses 6b and 7a underlined, shown here italicized); also 'Believe me that I am in the Father and the Father is in me; but if you do not, then believe me because of the works themselves' [12], which is marked in a similar manner. The atoning sacrifice of the Son bridges this divide. Further, the second person of the Trinity is often knowable, for Dostoevsky, to ordinary people through suffering. The existential decision to turn to God is then an experience of the Holy Spirit often characterized by prevenient grace leading to the denial of will - this pneumatological immediacy is paradoxical in the sense that it appears to contradict the distance/distinction between humanity and God. The litmus test is as always with Dostoevsky, sacred scripture: how the problems of existence measure against the Bible. Therefore the struggles of his characters to live either for the good or for self is a reflection of an existential Gospel.

For Barth and Thurneysen the transcendence of God was the basis of the theology underpinning Dostoevsky's novels. This realization, this *diastasis*, was of great importance to them at this juncture in their development.[13] God was not to be seen as infused through history and human events. Barth was a busy pastor at this time, yet he spent an entire day (*ganzen Tag*) reading Dostoevsky's novel, *Crime and Punishment*. Why? He had been impressed by Kutter's assertion that God will use secular powers, secular people, to embarrass the church and to bring it to its knees in humility. Barth was impressed by the observation that the truth of the Gospel might often be presented by agencies outside of the Church; further, that the reality and truth of the Gospel was to be found infused and suffused throughout ordinary existence. Barth saw the way Dostoevsky presented Gospel truth and as a result criticized human religious pride. In *Crime and Punishment* both Barth and Thurneysen noted how little had changed in terms of this world but God had

---

[11] John 14:6-7. See Geir Kjetsaa, *Dostoevsky and his New Testament* (Oslo: Solum Forlag A.S., 1984), p. 39.
[12] John 14:11. See Kjetsaa, *Dostoevsky and his New Testament*, p. 39.
[13] Thurneysen *Dostojewski*, from ideas formulated soon after their discovery of Dostoevsky in 1915 but published eventually in 1921.

been acknowledged, likewise God's unique ability to change and to save people.

Thurneysen wrote that at the end of *Crime and Punishment* there was neither, '...a revolutionary nor a pacifist, neither a particularly pure, noble soul, a martyr or saint nor a dilettante and reformer, not even a fully repentant man to be seen, but "only" a man, who had "a new outlook on life".'[14] At the end of *Crime and Punishment* is a new life, a rebirth - resurrection. Thurneysen continued, 'On earth that may be little, but in heaven there is more joy over one sinner who repents than over ninety-nine just persons who have no need of repentance.'[15] This change of heart, change of mind, which is cataclysmic, earth shattering to the individual, does not close the *diastasis* between humanity and God: life is existential, life is still to be lived - world still remains, and God is still God. There is no moral pride, no transformation into a superman (Übermensch). Furthermore, as Thurneysen asserts,

> At the end there are no matured, enlightened, purified personalities standing before us as there are in the famous developmental novels of German literature. Rather the opposite has happened. Siberian prisons are at the end of *Crime and Punishment* and *The Brothers Karamazov*. Stavrogin, one of the anti-heroes in *The Demons*, hangs himself on the last page of the book. And yet, something has happened, something has changed! The questionability of everything human has become greater, and now with truly shattering power the problem of all being cries out for its final solution in God. That is the result! Once more, if it were otherwise, the solution would not lie in God. Precisely because it is in God, and only in him, the final word of true knowledge of life can therefore be nothing else than the question about him.[16]

Therefore the end is not religious (that is, human religion) - what is, is a paradoxical dialectic that appears to be negative, a denial. The solution to life's problems is not humanly religious: the solution is God. In this death is a rebirth, resurrection, as it is in *Crime and Punishment*, characterized by a questioning of the pride of humanity. Religion, culture, prestige, power, status, politics - these are all human efforts at solving the problem of life - they all come to naught; humanity can achieve nothing in the face of the Gospel (n.b. Mark 10:26-27). This is even more starkly presented in *The Idiot* as Thurneysen notes: Myshkin, the Christlike figure fails in his efforts to save Nastasya Filippovna because he is human and not divine - a denial of the Hegelian agenda in Herrmannian liberalism and also of Nietzsche's Übermensch. 'The Idiot, Prince Myshkin, an epileptic, returns to Russia from a nerve clinic in Switzerland without being cured'[17] only to return there again after suffering his destruction at the hands of murderers, libertines and the bourgeois classes in St

---

[14] Thurneysen, *Dostojewski*, p. 17/ET: p. 21.
[15] Thurneysen, *Dostojewski*, p. 17/ET: p. 21.
[16] Thurneysen, *Dostojewski*, p. 38/ET: pp. 43-44.
[17] Thurneysen, *Dostojewski*, p. 22/ET: pp. 25-26.

Petersburg: the world still remains the same but there has been a change in people - some for the better, some for the worse. Hence Thurneysen's comparison of Raskolnikov and Stavrogin (noted in the quotation above) - the former is moving towards God, the latter away (and to suicide).

Dostoevsky - Judgement and Intellectual Sins

Underpinning Dostoevsky's understanding of sin and grace is his theological anthropology (see Figure 1 Dostoevsky's Theological Anthropology, on page 44). So what was Dostoevsky's understanding of humanity? His early, pre-Siberian works, for example *Poor Folk* (1846) and *The Double* (1846), present characters that are considered shallow, meek, and fearful of any trouble in life. In *White Nights* (1848) we find humanity characterized by little good deeds but like his enlightenment forbears Dostoevsky did not ask where goodness came from, or recognize that there was evil in human hearts. The experience of Siberia was an education for him. Up to this point in his life he had been raised in relative comfort and security: student days had been in St Petersburg, the most Westernized of Russian cities, an army career (engineer) ahead of him (initially as a Lieutenant), with little to give him any doubt about the innate goodness of humanity. Post Siberia Dostoevsky picked up the threads of his fledging career as a writer but now his anthropology was characterized by recognition of the evil that infects humanity. Within a few years of returning to Russia in 1859 he had published a few short stories and articles, and produced *Notes from the House of the Dead* (1860-62), based on his experience of a Siberian prison camp and *Notes From Underground* (1864). This is considered his dark period and culminated in the writing and publication of *Crime and Punishment* (1866) and *The Idiot* (1868). Dostoevsky is at his most pessimistic during this period. By the late 1870s we find a greater balance in his understanding of humanity before God: humanity is still prey to nothingness but with God people can be something. Without God there is no limit to the depths of depravity, sin, debauchery and cruelty that humanity can sink to; worse, as people perpetrate these acts they convince themselves that what they are doing is right. By contrast, and with God through Christ there is no limit to the goodness, sanctity and love that can be achieved, demonstrated. This is the fundamental dialectical conclusion of the theological anthropology in Dostoevsky's mature work. For Dostoevsky, only God can keep people from totally destroying themselves.

Raskolnikov's chief crime, his transgression, was to try to be God - *eritis sicut deus!* Raskolnikov's belief system that led him to behave like a Napoleon was actually an attempt to be as God. In claiming the authority to transcend right and wrong, to redefine the moral ought, in attempting to act like God he was subverting the righteousness of God. Sonya does not - why? Sonya is forced into the work of licensed prostitution as the only way to feed and clothe her consumptive mother and her stepbrothers and stepsister. She hates being a prostitute - but does it for the good that it gains. Raskolnikov is bemused at her calm sanity considering the life she leads - however, he soon realizes that her sanctity and sanity lay in the evenings spent studying the Bible with Lizaveta (whom Raskolnikov murdered to cover his crime of bludgeoning to death her sister, the elderly pawn broker). Sonya waits on God for forgiveness and mercy: the Übermensch, the Mensch-Gott does not. This is what impresses itself on Barth and Thurneysen. Within this is a criticism of intellectual sins - the pride resulting from bad ideas. For example, Sonya's father knows that he is a drunken wastrel who should be looking after his family rather than allowing his eldest daughter to earn money through prostitution. Dostoevsky is very tolerant of thieves and ruffians, libertines and villains, people who commit wrongful actions but may not necessarily suffer from bad ideas in the philosophical sense - '...as long as one is content to use fists and axes, there is always the possibility of continued life in Dostoevsky's world.'[18] Perhaps many expect the drunkards and prostitutes to be condemned by God. However, if this is so, such condemnation is not in keeping with the Gospels. Dostoevsky is saying that they are forgiven, that the all-powerful merciful God who watches and knows all forgives them; why? - because not one of them believed him or herself to be worthy. Worthy of what? - worthy of forgiveness by God. Not unworthy before respectable society, not unworthy within a humanist ethic, but unworthy to face God - the otherworldly God of Dostoevsky's dialectical doctrine of God. Why are they loved even when they are unworthy before God? - because (speaking of Sonya) she has loved much. Sonya's sins are great - as a prostitute - but her love and suffering for her family are great. This does not make her prostitution right before God, but when Christ has died for all so all may be forgiven their sins there is still the question, for Dostoevsky, of God's justice: justice is measured by the amount someone has loved, and that love is measured by Christ. The importance of this will become clear when we examine Barth's address/essay 'Die Gerechtigkeit Gottes', in the next chapter, written a few months after his reading of *Crime and Punishment*.

'The Idea' [19]

Raskolnikov parading himself as God is paradoxical: at times he appears not to believe in God, at others he agrees patronisingly to God's existence, but a result of his rebellion is that he ends up behaving *as if* he were God (*eritis sicut deus*) because if there is no God then there are no limits on human behaviour, no morals, no ethics. Humanity, therefore, claims the right to define what is right and wrong, entirely with reference to itself alone, or more pertinently, an

---

[18] Kjetsaa, *Dostoevsky and his New Testament*, p. 11.
[19] The phrase 'The Idea' comes from Boyce Gibson, *The Religion of Dostoevsky*, chp. 7, 'Each and All: The Brothers Karamazov', pp. 169-208. See in particular p. 172.

oligarchic elite (those who have thought and had ideas and are regarded as experts) claim this right in their wilfulness. Pertinently, certain individuals claim the right to transcend traditional morals and ethics and thereby redefine - hence Raskolnikov's Napoleonic delusion: the ground or basis of such morality is not outside of humanity, it is within humanity - or more pertinently, it is within the perception of an elite that has the innate right to define what is acceptable behaviour. This is, in Dostoevsky's work, 'The Idea'. That is, the realisation that if there is no God then there is no sound or permanent basis for ethics and morality; if humanity is alone in a universe of its own making then Christian morality is a fraud; if Christianity is abandoned then so too is Christian morality: everything is then permitted. The alternative is that we are the creature, the creation, of the creator, we have been made for a purpose and there are limits expected of our behaviour simply for the pleasure of the creator and for our own good. This rebellion, 'The Idea', is the central preoccupation of Dostoevsky. 'The Idea' reaches its climax for Dostoevsky in *The Brothers Karamazov* twelve years after writing *Crime and Punishment,* and is seen in Ivan Karamazov's philosophical dictum that everything is permitted, individuals will define what they believe is acceptable ethics (Ivan Karamazov is contrasted in *The Brothers Karamazov* with Father Zossima who expounds the Gospel dictum that each is responsible for all: love God and love your neighbour). Within this rebellion, the logical conclusion of 'The Idea' is that even if God exists, I (the ego in Ivan Karamazov) want nothing to do with the deity and will return my ticket of life - suicide (see Figure 2 'The Idea' - Dostoevsky, Nietzsche, Thurneysen and Barth, on page 45).

The first example of 'The Idea' was in a work published in 1864 five years after his return from imprisonment/exile in Siberia - *Notes from Underground* (подполье - *podpole* literally beneath the floor).[20] On the surface it appears totally unchristian, save that what Dostoevsky was presenting was the logical outcome of rejecting the Gospel: humanity without God. The work is about a retired civil servant living alone in a bleak grey nihilistic world. This is an early example of the dictum later presented by Ivan Karamazov that without God there is no morality, no humanity, there are no constraints on human behaviour. *Notes from Underground* is a portrait of the weakness and fragmentation, psychologically, of the human soul; this is the logical conclusion of liberal humanism and atheism. For Dostoevsky, any love for humanity is a fraud without God. Why is this so? First, the work contains the psychological basis of Dostoevsky's study of *sublapsarian* humanity; second, the work, along with

---

[20] Fyodor Mikhailovich Dostoevsky, *Notes From Underground* and *The Gambler* (trans. Jane Kentish, Oxford World's Classics; Oxford: Oxford University Press, 1999).

much of the rest of Dostoevsky's corpus (with the exception of *The Brothers Karamazov*) had a profound influence on the German philosopher Friedrich Nietzsche.

Unlike many nineteenth-century German Idealists and European humanitarians Nietzsche saw that if people were to abandon Christianity then the Christian basis for human behaviour went as well. All that was left was Dostoevsky's underground man: the corrupt will, fragmenting into alienated insanity. This understanding led Nietzsche to propound his theory of 'will-to-power'. In *Twilight of the Idols* Nietzsche acknowledges the profound debt he owed to Dostoevsky.

> The testimony of Dostoevsky is relevant to this problem - Dostoevsky, the only psychologist, incidentally, from whom I had something to learn; he ranks among the most beautiful strokes of fortune in my life, even more than my discovery of Stendhal. This profound human being, who was ten times right in his low estimate of the superficial Germans, lived for a long time among the convicts in Siberia - hardened criminals for whom there was no way back to society - and found them very different from what he himself had expected: they were carved out of just about the best, hardest, and most valuable wood that grows anywhere on Russian soil. [21]

The difference from our perspective is that Nietzsche saw this reality and followed the path of atheism, which logically led to moral nihilism. In *Notes From Underground* Dostoevsky's message was that this is the limit of human freedom without God - all that is left is the necessity for Christ and the slender hope of faith. Unfortunately the Czar's official censor expunged the passage that made this explicit. Dostoevsky writing to his elder brother, Mikhail Mikhaylovich, from Moscow on the 26 March 1864 made his frustration felt:

> It would have been better not to print the last chapter but one at all (it is the most important, where the essential idea is expressed), than to print it as it is, that is, with cobbled-up sentences and full of contradictions ... those brutes of censors - where I made a mock of everything and sometimes blasphemed for form's sake, that is passed, but where I deduced from all this the necessity of faith in Christ - that is suppressed! [22]

He never restored the passages that had been removed and there is no record of it in the archive of his work. However, he went on to present this more explicitly in *Crime and Punishment* two years later. To achieve the understanding of the absolute necessity of Christ and the inability of the human psyche to solve the problem of life on its own Dostoevsky had to cut through

---

[21] Friedrich Nietzsche, *Twilight of the Idols* (trans. Walter Kaufmann and R.J. Hollingdale; London, Harmondsworth: Penguin Books, 1985). See 'Skirmishes of an Untimely Man', § 45, 'The criminal and what is related to him', p. 99.

[22] Quoted in Jessie Coulson, *Dostoevsky: A Self-Portrait* (Oxford: Oxford University Press, 1962), p. 124. See Fyodor Mikhailovich Dostoevsky, *Dostoevsky - Complete Letters* (trans. and ed. David A. Lowe; 5 vols; New York: Ardis Publishers, 1989-91).

3. Sonya and Raskolnikov - a Dialectic of Sin and Grace

human culture and human-centred religion. This is important because Nietzsche was an influence on (and illustration of this idea) for Barth during the period of the rewriting of *Der Römerbrief* - and Dostoevsky was a profound influence in this respect on Nietzsche. Both Barth and Nietzsche held the respectable Christian society in nineteenth-century Germany in low estimation, as also did Dostoevsky. Barth did not as far as can be ascertained read *Notes from the Underground* - however, these ideas are expounded at their most explicit (theologically and psychologically) in *The Brothers Karamazov*, which had a significant impact on Barth whilst writing *Römerbrief 2*.

'The Idea' is existential because it is centred on human decision and actions. Initially there is the decision to disbelieve in God or to reject God for one's own agenda; this results in the paradox of consciously or unconsciously asserting one's own ego as God - to be, therefore, as God (*eritis sicut deus*), to act *as if*. The next stage is to redefine human morality and ethics according to one's own principles (for example, Raskolnikov's Napoleonic agenda in *Crime and Punishment*); then to storm heaven, that is the attempt to redefine human morality/ethics, thereby to realize that without God there are as a result no limits or constraints on human behaviour, human wilfulness. When Raskolnikov contemplates his crime he raves about how marvellously Napoleon redefined the good by killing many, abandoning thousands, razing whole cities, therefore nothing is impossible, everything is permitted:

> No, those people are made differently; the true master, to whom all is permitted, sacks Toulon, makes a slaughterhouse of Paris, forgets an army in Egypt, expends half a million men in a Moscow campaign, and gets off with a pun in Vilno; and when he dies they set up monuments to him - and thus everything is permitted.[23]

This results in rebellion: to rebel, even in the face of God-and-immortality. This leaves only one option: suicide. Suicide is the ultimate statement, the ultimate rebellion. For example, to return the ticket of life to God as Ivan Karamazov in *The Brothers Karamazov* puts it. Ivan flirts with suicide as an intellectual exercise but is overwhelmed by a mental breakdown before he can kill himself. Smerdyakov in *The Brothers Karamazov*, Stavrogin in *The Demons*, Svidrigailov in *Crime and Punishment*, do commit suicide because of the weight of their sin, though they do not perceive themselves as sinners or sinful.

---

[23] Dostoevsky, *Crime and Punishment*, pt. 3 chp. 6, pp. 274.

Year			Work
1881			*Diary of a Writer* (1880 and 1881)
	The Brothers Karamazov: a more balanced approach between good and evil in people		*The Brothers Karamazov* (1878/9-80)
			Diary of a Writer (1876 and 1877)
			Dream of a Ridiculous Man (1877)
			Diary of a Writer (inc. *The Dream*) (1878)
1875			*A Raw Youth* (1875)
			articles and short stories
			Diary of a Writer (1873)
	The Pessimistic Years: without God humanity is corrupt, depraved, with virtually no good left in people; the *imago dei* is totally obscured by a corrupt will		*The Demons* (1871-2)
			articles and short stories
1870			*The Idiot* (1868)
			articles and short stories
			The Gambler and *Crime and Punishment* (1866)
1865			*Notes from Underground* (1864)
			articles & short stories
			Notes from the House of the Dead (1860-2)
			articles & short stories
1859			

THE SIBERIAN YEARS

PRISON 4 years — EXILE 6 years

1849	Early writings characterised by optimism, in the inherent goodness of humanity	Influence of Belinsky & involvement with the Petrashevskii circle - arrest and conviction; death sentence commuted
		White Nights (1848)
1845		*Poor Folk* & *The Double* (1846)
		Articles & short stories

FYODOR MIKHAILOVICH DOSTOEVSKY (1821-1881): KEY WORKS AND THEIR RELATIONSHIP TO THE DEVELOPMENT OF HIS THEOLOGICAL ANTHROPOLOGY

Figure 1 Dostoevsky's Theological Anthropology
The major works are here shown chronologically in relation to the period of Siberian exile and the changing nature of Dostoevsky's theological anthropology from the naivety of his early novellas and short stories through the pessimism of his understanding of the human condition in the middle years following the return from Siberia, culminating in the more balanced approach to the human predicament in his mature years.

3. Sonya and Raskólnikov - a Dialectic of Sin and Grace

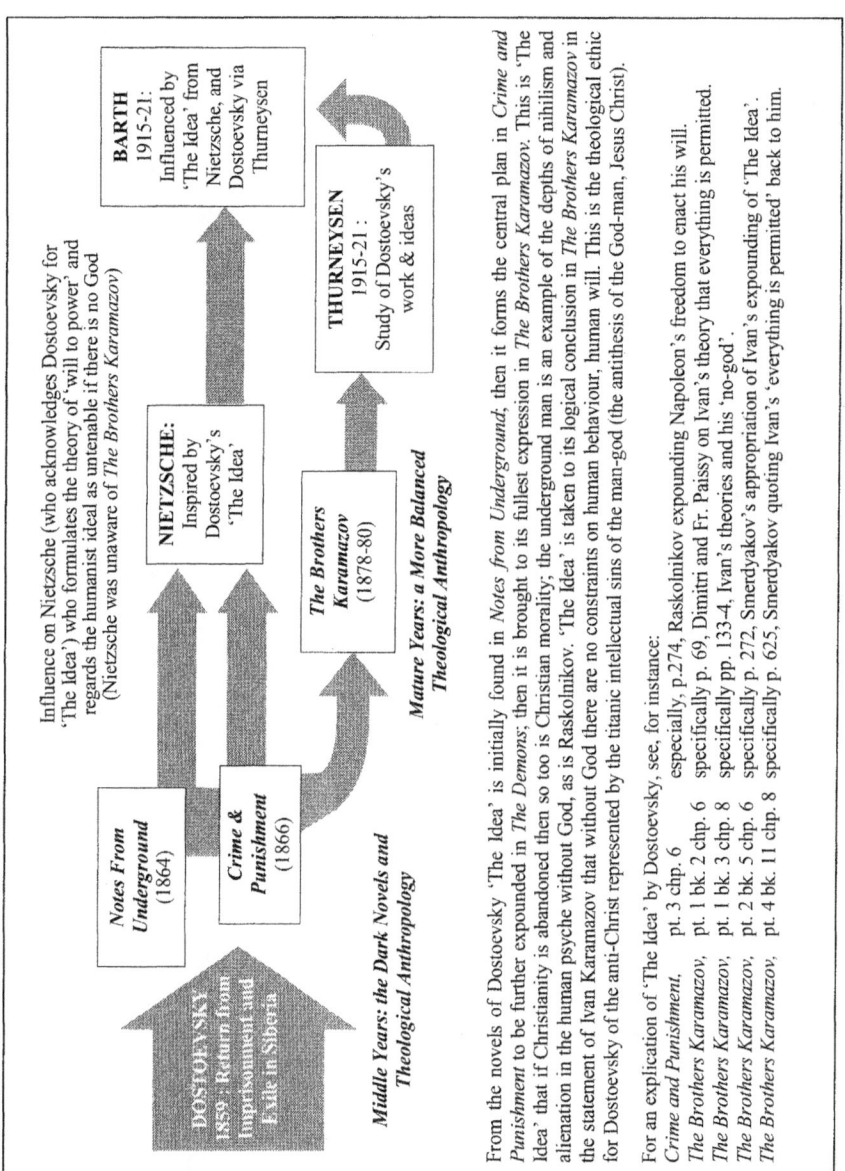

Figure 2 'The Idea' - Dostoevsky, Nietzsche, Thurneysen and Barth
The relationship between Dostoevsky and Nietzsche; and between Dostoevsky, Thurneysen and Barth, and how Barth receives 'The Idea' both from Dostoevsky (via Thurneysen) and Nietzsche of the logic of nihilistic, atheistic ethics: it is important to remember one important principle: Nietzsche (as with Feuerbach, Freud, Marx) is approaching ethics from the position of an avowed atheist; Dostoevsky and Barth are operating from a Christian perspective.

Chapter 4

Die Gerechtigkeit Gottes

Wilfulness

Barth presented an address to an assembly of clergy and religious dignitaries in Aarau Town Church, 'Die Gerechtigkeit Gottes' ('The Righteousness of God'), a matter of months after initially reading *Crime and Punishment*.[1] Barth's theological anthropology in 'Die Gerechtigkeit Gottes' is critically *sublapsarian*; this anthropology portrays a humanity that is dominated by a corrupt and fallen will, a wilfulness that is self-seeking and lacks constancy and is even at odds with itself. Righteousness belongs not with the human will but with God; the will of God is always faithful and true, right and correct, free and unfettered. Humanity can recognize this state of wilfulness, this arbitrary self-seeking, but decides to compromise. Therefore Barth invokes conscience. Conscience points us to the will of God, God's righteousness. But we try to silence the voice of conscience by creating our own righteousness: morality and judgement, the state and nations, law and religion. Human righteousness, in Barth's words, is merely a Tower of Babel attempting to mask the problem. In attempting to mask, even to deny the problem, humanity is trying to be as if it were God - *eritis sicut deus*. Institutional Christianity and a church that is settled and at one with the world are examples of this for Barth; the answer to this problem is to deny this human delusion and listen to conscience. Conscience will tell us that God alone can solve the problem. Barth is therefore setting-off *faith* against *religion* - a distinction characterized by *diastasis*.

eritis sicut deus - The Tower of Babel

In Dostoevsky's work, particularly in *Crime and Punishment*, the righteousness of God exists completely outside of the world of men and women, of all human affairs. The religion of the polite St Petersburg bourgeois class masks and hides, suffocates, conscience. Conscience and the righteousness of God are

---

[1] The address 'Die Gerechtigkeit Gottes' was written in early December 1915 and presented at Aarau Town Church on 16 January 1916; it was initially published later in the year in *Neue Wege* X (1916). It was reprinted verbatim as Karl Barth, 'Die Gerechtigkeit Gottes', in Barth, *Das Wort Gottes und die Theologie*, pp. 5-17; ET: Karl Barth, 'The Righteousness of God', in Barth, *The Word of God and the Word of Man*, pp. 9-27.

independent of the religiosity of all but the most fallen, broken and downtrodden people in St Petersburg. The righteousness of God is most certainly not the same as good human morality, it is not something that wealthy people come to practice only when they have become comfortable in life - it is most certainly not the highest of human ideals produced by and controlled by humanity (a belief, Hegelian in origin, that was central to the Herrmannian liberalism that Barth was reacting against). Raskolnikov in attempting to rewrite the rule-book whereby he was perfectly at right and at liberty to stamp out the elderly pawn broker because *he* regarded her as a louse, as a parasite on the poor (not because he is concerned for the poor, but because *he* is poor), is laying claim to own the righteousness that is only of God. In the light of his reading of *Crime and Punishment* and from his discussions with Thurneysen Barth reflects something of our capacity to judge, morally, and to lay claim to possess righteousness in 'Die Gerechtigkeit Gottes'. Barth and Thurneysen's reading of *Crime and Punishment* is then built on by their reading of *The Brothers Karamazov* and Nietzsche in subsequent years. What Barth and Thurneysen are observing is part of the central influence that Dostoevsky had on them: the re-education, so to speak, of their understanding of sin and grace and with it a theological anthropology in keeping with Russian Orthodox theology (which reawakened in them a similar understanding from their Reformed heritage) - men and women are sinners, their lives are characterized by fallenness and depravity, further, that there is little or no good left in them. This is part of what Dostoevsky taught them: the Church, if there is any value to it, is the community of sinners.

This storming of heaven (*eritis sicut deus*) was also seen by Barth and Thurneysen as representative of The Tower of Babel - a motif drawn explicitly from the Bible and from Dostoevsky. This Babel image is used considerably by Barth in 'Die Gerechtigkeit Gottes' and later by Thurneysen in *Dostojewski* (for example, for Thurneysen, in The Legend of the Grand Inquisitor from *The Brothers Karamazov*[2]): see Figure 3 Barth and Thurneysen - The Tower of Babel, on page 57. However, the metaphor of The Tower of Babel puts into words what is woven throughout *Crime and Punishment*. One of Dostoevsky's stated aims in his notebooks for *Crime and Punishment* was to write a story that encapsulated what was represented by The Tower of Babel.[3] Let us briefly remind ourselves of the biblical story of The Tower of Babel (Genesis 11:1-9).

---

[2] Fyodor Mikhailovich Dostoevsky, *The Brothers Karamazov* (trans. Richard Pevear and Larissa Volokhonsky; London: Everyman's Library, 1990), pt. 2 bk. 5 'Pro and Contra', chp. 5, 'The Grand Inquisitor', pp. 246-264.

[3] See Fyodor Mikhailovich Dostoevsky, *The Notebooks for Crime and Punishment* (trans. Edward Wasiolek; Chicago, IL: University of Chicago Press, 1967), p. 218. See also Dostoevsky, *The Diary of a Writer, vol. I*, February 1876, chp. 1, '1 On the Subject that we are all Good Fellows', pp. 198-201, and March 1876, chp. 1, '4 Meditations About Europe', pp. 250-254.

It is not so much the construction of a tower as a gateway to heaven, to the gods that is the offence, the essence of the story is contained in the Hebrew word *zamam* (זָמַם *zaw-mam'*): to plan, usually in a bad sense, to consider, devise, imagine, plot, to purpose and think in an evil manner: God concludes, 'Look, they are one people, and they have all one language; and this is only the beginning of what they will do; nothing that they propose to do will now be impossible for them' (Genesis 11:6). It is because of these proposals, these bad ideas as Dostoevsky would have put it, that God restrains the ancient peoples through the confusion of language, confusion of purpose, because of their attempts to storm heaven, to be as God - *eritis sicut deus* - to believe that everything is permitted (Raskolnikov), that nothing is impossible.

Barth and The Tower of Babel

Barth weaves the biblical story of the Babel tower into 'Die Gerechtigkeit Gottes'. Barth opened the address with Matthew 3:3 - John the Baptist crying in the wilderness. He immediately cites the importance of conscience as the perfect interpreter of life, 'what it tells us is no question, no riddle ... but a fact - the deepest, innermost, surest fact of life, that God is righteous'. Furthermore, Barth compares conscience with reason, reason is inadequate - 'It sees what is human but not what is divine.'[4] We will not learn of God by basing our theology on the human but we must let conscience speak of the righteousness of God in such a way that this righteousness becomes a certainty.[5] Conscience 'may be reduced almost to silence or crushed into oblivion, it may be led astray to the point of folly and wrongdoing, but it remains forever the place between heaven and earth in which God's righteousness is manifest.'[6] But conscience disturbs, it is a pressing accusation, often bitter, sometimes as a crushing curse, then as holy joy, but above all it convinces us that all our living and learning have a goal, it points to a will that is always true to itself, a pure will - the righteousness of God. By comparison Barth cites the human will as capricious, fickle, corrupt. Human will causes us to forget the constancy and purity of God's righteous will: 'For we suffer from unrighteousness.'[7] At times we dread this, we revolt against it, we try to justify our unrighteousness: 'grounded upon caprice, vagary and self-seeking - a will without faithfulness, logic or correlation, disunited and distraught within itself.'[8] Barth outlines the state of Europe, possessed by fiendishness, competition in business, passion and wrongdoing, also world war, further, class warfare, moral depravity and economic tyranny. As the argument develops, Barth paints a portrait of the

---

[4] Barth, 'Die Gerechtigkeit Gottes', p. 5/ET: p. 9.
[5] Barth, 'Die Gerechtigkeit Gottes', pp. 5-6/ET: p. 10.
[6] Barth, 'Die Gerechtigkeit Gottes', p. 6/ET: p. 10.
[7] Barth, 'Die Gerechtigkeit Gottes', p. 6/ET: p. 11.
[8] Barth, 'Die Gerechtigkeit Gottes', pp. 6-7/ET: p. 11.

result of this corrupt and fallen will:

> The unjust will which imbues and rules our life makes of it, with or without our sanction, a weltering inferno. How heavily it lies upon us! How unendurably! We live in a shadow. We may temporarily deceive ourselves about it. We may temporarily come to an understanding with it... For the righteous will is by nature the unendurable, the impossible. We live by knowing that there is really something else in the world. [9]

But so often unrighteousness triumphs: we make peace with conscience and convince ourselves that such wrong is really right. 'But now in the midst of this sense of need and apprehension, as resistless and unbroken as the theme of a Bach fugue, comes the assurance of conscience.' [10] We perceive the righteous will of God above our warped and weakened will. Our greatest pain comes in perceiving this will, this pure righteousness of God. Barth traces this cry through the Hebrew prophets and into John the Baptist as figures 'never to be erased from humanity.' [11]

But now 'comes a remarkable turn in our relation with the righteousness of God. The trumpet of conscience sounds ... we feel the touch of holiness upon us.' [12] It is here that what was implicitly analogous to *Crime and Punishment* becomes explicit. Here Barth invokes The Tower of Babel, woven in with *eritis sicut deus*. There are eleven explicit uses of The Tower of Babel in 'Die Gerechtigkeit Gottes' in addition to the way Genesis/Dostoevsky is woven into the meaning of the address generally (see Figure 3 Barth and Thurneysen - The Tower of Babel, on page 57). As conscience touches us we fail to respond to the righteousness of God, instead we build a Tower of Babel:

> Let us build us a city and a tower ... whose top may reach into heaven; and let us make a name, lest we be scattered abroad upon the face of the whole earth! We come to our own rescue and build The Tower of Babel. In what haste we are to soothe within us the stormy desire for the righteousness of God. [13]

We do not let conscience speak to the end, we stifle, we cover, we placate by inventing our own righteousness - worse, our own religion. 'We stand here before the really tragic, the most fundamental error of humanity. We long for the righteousness of God, and yet we do not let it enter our lives and our world.' [14] Again,

> ...we go off and build this pitiable tower at the Babel of our human righteousness, human consequence, human significance. Our answer to the call of conscience ... (is) a single gigantic *'as if'* (*als ob*) - as if our tower were important, as if

---

[9] Barth, 'Die Gerechtigkeit Gottes', pp. 6-7/ET: p. 12.
[10] Barth, 'Die Gerechtigkeit Gottes', p. 7/ET: p. 13.
[11] Barth, 'Die Gerechtigkeit Gottes', p. 8/ET: pp. 13-14.
[12] Barth, 'Die Gerechtigkeit Gottes', p. 8/ET: p. 13.
[13] Barth, 'Die Gerechtigkeit Gottes', p. 8/ET: p. 14.
[14] Barth, 'Die Gerechtigkeit Gottes', pp. 8-9/ET: p. 14.

something were happening, as if we were doing something in obedience to conscience.[15]

Therefore God's righteousness eludes us. This is the pattern for the entire address - we discern intimations of the righteousness of God in our conscience but we silence, abort, such intimations through busily building a Tower of Babel from our own righteousness by proudly inventing religions, cultures, human achievement. We are bedevilled by a longing for a new world but fail to achieve anything through our own efforts. Barth saw this particularly in the arrogance of the Western European nations that were locked into the annihilation of the First World War:

> The righteousness of God has slowly changed from being the surest of facts into being the highest among various high ideals, and is now at all events our very own affair. This is evident in our ability now to hang it gaily out of the window and now to roll it up again, somewhat like a flag: *eritis sicut deus*! You may act 'as if' you were God, you may with ease take his righteousness under your own management. This is certainly pride. One might equally well, however, call it despair.[16]

Later, Thurneysen was to write similar words in his theological study - *Dostojewski* (1921) - about how Raskolnikov was taken in by his idea, further, that he was bewitched, enchanted (bezaubert[17]), he was a man characterized by hurricanes of passion, capable of a titanic storming of heaven leading inevitably to a demonic plunge into hell:

> ...(such a) man becomes godlike and devilish... With the parable, however, there is also given the titanic temptation of the *eritis sicut deus*, the temptation to make out of the parable and allusion more than parable and allusion, the seduction to be superman, to be the man-god (zum Übermenschen, zum Mensch-Gott).[18]

It is because of our despairing pride 'that we build a Tower of Babel.'[19] Barth then rails against the suffocating judgemental morality of the West:

> Is it not remarkable that the greatest atrocities of life - I think of the capitalist order and of the war - can justify themselves on purely moral principles? The devil may also make use of morality. The devil laughs at The Tower of Babel which we erect to him - the righteousness of the state and of the law - a wonderful tower! ...very useful for quieting the conscience![20]

The charitable acts we indulge in so often fail to touch or change the character of our fallen will and the world we have constructed.[21] Here Barth weighs in with his most forceful criticism of religion (in the service of the

---

[15] Barth, 'Die Gerechtigkeit Gottes', p. 9/ET: p. 14.
[16] Barth, 'Die Gerechtigkeit Gottes', p. 10/ET: p. 16.
[17] Thurneysen, *Dostojewski*, p. 19/ET: p. 23.
[18] Thurneysen, *Dostojewski*, p. 20/ET: p. 23.
[19] Barth, 'Die Gerechtigkeit Gottes', p. 11/ET: p. 17.
[20] Barth, 'Die Gerechtigkeit Gottes', p. 11/ET: p. 18.
[21] Barth, 'Die Gerechtigkeit Gottes', pp. 11-12/ET: p. 19.

Gospel): 'Religious righteousness! There seems to be no surer means of rescuing us from the alarm cry of conscience than religion and Christianity. ...it is a wonderful illusion.'[22] All this does is enable us to hide from reality. Barth lists the problems bedevilling Europe: militarism, capitalism, prostitution, housing problems, alcoholism, et cetera. He weighs against the pride with which European countries consider themselves Christian nations: 'Are we not, with our religious righteousness, acting 'as if' in order not to have to deal with reality? Is not our religious righteousness a product of our pride and our despair, a Tower of Babel, at which the devil laughs more loudly than at all the others?'[23]

We then move into the concluding section. Barth comments on the pointlessness of both sides in the war questioning whether God is righteous and if so why does God allow the carnage and nihilism of the war: 'A very pointed and correct and weighty question it is, when we refer it to the god to whom in our pride and despair we have erected The Tower of Babel ... (to the) patron saint of our human righteousness, morality, state, civilization, or religion.'[24] Both sides in the war were claiming righteousness for themselves, both sides had erected a Babel tower, 'it is our calamity ... we have made ourselves a god in our own image... In the question 'Is God righteous?' our Tower of Babel falls to pieces.'[25] Humanity is therefore looking for righteousness without God: 'It is clear that such a god is not God, he is not even righteous. He cannot prevent his worshippers, all the distinguished European and American apostles of civilization ... from falling upon one another ... this god to whom we have built The Tower of Babel is not God. He is an idol, he is dead.'[26] Barth then asserts that the only way to approach the one true living God is not by speech, not by reflection or reason but by being still and listening to conscience.[27] Such intimations will tell us of the righteousness of God and the unrighteousness of human actions and strivings. Therefore it will be, 'above all, a matter of recognising God once more as God.'[28] Therefore there is identified the absolute need for a recreation of our corrupt will: 'we ought not so gratuitously to confuse our hearts by the continual building of Towers of Babel.'[29] In conclusion Barth cites examples of a correct listening to conscience in the Bible, examples where something has happened, something has changed.[30] This inner way, 'the way of simple faith, is the way of Christ for he is the love of

---

[22] Barth, 'Die Gerechtigkeit Gottes', p. 12/ET: p. 20.
[23] Barth, 'Die Gerechtigkeit Gottes', pp. 12-13/ET: p. 20.
[24] Barth, 'Die Gerechtigkeit Gottes', p. 13/ET: pp. 21-22.
[25] Barth, 'Die Gerechtigkeit Gottes', p. 14/ET: p. 22.
[26] Barth, 'Die Gerechtigkeit Gottes', pp. 13-14/ET: p. 22.
[27] Barth, 'Die Gerechtigkeit Gottes', pp. 14-15/ET: p. 23.
[28] Barth, 'Die Gerechtigkeit Gottes', p. 15/ET: p. 24.
[29] Barth, 'Die Gerechtigkeit Gottes', p. 16/ET: p. 25.
[30] Barth, 'Die Gerechtigkeit Gottes', p. 17/ET: pp. 25-26.

God.'[31] But we continue building these Babel towers: 'It remains to be seen whether the quaking of The Tower of Babel which we are now experiencing will be violent enough to bring us somewhat nearer to the way of faith.'[32]

Dostoevsky and The Tower of Babel

But what has The Tower of Babel to do with Dostoevsky? In the same manner that 'The Idea' occupies Dostoevsky's thinking throughout his post-Siberian work, two all pervading metaphors are The Tower of Babel and The Crystal Palace. Both are used in the same way and complement 'The Idea'. Kroecker and Ward see the use of both starting with Dostoevsky's *Notes from Underground* (1864):

> According to the underground-man, modern progressivism places great emphasis on the notion that world history is ultimately rational. ...(this) is apparent in the very phrase philosophy of history, which was invented by Voltaire... For the underground man, reason is merely the tip of the iceberg, amounting to 'perhaps one-twentieth' of what constitutes human being. Under his scrutiny, the modern idea of progress is revealed not as the expression of dispassionate reason but as the symptom of fervent hope - hope for the 'Crystal Palace' of the future.[33]

These two metaphors are supplemented by a third - The Ant-Heap - and are all used to represent related phenomena: human progress as symbolized by the economic and social ideals of the utopian socialists in France, the religio-capitalist system in England and the nineteenth-century liberal neo-Protestant humanist-Idealist agenda in Germany. Chapple: 'the underground man muses about the perversity of humanity's history and the hopelessness of efforts to plan rationally humanity's utopia on earth ... he asserts The Crystal Palace will be built as a symbol of the success of human reason.'[34] For Dostoevsky The Tower of Babel is the symbol of humanity's attempt to go it alone without God. Ellis Sandoz, on the political apocalypse that Dostoevsky predicted, wrote:

> (This) is represented by three symbols: (1) The Tower of Babel - the ideal society of the revolutionary wishing to insure without God the happiness of mankind: the symbol of idolatry; (2) The Crystal Palace - society illumined from within by the power of human reason but opaque to the light of faith which is rejected, together with tradition, as irrational mystery: rationalism, symbol of the pride of mind; (3) the Ant Heap - the future ecumenical society of man devoid of humanity and

---

[31] Barth, 'Die Gerechtigkeit Gottes', p. 17/ET: p. 26.
[32] Barth, 'Die Gerechtigkeit Gottes', p. 17/ET: p. 27.
[33] P. Travis Kroeker and Bruce K. Ward, *Remembering the End: Dostoevsky as a Prophet of Modernity* (Oxford: Westview Press Radical Traditions, 2001), p. 67. Kroeker and Ward are referring to Dostoevsky, *Notes from Underground*, chps. 8 and 10.
[34] Richard Chapple, *A Dostoevsky Dictionary* (Ann Arbor, MI: Ardis Publishers, 1983), pp. 138, 164, 251 and 302-303.

reduced to the level of an insect in the name of humanitarianism: the symbol of the end of secular history.[35]

In *Crime and Punishment* Dostoevsky uses these three ideas and goes one step further by inventing a fashionable restaurant/cafe, frequented by liberal humanists and proto-socialists, named The Crystal Palace, which is mentioned in the movements of Razumikhin and Raskolnikov.[36] Babel, as a motif, is often complemented by the use of the term Babylon as a metaphor of wickedness and confusion - Karamazinov and Pyotr Stepanovich (*The Demons*) agree that Western Europe is Babylon and will fall.[37] This image of The Crystal Palace comes from Dostoevsky's European tour (Summer 1862). He believed Europe had been corrupted by this Tower of Babel/Crystal Palace. Therefore we can find the genesis of all three metaphors in Dostoevsky's scathing critique of London. On return from his travels he wrote of overwhelming depravation and poverty in the East End of London.[38] He noted the noise and pollution and the filthy state of the Thames, as compared to the progress and engineering achievements represented by The Crystal Palace and the Great Exhibition held in it:

> Now London is in this respect something entirely different ... the typically Western principle of individual isolation ... even the very leaders of progress lack faith, and bow down in worship of Baal.
>
> The immense town, forever bustling by night and by day ... the daring of enterprise, the apparent disorder ... the polluted Thames, the coal-saturated air, the magnificent squares and parks, the town's terrifying districts such as Whitechapel with its half-naked, savage and hungry population, the City with its millions and its world-wide trade, The Crystal Palace, the Great Exhibition. ...you realize the grandeur of the design; you feel that something has been achieved here, here is victory and triumph. And you feel nervous. It is a Biblical sight, something to do with Babylon or Babel, some prophecy out of the Apocalypse being fulfilled

---

[35] Ellis Sandoz, *Political Apocalypse: A Study of Dostoevsky's Grand Inquisitor* (Baton Rouge, LA: Louisiana State University Press, 1971), p. 137.

[36] Dostoevsky, *Crime and Punishment*, pt. 2 chps. 4, 6 and 7, pp. 106-117, 154-174 and 175-193.

[37] Fyodor Mikhailovich Dostoevsky, *Demons* (trans. Richard Pevear and Larissa Volokhonsky; London: Everyman's Library, 1994), pt. 2 chp. 6, 'Pyotr Bustles About', pp. 343-387. It is important to note that in German *Babel* and *Babylon* can sometimes be used synonymously: Der Turm zu Babel (The Tower of Babel) and *der Babylonische Turm* (The Babel Tower) also interchange for vice, sin and iniquity - e.g., Sündenbabel.

[38] In June 1862 Dostoevsky visited Western Europe to consult specialists about his epilepsy and to see the Western ideas he believed were corrupting Russia. He visited Berlin, Paris, London, Florence, Milan and Vienna. He published his observations in 'Winter Notes on Summer Impressions', published in *Vremya* (*Time*, the periodical he edited) February-March 1863. These observations were later reordered and published in book form: Fyodor Mikhailovich Dostoevsky, *Winter Notes on Summer Impressions* (trans. Kyril Fitzlyon; London: Quartet Books, 1985), chp. 5, 'Baal', pp. 42-43.

4. Die Gerechtigkeit Gottes 55

before your very eyes. You feel that a rich and ancient tradition of denial and protest is needed in order not to yield, not to succumb ... not to idolize Baal, that is, not to take the actual for the ideal. [39]

Dostoevsky writes at length about the poverty and depravity of the working class, and how Catholic priests try to care and convert them,

But an Anglican minister would never visit a poor man. The poor are not even allowed inside a church because they have not the money to pay for a seat. ...Anglican ministers and bishops are proud and rich, live in wealthy parishes and dioceses and wax fat... It is a religion of the rich, and undisguised at that. They travel all over the earth, penetrate into darkest Africa to convert one savage, and forget the million savages in London ...in fact all the Golden Calves in that country are extremely religious... Baal reigns and does not even demand obedience, because he is certain of it. Baal does not close his eyes... [40]

Thus we have the origin of the image/metaphor of The Crystal Palace/The Tower of Babel as representing humanity trying to go it alone without God, fed by corrupt religion, with the mass of humanity as The Ant-Heap.

Further, because of what he saw he was convinced that Liberal neo-Protestantism in Germany was moving into atheism because of its fragmentation, whilst he declared socialism the illegitimate offspring of Roman Catholicism, and was convinced that socialist atheism would lead to inhumanity and materialism.[41] Much of this works through into *Crime and Punishment* (1866) - with Raskolnikov representing The Tower of Babel in his arrogant assertion of his own will. Babel functions in Raskolnikov as a measure of the modern hope that human history is progressing toward its fulfilment in a new kind of social order. This new order was indelibly associated with the French revolutionary principle of liberté, égalité, fraternité:[42] Hence Raskolnikov's Napoleonic delusion - *eritis sicut deus*, building his Babel tower. Where is this leading? - Dostoevsky gives Raskolnikov the dream he experiences when in prison in Siberia at the end of the book[43] of humanity having lost the ability to agree on what is good and what is evil and therefore the teeming millions killing each other in meaningless spite (the significance of this to the Babel of the First World War was not lost on Barth).[44]

Therefore the combined metaphor of The Tower Babel/The Crystal Palace/The Ant-Heap represented for Dostoevsky the dis-ease of humanity: primarily, proto-socialist liberal humanist atheism, secondarily, the authority of the Roman Catholic Church, coupled with the religious-capitalist pride and

---

[39] Dostoevsky, *Winter Notes on Summer Impressions*, pp. 43-44.
[40] Dostoevsky, *Winter Notes on Summer Impressions*, pp. 51-52.
[41] See Denis Dirscherl, S.J., *Dostoevsky and the Catholic Church* (Chicago: Loyola University Press, 1986), p. 95.
[42] Kroeker and Ward, *Remembering the End*, p. 67.
[43] Dostoevsky, *Crime and Punishment*, 'Epilogue', pp. 533-552.
[44] Kroeker and Ward, *Remembering the End*, p. 75, quoting from the Epilogue to *Crime and Punishment*.

elitism of Victorian England, complemented by the drive towards atheism in some quarters of Liberal neo-Protestantism in Germany. This is taken to its logical conclusion in The Grand Inquisitor who explicitly invokes/voices The Tower of Babel,[45] as does Stepan Trofimovich (*The Demons*).[46] Babel represents not just corrupt Roman authority but is a prophetic forewarning of Marxism in Russia. Therefore Dostoevsky used the metaphor of The Tower of Babel explicitly in The Grand Inquisitor to describe the state of *eritis sicut deus* (which in turn epitomized 'The Idea'):[47] totalitarianism whether Roman Catholic or political (socialist or free market) was a Tower of Babel, which could be communal (Rome, or French socialism) or individualistic (the schismatic Raskolnikov).

We have noted already how Dostoevsky wanted to write a story that encapsulated this motif; he presented The Tower of Babel/The Crystal Palace/The Ant Heap in literary form in *Crime and Punishment* (1866) along with *eritis sicut deus*, which affected Barth and Thurneysen during the period 1915-16. The motif of The Tower of Babel/*eritis sicut deus* is important in Barth's developing thinking, an image he uses strongly. There is no evidence for him using these motifs prior to the latter half of 1915. Furthermore, there is no evidence in the Swiss Reformed Church lectionary of the use of Genesis 11:1-9 (The Tower of Babel) for the year 1915 as evidenced from Barth's sermons.[48] These motifs come from Barth's reading of *Crime and Punishment* and the Bible (Genesis 11:1-9). Therefore the concepts woven into *Crime and Punishment* by Dostoevsky complement and influence Barth's use of The Tower of Babel/*eritis sicut deus* particularly when he came to write 'Die Gerechtigkeit Gottes' in December 1915. Therefore in 1915 Barth's theological thinking had developed along similar lines to the way Dostoevsky's ideas had in the mid-1860s.

---

[45] Dostoevsky, *The Brothers Karamazov*, pt. 1 bk. 1 chp. 5, 'Elders', pp. 25-33, and pt. 2 bk. 5 chp. 5, 'Grand Inquisitor', pp. 246-264.
[46] Dostoevsky, *Demons*, pt. 1, chp. 1, pp. 7-11.
[47] Kroeker and Ward, *Remembering the End*, pp. 63, 67, 75, 102, 185 and 227 n.1.
[48] Karl Barth, *Predigten 1915* (Gesamtausgabe 27; Zürich: Theologischer Verlag Zürich, 1996).

Barth 'Die Gerechtigkeit Gottes'

'We come to our own rescue and build a tower of Babel.'
p.8/ET: p.14

'We go off and build the pitiable tower of Babel of our human righteousness...'
p.9/ET: p.15

And because we are so proud and so despairing, we build a tower of Babel.
p.11/ET p.17

'The devil may also make use of the morality. He laughs at the tower of Babel which we erect to him. The righteousness of the state and of the law. A wonderful tower!'
p.11/ET: p.18

'The devil may also laugh at this tower of Babel.'
p.12/ET: p.19

'Are we not, with our religious righteousness, acting 'as if' — in order not to have to deal with reality? Is not our religious righteousness a product of our pride and our despair, a tower of Babel, at which the devil laughs more loudly than at all the others.'
p.13/ET: p.20

'In the question, "Is God righteous?" our whole tower of Babel falls to pieces.'
p.14/ET: p.22

'...this god to whom we have built the tower of Babel is not God. He is an idol. He is dead.'
p.14/ET: p.22

'We ought not so gratuitously to confuse our hearts by the continual building of towers of Babel.'
p.16/ET: p.25

'It remains to be seen whether the quaking of the tower of Babel which we are now experiencing will be violent enough to bring us somewhat nearer to the way of faith.'
p.17/ET: p.27

Thurneysen *Dostojewski*

'This is the reason for his deep, critical distrust of culture and society. He did not see in it merely this or that which was distorted or in need of improvement. He sensed in all its proud towers and battlements the tower of Babel, the deep-rooted tendency of man to make himself at home in the world without God and against God, as a god himself.'
p.42/ET: p.48

'The totally radical nature of his critique, however, is seen in that it also strikes socialism with the utmost severity, socialism that would bring a counterattack within society, end middle-class culture, and proclaim a new society. Even there, yes, there most of all, Dostoevsky sees the titanic countenance of the man who, as it says in *The Brothers Karamazov*, would 'erect the fearsome tower of Babel, who would establish an eternal life in this world' (a flagrant *contradictio in adjecto*). Not that Dostoevsky was in the least concerned with the existing order; because of its corruption it has earned its destruction ten times over.'
p.44/ET: p.49

'The meaning of life does not lie in this life, but in God. From this comes all the deeply questionable and uncertain nature of this life... And each new 'tower of Babel' 'remains unfinished just like the first one.'
p.46/ET: p.52

'The absolute is God, and only God can play the role of God. He who knows that will become patient again... He will no longer issue a call to the building of a tower of Babel that reaches into the heavens.'
p.67/ET: p.73

'Dostoevsky accuses directly and judges passionately only where he encounters the titanic gestures of man. These he finds most of all where man is not suffering and languishing, but is seeking justice in his own might and is building his towers of Babel. Thus the finger raised against socialism, thus the fist shaken against the culture of the West.'
p.68/ET: p.75

Figure 3 Barth and Thurneysen - The Tower of Babel
Barth and Thurneysen's use of the motif of the Tower of Babel in 'Die Gerechtigkeit Gottes' (1916) and *Dostojewski* (1921); this is derived, essentially, from the work of Dostoevsky.

Conscience and the Critical Realism of God

What is important about the influence of Dostoevsky's *Crime and Punishment* on Barth at the time of the writing of 'Kriegszeit und Gottesreich' and 'Die Gerechtigkeit Gottes' is contained in this statement from the latter: 'It will then be, above all, a matter of our recognizing God once more as God. ... There is nothing for our will except a basic re-creation.'[49] This is what Raskolnikov undergoes - a radical transformation of his will, whilst on the path to recognizing and accepting Sonya's God. Both Barth and Thurneysen realized that such a one as Raskolnikov, whom they could see was in many ways an archetype of the dis-ease that was plaguing Europe at the time (the mid years of the First World War), was faced with an existential dialectical choice: he can continue on his path of being as it were God (*eritis sicut deus*) or he can accept the grace given in freedom to a criminal class, the grace of the righteousness of God - grace given in judgement. The choice is existential because it is woven into existence. This is characterized by a dialectical *diastasis*: each and every human being on an individual basis, though affected by the community, adopts, to a greater or lesser degree, one position or the other at different times in his or her life. Either s/he reflects that judgement and mercy are of God, and like Sonya, s/he waits in humility aware of the total need for grace and forgiveness from God and refuses to judge, condemn; or the alternative position is adopted - to be, to act, just as God (*eritis sicut deus*) and, like Raskolnikov's grand Napoleonic delusion, to claim the right of life, death and judgement over others. Therefore, even at this early point in time, 1915-16, there is evidence of Barth using an irreconcilable dialectical *diastasis* inspired in part by his reading of Dostoevsky's *Crime and Punishment*. There is no synthesis or reconciliation of this antinomy onto a higher plane, no cultural understanding which will accommodate both positions before the God of truth and grace: God is, and is wholly other, and is sole judge. God is also means God is critically realistic: God is love; this love is wholly realistic and critical in the sense that it convicts when one such as Raskolnikov transgresses. In the context of *Crime and Punishment* the only option is to turn and dismantle The Tower of Babel - Raskolnikov must abandon his pretence. In theological terms this can be found in 'Die Gerechtigkeit Gottes.' The dialectic must stand and await the *eschaton* - this is characteristic of Dostoevsky's novels, though it is important to remember that the eschatological elements as such in Barth's thinking and work at this time were also from the Blumhardts.

---

[49] Barth, 'Die Gerechtigkeit Gottes', p. 14/ET: p. 24.

Conscience as Liberal Piety ?

Barth's appeal to conscience has been contentious amongst the Barthian scholarly tradition. McCormack raises the point when he deals with 'Die Gerechtigkeit Gottes' of how certain elements within the tradition see Barth's appeal to conscience as evidence that he was still in the mould of liberal theology. McCormack quotes Stephen Webb in *Re-figuring Theology The Rhetoric of Karl Barth,* where Webb asserts that Barth was still, 'caught in the web of liberal theology in an attempt to ground religion in subjectivity.'[50] Webb's assertion appears to be that in appealing to conscience Barth was showing too much respect for pietism. McCormack ably defends Barth by asserting that Webb's claim,

> rests upon a highly selective reading of the essay in question and an all-too-narrow acquaintance with Barth's other writings (essays and letters) of this period... For Barth to have engaged in a 'liberal' attempt to ground religion in subjectivity, he would (at the very least) have needed a positive interest in religion. But religion is treated in this essay as the contrary to the righteousness of God; an exercise in idolatry.[51]

McCormack is correct - religion is, at this point in time, almost abhorrent to Barth. In 'Die Gerechtigkeit Gottes' Barth does at one point argue that atheism would be a better position than corrupt, self-serving religion. He argues against the false gods of the distinguished European and American apostles of civilization, as he calls them, eager for piously 'Christian' progress:

> It is clear that such a god is not God ... He cannot prevent his worshippers ... from falling upon one another with fire and sword to the amazement and derision of the poor heathen in India and Africa. This god is really an unrighteous god, and it is high time for us to declare ourselves thorough-going doubters, sceptics, scoffers and atheists in regard to him. It is high time for us to confess freely and gladly: this god, to whom we have built The Tower of Babel, is not God. He is an idol. He is dead.[52]

This is not the critically realistic God, the wholly other transcendent God, independent from human affairs and history that presses in on Raskolnikov, the sceptic, the Raskolnikov who is arrogantly dismissive of all that is precious to the respectable bourgeois Christian classes of St Petersburg. Barth is criticizing the false god of nineteenth-century liberal neo-Protestant humanism: this god is

---

[50] McCormack, *Karl Barth's Critically Realistic Dialectical Theology*, p. 135 n.14 referring to Stephen H. Webb, *Re-figuring Theology: The Rhetoric of Karl Barth* (Albany, NY: University of New York Press, 1991).

[51] McCormack, *Karl Barth's Critically Realistic Dialectical Theology*, p.135 n.14.

[52] Barth, 'Die Gerechtigkeit Gottes', p. 14/ET: p. 22. Note there are striking similarities between this passage and others with Dostoevsky's *Winter Notes on Summer Impressions* that was examined earlier, especially the chapter on London entitled 'Baal'. Therefore, in all probability, Barth read this work: Dostoevsky, *Winter Notes on Summer Impressions*, pp. 42-43.

a projection, a human invention. In the case of Raskolnikov, conscience is a pressing external reality on him; he then experiences this critical realism as guilt, a guilt that could only be assuaged by giving in to its promptings and to the witness of Sonya, particularly in her reading of the story of the raising of Lazarus to him. Raskolnikov is a rebellious sceptic, but this does not prevent the external, wholly other transcendent reality of the God of love as Holy Spirit pressing and acting upon him: conscience is pneumatological, critical and real. This is not conscience as an example of bourgeois pietistic self-love; it is not conscience as a humanistic projection. Conscience here leads to a right understanding of sin and repentance. McCormack is correct to refute Webb, but he is unaware of the influence of *Crime and Punishment* generally on Barth, or Raskolnikov's existential crisis specifically, and how Dostoevsky's ideas influenced the thinking that fed into 'Die Gerechtigkeit Gottes'. Barth's appeal to conscience is not a regression into subjectively humanistic piety; conscience for Barth is the unpredictable and uncontrollable action of the Holy Spirit that will act on people regardless of religious beliefs.

Graceful Sin - Sinful Grace

Raskolnikov was no figment of Dostoevsky's imagination - he was very real and was built upon Dostoevsky's own liberal years in St Petersburg before he was arrested for sedition along with other 'Westernizers' and exiled to a Siberian prison where he underwent conversion to Christian faith.[53] In addition, Dostoevsky's faith was characterized by an existential, almost eschatological, *Krisis*, which was, yes, emotional, but was very different from the social *etiquette* of the St Petersburg religious classes. Consider the following from the diary of his wife, Anna Dostoevsky, for the summer of 1867 when they travelled to Switzerland to see doctors about Fyodor's epilepsy:

> On the way to Geneva we stopped overnight in Basel, with the object of viewing a painting in the museum there which someone had told Fyodor Mikhailovich about. This painting, by Hans Holbein, depicts Jesus Christ after his inhuman agony, after his body has been taken down from the Cross and begun to decay. His swollen face is covered with bloody wounds, and it is terrible to behold. The painting had a crushing impact on Fyodor Mikhailovich. He stood before it as if stunned. And I did not have the strength to look at it — it was too painful for me, particularly in my sickly condition — and I went into other rooms. When I came back after fifteen or twenty minutes, I found him still riveted to the same spot in front of the painting. His agitated face had a kind of dread in it, something I had

---

[53] Dostoevsky was something of a prophet in the crime/trespass of Raskolnikov for anarchic reasons: in November 1869 (three years after the publication of *Crime and Punishment*) a young student at the Petrovsky Agricultural Academy in Moscow was murdered by a revolutionary group headed by Sergei Nechaev (1847-1882, a Russian revolutionary nihilist who advocated the single-minded pursuit of revolution by any means necessary, including violence) for the supposedly humanitarian aims of radical ideology, or what Dostoevsky would have described as rational egoism.

4. Die Gerechtigkeit Gottes

noticed more than once during the first moments of an epileptic seizure. Quietly I took my husband by the arm, led him into another room and sat him down on a bench, expecting the attack from one minute to the next. Luckily this did not happen. He calmed down little by little and left the museum, but insisted on returning once again to view this painting which had struck him so powerfully.[54]

The painting had a profound effect on Dostoevsky as it did on Eduard Thurneysen and Karl Barth (housed as it was in a gallery in Basel).[55] Dostoevsky's reaction was not mere emotionalism: in his reaction is a profound realisation of the appalling suffering and rejection, torture and death meted out by humanity onto the God-man, Christ, God incarnate. Dostoevsky's life was one of a graceful sinner - as was Sonya's. Neither was without sin, wilfulness or flaw (*simul iustus et peccator*). But then Raskolnikov is not entirely graceless, he is in effect characterized by sinful grace: the difference is one of emphasis - Sonya has turned to God, accepted grace and awaits full sanctification and redemption; Raskolnikov is still moving away from God's grace. There is in effect a dialectic here: graceful sin - sinful grace. Sonya is a graceful sinner; Raskolnikov is sinful, and to a lesser degree graceful. It is a question of which dominates - there is a battle ranging in each one of them (as it is in each and every soul) between the forces of good and evil.

A key to Dostoevsky's understanding of sin and grace (and thereby Barth and Thurneysen's at this time) is in the long encounter/discussion between Raskolnikov and Sonya where he forces her to read the story of the resurrection of Lazarus from St John's Gospel to him.[56] He taunts her that she has also destroyed a life - her own through the depravity of her prostitution. Yet he can perceive the effect of grace in her - her sanity and sanctity. This leads him to bow down and kiss her feet.[57] This is a graceful act, acknowledging on a subliminal level her holiness and her God; however sensing the change in him and in an attempt to reassert his rebellion he states that 'I was not bowing to you but to all human suffering'. He enquires of her faith; then he teases her laughingly, gloatingly, that 'maybe there isn't any God', and that her stepsister, the innocent and charismatically holy Polenka, will end up following her into prostitution when Sonya inevitably falls sick. Sonya likewise admits in abject humility that she is a fallen creature, that she is 'dishonourable, a great, great sinner' (*simul iustus et peccator*). When he finally forces her to read the raising

---

[54] Anna Grigorievna Dostoevsky, *Dostoevsky Reminiscences* (trans. Beatrice Stillman; London: Wildwood House, 1976), p.134.

[55] Hans Holbein the Younger (b.1497, Augsburg, Germany, d.1543, London), *The Body of the Dead Christ in the Tomb*, 1521, oil on wood, 30.5 x 200 cm Kunstmuseum, Öffentliche Kunstsammlung, Basle. See P.H. Brazier, 'Barth and Expressionism - Some Further Considerations', *Zeitschrift für dialektische Theologie*, 20.1 (Fall 2005), pp. 34-52.

[56] Dostoevsky, *Crime and Punishment*, pt. 4, chp. 4, pp. 314-331.

[57] Dostoevsky, *Crime and Punishment*, pt. 4, chp. 4, p. 321.

of Lazarus she stumbles over the words, her voice falters and she trembles with fear:

> Raskolnikov partly understood why Sonya was hesitant to read to him, and the more he understood it, the more rudely and irritably he insisted on her reading. He understood only too well how hard it was for her now to betray and expose all that was hers. He understood that these feelings might indeed constitute her secret, as it were, real and long-standing, going back perhaps to her adolescence, when she was still in the family, with her unfortunate father and her grief-maddened stepmother, among the hungry children, the ugly shouts and reproaches. But at the same time he now knew, and knew for certain, that even though she was anguished and terribly afraid of something as she was starting out to read, she also had a tormenting desire to read, in spite of all her anguish and apprehension, and precisely for him, so that he would hear it, and precisely now - whatever might come of it afterwards! ... He read it in her eyes, understood it from her rapturous excitement ... She mastered herself, suppressed the spasm in her throat that had made her voice break at the beginning of the verse, and continued her reading... [58]

It is as though Sonya - the great sinner - is holding her very soul in her hands, exposing it in her frailty before Raskolnikov fearful that he may mock and destroy her faith, the slender thread of faith that holds her from falling into a depraved nihilistic nothingness. Sonya's existential Krisis in facing Raskolnikov is not nervous emotionalism, it is not to be seen as pietistic religion, it is about facing the truth of one's sinful nature whilst exercising the divine imperative to witness to the truth of the Gospel. This is not to be considered subjective because this existential experience is defined by and in relation to the pneumatological action of the love of God that is love, a love that measures and judges all.

Luther and Calvin

Although Webb has raised the question of whether Barth's appeal to conscience is a regression into the pietism that characterized nineteenth-century Liberal neo-Protestantism, and in the light of Barth's reading of Dostoevsky's *Crime and Punishment* we can see that this is not the case the question could be raised that Barth gets these ideas in 'Die Gerechtigkeit Gottes' from reading Luther - for example, the use of *eritis sicut deus* as well as the understanding underpinning the Latin theological statement of humanity trying to be as God; or for that matter the employment of the Biblical metaphor of The Tower of Babel, and behind this a forensic and legalistic understanding of atonement and redemption.[59] Barth's talk of the righteousness of a Christian is of course something granted on the basis of the intrinsic worth of Christ, having been

---

[58] Dostoevsky, *Crime and Punishment*, pt. 4, bk. 4, p. 326.
[59] The implication here is of a parallel in terms of ideas with, for example, Luther's *On the Babylonian Captivity of the Church* of 1520. See Carter Lindberg, *The European Reformations Sourcebook* (Oxford: Blackwell Publishers, 1999), pp. 38-39.

4. Die Gerechtigkeit Gottes

won by Christ and derived from the righteousness of God. This righteousness, as distinct from the righteousness of a fallen and corrupt will, which comes as a pure grace, externally; it is not from anything inside the man or woman, the sinner. Before any step on the road to sanctification is possible (for example, Raskolnikov's turn from the corruption of his ideas of being as God - the Napoleonic superman - to a gradual, even reluctant acceptance of Sonya's God) there is the unwarranted, unilateral gift of God's grace: prevenience. Our cooperation in this unilateral act does not claim any effort of goodness or purity on our behalf. This is evident in the theology that underpins Dostoevsky's work - theological beliefs also found in Luther's writings. However, it is important to remember that it is from August 1916 that Barth starts to consider the Reformers generally, and read Luther specifically. This is evidenced by the representation given to Luther in *Römerbrief 1*.[60] This understanding of Luther is important and it carries over into *Römerbrief 2* but it is important to remember that the influence of Dostoevsky predates this and further that Dostoevsky points towards the understanding of sin and grace that Barth found in Luther and the Reformers. Barth was therefore unfamiliar, in this sense, with

---

[60] For example, Barth, *Römerbrief 1*:
4 Kapitel 'Der Stimme der Bibel' on Romans 4:13-22 relating to righteousness - 'Die Gerechtigkeit und die Moral', p. 140.
5 Kapitel 'Der Tag' on Romans 5:1-11 where Luther is referred to (and used illustratively) in relation to humanity's situation - 'Die neue Lage', pp. 153-156; also Romans 5:12-21 on life's victory - 'Der Sieg des Lebens', pp. 175, 196, 199 and 201-210.
6 Kapitel 'Die Gnade' on Romans 6:1-14 relating to Christ's sacrifice - 'Karfeitag', pp. 208, 213-216 and 230; then on Romans 6:15-23 relating to Easter and Christ's Resurrection - 'Ostern', p. 233.
7 Kapitel 'Die Freiheit' on Romans 7:7-13 on the freedom given, won by Christ as compared to the reliance on religious emotionalism in German nineteenth-century Romanticism - 'Das Gesetz und die Romantik', p. 275; then on Romans 7:14-25 on the freedom given, won by Christ as compared to Pietism - 'Das Gesetz und die Pietismus', pp. 278-279, 284-286 and 288.
8 Kapitel 'Der Geist' The Holy Spirit (decision, truth, love) on Romans 8:1-11 - 'Der Vergangene' pp. 299 and 305. See also 'Das Gegenwärtige', pp. 315, 318, 323 326, and 329; also 'Das Zukünftige', p. 349.
10 Kapitel 'Eine Schuld' on Romans 10:1-21 the Guilt of the Church, clarification, the message - 'Klarstellungen', Die Botschaft' and 'Die tauben Ohren', pp. 395, 407 and 420.
12-13 Kapitel 'Der Wille Gottes' on Romans 12:3-16b on behaving prudently, circumspectly - 'Besonnenheit', pp. 482-484; also on Romans 12:16c-13:10 on the will of God - 'Überlegenheit', p. 501.
14-15 Kapitel 'Die Bewegung' in particular on Romans 14:13-23 and 15:1-6 (and relating to 16:25-27) on conscience and community - 'Gewissensgemeinschaft', pp. 548-550; also Romans 15:7-13 'Der Gott der kommenden Dinge', p. 558.
There are other brief references to Luther in the introduction/preface and in the appendices, for example, pp. 589, 624 and 641.

Luther at this time of writing 'Die Gerechtigkeit Gottes' at the end of 1915 - however, he was familiar with Dostoevsky's *Crime and Punishment*. Barth should, it can be argued, have gained some forensic understanding of sin and grace from Luther during his undergraduate days - but it appears he did not. He would have read Luther and Calvin, it is difficult to see how he could have graduated without such study; further, he was the son of a Reformed minister in Switzerland so Calvin would have been something of a household name! Yet he did not gain this realization of sin and guilt, redemption and atonement, such was the all-persuasive grip nineteenth-century liberal neo-Protestantism had on his mind. What is more it is only from August 1916 that he starts to study Luther critically (we will examine this assertion more in the next chapter).

Chapter 5

Barth on the Influence of Dostoevsky

What did Barth have to say about his reading of Dostoevsky, about the influence exerted by this Russian writer's work? Barth's comments are reflective, they are from the period of his mature work: 1928, and then from the 1950s and 1960s. These comments confirm the emphasis and place we have set out for Dostoevsky being a key influence on Barth during the year of the new starting point - 1915. What is more it will be seen that Barth's re-ordered understanding of sin and grace as represented by Sonya and Raskolnikov was a crucial step in his move away from nineteenth-century Liberal neo-Protestantism, and the eventual development of his mature doctrine of sin and grace.

Der römische Katholizismus als Frage an die protestantische Kirche (1928)

In early 1928 Karl Barth was working on a lecture 'Der römische Katholizismus als Frage an die protestantische Kirche'. This was delivered in Bremen on 9th March, then in Osnabrück on 15th March, and finally at the Lower Rhine Pastors' Conference in Dusseldorf on 10 April 1928. Later in the year it was published along with other essays and lectures in a volume entitled *Die Theologie und Die Kirche*.[1] In this lecture Barth commented, reflectively, about the influence of Dostoevsky on a key, some would say critical, component of his theology:

> We should prefer not to discuss the teaching of Schleiermacher and Ritschl on sin. But what other leadership of the new Protestantism, except, the one Kohlbrügge, can be cited as unquestioned and reliable? Where has there not been a hankering for the fleshpots of Egypt? Where has there been preserved the insight that there is no other grace except the free pardon of criminals, grace in judgement? Is it not shameful that we needed to have this truth retold to us by the Russian Dostoevsky? If we have refused to hear it from our Reformers who really

---

[1] Karl Barth, 'Der römische Katholizismus als Frage an die protestantische Kirche', in Karl Barth, *Die Theoligie und die Kirche* (Zollikon-Zurich: Evangelischer Verlag AG, 1928), pp. 329-363; ET: Karl Barth, 'Roman Catholicism: A Question to the Protestant Church', in Karl Barth, *Theology and Church: Shorter Writings 1920-1928* (ed. T.F. Torrance, trans. Louise Pettibone Smith; London: SCM Press, 1962), pp. 307-333.

understood it better than Dostoevsky, are we then still Protestants? If the homesick yearning for synthesis, for balance, for harmony, which found its theological fulfilment in the system of Schleiermacher, and its philosophical fulfilment in the system of Hegel, is to be the yearning of the Protestant Church of today, why does Protestantism not return to the (Roman Catholic) Church which, as we have just heard, awaits us with open arms? We should not be given too heavy a penance to perform. 'We cannot'. The real question is can we not?[2]

Within this passage there are crucial comments for identifying the nature of the influence of Dostoevsky: 'Where has there been preserved the insight that there is no other grace except the free pardon of criminals, grace in judgement? Is it not shameful that we needed to have this truth retold to us by the Russian Dostoevsky? If we have refused to hear it from our Reformers who really understood it better than Dostoevsky, are we then still Protestants?' What Barth is stating here is the nature of the relationship of grace between humanity and God - a relationship that leads to the salvation of humanity, a relationship like that of a prisoner who receives a free pardon, grace given freely with no conditions save the development, sanctification, of the individual. This is what is often termed a forensic or legalistic understanding of forgiveness.

Barth and Rome

Why did Barth say this - and on three occasions - and publish the lecture in a book of essays? The answer to this question lies in the context of his relations with the Roman Catholic Church in the late 1920s.[3] Early in 1928, whilst Professor of Dogmatics and New Testament Exegesis in the predominantly Roman Catholic city of Münster, Westphalia, Barth had regular meetings with Roman Catholics.[4] Discussions appear to have centred squarely on dogmatic and ecclesiological issues: '...reason and revelation, Trinity, Christology, and Church; a far-ranging conversation of the kind that one could not have with a Protestant theologian. One could honestly and joyfully give them one's hand.'[5]

---

[2] Barth, 'Der römische Katholizismus', pp. 356-357/ET: p. 328.
[3] See P.H. Brazier, 'Barth and Rome - a Critical Engagement', *Downside Review*, 123.431 (April 2005), pp. 137-152, and P.H. Brazier, 'Barth and Rome - II: Socialism, the Church and a Theocratic Illusion', *Downside Review*, 124.434 (January 2006), pp. 61-78.
[4] Wilhelm Neuser, 'Karl Barth in Münster 1925 bis 1930', *Theologische Studien und Kritiken*, 130 (1985), pp. 37-40. Neuser lists the participants as Dr. Bernhard Rosenmüller (philosophy of religion, Münster) and his wife; Dr G. Hasenkamp (editor of the *Münsterischen Anzeiger*) and his wife; Dr. Robert Grosche (pastor to the Catholic students at Münster); also Dr. Theodor Steinbüchel (Catholic philosopher of religion at Gießen).
[5] Barth to Thurneysen, 4 February 1927, in Karl Barth and Eduard Thurneysen, *Karl Barth-Eduard Thurneysen, Briefwechsel Band II 1921-1930* (Gesamtausgabe Bearbeitet und herausgegeben von Eduard Thurneysen; Zürich: Theologischer Verlag Zürich, 1973), p. 460.

By early 1928 the group met bi-monthly, sometimes more often. It is during these meetings where papers were presented that the topic of sin and grace was discussed along with the nature of evil, the doctrine of the Trinity and the appropriation of grace. Barth's reading extended at this time to the works of nineteenth-century Catholic writers and inevitably to Aquinas and Anselm. Barth could enjoy these meetings because all parties took seriously the Gospel that had founded and led to the various churches each represented - hence the long debates about revelation and reason, sin and grace, and so forth. However, Barth was forthright in his criticisms of the Roman Catholic Church - he saw the limit of discussions and rapprochement in the Roman attempt to control God's grace and to ration it out rather than allowing God's grace freely given to be the controlling power.[6] For example, in a little known lecture entitled 'Die Theologie und der moderne Mensch' (1927) Barth commented that when confronted by 'the utterly superior, specific, binding and critical truth considered in theology' humanity either rejected this truth atheistically, or sought to neutralize, to negate, calm and smother (verharmlosen to play down; and entschärfen to defuse) the truth of the Gospel through liberalism as in the humanism of the Protestant agenda, or humanity sought to control this truth of the freedom of God as in the power and authority of Roman Catholic ecclesiology.[7] Within these comments was an attack on neo-Protestantism for interpreting God's revelation as humanity's self-revelation or self-discovery. Barth pursued this relationship with Rome into 1928 and 1929 by reading Thomist scholarship (also studying book one of the *Summa Theologica*). In February 1929 Barth invited the Jesuit scholar Erich Przywara[8] to work with him at Münster - a lecture and a joint seminar. As Eberhard Busch commented,

> Przywara gave Barth a great deal to think about and to ask about in every respect

---

[6] See Karl Barth, 'Die Kirche und die Kulture', lecture delivered to the Congress of the Continental Association for Home Missions in Amsterdam on 1 June 1926 published in Barth, *Die Theoligie und die Kirche*, pp. 364-391; ET: Karl Barth, 'Church and Culture', in Barth, *Theology and Church: Shorter Writings 1920-1928*, pp. 334-354. See also Karl Barth, 'Der Begriff der Kirche', a lecture given at the University Association of the Centre Party in Münster on the 11 July 1927, published in Barth, *Die Theoligie und die Kirche*, pp. 364-391; ET: Karl Barth, 'The Concept of the Church', in Barth, *Theology and Church: Shorter Writings 1920-1928*, pp. 334-354.

[7] 'Die Theologie und der moderne Mensch', address to *Der Welt der deutschen Burschenschaften* conference at Burg Lauenstein in Thuringia, 8 October 1927, revised and published as Karl Barth, 'Die Theologie und der heutige Mensch', *Zwischen den Zeiten* 8 (1930), pp. 374-396. See also Barth to Thurneysen 24 October 1927, in Barth and Thurneysen, *Briefwechsel Band II 1921-1930*, pp. 533-540.

[8] Erich Przywara (1889-1972): a Roman Catholic philosopher of religion and theologian, who was part of the editorial board of *Stimmen der Zeit* (*Voices of the Time*), a journal based in Munich from 1922, until banned by the Gestapo in 1941. Przywara published many works on Augustine, Newman, Kant and Kierkegaard, for example, Erich Przywara, *Das Geheimnis Kierkegaards* (München: R. Oldenbourg, 1929).

... Barth made the seminar session a kind of symbol, for the paper he put two seats behind the desk and began by pointing out that after centuries, Protestant and Catholic theologians were again sitting at one table.[9]

Przywara's formula as Barth called it was similar to the *diastasis* that had enabled Barth and Thurneysen to separate God from the human-religious consciousness of the Schleiermacher-Hegel system: 'The formula "God in and beyond man from God's side"'[10] underpinned Przywara's discussions with Barth. The seminar was the morning after the presentation of Przywara's address - 'The Catholic Church Principle' - which was also published in *Zwischen den Zeiten*.

Sin, Grace and Dostoevsky

Within the context of these discussions with Roman Catholic theologians and philosophers of religion Barth wrote several lectures on the relationship between church and culture, the concept of church, but most particularly the appropriation of grace by humanity. In 'Der Begriff der Kirche', a lecture given at the University Association of the Centre Party in Münster on the 11 July 1927, Barth states that what is considered church by both Protestants and Catholics is the same reality, but each side thinks differently about this reality.[11] This is the context six months later when he wrote 'Der römische Katholizismus als Frage...',[12] which is both positive and negative about the Rome he was encountering. The question placed before Barth was in two parts: first, is the Protestant church a church; second, how far is it a Protestant or protesting Church.[13] Barth compliments Rome for how it has remained true to a kerygmatic Gospel but questions whether what it proclaims reflects the reality he and others perceive. However, in a scathing criticism of the liberal humanism of the reformed churches of his day Barth stated that,

> ... in spite of the new Protestantism, we cannot deny that we feel more at home in the world of Catholicism and among its believers than in a world and among believers where the reality about which the Reformation centred has become an unknown or almost unknown entity.[14]

---

[9] Busch, *Karl Barths Lebenslauf*, p. 197/ET: p. 183.
[10] *'Gott in-über Mensch von Gott her'*, comment by Barth to Thurneysen, 9 February 1929, in Barth and Thurneysen, *Briefwechsel Band II 1921-1930*, p. 652. See also Erich Przywara *Gespräch zwischen den Kirchen* (*zusammen mit Hermann Sauer*) (Nürnberg: Glock und Lutz, 1956), p. 7.
[11] Barth, 'Der Begriff der Kirche', pp. 285-287.
[12] The title could be more accurately translated as 'Roman Catholicism *as a* (*als*) question *at/to* the Protestant Church'; Barth is therefore acknowledging that by its very existence and continuation the Roman Catholic Church continually questions the existence of the Protestant Churches.
[13] Barth, 'Der römische Katholizismus', pp. 336 and 349/ET: pp. 312 and 322.
[14] Barth, 'Der römische Katholizismus', p. 338/ET: p. 314.

5. Barth on the Influence of Dostoevsky

In case his readers were in any doubt about what he was saying Barth added in the published text a footnote driving this point home further:

> If I today became convinced that the interpretation of the Reformation on the line taken by Schleiermacher-Ritschl-Tröltsch (or even by Seeberg or Holl) was correct, that Luther and Calvin really intended such an outcome of their labours, I could not indeed become a Catholic tomorrow, but I should have to withdraw from the evangelical Church. And if I were forced to make a choice between the two evils, I should, in fact, prefer the Catholic.[15]

Barth does not leave the question of Rome alone though - he goes on to criticize what Rome had become and not withstanding what he had said and despite the fact that Rome could be considered closer to the revelatory foundation of the early Church than the Lutheran Church of his day, Rome was still at fault. Using evidence both for and against from contemporary Catholic scholars (essentially Erich Przywara, but also Karl Adam and Karl Heim) he exposes the flaws in Rome as severely as he does in the neo-Protestantism of his day. This criticism culminates in an attack on the Roman concept of authority - 'the world of the Court of the Inquisition',[16] an allusion to the impact Dostoevsky's The Grand Inquisitor had exerted on Barth and Thurneysen several years earlier (1918-22). For Barth, the answer to the first question as to whether the Protestant Church is a church at all lies in the providence of God.

It is in the context of the second question, the extent to which the Protestant Church is *Protestant* or a *protesting* church, that Barth deals with the nature of sin and grace. Yes, the new Protestantism has lost the substance of church, it has 'thrown away the restoration. It has ceased to be Church and it has ceased to be Protestant.'[17] By contrast the Catholic Church speaks boldly and has preserved its substance to a better degree than the Protestant Church: '...it has in these four centuries remained astonishingly true to itself.'[18] It has, Barth observes, become Jesuit and, latterly, has revived Thomism and therefore speaks boldly. Yes, Rome has a serious understanding of sin but it is the manner in which it attempts to control grace, the grace as of the forgiveness of God, which causes Barth serious concern. It is in this context that Barth examines the concept of sin in the neo-Protestant and liberal humanism of his own theological heritage. Hence his comments about it being best to avoid the teaching of Schleiermacher and Ritschl on sin, and how the new Protestantism had been characterized by 'a hankering for the fleshpots of Egypt.'[19] It is certainly not here in the new Protestantism that he was to find the insight that the only grace we have from God is that which can be received like the free

---

[15] Barth, 'Der römische Katholizismus', p. 338/ET: p. 314.
[16] Barth, 'Der römische Katholizismus', p. 348/ET: p. 322.
[17] Barth, 'Der römische Katholizismus', p. 350/ET: p. 323.
[18] Barth, 'Der römische Katholizismus', p. 351/ET: p. 324.
[19] Barth, 'Der römische Katholizismus', p. 357/ET: p. 328.

pardon given to criminals. This is grace given in judgement and requires a realization on the part of the sinner of the true depth of one's sins. This cannot be taken lightly, this cannot be regarded as a tiny blemish on an otherwise perfected soul, it certainly cannot be received by redefining sin as the good (the fleshpots of Egypt[20]) as in the liberal agenda, which, for Barth, merely defused the seriousness of sin. No, Barth is asserting that there is no other grace except the free pardon of criminals, grace in judgement. Barth does not find this in Rome nor in the neo-Protestantism of his liberal theological heritage. He finds this, so he explicitly states, in the work of Dostoevsky: 'Is it not shameful that we needed to have this truth retold to us by the Russian Dostoevsky? If we have refused to hear it from our Reformers who really understood it better than Dostoevsky, are we then still Protestants?'[21] So it is in this question of the seriousness of sin, coupled with the understanding that forgiveness and grace only comes like the free pardon of a thief/criminal (Schächergnade in the biblisch sense) that decides whether the Protestant Church is still a church - if Barth's contemporaries have failed to see this then Barth seriously asks the question himself, 'are we then still Protestants?'[22] So the answer does not revolve around ecclesiological issues, or more specifically issues of authority (the Courts of the Inquisition) and commission (Peter's rock) but on theological anthropology. That is, the relationship between humanity and God, whereby humanity must realize the full depravity of its sinfulness and be prepared, facing this crime, to accept forgiveness given in judgement, forgiveness given as a free pardon. This is a forensic understanding and mirrors that of the Reformers. But, argues Barth, not only did he not learn this from the Reformers, but the liberal humanist neo-Protestant teachers of his youth had forgotten it, substituting it with this sly backward glance, as he put it, for the fleshpots of Egypt.

In the revision of 'Die Theologie und der moderne Mensch' published in *Zwischen den Zeiten* in 1930 (originally presented as an address, 8th October 1927) Barth expands on the critique of humanity's response to the scandal at the heart of theology.[23] Yes, he reiterates the scathing criticism of liberalism for defusing this fear of God, but he expands on his criticism of Rome to include natural theology. The criticism of Rome is now not only that it attempts to control the truth of the freedom of God by its own power and authority but also what he described as the increasing demand for natural theology - the desire, as Barth saw it, to ground revelation not in God but in human life. Theology, he argued, must return ceaselessly to its grounding in the Word of God, further, that we as mere mortal and fallen humans cannot reflect on the question of life with any accuracy because our existence has irretrievably lost its meaning. That

---

[20] An allusion to Exodus 16:3.
[21] Barth, 'Der römische Katholizismus', p. 357/ET: p. 328.
[22] Barth, 'Der römische Katholizismus', p. 357/ET: p. 328.
[23] Barth, 'Die Theologie und der heutige Mensch', pp. 374-396.

meaning can only be found in the Church - or more pertinently what the Church bears witness to.

> And isn't that rebellion? Isn't that domestication? And is not this possibility the possibility of the Grand Inquisitor really more dangerous than all atheism and liberalism? More dangerous, because theology is then so unbelievably done away with, with the exception of one small point, that it cannot say anything more than that by human thought alone one can never get to deal with the word of God.[24]

Thus Barth repeats his criticism of how humanity either rejects this truth atheistically, or seeks to play it down, to neutralize it through liberalism, or seeks to control it through the power structure of Rome and the palliative of natural theology. Barth asserts that this palliative as evidenced in Rome is by far the worst option because it lays claim to the principle that one can never get to deal with the word of God except through human thought. This, for Barth, is then linked indelibly to the arrogance and authoritarian control of the Großinquisitor (The Grand Inquisitor from *The Brothers Karamazov*). Barth commented that at the heart of Christian theology is a scandal, a paradox, and explicitly invoking Kierkegaardian terminology, a stumbling block to negate the 'Furcht und Zittern' (fear and trembling) that must accompany the realization of God's pressing claim on us.[25] The perplexities of faith cannot be denied.[26]

Grace, Forgiveness and Redemption - Christian Soteriology

For Barth, the essential difference between Rome and the Reformation churches was how the grace of God was controlled/given. For Barth, grace should not be controlled, owned, meted out or in any way guarded by humanity (ecclesial or otherwise). Grace is the free gift of God to sinful humanity - to every man, woman and child - and the response by such a one is the closest it is possible to get to appropriation. Therefore it was in Rome that he could at least identify a serious understanding of sin, but here he found difficulties. He repeated often in 'Der römische Katholizismus als Frage...' how he did not believe that Rome took sin seriously - despite the references to sin and depravity in humanity that were in various parts of the Roman liturgy. Barth still saw an emphasis on merit and preparation in Roman doctrine and spirituality. In addition the Roman claim to be able to forgive sins effectively meant that they controlled and could mete out this gracious forgiveness on God's part (Barth also objected to the emphasis on imputation). From 1916 on

---

[24] Barth, 'Die Theologie und der heutige Mensch', p. 395.
[25] Barth, 'Die Theologie und der heutige Mensch', p. 380. Kierkegaard's phrase 'Fear and Trembling' (*Frygt og Baeven*) - in the German, '*Furcht und Zittern*' - is also used in the introduction to Barth, 'Der römische Katholizismus', pp. 330 and 332/ET: pp. 308 and 310.
[26] Barth, 'Die Theologie und der heutige Mensch', p. 394.

Barth was to a degree re-discovering his roots in Calvinism - with the understanding that human depravity was such that any attempt at goodness was not possible by human efforts alone. Grace was the important catalyst - preveniently speaking. However, it is important to remember that Barth did not find this orthodox reading of sin balanced by the grace of God given freely in his Calvinistic heritage. No, he tells us that it was through the Russian writer Dostoevsky that he realized/discovered this. This is the relationship between God and humanity as sinners. Justification leads, or should lead, to sanctification. Grace given freely, as that of a pardon given to a criminal, should lead to rehabilitation - sanctification. This is a forensic understanding of sin and grace and is one that was relatively common in the early Church, the Patristic Church and in the writings of the Reformers. Likewise it continued to a degree to be found in Russian Orthodox theology, which in turn influenced Dostoevsky.

Therefore there is no other grace except 'the free pardon of criminals, grace in judgement.' This forensic/legalistic language when appropriated by Barth emphasizes the difference between the Reformers and the early Church on the one hand and the control by Rome or the negation of sin (and in consequence, grace) by liberalism on the other hand. Barth had already explicated some understanding of this several years earlier, for example in *Römerbrief 2* (1922):

> It is true, also, that freedom is the essential meaning of the manner of life which is here required: the freedom which was brought by Christ and which the Grand Inquisitors of all ages have found so awkward and so dangerous - the freedom of the imprisonment from God.[27]

This quotation reflects the central influence of Dostoevsky on Barth: the understanding that the grace of God is given like the free pardon given to a thief/criminal (schächer), the forgiveness and freedom (Freiheit) given to a captive/prisoner (Gefangene), in captivity (Gefangenschaft), the captivity from God (Gefangenschaft Gottes): therefore, '...die Freiheit in der Gefangenschaft Gottes'[28] - the freedom of grace given to the one who is imprisoned by God, in captivity to God. Barth presented this freedom on many occasions in the context of the Grand Inquisitor of all ages who seeks to deny this freedom often through religion/church. This figure is at the heart of the theological polemic that is infused throughout Dostoevsky's novel, *The Brothers Karamazov*; Barth's use of this figure is more than merely illustrative: it is not just the figure he took from Dostoevsky but also the concept of the Großinquisitor as a representative, of the theocratic illusion[29] - the illusion that it is possible to

---

[27] Barth, *Römerbrief 2*, p. 532/ET: pp. 504-505, commenting on Romans 14:1-15:13, 'Der Krisis des freien Lebensversuchs' ('The Krisis of Human Freedom and Detachment').

[28] Barth, *Römerbrief 2*, p. 532/ET: pp. 504-505.

[29] Barth, *Römerbrief 2*, p. 504/ET: p. 479.

bring God down to earth, to control God, indeed to laud the human agenda of church, religion and politics in the place of God's *aseity*. Barth therefore acknowledged in 1928 his debt to Dostoevsky for this understanding, that this influence along with other ideas from the Russian Orthodox derived and influenced writings of Dostoevsky occurred between six and thirteen years earlier: that is, in 1915-1916 (*Crime and Punishment,* also *The Idiot*) and then again from 1918-21(*The Brothers Karamazov*).

Barth's Theological Education - Neo-Protestant Liberalism

For Barth, grace and sin had become marginal concepts in the liberal humanism of neo-Protestant theology; for Barth, the liberal agenda had, to a degree, developed an understanding of humanity that often defined sin as the result of social conditioning. Dostoevsky is one of a few lone outsiders in the nineteenth-century who did not. Despite the fact that Barth had been raised in a Calvinistic household, any understanding of an orthodox, forensic doctrine of sin and grace derived from a reading of theological anthropology that saw humanity as fallen, corrupt and irretrievably lost without God, either failed to make an impression or was overlaid by the liberal neo-Protestantism of his teacher at Marburg, Wilhelm Herrmann. Between 1909 and 1921 Barth was assistant pastor to the German speaking Church in Zürich and then Minister of the Reformed Church in Safenwil. In both instances he would have been singing hymns with his congregation, which presumably voiced this forensic understanding of sin. Did this not press on him theologically prior to the point of influence of Dostoevsky in the summer of 1915? The answer is presumably no; is this because he had been taught a much higher, even elitist, understanding by his liberal teachers, which relegated this biblical understanding, as such, to the relatively uneducated members of his congregation? Either way, this understanding did not strike him as an important part of his understanding of atonement.

Barth on the Influence of Dostoevsky

Those who refused to hear this truth about salvation were presumably his liberal Protestant teachers - Herrmann, Ritschl, and of course, Schleiermacher. In 1921 Barth left Safenwil to be Professor of Reformed Theology at Göttingen. Six years later he wrote about what appears to have been a mad scramble to read and find out about the Reformers generally, the Reformed Confessions specifically, in time to lecture on them; writing some autobiographical sketches from Münster in 1927, Barth admitted the ignorance he had of the Reformed Confessions, even at the time of his appointment to Göttingen in 1921, let alone in 1915! - 'I can now admit, six years later (1927), that at that time I did not even possess the Reformed confessional writings, and had certainly never read them, quite apart from other horrendous gaps in my knowledge.'[30] It was from his reading of Dostoevsky that this forensic understanding of forgiveness comes - not from the great Reformers, nor from the Reformed Confessions. On the evidence of his having read and been impressed by *Crime and Punishment*, and the internal evidence we have seen in 'Die Gerechtigkeit Gottes' it was at this time, the second half of 1915, that these ideas about sin and grace pressed on his theological *Wendung und Retraktation*.

But what does Barth have to say on this influence apart from the comments in 'Der römische Katholizismus als Frage...'. The world that Dostoevsky created in his novels was essentially biblical. This was very different from the modern, progressive world of advanced, industrial West European nations such as Germany, Britain and France - powerful and civilized. Religious understanding was likewise different - we have already alluded to the nature of liberal neo-Protestantism and the belief that God was to be identified with the power and progress of these self-confident and assertively mammonistic European nations and empires. But the Great War had dealt such an understanding of Western civilization a mortal blow. Barth and Thurneysen saw preserved in Dostoevsky's thinking that which they believed was true to the Gospel from the early church and from Patristic theology. Thurneysen wrote that Dostoevsky saw the memory in the church of his day still preserved pure of the early history of Christendom, as he perceived it, prior to its compromise, its institutionalisation.[31] This was something that had been lost to Liberal neo-Protestantism. In substance this was the understanding that life is as it is, the world goes its way, but then there is the beyond - God, eternity, resurrection. There is humanity; then there is God. Further, that humanity is sinful and cannot find any way out of this condition of its own efforts. God is God, and there is no step that leads over from humanity to God - only what God can do for us, to save us from ourselves provided we are prepared to accept this grace, this forgiveness given freely to those who can perceive the true state of corruptness in their own human heart. This is the understanding of the Reformers precisely because it is a theocentric view - or more pertinently, it is characteristic of an understanding of salvation present in the writings of the New Testament.

Therefore in the light of Barth's comments to Thurneysen (letter, 18 August

---

[30] Barth, 'Autobiographische Skizzen', p. 309/ET: p. 156. See also Karl Barth, 'Foreword', in Heinrich Heppe, *Reformed Dogmatics set out and Illustrated from the Sources* (ed. Ernst Bizer, trans. G.T. Thomson; London: Allen and Unwin, 1950. [1861]. Barth comments in the 1935 reissue of Heppe's work about how this work fell into his hands and although seemingly unattractive and out-of-date in the as then theological climate, it proved its worth to him.

[31] Thurneysen, *Dostojewski*, p. 6/ET: p. 10.

1915) that he was so impressed by *Crime and Punishment* that he then wanted to be as wise as this Russian, we must assess again what he wrote in the preface to *Römerbrief 2*: 'I have also paid more attention to what may be culled from the writings of Kierkegaard and Dostoevsky that is of importance for the interpretation of the New Testament.'[32] For *Römerbrief 2* he paid greater attention (vermehrte Aufmerken, increased notice or increased attention), the implication being that he had already paid attention to Dostoevsky from the perspective of how to interpret the New Testament. Dostoevsky had already pointed him in the direction of this theocentric view in 1915. Then during the period of the rewriting he pays further attention (Barth commented on several occasions that he only came to Kierkegaard late - that is, in 1919). Barth's comment in a volume of essays and correspondence published for Thurneysen's seventieth birthday confirms this. When Barth wrote of the importance of Eduard Thurneysen and how many Barthian scholars in the 1950s saw Thurneysen as passive in their correspondence and assumed that he, Barth, had been the instigator, he commented,

> On the contrary he was the one who first put me on the trail of Blumhardt and Kutter, and then also Dostoevsky without whose discovery I would not have been able to write either the first or the second edition of the commentary on Romans.[33]

Note, Barth wrote that neither the first nor second edition of *Der Römerbrief* could have been written without Thurneysen having exposed him to the influence of Dostoevsky - not the second edition only, but the first as well (started in the August of 1916). This evidence, along with the letter dated 18 August 1915 confirms the importance of Dostoevsky from this early stage in Barth's theological *Wendung und Retraktation*. Further it reinforces the importance of Thurneysen in mediating this influence. The influence of Dostoevsky is part of the new starting point we looked at earlier - the year 1915.[34] The evidence from Barth himself confirms two crucial details: first, that Thurneysen was instrumental in introducing Barth to Dostoevsky (a fact widely acknowledged in the Barthian scholarly tradition) therefore this influence occurs after Thurneysen's arrival in the Aargau (installed as pastor, 1st June 1913 in the village of Leutwil); second, that the influence must have occurred before Barth's rediscovery of elements of a forensic understanding of sin and grace in Luther and Calvin from the second half of 1916 on.[35] The influence therefore must be in the period June 1913 to August 1916, and the correspondence from August 1915 identifies the point of influence, as does the internal evidence in 'Die Gerechtigkeit Gottes'.

---

[32] Barth, *Römerbrief 2*, 'Vorwort zur zweiten Auflage', p. XIV/ET: p. 4.
[33] Barth, 'Lebendige Vergangenheit', p. 13.
[34] Barth, 'Kriegszeit und Gottesreich', pp. 120-122.
[35] Barth, 'Nachwort', pp. 295-297.

Von Balthasar's Understanding

Von Balthasar who worked with Barth knew that the influence of Dostoevsky predated that of Luther and Kierkegaard; further that the influence of Dostoevsky was not identical with that of Kierkegaard. Writing in 1951 and commenting on the period of the writing of *Römerbrief 2* (1920-1921) Von Balthasar wrote,

> At this point, there is an inevitable transition from Platonic and Eastern Christian notions of 'identity' to the Reformation insistence on 'contradiction'. And so Origen and Dostoevsky encounter Luther, Calvin and Kierkegaard; and the rules of engagement for this clash are the whole point of the second edition of the Epistle to the Romans. [36]

Von Balthasar understood, what was to be lost to the Barthian scholarly tradition, that Barth was influenced by Dostoevsky prior to his discovery of Kierkegaard in 1919. The influence occurs from 1915, a year before Barth started writing *Römerbrief 1*, and a full five years before he considers rewriting. The transition that Von Balthasar writes of is from the early influence of Dostoevsky (*Crime and Punishment*, read in 1915, and *The Idiot*), which then gives way to a Reformation understanding (Luther, then Calvin). This Eastern concept of identity is essentially from Origen and Dostoevsky, asserts Von Balthasar. This, Von Balthasar asserts, gives way to a Reformation insistence on contradiction. This is not quite correct - the key person/identity that influences Barth from Dostoevsky (from 1915) is the character of Rodion Romanovich Raskolnikov in *Crime and Punishment*, who is racked by contradictions. Sofya Semyonovna Marmeladova - Sonya - by contrast is not; if anything she is characterized by what Von Balthasar refers to as a Platonic-Eastern (i.e. Orthodox) notion of identity. Raskolnikov is on the verge of a schizophrenic mental breakdown, and is pulled back from the brink, to a degree, by Sonya's Christian witness (a witness rooted in Bible readings!). Von Balthasar can therefore be considered as somewhat off the mark in his comments about identity and contradiction, or perhaps he is half right - his comments apply to Sonya, but not Raskolnikov. However, he does identify the correct timeframe (Dostoevsky, then Luther and Calvin, then Kierkegaard, then Overbeck), and it is important to remember that at the time of writing Von Balthasar was working with Barth. Furthermore, what we find in 'The Idea' of Dostoevsky is the *surd*-like nihilism that overwhelms such an individual as Raskolnikov. In this context Von Balthasar wrote that 'writers like Dostoevsky and Claudel, in common with the saints, knew in all its depth this social side of sin' [37]. John McDowell's comments on Barth's eschatology on how Barth gained a sense of cultural crisis from this existential reading are also relevant here; furthermore McDowell acknowledges that 'underlying Barth's radically

---

[36] Von Balthasar, *The Theology of Karl Barth*, p. 66.
[37] Von Balthasar, *The Theology of Karl Barth*, p. 375.

5. Barth on the Influence of Dostoevsky

powerful return to Reformation conceptions of sin are particularly St Paul, Kierkegaard, Luther and Müller, and also Dostoevsky's doctrine of the irrational and *surd*-like element of sin.'[38] What is important is that this influence, as we have seen, predates that of Paul (Romans), Luther and Kierkegaard.

---

[38] John C. McDowell, *Barth's Eschatology: Interrogation and Transformations beyond Tragedy* (Aldershot: Ashgate, 2000), pp. 77, 79 n. 90, 221.

CHAPTER 6

Barth and Thurneysen's Theological Agenda: 'The Solution'

From *Crime and Punishment* Barth can begin to see something of the approach to sin and redemption that, it can be argued, is analogous to that found in the early church as evidenced from the epistles of the apostle Paul and early Patristic writers. Dostoevsky was therefore pointing Barth towards what can be considered a theocentric or biblical interpretation of sin. Sin and grace were dialectically balanced - held in an eschatological tension. However, this is to get ahead of ourselves. So far we have examined 'The Problem' for Barth and Thurneysen. 'The Solution' for them was to lie in the Bible - or at least in the rediscovery of the Bible as the basis for theology, a theology that would address the problems they encountered in their ministry.

Reading: Barth and Paul - Thurneysen and Dostoevsky

Whilst on holiday in Leutwil in the summer of 1916, Barth and Thurneysen agreed '...that for further clarification of the situation it would be necessary to return to academic theology.'[1] Barth suggested a return to an in-depth study of Kant. However, Thurneysen suggested that they needed something wholly other:

> In fact we found ourselves compelled to do something much more obvious. We tried to learn our ABC all over again, beginning by reading and interpreting the writings of the Old and New Testaments, more thoughtfully than before. And lo and behold they began to speak to us - but not as we thought we must have heard them in the school of what was then 'modern theology'.[2]

As a result Barth took up serious academic Bible study - he began studying Paul's Epistle to the Romans in depth. Barth still believed it was important and even obligatory to belong to the Social Democratic Party, but beyond the problems of Liberalism and Religious Socialism, the understanding of the Kingdom of God in the real, transcendent sense, mediated to him in part by the Blumhardts, Dostoevsky and Kutter had eventually pointed them to, at Thurneysen's behest, 'The Solution'. Barth commented:

---

[1] Barth, 'Nachwort', p. 294.
[2] Barth, 'Nachwort', p. 294.

On a certain day in 1916, Thurneysen and I very naively agreed to go back to academic theology to clarify the situation. If we had known what was to happen we would not have found the confident audacity to do this.

The following morning, surrounded by a stack of commentaries, I found myself before the Romans of the apostle Paul with what seemed to me to be the newly put question of what was really in it. From the notes that I then made on Romans, there arose what became later the well-known, controversial book.[3]

Barth's thoughts had been moving in a particular direction and the years 1915 and 1916 confirmed this movement - what was to become a return to a Biblical basis for theology. It was, so Barth recalled, Thurneysen who '...whispered the key phrase to me...' whilst on holiday in June of 1916, '...what we need for preaching, instruction and pastoral care is a 'wholly other' theological foundation ('eine ganz andere theologische Grundlegung')'[4]

And so Barth commenced this study of Romans. At first the notebooks he was filling with his thoughts and comments were for his own private use, for Eduard Thurneysen to read and for use in explaining to others his developing theological rebellion against his liberal heritage. Barth explained to Ragaz in November 1916 that he had intentionally chosen Romans because of its misuse and its misinterpretation by what was now considered his liberal opponents.[5] Barth saw Paul's comments as evidence of action by God that transcended religion, events that were a concrete historical occurrence; furthermore, as he commented in the preface to *Römerbrief 1*, the problems of humanity had not changed, and this truth was known nineteen hundred years ago by the early church in a way that, so Barth believed, it was not known in many of the churches of his day. For Barth, Paul was giving him special evidence about the truth and clarity of the Bible's testimony.[6] Eberhard Busch summarized/paraphrased well, drawing on comments about Romans 8:1-11 from *Römerbrief 1*, where Barth questions all Christian groups, trends and movements, churches and political organisations arguing that they could not carry on as they were doing. Why? because these agencies (including the churches) had settled everything without recourse to God. Or they invoked God at the end to provide what Busch called the crowning touch. Furthermore Barth asserted in these comments from *Römerbrief 1* that he perceived a situation where human wisdom was not built on the fear of the Lord and that our movements often hindered God.[7]

This resonates with what Barth had been taught by Kutter and Dostoevsky -

---

[3] Barth, 'Autobiographische Skizzen', p. 307/ET: p.155.
[4] Barth, 'Nachwort', p. 294. Note this is the language of *basic fundamentals* or *reasons; grounds* or *foundations*, that was noted earlier in chapter two; in this instance, *Grundlegung* (figuratively, the laying of the foundations).
[5] Busch, *Karl Barths Lebenslauf*, p. 111/ET: p. 98.
[6] Barth, *Römerbrief 1*, 'Vorwort,' p. 3.
[7] Barth, *Römerbrief 1*, p. 299.

that all human achievement is nothing in the face of God. Barth was writing in the middle years of the First World War: 'The collapse of our cause must demonstrate for once that God's cause is exclusively his own. That is where we stand today.'[8] Yes, this echoes with what Barth and Thurneysen saw in Kutter's writings and in discussion with the man himself; likewise this also resonates with the relationship between human endeavour and the transcendence of God in the novels of Dostoevsky but this also defines the limits of any influence Dostoevsky is to have on Barth - whatever Barth finds in Dostoevsky, he will find it in the Bible generally, the New Testament specifically. Barth was to go on to study and write commentaries on other New Testament epistles, but this is the foundation period of grounding his theological *Wendung und Retraktation* on what Paul has to say in Romans.

Dostoevsky and the Russian New Testament

Barth commented reflectively in 1958 - 'Thurneysen with his "Johannine" disposition was so different from mine...'[9] By comparison we can fairly assert that Barth was *Pauline*! This explains why, once the decision had been taken to return to the Bible as a basis for theology, Barth set about analysing Romans and working on a commentary of his own whilst Thurneysen developed his interest in Dostoevsky. Why? - because Dostoevsky had developed a great love of John's Gospel and Epistles and was himself something of a Johannine personality.

As a young man at the St Petersburg Academy Dostoevsky fell in with the Petrashevskii group,[10] a revolutionary faction then under the tutelage of the editor and writer Belinsky.[11] Characterized by naive socio-political action, and inspired by the writings of philosophical theorists from the French Revolution (Jean Baptiste Joseph Fourier, 1768-1830, and Auguste Comte, 1798-1857), the

---

[8] Barth, *Römerbrief 1*, p. 299.
[9] Barth, 'Lebendige Vergangenheit', p. 12.
[10] Centred on Mikhail Butashevich-Petrashevskii (1821-66), the group met between 1845 and 1849 at his St Petersburg home. Members included minor officials and junior officers, writers and students, who were interested in the teachings of the French Utopian Socialists, and German Idealist philosophers, including Hegel, but primarily the future transformation of society into a federation of self-supporting communes in which human labour and other activities were organized in order to allow freedom and fulfilment. The group publicly criticized the autocracy of Czar Nicholas I and demanded free speech along with press and legal reforms.
[11] Vissarion Grigorievich Belinsky (1811-48), active 1831-1848 in Russia and then continental Europe, was a self-confessed atheist, humanist, anti-Czar, proto-socialist, though primarily a literary critic. He was expelled from the University of Moscow for his revolutionary views; he then worked as a journalist. He is generally considered the father figure of radical intellectuals in Russia and was highly respected by the Soviets. Belinsky died in 1848 a year before the authorities arrested the Petrashevskii circle.

group consisted of Westernized humanists, often self-confessed atheists: Belinsky had translated Feuerbach's *Essence of Christianity* (1841) for them. In 1849 Dostoevsky, regarded by the authorities as the leader was arrested and with the others, convicted of sedition, sentenced to death by firing squad, but was reprieved at the last second just as the firing squad had cocked their rifles. This experience had a devastatingly profound effect on Dostoevsky - it was the experience of being born again, of resurrection. This theme of resurrection was to dominate his mature novels and he was to project this near-death experience into his characters on more than one occasion. The sentences were commuted to transportation and imprisonment - to Omsk in Siberia for ten years (1849-59). The significance of the trial, mock execution and exile are of profound importance to anyone who wishes to understand Dostoevsky's theological beliefs.

In the same way that the Bible, or more pertinently biblical theology, became the foundational basis and 'The Solution' as we have seen to Barth and Thurneysen's theological problems, the New Testament is of crucial importance in Dostoevsky's rediscovery of his Christian faith and as the source and basis for the beliefs underlying his novels. On route to Siberia, as they marched in shackles through Tobolsk, an elderly woman thrust a Russian New Testament into his hands, which helped to rekindle his faith and was the most precious of possessions to him during his imprisonment. This helped him to reaffirm his commitment to Christian principles, as embodied in the traditions and spirituality of the Russian Orthodox Church (though he was always wary of ecclesial power and authority). He kept this Russian New Testament[12] until his death, reading John's Gospel on a daily basis, annotating it and writing his theological thoughts in the margins.[13] From the evidence of the annotations the following books were of most importance to him: The Gospel According to John, The Epistles of John, then The Revelation to John.[14] Twenty-one of the twenty-seven books of the New Testament are marked - however, The Gospel of Mark is annotated only in two places, Luke in seven; by contrast there are fifty-eight annotations in The Gospel of John. The teachings of Christ and The Passion are heavily marked and annotated. The short First Epistle of John is heavily marked and annotated in six places; The Revelation to John sixteen places.[15] By contrast The Sermon on the Mount is largely ignored. Even after

---

[12] See Kjetsaa, *Dostoevsky and his New Testament*. Dostoevsky's edition of the Russian New Testament was GBL, fond 93/I, K. 5b./1. *Evangelie. Gospoda nashego Iisusa Khrista Novyj Zavet,* Pervym izdaniem; Sanktpeterburg : V tipografii Rossijskogo Biblejskogo Obshchestva, 1823.

[13] Irina Kirillova, 'Dostoevsky's Markings in the Gospel of St John', in George Pattison and Diane Oenning Thompson (eds.), *Dostoevsky and the Christian Tradition* (Cambridge: Cambridge University Press, 2001), pp. 41-50.

[14] Kirillova, 'Dostoevsky's Markings in the Gospel of St John', p. 43.

[15] Kirillova, 'Dostoevsky's Markings in the Gospel of St John', p. 8.

his return from Siberia he regularly consulted, annotated, wrestled with what were to him key passages, marking in ink, pencil; the practice of wrestling with what he termed 'Sacred Scripture' continued even until the day before his death.[16] Therefore The Gospel According to John and The First Epistle of John, both with the emphasis on the figure of Christ and, what is termed in Eastern Orthodoxy, the theology of love',[17] these are by far the most important New Testament books to Dostoevsky and are the foundational basis for his belief system during the Siberian and post Siberian periods of his life.

To understand Dostoevsky's complicated life and beliefs we need to look at his appropriation of The Gospel of John. The greatest number of markings in John's Gospel relate to the divinity of Christ, and the relationship between the Son and the Father.[18] Irina Kirillova notes, '...like no other of the Evangelists John sees the miracle embodied in the Christ who preached love in an evil world.'[19] This can be seen in the heavily marked passages from the Johannine corpus, which deal explicitly with love - from the 'new commandment' passages in the Gospel through to the comments in the epistle dealing with the nature of love between people.[20] Irina Kirillova notes that as a religious type Dostoevsky is a '...Thomas the Doubter who needs to confront Christ in his own way.'[21] A large group of markings relate to resurrection - one of Dostoevsky's central concerns.[22] These annotations emphasize that belief and life are inseparable; therefore we find that the concept of, in Russian, живая жизнь (*zhivaia zhizn* - living life), is idiomatic of Dostoevsky's annotations in the Johannine corpus. The resurrection of Lazarus was central to his faith - the passage is heavily marked in his New Testament. In addition it is the central biblical passage in *Crime and Punishment*.[23] Overall, Irina Kirillova notes:

> The Gospel of St John has particular significance for Dostoevsky because, more than any of the other New Testament books, it enables him to affirm his faith in the divine Son of God through the affirmation of Christ's Sonship made manifest in the 'theology of love' that is so central to both The Gospel of St John and the First Epistle of John. Dostoevsky's profession of faith had to overcome not so much the claims of nineteenth-century Natural Science as the tragic, insoluble contradiction between belief in an omnipotent and merciful God and the cruel, bleak reality of innocent suffering. The luminous revelation of love in the person of Christ enables Dostoevsky to believe that it is possible to resolve the terrible

---

[16] Anna Grigorievna Dostoevsky, *Dostoevsky Reminiscences* (trans. Beatrice Stillman; London: Wildwood House, 1976), p. 375.
[17] Vladimir Lossky, *The Mystical Theology of the Eastern Church* (Cambridge: James Clarke, 1957).
[18] Kirillova, 'Dostoevsky's Markings in the Gospel of St John', pp. 8-9.
[19] Kirillova, 'Dostoevsky's Markings in the Gospel of St John', p. 9.
[20] John 13:34 and 15:12; 1 John 2:10, 4:7, 4:12 and 4:19-20.
[21] Kjetsaa, *Dostoevsky and his New Testament*, p. 45.
[22] John 6:54; 8:51-52; 11:26 and 12:32.
[23] Dostoevsky, *Crime and Punishment*, bk. 4 chp. 4, pp. 314-331.

antinomy of innocent suffering and divine mercy through faith in Christ, the God-Man, who is both innocent victim and Redeemer.[24]

This antinomy between divine mercy and what appears to be innocent suffering presented by the dialectical contradiction between the understanding of an omnipotent and merciful God and the reality of suffering and death here on earth is reconciled only in the lordship of the Son of God. This is the central dialectic in Dostoevsky's beliefs and in the theology presented in his novels. All other examples of Dostoevsky's dialectics flow from this resolution of the contradictions of faith and life in the God-man - hence живая жизнь - *zhivaia zhizn*.

It is therefore of no surprise that Thurneysen should have developed his theology along similar lines to Dostoevsky - being of a Johannine disposition, as Barth called him. When Barth was preoccupied with Pauline theology (initially from Romans) it was Thurneysen who drew his attention over the coming years to passages containing important theological polemics and beliefs from the novels of Dostoevsky - this discovery reached a climax with Thurneysen's study and analysis of *The Brothers Karamazov* and his mediation of Dostoevsky's great theological polemic The Grand Inquisitor to Barth from 1918 on.

Die neue Welt in der Bibel

By August 1918 the manuscript of Barth's commentary on Romans was ready to submit to the publishers. Some of his thoughts on a return to the Bible as the basis for theology were contained in an address - 'Die neue Welt in der Bibel' ('The Strange New World Within the Bible')[25] presented in Leutwil Church on 6 February 1917. This was the logical step on from the new starting point of twenty months earlier (the summer of 1915). In 'Die neue Welt in der Bibel' the *diastasis* is between the world of men and women and the world of God. Barth opens with the question, what is in the Bible? The answer being not what we expect. He then outlines characters and events that contradict our expectations in terms of morality and religion - particularly from the Old Testament. The answer is that '...within the Bible there is a strange new world - the world of God.'[26] Though on the surface the Bible may appear to present us with good upright moral characters we are in for a shock. Barth cites Samson, Saul and David, Amos or even Peter amongst others to illustrate this point. These characters do not present us with the archetypal role models claimed by

---

[24] Kjetsaa, *Dostoevsky and his New Testament*, p. 50.
[25] Karl Barth, 'Die neue Welt in der Bibel', in Barth, *Das Wort Gottes und die Theologie*, pp. 18-32; ET: Karl Barth, 'The Strange New World in the Bible', in Barth, *The Word of God and the Word of Man*, pp. 28-50.
[26] Barth, 'Die neue Welt in der Bibel', p. 21/ET: p. 33.

6. Barth and Thurneysen's Theological Agenda: the Solution

pietism or nineteenth-century Liberal neo-Protestantism. This point is pressed further:

> ... a David is a great man in spite of his adultery and bloody sword: blessed is the man unto whom the Lord ascribes no iniquity! Into this world the publicans and the harlots will go before your impeccably elegant and righteous folk of good society! In this world the true hero is the lost son, who is absolutely lost and feeding swine - and not his moral elder brother! [27]

There are of course echoes here of Sonya the prostitute in *Crime and Punishment,* and Raskolnikov who must turn to accept the grace and forgiveness of God despite his crimes. But more pertinently there are echoes here of Dostoevsky's understanding of the Last Judgement as spoken by the character Semyon Zakharovich Marmeladov, Sonya's father, to Raskolnikov whilst in a drunken stupor, whereby those who genuinely know of their unworthiness are paradoxically right before God-

> On that day He (Christ) will come and ask, 'Where is the daughter who gave herself for a wicked and consumptive stepmother, for a stranger's little children? Where is the daughter who pitied her earthly father, a foul drunkard, not shrinking from his beastliness?' And He will say, 'Come! I have already forgiven you once, I have forgiven you once, and now, too, your many sins are forgiven, for you have loved much.' And He will forgive my Sonya, He will forgive her, I know He will... And He will judge and forgive all, the good and the wicked, the wise and the humble ... He will say, 'Come forth, my drunk ones, my weak ones, my shameless ones!' And we will all come forth, without being ashamed, and stand there. And He will say, 'Swine you are! - of the image of the beast and of his seal; but come, you, too!'
>
> And the wise and the reasonable will say unto Him, 'Lord, why do you receive such as these?' And He will say, 'I receive them, my wise and reasonable ones, forasmuch as not one of them considered himself worthy of this thing' ... And He will stretch out His arms to us, and we will fall at His feet and weep ... Lord, Thy kingdom come! [28]

This is explicitly based on The Parable of the Sheep and the Goats (Matthew 25:31-46). In addition, as Boyce Gibson notes, 'Marmeladov's outburst (is) gorgeously decorated with fragments of Church Slavonic ... The only version of Christianity which appeals to him (Dostoevsky) at all is that which includes the wastrels and scoundrel...' [29]

This is not to assert that Barth was explicitly using Dostoevsky behind these comments - but the seed had been sown, the influence exerted in the summer of 1915. Dostoevsky had shown Barth how to interpret the Scriptures. He had learned this central premise - that grace and forgiveness can only be accepted in humility, the humility of a criminal class. Raskolnikov and the prodigal son are

---

[27] Barth, 'Die neue Welt in der Bibel', p. 26/ET: p. 40.
[28] Dostoevsky, *Crime and Punishment,* bk. 1 chp. 2, p. 23.
[29] Boyce Gibson, *The Religion of Dostoevsky,* pp. 93-94.

of the same criminal class - they have both transgressed, both have sinned before God the Father, reparation is seen in turning and submitting the will to God. 'The Solution', so to speak to, 'The Problem' - the theological contradictions they had perceived - lay in the Bible: a solution that Dostoevsky's biblical world of sin and grace, forgiveness and redemption presented existentially in *Crime and Punishment* had pointed Barth and Thurneysen towards - thus they returned to a biblical basis for theology triggered by Thurneysen's comment whilst they were on holiday in the summer of 1916.

The Early Influence of Dostoevsky on Barth - Interim Conclusion

So, what can we establish as to the influence of Dostoevsky on Barth's theological *Wendung und Retraktation* so far? This early influence comes at an impressionable time, the war has more or less shattered any faith he had left in his liberal theological heritage, and together we have the influence of Hermann Kutter (along with Leonhard Ragaz), the eschatology of the Blumhardts, and Dostoevsky's *Crime and Punishment* and *The Idiot* as part of the new starting point of 1915 (remembering the underlying and all pervasive influence of Kantian epistemology). To summarize:

First, the central influence of Dostoevsky on Barth is the realization that the relationship of grace between humanity and God is like that of a criminal receiving a free pardon provided s/he realizes the true nature and depravity of his/her crimes/sins. For example, the so-called 'Good Thief' in the Gospels who knew his crimes yet saw and accepted Jesus Christ and realized this man's innocence compared to his, the thief's, own guilt.

Second, this understanding is fundamental and crucial to Barth's break with his liberal theological heritage. Barth's comments from his lecture on the question put to the Protestant Church by the Roman Catholics he was in discussion with in the late 1920s confirm these beliefs, that such an understanding was important in his *Wendung und Retraktation* and should have come from the Reformers but it did not - it came from reading Dostoevsky's work.[30]

Third, therefore if this understanding, and thereby a reading of Dostoevsky, predates Barth's reading of sin and guilt, grace and forgiveness in Luther and Calvin, then this influence must predate his writing of not only *Römerbrief 2* (written between October 1920 and September 1921) but also *Römerbrief 1* (written between August 1916 and August 1918) where there are substantial references to Luther and Calvin. This is confirmed by Barth's comments that we looked at earlier, that without Thurneysen introducing him to Dostoevsky's

---

[30] Barth, 'Der römische Katholizismus', pp. 356-357/ET: p. 328.

novels and theological beliefs he could not have written either the first or the second editions of *Der Römerbrief*.[31]

Fourth, Barth must have been familiar with the works of Martin Luther and John Calvin prior to 1915 (it would have been highly unusual had he gained no awareness of them during his liberal theological education at Marburg, though the evidence of an influence is simply not there), however, the understanding of sin-guilt, grace-forgiveness in the theology of the Reformers did not press on him.

Fifth, Barth's comments in his letter to Thurneysen written on the 18 August 1915[32] that he had spent the entire previous day reading *Crime and Punishment* and that he was profoundly struck by the wisdom of this Russian writer can be used to set parameters for this crucial early influence: August 1915 to August 1916, after which his thinking on the subject of the nature of the grace relationship between humanity and God is affected primarily by the apostle Paul, secondarily by a reading of Luther and then Calvin.

Sixth, within this early period of influence (the year August 1915 to August 1916) we can find significant textual evidence in 'Kriegszeit und Gottesreich' (delivered on the 15 November 1915), but more pertinently, 'Die Gerechtigkeit Gottes' (delivered on the 16 January 1916) that confirms the early influence of Dostoevsky.

Seventh, this time frame is confirmed by the comments we saw from Von Balthasar writing in 1951[33] about how by the time of the writing of *Römerbrief 2* there is a transition from Platonic and Eastern Christian concepts of identity in relation to theological anthropology, across to those of the Reformation, likewise Dostoevsky encounters Luther, Calvin and Kierkegaard

Eighth, the specific influence of Dostoevsky on Barth in this early period of influence is the nature of the grace relationship between humanity and God characterized by a forensic understanding of redemption that can be found in *Crime and Punishment* and in particular the central characters of Sofya Semyonovna Marmeladova (Sonya) and Rodion Romanovich Raskolnikov. Indeed Преступление и наказание (*Prestuplenie i nakazanie - Crime and Punishment*, or, *Trespass and Reparation*, more pertinently) is a parable about the forensic nature of transgression and reparation, and therefore redemption, in Christian soteriology.

Ninth, the specific influence of Raskolnikov is seen in the use of the 'Tower of Babel' image in the context of the theological understanding of *eritis sicut deus* in 'Die Gerechtigkeit Gottes': the human arrogance of behaving *as if* (*als ob*) God.

Tenth, the influence of Dostoevsky may also be seen in Barth's new starting

---

[31] Barth, 'Lebendige Vergangenheit', p. 13.
[32] Barth to Thurneysen, 18 August 1915, in Barth and Thurneysen, *Briefwechsel Band 1 1913-1921*, pp. 71-72.
[33] Von Balthasar, *The Theology of Karl Barth*, p. 66.

point 'Welt bleibt Welt, daß Gott Gott ist' (confirmed by Thurneysen's invocation of this axiomatic doctrinal proposition in his work on Dostoevsky), though it is important to remember that this idea primarily comes from conversations with Hermann Kutter and from Barth's philosopher brother, Heinrich.

Eleventh, the initial result of the early influence of Dostoevsky, characterized by this forensic understanding of sin-guilt, grace-redemption, along with the Blumhardts' understanding of the Kingdom of God, is to point Barth towards what can be called a theocentric view (confirmed in part by Barth's comments in the preface to *Römerbrief 2* about how Dostoevsky - and from 1919 Kierkegaard - assisted him in interpreting the New Testament), thereby preparing the ground for Thurneysen's identification of their need for 'a wholly other theological foundation'[34] for their ministry and thereby a return to the Bible in the summer of 1916.[35]

---

[34] Barth, 'Nachwort', p. 294.
[35] Barth, *Römerbrief 2*, p. XIV / ET: p. 4.

PART THREE
THURNEYSEN AND BARTH-
THEOLOGY, MINISTRY
AND PASTORAL CARE

*'It is for this that we love them,
not for the radical nature of their negations
but for their still greater affirmations,
which arise from their denials.'*

Eduard Thurneysen, *Dostojewski*, p.10
(comment on Dostoevsky's characters and novels)

CHAPTER 7

Eduard Thurneysen

Before we examine the influence and use of Dostoevsky in Barth's *Römerbrief 2* we need to consider the pastor, colleague and fellow theologian who exerted a background influence on him. That Dostoevsky influences Barth during this crucial period of his theological *Wendung und Retraktation* is because of Eduard Thurneysen. Limited by the small number of his works available in translation, Eduard Thurneysen is little known in English speaking theological circles, his name being associated with the development of Karl Barth's theology but with little understanding or awareness of his contribution to ministry, pastoral care and theology outside of his native Switzerland. Indeed too often his influence is rated only as marginal but we have seen enough already to know that Barth rated Thurneysen's influence on him as important. James D Smart, writing in 1959, commented in relation to Thurneysen's own work, 'It has been a loss to the Church in America that during the past forty years the theological writings of Eduard Thurneysen have remained almost unknown.'[1] Sadly the situation has not changed in the nearly half a century since Smart wrote.

Eduard Thurneysen (1888-1974)

A native of Wallenstadt (in the Canton of Saint Gallen) Eduard Thurneysen was the younger of twins born on the 10th July 1888 to the Reformed minister Eduard Thurneysen and his first wife Elise (née Blüss). He died on the 21st August 1977 in Basel having not only lived through two world wars which ravaged central Europe but was co-partner and collaborator with his friend Karl Barth in what can be seen as a theological revolution. Thurneysen's elder twin brother died within three months; his mother, Elise died in 1891 when Eduard was three. His father also called Eduard (who had been deeply impressed by the Bible scholar Johann Tobias Becks in his formative years) worked as a hospital minister in Basel and had known Fritz Barth, Karl's father, from school days (Eduard senior was Fritz's best man at his wedding). The young Eduard married Marguerite Meyer (born 28 November 1893) in 1916 - they had five

---

[1] James D. Smart, 'Eduard Thurneysen: Pastor-Theologian', *Theology Today* 16.1 (April 1959), p. 74.

children Dorothee (born 1917), Mathis (born 1919), Käthi (born 1921), Monica (born 1925) and Christine (born 1931).

By far the greatest formative influence on the young Eduard was a meeting with Christoph Friedrich Blumhardt. Emilie (née Hindermann) his stepmother went to stay in Bad Boll for healing and recuperation in 1904. The sixteen-year-old Eduard travelled with her and was deeply impressed by Christoph Friedrich (son of Johann Christoph the great eschatological prophet), who captivated Eduard, as he recounted later, by his fatherly piety and the authoritative pastoral care of the people he engaged with. He was to travel again to Bad Boll to introduce Barth to Christoph Friedrich at Easter 1915 (10-15 April), the year of the new starting point. Barth and Thurneysen returned again in 1919 immediately after Barth's address 'Der Christ in der Gesellschaft' ('The Christian in Society' - the so-called Tambach Lecture). The Blumhardts with their doctrine of the Kingdom of God, their radical eschatology and pastoral ministry were an important formative influence on Eduard Thurneysen.

In terms of education and early career, Thurneysen studied theology in Basel to the level of the graduation examination (Maturität); his teachers included Bernhard Duhm, as well as Paul Wernle. After his first theological examination (Propädeutikum) he went to Marburg where Thurneysen encountered Wilhelm Heitmüller and fell under the influence of the writings of Ernst Tröltsch. From 1911 to 1913 Thurneysen worked initially in Zürich as assistant secretary to the CVJM (Der Christlicher Verein von jungem Mann - the YMCA) in addition he frequented meetings and organizations associated with Swiss Religious Socialism - this exposed Thurneysen to the prophetic and visionary beliefs of Leonhard Ragaz, also Hermann Kutter. Thurneysen moved into parish work in June 1913 as pastor of Leutwil (in the Canton of Aargau - as we have seen, in the next door valley to Barth); then pastor in Bruggen (near St Gall) 1920 to 1927. It is during this time that apart from developing his love of Dostoevsky's theology and novels and working with Barth on the return to a biblical basis for theology, he also developed a life-long interest in pastoral theology and pastoral care (Seelsorge) contributing much from this perspective to the development of dialektische Theologie. Eduard developed many written projects whilst a village pastor, including being involved with the founding of the journal *Zwischen den Zeiten*, publishing his work on Dostoevsky, and being co-author of several volumes of sermons with Barth, but his primary interest was his dedication to the community of which he was pastor. Many of his sermons during this period reflect the topic of obedience to God - thus his commitment to his parishioners in the form of a pastoral ministry. Between 1915 and 1920 he devoted much time to the novels of Dostoevsky - reading and study, reflection and discussion (with Barth). Thurneysen attended the Aarauer Studentenkonferenz from 1910. The conference had been a regular event for those interested in the cutting edge of modern theology - lectures and addresses being given regularly by such names as Wilhelm Herrmann, Ernst Tröltsch,

Johannes Weiss, Theodor Häring and Paul Wernle, also the philosopher Rudolf Eucken and the educationalist Paul Häberlin. From 1912, the religious socialists came to dominate the conference. It was through Thurneysen that Barth came to value this three-day conference in March of each year, which also introduced Karl to other young aspiring theologians including Emil Brunner. Despite the heavy influence of Swiss Religious Socialism at this time, Thurneysen, unlike Barth, did not become a party member. In the mid nineteen-twenties Barth would invite Thurneysen, who by then was in the industrial urban parish of Bruggen, to lecture to the 'Göttingen liberals' so as to give them some idea of what Church life was about in Switzerland.[2] During these early years as a professor Barth often sought the advice of Thurneysen - for example, during the summer vacation of 1924 at Pany (Graubünden) where they discussed the manner in which Barth was developing his teaching at Göttingen[3] and later when Barth was teaching at Münster, when they met at Nöschenrode for long constructive conversations.[4]

In 1927 Thurneysen was appointed as the senior minister (Basler Münstergemeinde) of the Reformed Cathedral in Basel. He was appointed part time lecturer (Privatdozentur - created specially for him) at the University of Basel in 1929; then as extraordinary professor for practical theology (with special reference for Homiletik - the art of preaching or writing sermons) in 1941. In the summer semester of 1939 Thurneysen developed a lively lecture tour in Europe, which he maintained among other things after his retirement. Thurneysen's theological achievement was lauded by the theological faculties of the University of Gießen in 1927 and University of Aberdeen in 1934. Thurneysen was a close theological and personal companion of Barth throughout his time in Basel, however, he was no mere shadow of Barth, as Barth has attested to whenever he has written about Eduard; furthermore he was an active protagonist in the development of dialektische Theologie often meeting with Barth to study or advise on various publications - including Barth's work for *Zwischen den Zeiten*. It is significant that the title *Zwischen den Zeiten* (*Between the Times*) was suggested by Thurneysen - the journal was established in the autumn 1922 by Barth and Thurneysen, with Friedrich Gogarten and Georg Merz, to promote dialektische Theologie.

During the 1920s, Thurneysen's interests developed on from Dostoevsky into pastoral theology. This enthusiasm grew very much out of his youthful meeting with Christoph Blumhardt whose belief that sinners do not stand in their own strength, their own volition, but rather God's grace alone is their need. Blumhardt's belief was fundamental to Thurneysen's doctrine of pastoral care. As such, pastoral care was to do with the healing of souls - of getting right

---

[2] Busch, *Karl Barths Lebenslauf*, p. 149/ET: p. 136.
[3] Busch, *Karl Barths Lebenslauf*, p. 169/ET: p. 156.
[4] Busch, *Karl Barths Lebenslauf*, p. 188/ET: p. 174.

the relationship with God of any given individual. This was not in competition with psychotherapy. Pastoral theology complemented psychotherapy; further it represented the pastoral side of dialektische Theologie - it is about seeing and understanding the person of God in the situation, the problem, the individual: each and every person is under the grace of God, but sin must be seen as a real and ever present reality in people's lives. Engrossed in the responsibilities of their ministry Thurneysen therefore tackled the problems he encountered by tracing the theological roots behind the person he encountered - the Bible being the measure of all. Thurneysen's emphasis on a ministry of service was seen especially when in June 1925 he invited Barth (who was about to leave his chair in Reformed Theology at Göttingen to become Professor of Dogmatics and New Testament Exegesis at Münster), to succeed Hermann Kutter who was due to retire in early 1926 from his position as pastor of the Neumünster in Zürich. However, Kutter had by this time come to regard Barth's theological position as different fundamentally from his own and therefore would not have approved. Barth was not tempted back to Switzerland from his initial foray into German dogmatics - though he agreed with Thurneysen that the pulpit was the real arena of God.[5]

Works - Ministerial

Thurneysen could have followed the path Barth did and been given a full-time chair in theology, but he chose to combine a part-time professorship in homiletics with his office as senior minister in the Reformed Cathedral in Basel. However, this does not diminish the value of his works which are numerous; if anything it enhances their worth - written by one who was in ministry. Thurneysen chose to remain a pastor, this was his unique contribution to the development of dialektische Theologie in the inter-war years: his contribution was therefore from the standpoint of the pastor-theologian. Barth commented,

> One can say that to ground theology in the church and especially in the work of the pastor and to make it relevant is a characteristic of the whole theological renewal movement. It should be known, however, on the one hand that Eduard Thurneysen saw the need for a church theology of this kind before anyone else; at any rate, he stimulated me to work in this direction. On the other hand, it should be noted that of all those who have made a reputation and a name within this new theology, there is hardly anyone who embodies it as a movement from the church for the church as characteristically as does Eduard Thurneysen.[6]

For Eduard Thurneysen the Church was an actuality and the basis of

---

[5] Barth to Thurneysen, 7 June 1925 (circular letter), in Barth and Thurneysen, *Briefwechsel Band II 1921-1930*, p. 313.

[6] Karl Barth, 'Geleitwort', in Eduard Thurneysen, *Das Wort Gottes und die Kirche* (München: Christian Kaiser Verlag, 1971 [1927]), p. 227.

theology - theology was existential (as it was in Dostoevsky's works) and the community of faith was the essential response to the freedom and grace of salvation (as Thurneysen found in Dostoevsky's works). Barth commented further on Thurneysen that by the very nature of his existence he forced the reader to come to grips with the fact of the Church, which was also something other than the fact of the Church, therefore behind Thurneysen's ministry was what Barth considered the Socratic quality of his scholarship relating to the religious, philosophical, or moral sphere - '...he can say No! as emphatically as we others who are not so blessed with his Johannine nature.'[7]

Works - Theological

Barth and Thurneysen sent sermons to each other as they mapped out the Biblical and theological studies they were involved with in this crucial period of 1916-17. Barth sent the chapters and sections of *Römerbrief 1* to Thurneysen as they were completed - and likewise Thurneysen shared his emerging work on Dostoevsky with Barth. At this time they also worked together on publishing a volume of sermons jointly - *Suchet Gott, so werdet ihr leben! (Seek God and You Will Live)*. They prepared six sermons each for publication, the work eventually being published by Bäschlin in 1917.[8] The title bears a resemblance to the psalms - '...seek ye after God, and your soul shall live'[9] - which may or may not have been intended by them. The sermons were not credited to either Barth or Thurneysen - it was their decision that they should stand as they were, for whatever either one of them said the other agreed with wholeheartedly. Furthermore, in the foreword to the work, they wrote that the volume was for, '...the people who share our disquiet at God's great hiddenness in the present world and the church and share our joy at his even greater readiness to break through all our bonds'[10] These sermons exemplify the drive with which they were pursuing, in visionary terms, 'The Solution' to the theological problems and contradictions they had identified. This vision was to do with their new understanding of revelation coming from Scripture - what was important was the manner in which God made himself known as the God that he is; and how this God wants, wills, the salvation of humankind. This was seen especially in the nature and content of this first volume of sermons but also in the title they chose for the volume - *Seek God and You Will Live!* that is, not the god of religious projection, not a god infused into human consciousness and a civilized Western society, but the real, other-worldly, transcendent God, the pure

---

[7] Barth, 'Geleitwort', p. 227.
[8] Karl Barth and Eduard Thurneysen, *Suchet Gott, so werdet ihr Leben!* (Berne: G.A. Bäschlin, 1917).
[9] See Psalms 37:3; 69:32b; 118:17, 140:13 and 146:2; but in particular Psalm 119, specifically vv. 17, 77 and 116-117.
[10] Barth and Thurneysen, *Suchet Gott, so werdet ihr Leben*, p. 5.

Ursprung of all, the judge of all human righteousness, the critically real God. Hence the intensity with which they struggled with Scripture, working through the historical-critical commentaries, but also the commentaries of the Reformers, and giving due respect to patristic material on the New Testament (it is this respect for an understanding that predates the historical-critical method of nineteenth-century neo-Protestant scepticism that appears to have caused offence with their critics). Thurneysen's Johannine nature insisted that they remained true to their vision - that the wholly new basis of their theology should witness to the revelation that was recorded in and had inspired the Scriptures: 'The testimony of Barth is that it was Thurneysen's vision before it was his. Perhaps Thurneysen would say the same of Barth. Each is certain only of the greatness of his debt to the other.' [11]

In 1920 Thurneysen finished his study of Dostoevsky - approximately nine months after Barth's *Römerbrief 1* had been published. He presented much of the content and substance at the Aarauer Studentenkonferenz on 21st April 1921, which was then published under the title *Dostojewski* in the summer. In September Barth was to finish writing the second edition of his commentary on Romans - *Römerbrief 2*.

Although he never produced anything on the scale of Barth's *Church Dogmatics* Thurneysen went on to publish a considerable corpus. From 1923 on he was a co-editor of what was considered the organ of dialektische Theologie - *Zwischen den Zeiten*. In 1924 Thurneysen co-published another volume of sermons with Barth - *Komm Schöpfer Geist* (the English translation *Come Holy Spirit*, appearing also in 1924).[12] During this period of the mid-nineteen-twenties, and despite the other theologians who had gathered in some loose grouping around Barth under the banner of dialektische Theologie or Krisis Theologie (Friedrich Gogarten, Emil Brunner, Rudolf Bultmann), it was only Thurneysen that Barth was at one with theologically. Indeed the two were so much of one mind that they could still publish this second volume of sermons as joint authorship - with no indication being given as to which of them had written and preached each sermon. In 1926 Thurneysen published another small book, comparable in scope and treatment with *Dostojewski*, this time on Christoph Friedrich Blumhardt - entitled simply *Christoph Blumhardt*, again published by Chr. Kaiser Verlagbuchandlung of Munich.[13] In 1927 Thurneysen published a volume of addresses and essays of his own from the

---

[11] Smart, 'Eduard Thurneysen: Pastor-Theologian', p. 78.

[12] Karl Barth and Eduard Thurneysen, *Komm Schöpfer Geist! Predigten* (München: Christian Kaiser Verlag, 1924); ET: Karl Barth and Eduard Thurneysen, *Come Holy Spirit* (trans. George W. Richards, Elmer G. Homrighausen and Karl J. Ernst; New York: Round Table Press, 1933).

[13] Eduard Thurneysen, *Christoph Blumhardt* (München: Christian Kaiser Verlag, 1926).

previous twelve years *Das Wort Gottes und die Kirche*[14] (comparable in many ways to Barth's collection of addresses, *Das Wort Gottes und die Theologie* published two years earlier). New Testament studies including the prologue to John's Gospel,[15] the Epistle of James, the Epistle to the Philippians[16] and the Sermon on the Mount were also published; likewise works on preaching, confession and the Lord's Supper.[17]

The earlier slim volume of six sermons each from Barth and Thurneysen - *Suchet Gott, so werdet ihr Leben!* - was much expanded and reissued in 1928. By the end of the 1920s fractures had appeared between Barth and many of the other adherents to *dialektische Theologie*, so much so that with the rise of National Socialism in Germany and the manner in which many of his colleagues supported the developing Blood and Soil religion of the Nazis, the point had been reached where he broke-off relations completely with theologians who once had been his colleagues, in particular Gogarten. Barth wrote a final acerbic Abschied (a parting, a farewell, a resignation) to the journal *Zwischen den Zeiten* that they had founded together. He wrote criticizing the adoption of a religion and theology that was contrary to what they had been proposing, further that it now represented the worst sort of German neo-Protestantism based on the religious mythology and beliefs of Wilhelm Stapel[18] that the law of God was the law of the German people; further, that it was a comfort to hear Thurneysen, and that he was a constant confirmation as to what they had once believed in and expected from the theological revolution they had started.[19] Barth and Thurneysen distanced themselves from the rest of the group centred on the journal *Zwischen den*

---

[14] Thurneysen, *Das Wort Gottes und die Kirche*.

[15] Eduard Thurneysen, 'Zum Prolog des John', *Zwischen den Zeiten* 3 (1925), pp. 12-37.

[16] Eduard Thurneysen, *Der Brief des Paulus an die Philipper* (Basel: F. Reinhardt, 1943).

[17] Thurneysen, Eduard, *Die Kraft der Geringen. Drei Predigten* (Theologische Existenz heute; Schriftenreihe 8; München: Christian Kaiser Verlag, 1934).

[18] Wilhelm Stapel (1882-1954), writer, journalist and translator, was noted as a Protestant-German-Nationalist who supported the National Socialists and was crucial in formulating their religious mythology and anti-Semitism. Stapel poured scorn on German Christians who opposed Hitler but also on those who offered qualified support by endorsing the brotherhood fostered by the Nazis. See Wilhelm Stapel, *Der christliche Staatsmann - eine Theologie des National-sozialismus* (Hamburg: Hanseatische Verlag, 1932). See also Wilhelm Stapel, *The Heiland* (München: Hanser, 1953 [1932]). He worked on the concept of 'heathen imperialism' in which he saw the will of the German people as synonymous with the will of 'god' (his 'theism' as such drew much from a simplified reading of Hegel and Nietzsche, but equally from the pagan Norse myths popularised by Wagner!). See Wilhelm Stapel, *Die drei Stände Versuch einer Morphologie des deutschen Volkes* (Hamburg: Hanseatische Verlag, 1941).

[19] Karl Barth, 'Abschied', *Zwischen den Zeiten* 11 (1933), pp. 536-544. See also Busch, *Karl Barths Lebenslauf*, pp. 242-244/ET: pp. 229-230.

Zeiten. Eberhard Busch comments: 'Eduard Thurneysen was the only one of his colleagues with whom Barth had a very close relationship'[20] By the mid-1930s Barth had returned to Switzerland, having left Germany as the political situation worsened: in 1934 he had refused to give an oath of loyalty to Adolf Hitler (such an oath would have been interpreted as giving unequivocal support to the Nazis); therefore on 26 November 1934 Barth was suspended from his teaching duties in Bonn, he was then dismissed by the Minister of Cultural Affairs in Berlin on 22 June 1935. As soon as the news was out he was offered a chair of theology in Basel - early in July, Barth and his family left Bonn to return to Switzerland, once again to be in close proximity to the Thurneysens.

---

[20] Busch, *Karl Barths Lebenslauf*, p. 281/ET: p. 268.

CHAPTER 8

Pastoral Theology

Die Lehre von der Seelsorge

The same year that saw Barth's return to Basel also witnessed the publication of a third volume of their sermons, again published jointly: *Die Grosse Barmherzigkeit (The Great Mercy)*.[1] In the Vorwort Barth and Thurneysen wrote how each sermon was essentially an interpretation of Scripture that should address the questions of the day but should be rooted in the revelation attested to in the Bible and how they bear witness to the mighty fact of God's self-revelation in Jesus Christ:[2] 'In this the church alone is directly free and strong and confident to its Lord.'[3] In addition, Barth and Thurneysen published a volume for specific festivals.[4] In March 1937 Barth and Thurneysen travelled to Scotland and England, but Barth did not take part in the ecumenical conferences at Oxford and Edinburgh whereas Thurneysen did.[5] Busch notes that over the next ten years or so their relations became less close:

> Not only did Barth disagree with Thurneysen's tendency to generalize in his sermons, but he found that in spite of their continuing friendship, Thurneysen's intellectual development since 1921 had somewhat alienated him from the problem of a church dogmatics and from the lessons Barth thought that he had learnt from the German church struggle. Once he had settled in Switzerland, Barth also preached from time to time. This was mostly to stand in for Thurneysen ... in the cathedral.[6]

This is the mature period of Barth's work where he is writing the initial volumes of *The Church Dogmatics*. Thurneysen by contrast was the senior minister at the cathedral in Basel and the close proximity of Barth in the form of the late-night theological discussions they had prompted Thurneysen to

---

[1] Karl Barth and Eduard Thurneysen, *Die Große Barmherzigkeit (Predigten)* (München: Christian Kaiser Verlag, 1935); ET: Karl Barth and Eduard Thurneysen, *God's Search for Man* (trans. George W Richards, Elmer G Homrighausen and Karl J. Ernst; New York: Round Table Press, 1935).
[2] Barth and Thurneysen, *Die Grosse Barmherzigkeit*, pp. 3-4.
[3] Barth and Thurneysen, *Die Grosse Barmherzigkeit*, p. 4.
[4] Karl Barth and Eduard Thurneysen, *Andachten für die Advents-, Weihnachts-, Passions- und Osterzeit* (Berlin: Furche Verlag, 1936).
[5] Busch, *Karl Barths Lebenslauf*, pp. 294-295/ET: p. 281.
[6] Busch, *Karl Barths Lebenslauf*, pp. 282-283/ET: pp. 269-270.

tackle writing in-depth theology again. The result was that in 1946 Thurneysen published what to many is his definitive work, *Die Lehre von der Seelsorge* (*A Theology of Pastoral Care*):[7] this is Thurneysen's major contribution to the doctrinal basis of pastoral theology - that is, the curing of souls.[8]

So what does Thurneysen say in *Die Lehre von der Seelsorge?* The English edition is somewhat simplified and reduced - the long references are by and large omitted, as are the copious German multiple indices. The German first edition adopted the same structure and layout as Barth's *Church Dogmatics* - sections (§§) rather than chapters, with long footnote references integrated into the text set in a smaller typeface. Thurneysen had consciously wanted this work to be comparable in dogmatic structure to Barth's *magnus opus*. The work is in three parts: Part I The Basis of Pastoral Care;[9] Part II The Nature and Practice of Pastoral Care;[10] and Part III The Implementation of Pastoral Care.[11] The first part deals with the basis of pastoral care as existing within the Church: 'Pastoral care exists in the church as the communication of the Word of God to

---

[7] Eduard Thurneysen, *Die Lehre von der Seelsorge* (Zollikon-Zürich: Evangelische Verlag AG, 1946); ET: Eduard Thurneysen, *A Theology of Pastoral Care* (trans Jack A. Worthington and Thomas Wieser; Richmond, VA: John Knox Press, 1962).

[8] *Oxford Duden German Dictionary*: *die seele*, spirit, soul, relating to heart and soul; *die sorge*, care; therefore, *die seelsorge*, cure of souls or pastoral care.

[9] Thurneysen, *Die Lehre von der Seelsorge*, I. Die Begrondung der Seelsorge. §. 1 Seelsorge als theologisches und kirchliches Problem (Pastoral Care in Theology and the Church), pp. 9-26/ET: pp. 11-31. §. 2 Seelsorge als kirchenzucht (Pastoral Care as Church Discipline), pp. 27-45/ET: pp. 32-53. §. 3 Die Seele des Menschen als Gegenstand der Seelsorge (The Soul of Man as the Object of Pastoral Care), pp. 46-60/ET: pp. 54-67. §. 4 Der Kampf um das Verständnis des Menschen in der Seelsorge (The Struggle to Understand Man in Pastoral Care), pp. 61-89/ET: pp. 68-97.

[10] Thurneysen, *Die Lehre von der Seelsorge*, II. Wesen und Gestalt der Seelsorge. §. 5 Seelsorge als Gespräch (Pastoral Care as Conversation), pp. 90-103/ET: pp. 101-114. §. 6 Die Gestalt des seelsorgerlichen Gesprächs (The Form of Pastoral Conversation), pp. 104-118/ET: pp. 115-130. §. 7 Der Bruch im seelsorgerlichen Gespräch (The Breach in the Pastoral Conversation), pp. 119-134/ET: pp. 131-146. §. 8 Der Inhalt des seelsorgerlichen Gesprächs (The Content of Pastoral Conversation), pp. 135-161/ET: pp. 147-178. §. 9 Die Ansprechbarkeit des Menschen für die Vergebung der Sünden (Man's Responsiveness to the Forgiveness of Sins), pp. 162-181/ET: pp. 179-199. §. 10 Seelsorge und Psychologie (Pastoral Care and Psychology), pp. 182-201/ET: pp. 200-220. §. 11 Seelsorge und Psychotherapie (Pastoral Care and Psychotherapy), pp. 202-234/ET: pp. 221-252.

[11] Thurneysen, *Die Lehre von der Seelsorge*, III. Der Vollzug der Seelsorge. §. 12 Evangelium und Gesetz in der Seelsorge (Gospel and Law in Pastoral Care), pp. 235-252/ET: pp. 255-273. §. 13 Evangelische Buße in der Seelsorge (Evangelical Repentance and Pastoral Care), pp. 253-262/ET: pp. 274-283. §. 14 Seelsorge als Beichte (Pastoral Care as Confession), pp. 263-293/ET: pp. 284-314. §. 15 Seelsorge als Exorzismus (Pastoral Care as Exorcism), pp. 294-312/ET: pp. 315-333. §. 16 Der Seelsorger (The Pastoral Counsellor), pp. 313-322/ET: pp. 334-343.

individuals'[12] - pastoral care therefore issues forth from the living Word of God given to the church. Thurneysen stresses the importance of sermon and sacrament and of the Christian community 'So understood, it is an act of sanctification and of discipline ... by which the individual is redeemed.'[13] Pastoral care is care for the soul of a person. This is not simply the psychic element in a person, 'but soul is to be understood according to Holy Scripture as the totality of humanity's personal existence in body, "soul," and spirit under the claim of God.'[14] This is rooted in the incarnation of Jesus Christ. Accordingly, the task of pastoral care is to be defined as the sanctification of the whole person for God. The basis of pastoral care must be rooted in Holy Scripture - despite the fact, acknowledges Thurneysen, that there are other interpretations of humanity.[15] In *Part II, The Nature and Practice of Pastoral Care*, Thurneysen establishes the principle that pastoral care is accomplished in the form of a conversation, emanating from the Word of God and enabled pneumatologically: 'The form of pastoral conversation is determined by its claim to see even the remotest human concern in its relationship to God and his Word as established by the incarnation of Jesus Christ.'[16] Pastoral conversation involves, evokes, the judgment of the Word of God on everything human. Humanity's natural response is to resist. But, this judgement communicates 'the forgiveness of sins in Jesus Christ'[17]. Humanity is addressed as a sinner under grace. This is the presupposition - 'the unconditional communication of forgiveness, which means that it is free of all legalism and thus obedient to the Word of God.'[18] Only God can bring about this forgiveness; thus, prayer for the gift of the Holy Spirit is central to all pastoral care. Pastoral care needs psychology as an auxiliary science, but must - as with psychotherapy - be treated cautiously especially when these sciences do not respect the theological anthropology expounded in Scripture. Part three deals with the Implementation of pastoral care. The actual practice of pastoral care consists in what Thurneysen describes as the true ordering of Gospel and law, but also of justification and sanctification. Thurneysen is here critical of Rome: 'The dissolving of the unity of Gospel and law, of justification and sanctification, as it takes place, for example, in the pastoral care of the Catholic Church, is to be considered a mortal threat to true pastoral care.'[19] Evangelical repentance and care is contrasted with Roman confession. Repentance is of absolute importance. At the point of repentance the person '...is pardoned by the Word

---

[12] Thurneysen, *Die Lehre von der Seelsorge*, p. 9/ET: p. 11.
[13] Thurneysen, *Die Lehre von der Seelsorge*, p. 27/ET: p. 32.
[14] Thurneysen, *Die Lehre von der Seelsorge*, p. 46/ET: p. 54.
[15] Thurneysen, *Die Lehre von der Seelsorge*, pp. 61-89/ET: pp. 68-97.
[16] Thurneysen, *Die Lehre von der Seelsorge*, p. 104/ET: p. 115.
[17] Thurneysen, *Die Lehre von der Seelsorge*, p. 135/ET: p. 147.
[18] Thurneysen, *Die Lehre von der Seelsorge*, p. 135/ET: p. 147.
[19] Thurneysen, *Die Lehre von der Seelsorge*, p. 235/ET: p. 255.

of forgiveness and thereby judged and placed in obedience to Christ. This is regeneration and conversion.'[20] Pastoral care is therefore centred on confession: 'Repentance is the act whereby I allow the Word of God to disclose my sin to me and lay it before God, so that God may take it from me.'[21] But this involves taking individual responsibility - again this contrasts with Roman Catholic confession. Thurneysen then deals with the reality of exorcism and evil, factors that are real and biblical, but he emphasizes the Patristic Christian doctrine of the final victory being in Christ: 'The pastoral counsellor is the bearer and mediator of the message of forgiveness'[22] who acts not in her/his own strength and judgment but as one who is called by God to this work. The counsellor must be rooted in the Word of God and in the Church - further, must live from faith in forgiveness. The Christian counsellor does not bind people to her/himself 'but to the Lord of the church by leading them to the Word and by continually praying for them.'[23]

Sin and the Human Condition before God

In many ways *Die Lehre von der Seelsorge* is the culmination of a vocation, which for Thurneysen started with his encounter at the age of sixteen with Christoph Blumhardt in 1904. Blumhardt is the theologian behind this work; indeed at the end of §11 Thurneysen quotes from a letter of Christoph Blumhardt to a woman he had been counselling dated 8 August 1890 as an example of good pastoral counselling.

> Yet I increasingly feel we should not pray too urgently for health and help in illness, but rather for our right attitude toward God in order to make the streams of living water flow more richly. God is often hindered from doing what he would gladly do if we were more his people serving him.
>
> ...I long for the experience of seeing people care more for his Kingdom and take a back seat for themselves. In this way, even illness can become a service for God, and God is again close at hand.[24]

This explains to a degree his interest in Dostoevsky - and why *Crime and Punishment* made such an impression on Barth and Thurneysen in 1915. Raskolnikov is an example of a lost soul who needs care to bring him back from the path he has followed - not legalistic condemnation, not moralistic self-righteousness, nor liberal-humanistic acceptance in total of a person's behaviour, but pastoral care informed by the Gospel that is, the salvation offered, proffered, by the atonement of Jesus Christ. But it is not psychotherapy practised from a humanistic perspective that redeems Raskolnikov - it is the

---

[20] Thurneysen, *Die Lehre von der Seelsorge*, p. 253/ET: p. 274.
[21] Thurneysen, *Die Lehre von der Seelsorge*, p. 263/ET: p. 284.
[22] Thurneysen, *Die Lehre von der Seelsorge*, p. 313/ET: p. 334.
[23] Thurneysen, *Die Lehre von der Seelsorge*, p. 313/ET: p. 334.
[24] Thurneysen, *Die Lehre von der Seelsorge*, p. 234/ET: p. 252.

8. Pastoral Theology

biblical witness of Sonya the prostitute! Pastoral theology must have a biblical basis and must testify to what is witnessed to in the Bible generally, the New Testament specifically. *Die Lehre von der Seelsorge* offers a critical theological approach to the field of pastoral counselling. Thurneysen by the 1940s had a wealth of experience in counselling, but importantly, a sound theological understanding and respect for the Bible. Thurneysen worked from the perspective of the Gospel and as a minister of the Church - and as such, counselling was to be seen as having doctrinal issues; psychological training was important, but so was Biblical or theological training. Thurneysen believed with great perceptiveness that the professional manner of a counsellor, and the outcome of any counselling, were determined to a large extent by the presuppositions of the minister/counsellor, whether from a theistic or atheistic perspective.

Underlying this theory of pastoral care is a doctrine of sin. For both Barth and Thurneysen, this doctrine of sin came initially from reading Dostoevsky's *Crime and Punishment*. This doctrine of sin is the key to understanding the human dilemma and the existential relationship between God and humanity: 'We cannot study enough the description of life as given by the great portrayers of mankind like Balzac, Dostoevsky and Jeremias Gotthelf', commented Thurneysen in the section on the form of the pastoral conversation.[25] Further, that it is these writers that truly show us a 'description of the intricate perversities of sinful humanity', but especially this 'great Russian'.[26] In their formative years Barth was a disciple of Wilhelm Herrmann; Thurneysen was a disciple of Ernst Tröltsch.[27] For both of them sin was relatively lightly treated, something of little concern such was the humanistic centre of their formative doctrinal basis. Ironically, both then became politicized: campaigning against the abuses of powerful industrial capitalists thereby championing the cause of the workers - sin, as such, became political. Only with the encounter with Christoph Blumhardt (Easter 1915) and to a lesser degree Hermann Kutter did a concept of sin begin to press on their theological development. We have seen the evidence and context already for the influence of Dostoevsky's *Crime and Punishment* in the year 1915 - this is the time when they begin to take sin seriously as the decisive factor in the human condition before God. This is the single most important aspect of Dostoevsky's work that presses itself on Barth and Thurneysen in their theological re-development: the nature of the grace relationship between humanity and God characterized not by the forgiveness granted by a priest, not some sort of atonement achieved through a Schleiermachian religious experience, but by grace alone - justification by grace alone. Sin became theological in the sense that it was defined by, and in

---

[25] Thurneysen, *Die Lehre von der Seelsorge*, §. 7 Der Bruch im seelsorgerlichen Gespräch, p. 117/ET: p. 129.
[26] Thurneysen, *Die Lehre von der Seelsorge*, p. 185/ET: p. 203.
[27] McCormack, *Karl Barth's Critically Realistic Dialectical Theology*, p. 38.

relation to God's grace. And here it is spelt out in *Die Lehre von der Seelsorge*. This is a forensic understanding of redemption involving an awareness of trespass, transgression; but with this realization is forgiveness and redemption: thus the model of Rodion Romanovich Raskolnikov - the parable of transgression and redemption in Christian soteriology.

In *Die Lehre von der Seelsorge* Thurneysen contrasts what he considers an evangelical approach to the problem of sin and the human condition before God with the doctrine of sin, as he perceived it, in the Roman Catholic Church. The Roman Church certainly at the time Thurneysen was writing held to a doctrine of imputation. However, Thurneysen, and Barth, adopted a position more akin with the Reformers whereby a doctrine of the Fall held that the whole person is corrupted by sin and that even what appear to be insignificant sins after baptism are manifestations of a greater alienation: a fundamental alienation from God (this, of course, can be found in Calvin's *Institutes* [28] and yes Calvin informs this teaching when Thurneysen is writing *Die Lehre von der Seelsorge* but the origin, as we have seen, is with Barth and Thurneysen's reading of Dostoevsky). Only God's forgiveness, freely given and received in the sinner as that of the free pardon given to a criminal is sufficient - leading to sanctification. Thurneysen:

> Because this is so, because there is no forgiveness without sanctification the commandment must be established in each pastoral conversation by the very nature of the case. Pastoral care without sanctification would be a wooden horseshoe, a ship on the sand, a contradiction in itself.[29]

Sonya is in many ways an archetype of this pastoral counsellor. She does not flinch at Raskolnikov's confession, or waiver in the pressure she exerts on him to confess his crime/sin publicly (to shout it out in the Haymarket before everyone and prostrate himself on the ground kissing the very earth he has defiled) then to confess to the authorities in the form of the investigating officer - Porfiry Petrovitch - again an example of not just a detective but a pastoral counsellor in his intelligent discernment that Raskolnikov is guilty of the murder of the pawnbroker and her sister even though he has no evidence: this is forensic, and so also is sin and grace between humanity and God. Thurneysen and Barth also read this in Dostoevsky's major work *The Brothers Karamazov*, not only in the nature of the crimes/sins amongst the four Karamazov brothers and their father but also in the demonic attitude of The Grand Inquisitor who spoke of *binding* the people to himself (as a representative of the Roman

---

[28] John Calvin, *Institutes of the Christian Religion* (ed. John T. McNeill; Library of Christian Classics; Louisville, KY: Westminster John Knox Press, 2006 [1960]). See bk. 2 chp. 1-3, pp. 239-309 (see in particular bk. 2 chp. 1 §§. 8-11, pp. 250-255); bk. 3 chp. 23 §. 7, pp. 955-956, and bk. 4 chp. 15, pp. 1303-1323 (see in particular §. 10, p. 1311).

[29] Thurneysen, *Die Lehre von der Seelsorge*, p. 240/ET: p. 260.

Catholic priesthood) in the same way that Thurneysen spoke of not binding [30] people who are the object of pastoral care to himself (as representative of the pastoral counsellor) but by leading them to God as Lord. It is not the pastoral counsellor who forgives, it is God: '...the pastoral counsellor does not help. God helps. And this is so easily forgotten.'[31]

---

[30] Thurneysen, *Die Lehre von der Seelsorge*, see the opening introduction/summaries to §§. 12, 14 and 16, pp. 235, 263 and 313/ET: pp. 255, 284 and 334. See, for the use of binding by a priestly caste/ministerial elite, Dostoevsky, *The Brothers Karamazov*, pt. 2 bk. 5, 'Pro and Contra', chp. 5 'The Grand Inquisitor', pp. 246-264.

[31] Thurneysen, *Die Lehre von der Seelsorge*, p. 319/ET: p. 340.

CHAPTER 9

Dostojewski

Published initially in 1921 following Thurneysen's presentation on Dostoevsky's theology at the Aarauer Studentenkonferenz in the April of that year, and approximately 23,000 words in length the seventy-seven-page book *Dostojewski* made a deep impression on German speaking theological circles:[1] in the first edition the frontispiece stated: 'This writing is an expanded version of that presented at the Aarauer Studentenkonferenz held on the 21st April 1921.' The later editions open with a quotation from Kierkegaard:

> If the experiment has made any impression at all, then it must be as when the beating of the wings of a wildfowl is heard above the heads of the tame fowl of the same species, who live secure in the sureness of reality, and brings them involuntarily to beat their wings, because each beat of the wings is at the same time anxiety - and allurement.[2]

This sets the scene for the opening pages.

What is Humanity?

In the first chapter - *1 What is Humanity?* - Thurneysen asserts that the works of Dostoevsky are like a wild untamed beast compared to the domesticated pets of pre-First World War German literature, culture and society: such a one who

---

[1] Eduard Thurneysen, *Dostojewski* (München: Christian Kaiser Verlag, 1921). Eduard Thurneysen, *Dostoevsky: A Theological Study* (trans. Keith R. Crim; London: The Epworth Press, 1964). Subsequent editions of *Dostojewski* were published by Christian Kaiser Verlag of Munich in 1922, 1925, 1930, 1937, and 1948; then in Zürich and Stuttgart in 1963. A Dutch translation was published in Amsterdam in 1928 and an Italian translation in Rome in 1929. A Japanese translation was produced in Tokyo: Eduard Thurneysen, *Dosutoefusukii kenkyu: benshoho shingaku yori mitaru. Dosutoefusuki kenkyu: igakuteki shinrigakuteki tachiba ni okeru* (trans. Thimoteus Segaloff; Dosutoefusukii bunken shusei; Tokyo: Ozorasha, 1933); reprinted in 1960 and 1995. This was followed a year later by a French translation: Eduard Thurneysen, *Dostoievski ou les confins de l'homme* (traduit de l'allemand par P. Maury; Paris: Editions "Je sers", 1934). The English translation was only finally published in 1964. With the exception of a reprint of the Japanese translation in 1995 there have been no editions/print runs of the work since the early to mid-1960s.

[2] Thurneysen *Dostojewski*, p. 5/ET: p. 6.

reads on has entered primeval territory.[3] Thurneysen borrowed from Hermann Hesse the phrase the glance into chaos to describe this.[4] This perception of primeval territory results in an unassuredness, where cultural norms become questionable - we are faced, Thurneysen asserts, with the riddle of our lives. What is mankind? 'This is Dostoevsky's question and ours'.[5] Thurneysen saw that for Dostoevsky human experience moved him and tormented him - but nothing within the remit of human behaviour and nature remained foreign to him. Therefore in this first chapter we have the outline of Thurneysen and Barth's understanding of the human condition before God informed as it was, by Dostoevsky's men and women. Thurneysen then proceeds to outline characters from the key novels to illustrate this theological anthropology, concentrating essentially on Rodion Romanovich Raskolnikov (*Crime and Punishment*) Prince Lev Myshkin (*The Idiot*) and Ivan and Mitya Karamazov (*The Brothers Karamazov*). But, in all this human sordidness and depravity, Thurneysen presents the resurrection at the end of *Crime and Punishment* - coming to a full and true understanding of the depravity of humanity is only tolerable and acceptable in the light of sanctification and resurrection.[6] Negation and denial are important but it must be in the context of affirmation. Thurneysen commented, 'It is from those darkest depths into which his analysis has penetrated that the wonderful light of this new synthesis streams forth...'[7] He continued, 'It is for this that we love them, not for the radical nature of their negations, but for their still greater affirmations, which arise from their denials.'[8] Furthermore, writes Thurneysen, 'Dostoevsky's own words are witness of this, "My Hosanna has passed through the great purging fire of doubt".'[9]

Dostoevsky's Men and Women

In the second chapter - *II Dostoevsky's Men and Women* - Thurneysen takes this theological anthropology further. He cites many examples of this remarkable, as he calls them, group of men and women. The leading characters examined are Raskolnikov and Ivan Karamazov. It is at this point that Thurneysen investigates Raskolnikov's Napoleonic delusion - which creates the distinction between God and humanity.[10] Further, how this *diastasis* this unresolved antinomy between God and humanity must be grasped by, in this case, Raskolnikov, but that closure can only come from God's side. This is at

---

[3] Thurneysen, *Dostojewski*, p. 3/ET: p. 7.
[4] Hermann Hesse, *Blick ins Chaos: Drei Aufsätze* (Berne: Verlag Seldwyla, 1920).
[5] Thurneysen, *Dostojewski*, p. 5/ET: p. 9.
[6] Thurneysen, *Dostojewski*, p. 9/ET: p. 13.
[7] Thurneysen, *Dostojewski*, p. 9/ET: p. 13.
[8] Thurneysen, *Dostojewski*, p. 10/ET: p. 14.
[9] Thurneysen, *Dostojewski*, p. 10/ET: p. 14.
[10] Thurneysen, *Dostojewski*, p. 14/ET: p. 19.

the heart of Thurneysen and Barth's understanding of Dostoevsky's theological anthropology and of the utter necessity of resurrection as the solution to the human problem:

> Only now does he understand himself. Only now does he understand God. And only now does he understand himself in God and from God precisely in his finiteness and humanity. He no longer strives to overcome it, for he knows that from man's side there is no bridge that leads across; there is none for the sake of God's honour and man's purity. But, perhaps from God's side?
>
> That is no longer a Promethean question for it is no longer a question of human possibilities. In this question Raskolnikov opens for himself the view of a final possibility of really passing over into the eternal kingdom of life, the possibility of resurrection. But this final possibility of man is no longer a possibility of man. Yet whoever has passed like Raskolnikov into the knowledge and fear of God must know of just this final and unique, this impossible possibility, and will be able to know of it without danger.[11]

How is this presented? Thurneysen continued:

> Once already it had appeared before him when Sonya, the harlot, had read to the murderer in that incomprehensible night, full of confession and humiliation, the story of the raising of Lazarus (this story of resurrection!) from the Gospel of John.
>
> ...He did not understand it then, but now that inconceivably great word is even on his lips, that word that says more than man can know, the word 'resurrection'.[12]

This links in with the understanding we saw earlier - the influence of *Crime and Punishment* generally, Sonya and Raskolnikov specifically, on Barth and Thurneysen during the second half of 1915, an influence that fed into Barth's address, 'Die Gerechtigkeit Gottes'. This quotation represents for Thurneysen and Barth the turning point of conversion, of faith, from the Napoleonic delusion of the *eritis Sicut deus* to a new beginning - the whisper of the word resurrection prior to the full God-given reality of resurrection.

Thurneysen then turns to *The Brothers Karamazov* as another example of this theological anthropology: the father (Fyodor) and three sons (four, including the illegitimate Smerdyakov). Here Thurneysen examines Dostoevsky's women - examples drawn from *The Idiot* and *The Brothers Karamazov*, for example Grushenka as the epitome of *eros* preyed upon by Fyodor and his son Mitya. This is the point where Raskolnikov is brought back in by Thurneysen and the concept of *eritis Sicut deus* is examined. Both *eros* and the understanding of being *as if God* are bewitching (bezaubernd) and captivating, dangerously alluring. The ascent is followed by the descent into hell and at this point they must turn to God. Thurneysen: 'At the end of the book, with this longing on their lips, Mitya Karamazov and Grushenka... stand

---

[11] Thurneysen, *Dostojewski*, pp. 15-16/ET: pp. 19-20.
[12] Thurneysen, *Dostojewski*, pp. 15-16/ET: pp. 19-20.

before the gates of heaven, tired of the Odyssey of their passions.'[13] Finally Thurneysen looks at Prince Myshkin in *The Idiot*. Here Thurneysen focuses on the paradox at the heart of this theological anthropology - 'This absolute fool begins to turn the world upside down; this one who is poor in spirit gives the clever and wise something to think about; this defenceless man reveals himself as the only one who is truly strong, this harmless one as a destroyer.'[14] Thurneysen notes how this man, the figure of Christlikeness is characterized by a clumsiness and a fearlessness, which become an offence to the world of social convention. Therefore Thurneysen asserts that the meaning of life is buried so deep that the wise and clever, the proud and powerful cannot find it - further, that the one who does understand the meaning of this life as a denial before God will be seen as a fool, as weak, as sickly.[15] Therefore we are forced to conclude, says Thurneysen,[16] that life so crowds out this truth that those who do perceive are the harlots and the murderers, the insane and the desperate: this is a paradox for both Barth and Thurneysen. But this paradox speaks of the mystery of God.[17] Raskolnikov is prepared to pursue this path, to probe this paradoxical denial though it is important to remember that his faith is initially in Sonya. Thurneysen concluded this second chapter with the catalyst and explanation of this paradoxical denial, this negation - 'Forgiveness, the forgiveness of sins. Exactly at this point the essential connection of Dostoevsky's knowledge with the ultimate knowledge of the Bible is unmistakable.'[18]

Dostoevsky's Perspective

In the third chapter - *III Dostoevsky's Perspective* - Thurneysen, having examined examples of Dostoevsky's characters as examples of his theological anthropology, turns to try to find the answer posed by the question of humanity - the answer and solution is in God. These people are sick as if, asserts Thurneysen, from a secret wound: captured and imprisoned as they are in the tempest of their passions, in the confusion of their thoughts, in the struggle of life, these people are moved and subjugated, oppressed, but by what? Thurneysen describes this pressure as '...something unspeakably great, distant, and yet near, something beyond and yet here.'[19] In this, willingly or unwillingly, these people become God's messengers and martyrs, his prisoners,

---

[13] Thurneysen, *Dostojewski*, p. 21/ ET: p. 25.
[14] Thurneysen, *Dostojewski*, pp. 22-23/ET: p. 26.
[15] Thurneysen, *Dostojewski*, p. 23/ET: p. 27.
[16] Thurneysen, *Dostojewski*, p. 23/ET: p. 27.
[17] Thurneysen, *Dostojewski*, p. 28/ET: p. 32.
[18] Thurneysen, *Dostojewski*, p. 31/ET: p. 35, 'Forgiveness, forgiveness of sins' (*Vergebung, Vergebung der Sünden*)', note, *Sünden*, traditionally meant *transgression, misdeed* as well as *sin(s)*.
[19] Thurneysen, *Dostojewski*, p. 32/ET: p. 38.

9. Dostojewski

his heralds. This something other, something beyond (Jenseitig) that presses is what Barth identified in *Crime and Punishment* in 1915 and then presented as what was behind conscience in 'Die Gerechtigkeit Gottes'; and what Bruce McCormack defined as the *critical realism* of God.[20] In the later editions Thurneysen added at this point,

> You hem me in, behind and before,
>   and lay your hand upon me
> If I ascend to heaven, you are there;
>   if I make my bed in Sheol, you are there.
> PSALM 139:5-8

Dostoevsky's perspective, as such, is to present humanity in utter realism so as to expose the solution to the problem and question of humanity - God. Both Barth and Thurneysen cite the movement in modern art known as Expressionism, however, Thurneysen also uses the example of the paintings of El Greco where form is exaggerated, distorted so as to convey a deeper meaning and in consequence a greater reality.[21] Both cite Expressionism where the resolution of lines of perspective are in a vanishing point outside of the picture, in addition the physical appearance of people is not according to expectation but is a reflection of the inner psychological state and truth of the person. These examples provide Thurneysen with an analogy for the closure of the dialectic between God and humanity - only in eternity is the antinomy resolved.[22] Therefore the utter realism of Dostoevsky's literary perspective is analogous with the perspective of a painting that can only be resolved in the vanishing point outside of the picture plane - outside of this reality, the other side of this life, this world. Dostoevsky's work, for Thurneysen, is both *Realistic* and *Expressionistic*. Thurneysen then cites *The Brothers Karamazov* as an example of Dostoevsky's psychology - a psychology that points to God. This leads to the first exposition by Thurneysen of an attempt at explicating Dostoevsky's doctrine of God: the solution must lie in God, because only in God is there true knowledge of life: *'God is God. That is the one central recognition of truth for Dostoevsky.'*[23] Revelation, asserts Thurneysen, is here proclaimed: the eschatological tension is resolved only by God through an eschatological act - resurrection.

The absolutely final word of his novels is 'resurrection' (Auferstehung). Over the

---

[20] McCormack, *Karl Barth's Critically Realistic Dialectical Theology*. See also Michael Beintker, *Die Dialektik in der 'dialektischen Theologie' Karl Barths* (München: Christian Kaiser Verlag, 1987).

[21] On the question of Barth and the visual arts, see P.H. Brazier, 'Barth and Expressionism - Some Further Considerations', *Zeitschrift für dialektische Theologie*, 20.1 (Fall 2005), pp. 34-52.

[22] Thurneysen, *Dostojewski*, pp. 35-36/ET: pp. 40-41.

[23] Thurneysen, *Dostojewski*, p. 36/ET: p. 42.

dark abysses of the humanity which he depicts there glows from the beyond the light of a great forgiveness.'[24]

Thurneysen then cites examples to illustrate this from Dostoevsky's work - forgiveness is God's response to the huge rebellion of *eritis Sicut deus*, the fearsome 'Tower of Babel.[25]

Ivan Karamazov, The Grand Inquisitor, and the Devil

In the fourth chapter - *IV Ivan Karamazov, The Grand Inquisitor, and the Devil* - Thurneysen focuses on Dostoevsky's most fearsome attack, which is levelled at the assembled power of the Church and religion as the ultimate example of *eritis sicut deus*. Ivan Karamazov is the chief protagonist and spokesperson for a frustrated pessimistic atheism in *The Brothers Karamazov*. The references to *The Brothers Karamazov* not only in this the fourth chapter but also in the rest of Thurneysen's book amount to a quarter of the entire work. This is not only representative of Thurneysen's priorities and thinking but also Barth's. So what did Thurneysen have to say in this chapter devoted to Ivan Karamazov? Ivan and his Babel like tower of rebellion against God represent religious escapism:

> Again we see the attempt, by turning the God who is other-worldly and unknown into one who is this-worldly and known, to escape that deeply problematical feature of life, in which alone the God who is beyond can and will attest himself to man.[26]

Thurneysen asserts that humanity cannot cope with its creatureliness, with the negativity of the relationship with this critically realistic God; humanity cannot cope with standing under God's judgement. The human solution is to be rid of God, or to control God by creating religion, church, an idol - the 'God-no-longer, an idol (Nicht-mehr-Gott, zum Götzen).'[27] We have seen this in Barth's 'Die Gerechtigkeit Gottes'! For both Thurneysen and Barth this is the ultimate and most dangerous of revolts because it takes place under the illusion of religion and the claim to be obedient to a god, or idol (Götzen). Thurneysen then asserts that the presentation and explication of this insurrection (Thurneysen uses Empörung - an outrage, a rebellious uprising - rather than Aufstand) is seen at its fullest in The Grand Inquisitor.

Thurneysen proceeds to outline in some detail the story of The Grand Inquisitor as the protest and rebellion of Ivan Karamazov. Thurneysen also goes further into the visual analogy of lines of perspective meeting outside of the picture plane because Ivan uses this metaphor also - in the form of two parallel lines never meeting according to Euclidean geometry, arguing that in

---

[24] Thurneysen, *Dostojewski*, p. 39/ET: p. 44.
[25] Thurneysen, *Dostojewski*, p. 36/ET: p. 42.
[26] Thurneysen, *Dostojewski*, p. 45/ET: p. 51.
[27] Thurneysen, *Dostojewski*, p. 45/ET: p. 51.

eternity they will meet in the same way that all the irreconcilable antinomies of suffering and evil on earth in this life will be resolved in eternity. But, asserts Thurneysen, the angry rebellion, the atheism (pseudo atheism - for in the end Ivan argues that even if God is proved to him he will still rebel), can often lead over into true faith, faith beyond religion as it begins to for Raskolnikov: 'The great, passionate negations of the false gods make room once again for the knowledge of the true God.'[28] Thurneysen quotes at length from Ivan's theological ramblings, his rebellion, his story of The Grand Inquisitor and the long dialogue with the devil. Thurneysen also invokes a similar earlier anti-hero in the same mould as Raskolnikov and Ivan - Stavrogin from *The Demons* and the problem of suicide in such men and women, suicide as the ultimate act of rebellion.[29] In the later editions Thurneysen again quotes from Psalm 139: '...if I make my bed in Sheol, you are there.' This prompts Thurneysen to ask the question, can one actually be sick with God and die without there being the supreme inconceivable possibility (impossible, humanly) of being healed by God, and of rising again, being born again?[30] This is where, as Thurneysen saw, the importance of Alyosha, the younger novice brother, and the Starets Zossima who had made such an impression on Alyosha, come in - what is impossible with humans (menschenunmögliche) is not impossible with God. But, for Dostoevsky, the real evil working against God was to be seen in the cultural atheism embodied in the West (that is, the civilized nations of Western Europe) - Ivan is therefore a Western construction. Thurneysen therefore raises the question of how successfully or not Dostoevsky presents the Russian Orthodox Church as the alternative to this Western atheism having already demolished the Roman Catholic Church through The Grand Inquisitor.[31]

Knowledge of God

Chapter five - *V Knowledge of God* - attempts to deal with the epistemological issues that Thurneysen's theological investigation into Dostoevsky's work raises. Here we find asserted the importance of the life we live, the *this-worldly* quality is important and should not be rejected, it is in this world that redemption comes - the forgiveness of sins in Christ. Hence Thurneysen could write: 'So in Dostoevsky there comes a full acceptance of life, of nature, and of man, a paradoxical affirmation of that which is, as it is, for the sake of that which it is not.'[32] This is then confirmed by Thurneysen quoting a verse from John's Gospel - which also forms the frontispiece after the title page in *The Brothers Karamazov* - 'Very truly, I tell you, unless a grain of wheat falls into

---

[28] Thurneysen, *Dostojewski*, p. 45/ET: p. 51.
[29] Thurneysen, *Dostojewski*, p. 60/ET: p. 65.
[30] Thurneysen, *Dostojewski*, p. 61/ET: p. 66.
[31] Thurneysen, *Dostojewski*, p. 62/ET: p. 67.
[32] Thurneysen, *Dostojewski*, p. 64/ET: p. 70.

the earth and dies, it remains just a single grain; but if it dies, it bears much fruit.'[33] This is to emphasize the importance of resurrection. In this context Thurneysen quotes at length from the teachings of the Starets Zossima (from *The Brothers Karamazov*). The negativity is held up by emphasising how love is often presented paradoxically in the negative - love is not, and so forth (1 Corinthians 13). Life is important but eternity more. In this sense Thurneysen compares Dostoevsky's work with that of Tolstoy - concluding that the latter is too moralistic. Humble love, by contrast, is a fearsome power and in this context, as Thurneysen showed, Dostoevsky never lost respect for the lowest in Russian society. But we then find Thurneysen criticizing Dostoevsky's conservative approach to the Russian Orthodox Church. In addition the manner in which he infused Christ into the peasants - the Russian Christ.

> One final question remains. Was not Dostoevsky himself untrue to this knowledge? Did he not himself, in an extremely titanic manner, betray the eternal, the divine, the Christ of the new life, the resurrection, the final things, by the here and now of a specific historical situation?[34]

Thurneysen's answer is that we must not excuse him - to do so would be to deny the best theological elements of his work. Grounding Christ in the Russian people (albeit the serfs and peasants) he was committing the same theological error that Thurneysen and Barth could identify with the neo-Protestant Liberal humanism of their own theological education in Marburg. There are no holy peoples, asserts Thurneysen, and there is no Russian Christ. What role/task would there be for a Christ of The Grand Inquisitor in Russia, questions Thurneysen.[35] But, 'Perhaps, however, even this grotesque aberration of Dostoevsky's is still better than the dream of the West, for its deepest root - even though distorted to titanism - is the counterattack against that western idea of the rise of mankind without God'[36] adds Thurneysen.

Summary of Thurneysen's *Dostojewski*

Thurneysen represents Dostoevsky's theological thinking as characterized by two extremes: life, the world, humanity as it is, an existence that goes its own way; then there is the beyond, resurrection, eternity, God. Here is humanity; there is God. Dostoevsky for Thurneysen is therefore not primarily a psychologist (though he is highly respected and rated by the psychology profession), nor a social philosopher even though this he is also, but he is seen as a theologian because his overarching concern is with God and the attempt to understand and explicate the relationship of humanity with this hidden, distant,

---

[33] John 12:24.
[34] Thurneysen, *Dostojewski*, p. 75/ET: pp. 81-82.
[35] Thurneysen, *Dostojewski*, p. 76/ET: pp. 82-83.
[36] Thurneysen, *Dostojewski*, p. 76/ET: p. 83.

other-worldly God that presses onto humanity. Therefore, for Thurneysen, Dostoevsky's men and women are characterized by a sickness, the secret answer to which lies not in this world, this life: these men and women hunger for eternity, they are driven by a passion for the infinite, a desire that cannot be assuaged by anything in this world, this life. Nothing, therefore, leads from this life to God, only from God to us. Where is Christ in this? Christ is the answer - and for Dostoevsky, the understanding of Christ gained from John's Gospel.

CHAPTER 10

Influences on Thurneysen and Barth's Understanding of Dostoevsky

Thurneysen and Barth's Understanding of Dostoevsky

We have seen the early influence of Thurneysen's mediation of Dostoevsky's *Crime and Punishment*, and to a lesser extent *The Idiot*, on Barth from the summer of 1915 already; from 1918-1921 Thurneysen brought to Barth's attention *The Brothers Karamazov*, *The Demons*, *The Dream of the Ridiculous Man*, plus other shorter works of Dostoevsky. This influence fed through into The Tambach Lecture and *Römerbrief 2*. It is of paramount importance and cannot be stressed enough that in the same way that Barth and Thurneysen published several volumes of sermons together with no distinction as to authorship, in the same way that Barth shared the drafts for *Römerbrief 1* and *Römerbrief 2* with Thurneysen and took seriously his comments and ideas and fed them back into the work, Thurneysen's *Dostojewski* is in part attributable to Barth. The understanding contained in the work is the result of the many long discussions they had together. The philosophical and epistemological elements of this study of Dostoevsky show all too clearly the fingerprint of Barth's theological thinking; likewise the fingerprint of Thurneysen's theological anthropology in *Dostojewski* can be discerned in Barth's *Göttingen Dogmatics* from 1924-5 (a point Barth acknowledged in these Göttingen lectures); and of course this theological anthropology is only there in *Dostojewski* because of the shared reading and discussion from their study together of *Crime and Punishment* in 1915, then to be informed by Barth's reading of Luther and Calvin in 1916-18 whilst writing *Römerbrief 1*! Therefore in looking at Thurneysen's work, *Dostojewski,* we are also seeing ideas by Barth. Thurneysen's *Dostojewski* informs us not only of Thurneysen's understanding of Dostoevsky but also Barth's. This is of fundamental importance to any understanding of the influence of Dostoevsky on Karl Barth.

How did Thurneysen come to read Dostoevsky in the first place? There is no evidence in his correspondence or sermons prior to the summer of 1915 of his having read Dostoevsky generally, *Crime and Punishment* specifically. An informed conjecture, a supposition, would be that Christoph Friedrich Blumhardt introduced him to Dostoevsky when he took Barth to stay at Bad Boll for Easter - the 10-15 April 1915. There is no hard evidence for this connection - Thurneysen might just as well have bought a copy of *Crime and*

Punishment from a railway station book stall thinking it might be a good read. However, Dostoevsky, the writer, his work and his theology, all fit in with and complement the Blumhardt's ministry, and I think it reasonable to postulate that this is the initial contact for Thurneysen, that primarily he was influenced by Christoph Friedrich in his coming to know the work of Dostoevsky in the first instance. It is important, therefore, to remember that Thurneysen was not working in isolation on Dostoevsky. The major novels had been translated into German in the early years of the twentieth-century, and notable writers in Germany and Eastern Europe were publishing studies of Dostoevsky. Thurneysen was aware of some of these academics: writers such as Herman Hesse, Karl Nötzel, Stefan Zweig and Akim Lwowitsch Wolynski are cited in references and in the text of *Dostojewski* and in their correspondence.

Influences on Thurneysen: Herman Hesse

Hermann Hesse[1] was a German existentialist writer who had rejected his Pietistic background to write in a similar oeuvre to Dostoevsky. Thurneysen cites two essays of Hesse's, initially published in 1920 in an anthology entitled *Blick ins Chaos*, as part of the formative influence on his understanding of Dostoevsky. These essays deal with issues relating to the turmoil of the war years and the problems facing the German intelligentsia after the war.[2] Thurneysen noted how this 'glance into chaos' had severe lessons to which most people shied away. The chaos that was represented by the Karamazov family was representative of the turmoil that had engulfed Europe - and was indicative of the theological anthropology in Dostoevsky's novels. Thurneysen wrote,

> Hesse's call, as that of a sentinel filled with hidden concern, in which he has so urgently pointed out the connection between the Russian men and women of

---

[1] Hermann Hesse (1877-1962), a German poet and novelist who explored what he considered to be the duality of spirit and nature - the *Grund* for the individual's spiritual search outside of the norms of civilized society. Born into a family of Pietistic missionaries, he was expelled from the Protestant seminary at Maulbronn in 1891; he then became a writer - several of his novels depicted the journey into the inner self. His reading of Dostoevsky was in part inspired by his father's Russian heritage. He was awarded the Nobel Prize for Literature in 1946 primarily for his *magnus opus* - Herman Hesse, *Das Glasperlenspiel* (Zürich: Fretz and Wasmuth Verlag, 1943).

[2] Hermann Hesse, 'Die Brüder Karamasow oder Der Untergang Europas', *Blick ins Chaos - Drei Aufsätze* (Berne: Verlag Seldwyla, 1920); ET: Hermann Hesse (trans. Stephen Hudson), 'The Brothers Karamazov or the Downfall of Europe', *The Dial Magazine*, New York, 72.6 (June 1922), pp. 607-618. Also Hermann, Hesse 'Gedanken über Dostojewskis Idiot', *Blick ins Chaos - Drei Aufsätze* (Berne: Verlag Seldwyla, 1920); ET: Hermann Hesse (trans. Stephen Hudson), 'Thoughts on Dostoevsky's The Idiot', *The Dial Magazine*, New York, 73.2 (August 1922), pp. 199-204.

Dostoevsky and the decline of the West, was not raised without good reason.[3]

So what did Hesse say in these two essays that significantly effected Thurneysen's thinking on Dostoevsky? Hesse discusses the characters of the Karamazov father and sons as a prophetic analogy of the decline of Europe - though he is specifically considering Germany and the old Austro-Hungarian Empire that collapsed so disastrously through the First World War. Hesse:

> It appears to me that what I call the Downfall of Europe is foretold and explained with extreme clearness in Dostoevsky's works and in the most concentrated form in *The Brothers Karamazov*. It seems to me that European and especially German youth are destined to find their greatest writer in Dostoevsky - not in Goethe, not even in Nietzsche.[4]

Humanity, as represented by all cultures, societies and civilizations is an endowment of something both allowed and forbidden - humanity, asserts Hesse, is something 'halfway between animal and a higher consciousness.'[5] It is the animal in the Karamazov that cause its downfall, and the same is asserted for Europe. In addition to this searing analysis and indictment of the human condition under the illusion of civilization, Hesse also analyses, though in a much shorter essay, Dostoevsky's *The Idiot* focussing on the problems of Christlikeness: Hesse sees this as part of a pertinent questioning - the stumbling foolishness of this Christlike figure (Myshkin) judges and negates the success of this world. For Hesse, this questioning is the question raised by the prophetic warnings that were issued by Dostoevsky - look at the trespass, transgression and sin of these men and women (Dostoevsky's characters) and see how much worse is the situation in Western Europe. This does have echoes with what we saw of Barth's concerns in 'Kriegszeit und Gottesreich' from late 1915, and of how the answer to this question for both Barth and Thurneysen lay in the biblical world of the New Testament. This solution, as we have seen, related to Dostoevsky's question, with which Thurneysen opened his study: 'What is Humanity?' Hesse focuses on the nature of these men and women and so does Thurneysen. Hesse assists Thurneysen, but Thurneysen's answer is different to Hesse's: it is theological.

Influences on Thurneysen: Stefan Zweig, Karl Nötzel Akim Lwowitsch Wolynski and Jeremias Gotthelf

Also in the context of Dostoevsky's question Thurneysen refers to a study on Dostoevsky by Stefan Zweig:[6] From it he identified the way Dostoevsky has this thread of vulnerability flowing throughout all his novels and characters, an

---

[3] Thurneysen, *Dostojewski*, p. 4/ET: p. 8.
[4] Hesse, 'Die Brüder Karamasow', ET: p. 607.
[5] Hesse, 'Die Brüder Karamasow', ET: p. 613.
[6] Stefan Zweig, *Drei Meistes* (Leipzig: Insel Verlag, 1920).

unresolved vulnerability. Zweig was an influential contemporary;[7] Thurneysen saw how Zweig identified the destiny and mastery of Dostoevsky in that he was controlled by this vulnerability to an unparalleled scale and that he wove it in his works so compellingly - 'Stefan Zweig has expressed it marvellously in his study on Dostoevsky.'[8] Therefore Thurneysen can assert of Dostoevsky, echoing Nietzsche, that '...he foresaw and anticipated Zarathustra-Nietzsche's discovery and message of the decline of humanity, and, also his titanic lunge toward the Superman.'[9] The opening of chapter one of *Dostojewski* is based on a concept from Zweig - the understanding we saw earlier that entering the world of Dostoevsky's characters and novels is like entering primeval territory:

> He is surrounded by awesome wildness, by strangeness, by the riddle of nature that has not yet been conquered, not yet contained and controlled, not yet crippled and chained by a hundred safety devices. 'He has entered primeval territory' (Stefan Zweig).[10]

Again Thurneysen uses a quote from Zweig to highlight the nature of the near death experience that Dostoevsky went through when he was within only seconds from being executed by firing squad - 'He never forgot those minutes before the execution. They were "the most intense moment of his life" (Stefan Zweig).'[11]

Karl Nötzel[12] is another German writer who influences Thurneysen's thinking. The German translation that Barth and Thurneysen used of *The Brothers Karamazov* was by Nötzel. Drawing on Nötzel's study *Dostojewski und Wir,* Thurneysen commented,

> His secret lies in the fact that he knew that we still know nothing even when we know many things. It does not lie in personal presuppositions of a psychic nature, which others may possess in common with him without being what he was. On

---

[7] Stefan Zweig (1881-1942), an Austrian biographer, essayist and short story writer, was born into a family of wealthy Viennese industrialists. He was noted for his historical biographies of characters in which he used psychoanalytical theories - *Drei Meister*, which examined Dostoevsky, Balzac and Dickens and is among Zweig's most noted works. His understanding of Dostoevsky is in such a psychoanalytical mode and was written to show how Dostoevsky had in effect held up a mirror to humanity, exposing people with distorted and broken souls.

[8] Thurneysen, *Dostojewski*, p. 5/ET: p. 9.

[9] Thurneysen, *Dostojewski*, p. 6/ET: p. 10.

[10] Thurneysen, *Dostojewski*, p. 3/ET: p. 7, quoting from Zweig, *Drei Meistes*.

[11] Thurneysen, *Dostojewski*, pp. 24-25/ET: p. 28, quoting from Zweig, *Drei Meistes*.

[12] Karl Nötzel (1870-1945) was a writer and translator born and raised in the Eastern part of Germany in the late nineteenth-century that is now Poland. He worked on a German translation of *The Brothers Karamazov: Die Brüder Karamasoff* (Leipzig: Insel, 1919). He also wrote a biography of the Russian novelist, Karl Nötzel, *Das Leben Dostojewskis* (Osnabrück: Biblio Verlag, 1925). His psychologicalical study, *Dostojewsky und wir: ein Deutungsversuch des voraussetzungslosen Menschen* (München: Musarion, 1920), was an interpretation of the underlying conditions, even prerequisites, of humanity as seen in Dostoevsky.

the contrary, it lies in what Karl Nötzel has called his complete lack of presuppositions. His secret is really nothing but that question, his question about humanity. It lies in the fact that he carried nothing in himself except the one great, endless penetrating concern to get to the basis of all things.[13]

Akim Lwowitsch Wolynski[14] is another East European German writer whom Thurneysen quotes to support his developing ideas: for example, the monastic world (and the Starets Zossima to whom Alyosha Karamazov is drawn) that parallels the depraved world of the Karamazovs and yet offers hope, an idea Thurneysen acknowledges was drawn from Wolynski's *Das Reich der Karamosoff*, and a quotation from *Das Buch vom grossen Zorn*, emphasising the manner in which Nastasya Filippovna is wasted by the uncontrollable passion of Rogozhin - Thurneysen quoting Wolynski, 'as if spewed out by the sea of passions.'[15]

By contrast with these writers who were more or less contemporary to Barth and Thurneysen, there are significant references by Thurneysen to another Swiss Minister and writer - Jeremias Gotthelf.[16] Gotthelf lived through the first half of the nineteenth century, indeed he died at the time Dostoevsky was

---

[13] Thurneysen, *Dostojewski*, p. 7/ET: p. 11.

[14] Akim Lwowitsch Wolynski (1863-1926), who often published under the pseudonym Chaim Lejbowitsch Flexer, was a representative of a literary criticism grounded in Idealism; he was publisher of the magazine *Severnyj vestnik* (*The Northern Messenger*). Wolynski's, *Das Reich der Karamosoff* (München: R. Piper Verlag, 1920) - *The Realm of the Karamazovs* - was rated as a tour-de-force of religious philosophy by critics, it exerted a strong influence on interpreters of Dostoevsky once it was translated into German by Alexander Eliasberg (the original Russian was published in St Petersburg in 1901). In it, the literary critic Bahr praises the book in highest tones: 'It is a masterpiece, which bears comparison with the highest of its kind. Here a work of art is not described or repeated or analyzed, it takes on a new life.' Wolynski's, *Das Buch vom grossen Zorn* (Frankfurt: Literarische Anstalt Rütten and Loening, 1905) - *The Book of Great Wrath* - was also rated highly by German followers of Dostoevsky.

[15] Thurneysen, *Dostojewski*, p. 23/ET: p. 26.

[16] Jeremias Gotthelf (1797-1854), a Swiss Reformed minister - real name, Albert Bitzius - was trained in theology in Berne and one term in Göttingen. Gotthelf's early ministry was in Utzenstorf, then in Herzogenbuchsee (Berne Kanton); he was involved in educational activities, particularly in the area of school support and teacher training, however, his politicization did not endear him to the authorities. In 1824 he was appointed as 'Vikar' to the *Kirche zum Heiligen Geist* in Berne, then in 1831 at Luetzelflueh in the Emmental. His major work was *Die Schwarze Spinne - The Black Spider* - originally published in Jeremias Gotthelf, *Bilder und Sagen aus der Schweiz* (Berne: Solothurner Verlag Jent und Gassmann, 1842-6) a work characterized by fears of the devil, pacts with a Satanic huntsman and a horrible flesh spider, set against a background of rural Pietism. By and large his other works are characterized by the sort of unromantic rural realism that also characterized the novels of Thomas Hardy, for example, *Der Oberamtmann und der Amtsrichter* (Leben: Proehle H. Deutsches, 1853) - *The Senior Official and the Office Judge* - works that were in many ways a precursor of existentialism.

imprisoned in Siberia, but what is important is that he is an early example of a writer of Realist literature. Realism as a movement in art and literature is an early precursor of existentialism: life is presented in all its darkness, warts and all so to speak. Realist painters often focussed on the grinding toil and poverty of rural life as compared to the romantic sylvan paradise presented by more romantic painters. Gotthelf was a Swiss-Reformed Minister who only left his homeland once to travel to northern Germany, but whose novels were characterized by a veiled satire of the respectable classes in Switzerland, and often focused on the unromantic, hard, broken lives of ordinary Swiss rural peasants. What does Thurneysen have to say about Gotthelf? At the opening of Chapter 2, *Dostoevsky's Men and Women* Thurneysen writes about how in Dostoevsky's work we find a group of remarkable people, people from all classes of society and all imaginable and possible spiritual provinces and zones between heaven and hell and how these people have all been seized 'like the peasant figures of Jeremias Gotthelf.' These people are not ghosts or figments of our imagination,

> ...but real people of reality, with earthly names and faces, having grown, in all phases of their being, one with the ground on which they stand, and yet all just in their earthly nature so strangely unearthly, just in their reality so completely not of this world, just in their belonging so uprooted! [17]

Thurneysen notes how the same persons who reject Dostoevsky's characters as 'unhealthy distortions' are just as offended by the unprecedented realism of Gotthelf's characters. Yet Thurneysen fears that many of his Swiss compatriots read Gotthelf only from the perspective of romantic ruralism and miss the deeper reality, the deeper struggles he presents. What is important is that, 'what is intimated in the deeper stories of Jeremias Gotthelf breaks forth in the great creations of Dostoevsky.' [18]

Both Thurneysen and Barth were studying Dostoevsky in the context of other German-speaking scholars during the post-war period - the period of the writing of *Römerbrief 2*. As such, their investigations are informed by the war-time and immediate post-war intellectual, spiritual and moral climate in central Europe: hence, their use of, and recognition of a parallel understanding, in Hesse, Nötzel, Zweig and Wolynski. We will encounter something similar in *Römerbrief 2* where Barth is influenced by and cites a wide variety of artists, writers and philosophers, also theologians, pastors and church historians.

Dostoevsky - 'this Russian'

Many of these writers were from Eastern Europe (today, Poland, Belarus and the Ukraine), German speaking because much of this area had been part of

---

[17] Thurneysen, *Dostojewski*, p. 11/ET: p. 15.
[18] Thurneysen, *Dostojewski*, pp. 33-34/ET: p. 39.

Germany during the nineteenth-century and until the end of the First World War (and for most of the twentieth-century part of the Soviet empire). Barth and Thurneysen, as were these writers, were looking East - Russia had always been considered as exotic, relatively, to Western Europe, by Germans. On several occasions in correspondence with Thurneysen, or in essays/addresses Barth commented about Dostoevsky as 'the Russian' or 'this Russian'.[19] In his middle age and mature years Dostoevsky was a Slavophile and a passionate supporter of the Russian Orthodox Church. However, the more interested he becomes in the Russian Church the more he was prepared to be one of its severest critics. We saw earlier how Dostoevsky's faith was grounded in his rediscovery of the Russian New Testament whilst in a Siberian prison camp, which in effect was his theological education and formation. It was this biblical/theocentric mindset that informed his return to faith. He was also informed by the fellow prisoners around him - some of whom were open to faith and the grace and forgiveness of God, others withdrew into the hardened, deranged and criminally perverse world they had created for their own self-justification. Thurneysen noted that what appealed to the mature Dostoevsky in the Russian Orthodox Church were the remnants of a Biblical and Patristic understanding that he saw in the church of his day:

> Without knowing Kierkegaard or Overbeck, he (Dostoevsky) bore in himself the deepest mistrust toward a Christendom that had become church, and he loved in his Russian church just that which is not church in it - the reminders, still preserved pure, as he believed, of the early history of Christendom, free from compromise.[20]

Whether this perception by Thurneysen is entirely correct is not of importance - this was how Barth and Thurneysen saw Dostoevsky. So, what informed Barth and Thurneysen from 'this Russian', in particular during 1915 was primarily the 'biblical' and 'patristic' theocentricity that in part pointed Barth and Thurneysen towards the New Testament as the wholly other starting point for theology.

Russian Orthodoxy and Eastern Platonism?

We can also consider certain questions relating to Russian Orthodoxy and Eastern Platonism (denominational traits or theological characteristics that Von

---

[19] For example, '...ich wollte ich würde ganz klug aus diesen Russen', Barth to Thurneysen, 18 August 1915, in Barth and Thurneysen, *Briefwechsel Band I 1913-1921*, pp. 71-72; also 'Ist es nicht beschämend, daß wir uns das von dem Russen Dostojewski wieder ganz neu haben sagen lassen müssen?', Barth, 'Der römische Katholizismus', pp. 356-367/ET: p. 328. See also '...weiter die Großen Russen, Dostojewski...', Thurneysen, *Die Lehre von der Seelsorge*, p. 185/ET: p. 203.

[20] Thurneysen, *Dostojewski*, p. 6/ET: p. 10.

Balthasar identified as being at the heart of the influence of Dostoevsky on the young Barth, which we noted earlier). For example, to what extent is this understanding of Dostoevsky shared by Barth and Thurneysen rooted in Russian Orthodox Theology? - or, are the theological beliefs inherent in Dostoevsky's work a reflection of the beliefs of the Russian Orthodox Church? These questions are particularly pertinent in 1915 - the period of the influence of *Crime and Punishment*. To what extent does this influence carry with it exposure to Russian Orthodox theology implicitly, and an Eastern understanding of soteriology specifically?

During this period of their theological *Wendung und Retraktation* Barth and Thurneysen are open to a range of influences that are not explicitly ecclesial. However, it is important to remember that Barth is, so to speak, his own man - it can be argued that he takes more from these influences on his terms than he is given. Thurneysen is less variable, less changeable - Thurneysen arrived in the Aargau, yes having been subjected to the influence of neo-Protestant liberalism generally, the theology of Ernst Tröltsch specifically, but he was less the liberal than Barth. And it is Thurneysen that introduces Barth to Leonhard Ragaz, and Hermann Kutter, Christoph Friedrich Blumhardt, and then Dostoevsky, and so on. It is Thurneysen whose Johannine disposition (for Barth) was always rooted in a theology of love comparable to that found in Eastern Orthodox theology (drawn from the Gospel and Epistles of John), so, Thurneysen was in many ways finding a theological companion in Dostoevsky - for Barth this was a radical departure from that which had informed him in his student days. Barth, to a degree, takes what will support his developing ideas from one such as Dostoevsky, ideas that may already be forming in his mind, rather than allowing him to be interrogated and changed by such an influence.

So what of Russian Orthodox theology generally, an Eastern understanding of soteriology specifically? Bradshaw has clearly identified a distinction between the East and the West in relation to rationality, faith and reason (the appropriation of Aristotle and Neoplatonism); therefore he identifies how the Orthodox East combined these ideas from Classical philosophy with a Biblical awareness of, as he terms it, the divine presence within humanity - particularly sinful men and women - to enable a psychological and physical transformation, even 'deification', progressively during a sinner's life following repentance.[21] This has been a consistent element of Russian Orthodox soteriology and ecclesiology, perhaps submerged by the pietistic Western-orientated St Petersburg bourgeoisie, which Dostoevsky so readily attacked in his novels. Dostoevsky became more and more interested in the doctrine of the Russian Church and in particular this biblically-based soteriological transformation of

---

[21] See David Bradshaw, *Aristotle East and West: Metaphysics and the Division of Christendom* (Cambridge: Cambridge University Press, 2004). See also Emil Bartos, *Deification in Eastern Orthodox Theology* (Paternoster Theological Monographs; Milton Keynes: Paternoster, 1999).

the sinner by stages: this Eastern understanding of Christian soteriology is the basis of his novel *Crime and Punishment*. The ground of Dostoevsky's faith and therefore his theological beliefs was the Russian New Testament. By communicating Russian Orthodox beliefs generally, this Eastern understanding of Christian soteriology specifically, to Thurneysen and Barth, Dostoevsky is reawakening in them Biblical and Patristic beliefs that are fundamental to Reformed theology; indeed he is communicating this initially through his novel *Crime and Punishment* at a time when having abandoned their Reformed heritage through a nineteenth-century liberal neo-Protestant mindset, they are effectively searching in the dark in a vain attempt to regain the truth of the Gospel, even though they do not fully realize this at the time (1915, the year of the new starting point).

So it is primarily Dostoevsky's presentation of some elements of Russian Orthodoxy (that is, atonement comparable, doctrinally, with the forensic understanding of the forgiveness of sins in the early church, Eastern Patristic thinking on the divine presence generating change/sanctification in the truly repentant) that not only had reawakened faith in the imprisoned Dostoevsky in his twenties, but also elements that reawakened a Biblical, Patristic and Reformed understanding in Barth. Even though such an understanding is present in Russian Orthodoxy and Eastern soteriology Dostoevsky was informed primarily by the Russian New Testament, and by the fellow prisoners around him. The world of the prison camp in Omsk was in this sense biblical and patristic; but yes, the doctrine of the Russian Orthodox Church did impinge on it. Thurneysen had come to a similar conclusion - what appealed to Dostoevsky in the Russian Orthodox Church of his day were the remnants of a Biblical and Patristic understanding that he saw in the church of his day. It is important to remember that Russian Orthodoxy never officially went along the path of Feuerbachian religious atheism, or exhibited a doctrinal liberalism which could be seen in some elements of nineteenth-century Liberal neo-Protestantism in Germany and to a lesser extent in Switzerland; likewise it is important to remember that there was no Reformation within Russian Orthodoxy - there has been a consistent relationship between ecclesial power, the laity and the Bible. Unlike the Catholic Church in the West where lay access to the Bible was a critical point of disagreement.

But what do we make of what we may call, Eastern Platonism? - we saw earlier how Von Balthasar identified such a trait in the early influence of Dostoevsky? It is widely acknowledged in the Barthian scholarly tradition that Plato and Platonic concepts are part of Barth's theological *Retraktation*, albeit mediated essentially by and from his brother Heinrich Barth. But we have seen enough already to see that there is something of a Platonic distance between humanity and God that Thurneysen identifies in Dostoevsky. It is not only

Barth who invoked this *diastasis* - 'Welt bleibt Welt, daß Gott, Gott ist.'[22] Thurneysen invoked this as well. This understanding is fundamental to Thurneysen's study *Dostojewski*.[23]

We must therefore note in the context of Barth's invocation of 'Welt bleibt Welt', Thurneysen's use of *jenseitig-unbekannten* (*other-worldly* and *unknown*) for God and how he compares this with the idol (Götze - idol, false god) that is *diesseitig-bekannten* (*this-side-of* and *known*). Thurneysen uses *Jenseit* (*other-worldly*) and *Diesseit* (*this-side-of*), with obvious Platonic overtones, to represent this dialectical antinomy. But it is important that he does not just state that this world is self-contained - he states that this world is this-side-of, that there is another reality to be taken into account that we are in relation to this otherness (*ganz andere* - *wholly other*), as Plato's world of shadows relates to the truer reality.

It is important to steer clear of a well established past generalisation that the Eastern Church was Platonic, other-worldly and mystical; the Western Church Aristotelian, this-worldly and efficient.[24] Such a distinction is often dualistic and indeed we must be wary of identifying such a dualism in Dostoevsky and in Barth and Thurneysen's appropriation of Dostoevsky. But, Platonism there is in Barth's theological *Retraktation* and the question is to be addressed, how much of this Platonism is from Eastern Theology via Dostoevsky? In many ways Dostoevsky's theological insights are the product of a) his own experiences of conversion in a Siberian prison camp, and b) the influence of the Russian New Testament. Yes, Dostoevsky's doctrine of God can be said to be analogous with a Patristic even neo-Platonic doctrine but that is only a comparison. Thurneysen's use of this other-worldly analogy is likewise scriptural (Johannine) rather than explicitly Platonic. For example, one of the statements we have just quoted asserting that world is world, God is God continues,

> It remains at this: God is God. 'He dwells in light unapproachable.' Therefore even when one stands very near to him, yes, most especially there, it is possible to speak of his light only as of something absolutely paradoxical. Otherwise it is no longer his light that is spoken of. And yet it is precisely only of this light of his that Dostoevsky wanted to speak.[25]

Therefore not only is Dostoevsky primarily influenced by the theocentric world of the Russian New Testament, but Thurneysen uses the language of *diastasis* from the German New Testament ('...wohnet in einem Lichte, da

---

[22] Barth, 'Kriegszeit und Gottesreich', p. 120.
[23] See Thurneysen, *Dostojewski*, p. 36/ET: p. 42: 'God is God; that is the one central recognition of truth for Dostoevsky'. See also p. 62/ET: p. 67, 'Only now is it clear that this world is this world, and the beyond is the beyond, that humanity is humanity and God is God'; and p. 73/ET: p. 79, 'It remains at this: God is God'.
[24] Lossky, *The Mystical Theology of the Eastern Church*, pp. 50, 53 and 101.
[25] Thurneysen, *Dostojewski*, p. 73/ET: p. 79.

Niemand zukann'²⁶). There is then also the criticism we have seen already of Dostoevsky's invocation of the Russian Christ - rooting Christ in the Russian peasants and serfs which both Thurneysen and Barth distanced themselves from. But the background remains - behind Dostoevsky and Thurneysen (and to a degree Barth) there is the heritage of Russian Orthodoxy and Eastern Platonism because this was the Christianity that Dostoevsky was raised and nurtured in and despite the years in his twenties when he was a Feuerbachian Western inspired liberal atheist, and although it is the theocentricity brought about by the Russian New Testament that was his sole reading matter in the Siberian prison camp that brings him back to faith, the cultural upbringing from his childhood is still there. But he did develop what to Barth and Thurneysen would have been a healthy criticism and suspicion of religion and religious practice. For example, whilst in Siberia he mistrusted the priests and formal religious services he was obliged to attend, instead he valued the соборность (*sobornost*) of togetherness as he rekindled his faith with his fellow convicts who were Russian Orthodox cradle-to-grave Christians. For example, Vrangel, a 'good Christian' whom Dostoevsky befriended observed, 'he was rather pious, but did not go often to church, and disliked priests, especially the Siberian ones...'.²⁷ Vrangel linked this spiritual revival with his Bible reading, which he preferred to the formalities of public religion. But this was not individualistic piety - he shared his Bible reading with sympathetic fellow prisoners, they were his congregation, his church. Here he discovered true соборность (*sobornost*) - the spiritual togetherness of Christians in which the ego is both submerged and enhanced, the spontaneous togetherness of a congregation at the moment of worship which is then carried over into everyday living. Dostoevsky wrote on this period of his life, 'From the people (in prison) I received again into my soul Christ, whom I had known in the family home when still a child, and nearly lost when in my turn I was transformed into a European liberal.'²⁸ In correspondence from Siberia he commented about his repudiation of 'Schillerism' (a term he coined, along with endarkeners/endarkenment as a euphemism for all that he now saw was wrong with European liberalism) and admitted that he had '...believed in theory and utopia'.²⁹ In correspondence from prison he sent to Madame Fonzina in 1854 a Russian Orthodox Christian living in Siberia³⁰ he commented:

---

[26] 1 Thimotheus 6:16b, Thurneysen, *Dostojewski*, p. 73/ET: p. 79.
[27] Quoted in Boyce Gibson, *The Religion of Dostoevsky*, p. 214.
[28] Dostoevsky, *The Diary of a Writer vol. II*, August 1880, chp. 3, '1 Concerning One Most Important Matter', p. 984.
[29] John Middleton Murray, *Fyodor Dostoevsky: A Critical Study* (London: M. Secker, 1916), pp. 77-78. Murray quotes from Dostoevsky's correspondence. See Dostoevsky, *Fyodor Mikhailovich Dostoevsky: Complete Letters*, p. 142.
[30] Murray, *Fyodor Dostoevsky: A Critical Study*, p. 79. Quoting from Dostoevsky, *Complete Letters*, pp. 142-143.

> I am a child of the age, a child of unbelief and doubt, up till now ... this longing for faith, which is all the stronger for the proofs I have against it ... I thank God for the times when I can love and believe I am loved...
>
> In such moments I have formulated my creed, in which all is precious and holy to me ... there is nothing lovelier, deeper, more appealing, more rational, more human and more perfect than the Saviour ... not only is there no one else like him, there never could be ... If anyone could prove to me that Christ is outside the truth, and if the truth really did exclude Christ, I should stay with Christ rather than with the truth.[31]

Truth began to be of supreme importance to him. And religion? the public show of religion that was sometimes required of the prisoners left him very uncomfortable. Whilst in Siberia he realized that his time as a European liberal had also been a search for truth - but a mistaken, misguided search where he arrived at wrong truth, the relativistic truth of the man-god. Christ and truth became synonymous to him. This, however, was very Russian in the sense of правда (*pravda*): a word that combines both 'truth' and 'justice'. And it is in keeping with Russian tradition, including the Russian Orthodox Church, to seek not simply правда (*pravda*) reduced to истина (*istina* - theoretical truth) but правда-справедливость (*pravda-spravedlivost* - truth as righteousness, righteousness as truth).[32] For Dostoevsky God in Christ was primarily about truth, righteousness and justice; religion was a vehicle, a form of human expression for collective worship (for example, the services the prisoners were marched off to in the nearby town, heavily guarded and in shackles). Dostoevsky attempts to articulate something like this in his mature writings. In looking at some of these we will understand his criticism of religion - that is, a criticism of religion when it worked against the Gospel. This is a critique of religion and the Church seen as human culture, piety seen as social respectability. Dostoevsky's ecclesiology as such was then the result of this biblical faith brought about whist in the prison camp at Omsk, Siberia, which was uncompromising in its criticism of religion and church when it was self-serving, but was also coloured by his childhood love of the Russian Orthodox rituals. This then must be considered as formative. Church and religion was regarded ambivalently to a degree by Dostoevsky, but God was everything - the God revealed specifically by the Christ of John's Gospel.

---

[31] Murray, *Fyodor Dostoevsky: A Critical Study*, pp. 79-80, quoting from Dostoevsky, *Complete Letters*, p. 142.

[32] Boyce Gibson, *The Religion of Dostoevsky*, p. 23. Boyce Gibson refers to James M. Edie, James P. Scanlan and Mary-Barbara Zeldin (eds.), *Russian Philosophy vol. II: The Nihilists, the Populists, Critics of Religion and Culture* (Chicago: Quadrangle, 1965) p. 175.

Chapter 11

Theological Existentialism

Theological existentialism is the explication of the character and nature of the relationship between God and humanity: human existence before God. This is often seen from an individual perspective - the crisis of faith of an individual characterized by decision-making. Humanity is not alone without knowledge or understanding of God and the nature and purpose of life, neither is humanity without understanding as to the fate, eschatologically, of men and women. This knowledge is independent of the contingent nature of religious knowledge (contingent in the sense of geographical, educational or ability to comprehend) - the atonement wrought by Christ may be a topic of religious knowledge and it is important for people to *know* cognitively what God has done for them, but even if they have not come across this knowledge in religious terms the reality is still there. The event of the crucifixion, death and resurrection of Christ has still happened and will impinge on the life of each and everyone - whether s/he knows about it or not in terms of cognitive knowledge and understanding. The primacy of this event is at the heart of the theological understanding of Barth and Thurneysen at this time, especially in their development; it is also fundamental to Barth's mature work in *The Church Dogmatics*.

In the reality occupied by men and women what does this mean? In the case of Raskolnikov conscience is a pressing external reality on him; he then experiences this reality as guilt, a guilt that could only be assuaged by giving in to its promptings and to the witness of Sonya, particularly in her reading of the story of the raising of Lazarus. Raskolnikov may declare atheistic beliefs at times (belief in God at others), but this does not prevent the external, wholly other transcendent reality of the God of love as Holy Spirit pressing and acting upon him: conscience is pneumatological, critical and real. This is not conscience as an example of humanistic projection. Conscience here leads to a right understanding of sin and repentance. The knowledge of what Sonya read to him from the Bible cannot be undone and it acts on him as well - he is sick with guilt before God even though he does not appear to believe in her God, or acknowledge God's overlordship. By contrast Ivan Karamazov becomes progressively more and more sick with the God he passionately seeks to deny the existence of, and even if he fails he will rebel against this God with all his might - without a Sonya figure he eventually succumbs to a mental breakdown. This is theological existentialism: this is part of an existential interpretation of the Gospel.

Thurneysen commented, in the context of a seventieth birthday volume of correspondence and essays for Barth,

> Because his concern was with this message, or, as one could also say, because Karl Barth thinks not abstractly but concretely, which means on the basis of the Bible, and because biblical thinking is in itself existential thinking ('und weil biblisches Denken in sich selber existentielles Denken ist...'), Karl Barth's theological thinking was from the beginning directed to the life of humanity.[1]

This existence, this life of humanity contrasts with God. For both Barth and Thurneysen the Word of God meets this life, lays hold of it, and transforms it - '...these are the two poles between which the sparks must again begin to pass in order that there may be an arc of light that will illuminate all things.'[2] Religion and all merely pietistic devotional thinking can often mask the promptings of the Word of God.

Religion as the Result of the Fall

Thurneysen commented, remarks that were shared by Barth, that 'In *The Dream of a Ridiculous Man*, a late, deeply meaningful short story that says in a few pages all that Dostoevsky had to say, it is told how humanity turns away from God, from the true, living God, and thereby make the earth into hell.'[3] This short story was considered archetypal of Dostoevsky by them - it said all that the Russian writer had to say - it is a story that puts forward the proposition that religion is the result of the Fall: before the Fall the relationship between God and humanity was characterized by immediacy; only with the Fall is the relationship characterized by distance, a distance that is subjugated into and is expressed by and through religion. Dostoevsky is concerned throughout the 1870s with the question of *Christlikeness* in relation to religious belief. This culminated to a degree in *The Dream of a Ridiculous Man*, published in 1878.[4]

In *The Dream* Dostoevsky focuses on the relationship between religious belief and theological anthropology; that is, religious belief and the invention of human gods seen in relation to the theological anthropology that he outlined in his other works. Written in the form of a story/parable, and recounted as narrative by the 'ridiculous man', the work deals with the state of humanity

---

[1] Eduard Thurneysen, 'die Anfänge', in Eduard Thurneysen (ed.), *Antwort - Festschrift zum 70 Geburtstag von Karl Barth* (Zollikon-Zürich: Evangelischer Verlag AG, 1956), p. 832.
[2] Thurneysen, 'die Anfänge', p. 832.
[3] Thurneysen, *Dostojewski*, p. 74/ET: p. 80.
[4] The story first appeared in Dostoevsky, *The Diary of a Writer vol. II*, April 1877, chp. 2, 'The Dream of a Ridiculous Man', pp. 672-690. Quotations here are from Fyodor Mikhailovich Dostoevsky, *A Gentle Creature and Other Stories* (Oxford World's Classics; trans. Alan Myers; Oxford: Oxford University Press, 1995), pp. 107-128.

prelapsarian/sublapsarian, the nature of original sin as a decision (therefore existential), and it raises issues to do with the 'invention' of religion by fallen humanity. The ridiculous man is very similar to the underground man - he is withdrawn, isolated, in a shroud of self-imposed loneliness. This results in alienation, spiritual desolation, moral indifference, and nihilistic beliefs. The ridiculous man is above all modern and individualistic. This individuality is important to Dostoevsky's critique - the counter is the communal characterized by compassion and a sense of responsibility for other human beings, but above all by соборность (*sobornost*). This ridiculous, sad man is on the verge of suicide when he falls into a deep dream where he is convinced he is dead but alive and rotting in his coffin in the ground. He prays fervently to be released and is transported to another world which turns out to be the earth - *prelapsarian*. He is impressed by the innocence of these people, but he causes them to fall. There is no sin in this world prior to the arrival of the 'ridiculous man' with all his Western inspired Petersburg sophistication - this world is created, the ridiculous man arrives, the people fall. The ridiculous man is placed in the role of the serpent:

> I only know that I was the cause of their sin and downfall. ...like a germ of the plague infecting whole kingdoms, so I contaminated all this earth, so happy and sinless before my coming. They learnt to lie, grew fond of lying, and discovered the charm of falsehood. Oh, at first perhaps it began innocently, with a jest, coquetry, with amorous play ... that germ of falsity made its way into their hearts and pleased them.[5]

What followed? 'Sensuality was begotten', then jealousy, then cruelty, soon the first murder. They began to separate into groupings, classes, and eventually racial groups. 'They formed into unions'; reproaches and upbraidings followed. They came to know shame, which led them to invent virtue. Honour sprang up, and flag waving nationalism. 'They began to struggle for separation, for isolation, for individuality, for mine and thine. They began to talk in different languages.' They knew sorrow and loved it, even thirsted for it - eventually believing that truth could only be attained through suffering.

> Then science appeared. As they became wicked they began talking of brotherhood and humanitarianism, and understood those ideas. As they became criminal, they invented justice and drew up whole legal codes in order to observe it, and to ensure their being kept, set up a guillotine.[6]

As time passed they forgot what they had been in their innocence. They called it a dream; they lost all faith and invented the notion of legends to account for these memories. They longed to be happy and innocent once more so they crafted an idol of it, statues proliferated; they set up temples and worshipped this idea - which they acknowledged as no more than their own

---

[5] Dostoevsky, *The Dream of a Ridiculous Man*, section 5 paragraph 1, pp. 123-124.
[6] Dostoevsky, *The Dream of a Ridiculous Man*, section 5 paragraph 2, p. 124.

projected desire. They reverenced and worshipped these idols, they bowed down to them and adored, and encouraged the people to do so (that is, their leaders did). Thus they invented religion, including theories of religion to explain that it was really all nothing - however, this was a secret kept for the priestly caste, the ruling class: *eritis sicut deus*. Religious consciousness arose outside of the officially sanctioned elite: saints came to these people, weeping, and talked to them of their pride, of their shame. These prophets were laughed at or stoned: 'holy blood was shed on the threshold of the temples' (religious sacrifice and martyrdom).

> Then there arose people who began to think how to bring all the people together again, so that everybody, while still loving himself best of all, might not interfere with others, and all might live together in something like a harmonious society. Regular wars sprang up over this idea. All the combatants at the same time firmly believed that science, wisdom and the instinct of self-preservation would force men at last to unite into a harmonious and rational society; and so, meanwhile, to hasten matters, the wise endeavoured to exterminate as rapidly as possible all who were not wise and did not understand their idea, that the latter might not hinder its triumph.[7]

In presenting the elite, the revolutionary guard/the Inquisitor, exterminating those who were not considered wise because they did not understand the beliefs of the elite (that is, seeking to impose common beliefs, a uniform utopian concept of humanity), Dostoevsky was writing at his most prophetic. Although in one way he is referring back to the French Revolution the tragedy here is uncannily like the belief system, the religion, of Soviet Marxism: the collectivisations, the Stalinist purges of anyone who did not conform to the party line and so on (in addition his comments are applicable to many twentieth-century dictatorial systems from the National Socialism of the Nazis in Germany with their religion of Blood and Soil to third world dictators towards the end of the twentieth-century). Finally in Dostoevsky's parable there arose religions with a cult of non-existence and self-destruction for the sake of the everlasting peace of annihilation: suicide. The wise, the humanitarians (the ruling elite) were happy for there to be religion - though they, the wise, knew there was nothing in it - as it kept the people happy.

The ridiculous man realising what he had caused was beside himself with grief and guilt. He awakes from his dream and back in St Petersburg lives a changed resurrected life, honouring God and accepting God's righteousness.

---

[7] Dostoevsky, *The Dream of a Ridiculous Man*, section 5 paragraph 3, pp. 125-126.

Feuerbach and Dostoevsky

After study with the philosopher Hegel, Ludwig Feuerbach (1804-1872) underwent something of a philosophical conversion represented by his first major work, *The Essence of Christianity*.[8] This work explicated his anti-Hegelian stance, by ironically drawing on Schleiermacher's focus on religious experience. But where Feuerbach differed from both Kant and Schleiermacher (who were theists) was that he did not hold to belief in God - Feuerbach argued that if they were correct then God (indeed all gods) was merely an enlargement of our ideas, experiences and aspirations. He wrote, 'God is the realized wish of the heart, the wish exalted to the certainty of its fulfilment',[9] furthermore the secret, so to speak, of theology is that it is nothing more than anthropology.[10] Both Feuerbach and Schleiermacher had focused, or grounded Christianity, on human religious experience. McGrath:

> This approach has enormous attractions. However, as Ludwig Feuerbach demonstrated, it is also enormously problematical...
>
> the leading idea of the work is deceptively simple: Human beings have created the gods, who embody their own idealized conception of their aspirations, needs, and fears. Human 'feeling' has nothing to do with God; it is of purely human origin, misunderstood by an overactive human imagination.[11]

McGrath notes that this proposition is a severe critique of human-centred religion - and Christianity is not excluded. But,

> It may be noted that Feuerbach's critique of religion loses much of its force when dealing with non-theistic religions, or theologies (such as that of Karl Barth) which claim to deal with a divine encounter with humanity from outside...[12]

Hence the answer to Feuerbach that we saw emerging in Barth's theology.

Dostoevsky read, drank in, Feuerbach as a naive Europeanized liberal student at the St Petersburg Academy. And like many inspired at this time (the 1840s) by Feuerbach's writings, he, along with the Petrashevskii circle, invented a morality and ethic centred on their own values and ego. He dismissed religious belief on the grounds of Feuerbach's theology but substituted a system of ethics based on supposed universal brother/sisterhood!) with everyone being innately nice to each other - a sort of pseudo-Christian

---

[8] Ludwig Feuerbach, *The Essence of Christianity* (ed. W. Schuffenhauer, Gesammelte Werke, vol. 5; Berlin: Akademie Verlag, 1973).
[9] Feuerbach, *The Essence of Christianity*, p. 121.
[10] Feuerbach, *The Essence of Christianity*, p. 207.
[11] Alister McGrath, *Christian Theology* (Oxford: Blackwell Publishers, 1994), p. 230.
[12] McGrath, *Christian Theology*, p. 231. See also Brian A. Gerrish, 'Feuerbach's Religious Illusion', *Christian Century* 114 (1997), pp. 362-365 and 367.

ethic, or more pertinently, a parasitic-atheistic creed derived from the Christian Gospel.[13] Robert Jenson:

> But just if Feuerbach is right, if there is in fact no antecedent one God, there also can be no one antecedent community of humankind. Feuerbach dreamed of a universal humanity and so of a shared eternal vision of human value, but therein he remained parasitic on the faith he debunked. Thus Western unbelief has since had to abandon that dream and now knows only classes and genders and races and cultures. Insofar as religion interprets itself by the resultant neo-Feuerbachian theory, religion is revealed as a struggle for metaphysical power, for each such group necessarily projects its ideal or compensatory vision of itself to be the final good. It is just so that Scripture sees the gods of the peoples as idols and 'nothings'. Exactly as neo-Feuerbachian theory says, what each of the gods does is validate and enforce the particular human situation, with its structure of values, from which she/he/it is projected - in all the alienation and tyranny of every such situation.[14]

This observation reflects Dostoevsky's understanding, 'The Idea' we encountered earlier that without God, if there was no God, then there are no limits to human morality, human depravity. Without God all human ethics are pretence - the demand by the most powerful group to set out how others should behave, in effect an educated, oligarchic, elite. Feuerbach, as well as others at this time, asserted that he could perceive a common harmonious human ethic, and that given time this could be achieved.[15] Dostoevsky, along with Kierkegaard,[16] are the two nineteenth-century Christian prophets who challenge this bourgeois notion. Dostoevsky had moved full-circle from his liberal humanist student days in the Petrashevskii group.

What is important for us is this idea that religion is often invented by people to mask the existential crisis of their lives, but this religion may not be acceptable in God's sight. This is in effect godless religion. Feuerbach ironically allows for a criticism of religion (though in the case of Barth and Dostoevsky this is in the service of the Gospel). *The Dream of the Ridiculous*

---

[13] For example, the British novelist George Eliot who translated works by Ludwig Feuerbach and David Friedrich Strauss. See Susan E. Hill, 'Translating Feuerbach, Constructing Morality: The Theological and Literary Significance of Translation for George Eliot', *Journal of the American Academy of Religion* 65 (1997), pp. 635-653. See, generally, George R. Creeger (ed.), *George Eliot: A Collection of Critical Essays* (Englewood Cliffs, NJ: Prentice-Hall, 1970), in particular B.J. Paris, 'George Eliot's Religion of Humanity', pp. 11-36 and U.C. Knoepflmacher 'George Eliot, Feuerbach, and the question of criticism', pp. 79-85.
[14] Robert Jenson, *Systematic Theology vol. 1: The Triune God* (Oxford: Oxford University Press, 1997), p. 53.
[15] See George L. Kline, 'Russian Religious Thought', in Ninian Smart, John Clayton, Patrick Sherry and Steven T. Katz (eds.), *Nineteenth Century Religious Thought in the West vol. I* (Cambridge: Cambridge University Press, 1985), pp. 179-229. See also, Van A. Harvey's chapter, 'Ludwig Feuerbach and Karl Marx', pp. 291-328.
[16] George E. Arbaugh, 'Kierkegaard and Feuerbach', *Kierkegaardiana* 11 (1980), pp. 7-10.

Man is in many ways Dostoevsky's answer to Feuerbach. For Dostoevsky, what blinds Feuerbach to God is sin. If he were not blinded by sin then he would see through the cacophony of human religion and understand that *God is*. From the time of his rediscovery of Christian faith in the prison camp at Omsk, Siberia, Dostoevsky struggled with how to refute Feuerbach; such was the influence this German theologian had been on him in his student days.[17] Robert Jenson's remarks quoted above echo what Dostoevsky has the ruling elite believing and saying in *The Dream*, that is, that Western humanity knows only classes and genders and races and cultures, that the common values of liberal humanism can only be, at best, imposed.[18] Is this what Dostoevsky is presenting where the elite seek to impose harmony and common values, beliefs? What we have here in this short story is the closest that Dostoevsky gets to a theological statement on religion - albeit presented in the style of a parable.

Primarily *The Dream* is a savage indictment of humanity; more pertinently humanity without God, humanity that has turned its back on God and deludes itself with all sorts of beliefs systems - religious, political, individualistic, socialist, nihilist. This is a *sublapsarian* humanity, which will try everything but turn to God. This is an existential crisis and both Thurneysen and Barth perceived the profoundness of Dostoevsky in writing it; further, they saw in their reading of *The Dream* a criticism of religion that complemented their own concerns. What is left after this critique of human religion, of human belief systems, is faith. Faith is, for Dostoevsky, in the one true God and the revelation of Jesus Christ. There are actually two stories here in *The Dream of the Ridiculous Man*. There is the parable of the human race as another race on another earth-like planet who (unlike the human race on earth) have no name for God, that is, no revelation as in the Old Testament - 'that merciful Judge Who will judge us and whose Name we know not'[19]. Furthermore they have no real revelation of the *nature* of that God/Judge as in Jesus Christ (they only have natural theology and religious cults) and therefore there is for them no atonement - these people are truly lost. Then there is also the story of the ridiculous man. Is Dostoevsky saying that this man must go through the period of doubt, alienation, finally to come back to the truth and be saved? There is evidence for dialectic here: the ridiculous man (as representative of the human race, not the people in his vision), moves from innocence through sin and death to saintliness. If this is so, there is dialectic but not dualism - the world of the people in his vision is not inherently evil, it is good (there is no hint of Manichaeism here).

---

[17] Boyce Gibson, *The Religion of Dostoevsky*, pp. 10-11 and pp. 161-164.

[18] Regarding 'there also can be no one antecedent community of humankind', Jenson refers to Wolfhart Pannenberg, *Systematic Theology vol. 1* (Edinburgh: T&T Clark, 1991), pp. 151-166.

[19] Dostoevsky, *The Dream of a Ridiculous Man*, section 5 paragraph 2, pp. 124-125.

Amongst the people the 'ridiculous man' corrupts in his dream there is no Christ, no saviour, they are in their fallen corrupt state forsaken. What is essential to Dostoevsky, therefore, is the figure of Christ and it can be argued that Christ was in this community that the ridiculous man visits in his dream prior to their Fall - implicitly. Boyce Gibson comments: '...for Dostoevsky, God was in Christ to such a degree that he had difficulty in envisaging the divine transcendence. Merging God in the community of Christ-seekers was a temptation to him at all times.'[20]

Further, Boyce Gibson and others have suggested that it is as if Dostoevsky was trying to set out 'the Christian truth anonymously: to confront us with the content...'.[21] But the people in his dream are left suspended with no forgiveness: what is missing, what they cry out for (though they do not realize it), is the grace and forgiveness of a criminal class bestowed from the God of love - tangibly revealed in Christ. In many ways *The Dream* is a lead up to Father Zossima in *The Brothers Karamazov* who sees the Gospel in the dictum, each is responsible for all. In the words of the ridiculous man, the chief thing is Christlikeness - to love others like yourself, who, after his dream/vision called upon this eternal truth with tears and not words.[22]

God-Humanity

How does Thurneysen represent and explicate this relationship between humanity and God in the frame of an existential Gospel? How does he use Dostoevsky's writings (see Figure 4 Thurneysen's Use of Dostoevsky - References, opposite)? For Thurneysen, Dostoevsky asserts that the more we see life realistically the more something mysteriously unreal, something powerfully unearthly is pointed to at the basis of all things, '...as in Dostoevsky, with the one great question, the question of the unknown God.'[23] The danger of atheism and bad religion, dialectically criticized, is that 'the original power of true knowledge of God is displayed in this atheism'[24] as was clear from the *surd*-like nihilism that overwhelmed Raskolnikov leading up to, motivating him and seen in his near mental breakdown after the murders.[25] In the context of Sonya, a woman marginalized as the lowest of the low by the respectable in society, and Myshkin in the heights of the intensity of beauty and joy in an

---

[20] Boyce Gibson, *The Religion of Dostoevsky*, p. 168.
[21] Boyce Gibson, *The Religion of Dostoevsky*, p. 166.
[22] Dostoevsky, *The Dream of a Ridiculous Man*, section 5 paragraph 4 and 5, pp. 126 and 127-8.
[23] Thurneysen, *Dostojewski*, pp. 34-35/ET: p. 40.
[24] Thurneysen, *Dostojewski*, p. 52/ET: p. 58.
[25] Thurneysen, *Dostojewski*, pp. 52-53/ET: p. 58.

The Brothers Karamazov

The Karamazov brothers	51
Ivan	39
Alyosha	20
Mitya	9
Fyodor	2
Fyodor as father	5
Zossima	12
The Grand Inquisitor	18
Grushenka	7
The devil	26

Crime & Punishment

Crime & Punishment	26
Rogozhin	4
Raskolnikov	19
Sonya	5
Svidrigailov	3

House of the Dead

House of the Dead	1

The Demons

The Demons	5
The Possessed	5
Stavrogin	5

The Adolescent

The Adolescent	2

The Dream of a Ridiculous Man

The Dream of a Ridiculous Man	1

The Idiot

The Idiot	25
Yepanchins	1
Ivolgin	1
Myshkin	9
(Prince) Myshkin	11
Nastasya	6

Poor People

Poor People	1

Figure 4 Thurneysen's Use of Dostoevsky - References

One of the five chapters in *Dostojewski* (1921) is devoted to 'Ivan Karamazov, the Grand Inquisitor and the Devil'; with other references/uses this amounts to a quarter of the book. In terms of a raw-data count there are 51 references to *The Brothers Karamazov* compared to 26 for *Crime and Punishment*, 25 for *The Idiot* and 10 for *The Demons*. Despite the influence of *Crime and Punishment* generally, Sonya and Raskolnikov specifically, in 1915, it is the demonic anti-hero Ivan Karamazov, his hallucinatory encounter with the devil, his presentation of the prose poem The Grand Inquisitor that exerted the greatest influence on Barth and Thurneysen.

aura in the minutes before an epileptic seizure, Thurneysen realized that these are the moments of true knowledge of God and of humanity's existence - 'To push the paradox to the limit ... wherein God is seen'[26] is in the depths of negation (illness, suffering). Myshkin therefore gains his deepest knowledge out of the moment of near death: 'Humanity can be true to the real meaning of this life only in those great negations of all human standpoints and possibilities.'[27] Furthermore, 'the kingdom of God is not set up anywhere, but it is powerful in its coming, and harlots and sinners are the first to await it. Understand those who can!'[28] Commenting on the dialectical problem at the heart of humanity caused by this unknown God, he wrote, 'The question of God is the question of all his works: God, the root of all life, and the basis of the world, which gives everything its basis, but also its abrogation, its torment, its 'dis-ease'.'[29] The central reposition of truth, as we saw, is therefore that 'God is God', furthermore, 'God is nothing of this world.'[30] Therefore Thurneysen

---

[26] Thurneysen, *Dostojewski*, p. 24/ET: p. 27.
[27] Thurneysen, *Dostojewski*, p. 48/ET: p. 53.
[28] Thurneysen, *Dostojewski*, p. 74/ET: p. 80.
[29] Thurneysen, *Dostojewski*, p. 37/ET: p. 42.
[30] Thurneysen, *Dostojewski*, pp. 37 and 52-53/ET: pp. 42 and 58.

and Barth could conclude that this world was indeed this world, beyond was beyond and God is God - 'Now God is recognized as the one he is, and he has the honour which is his right'.[31] Humanity's creaturely relation to God is deeply distinctive grounded as it is in relationship to God; but humanity '...does not recognize this ultimate relationship because of its Promethean rebellion against it.'[32] Again, Myshkin's (*The Idiot*) foolishness, his behaviour perceived as idiocy, is a dialectical paradox when viewed against the successful avarice and debauchery of the others he meets in St Petersburg, the worldly successful.[33] How does this work out in Thurneysen's study? An existential Gospel is characterized by decisions - good decisions, bad decisions. These are decisions that bring people closer to God in Christ - or further away. It is this so-called Promethean behaviour that concerns Thurneysen most of all, the arrogance of behaving *as if* one was God, behaviour summed up in the Latin theological phrase *eritis sicut deus*.

---

[31] Thurneysen, *Dostojewski*, p. 62/ET: p. 67.
[32] Thurneysen, *Dostojewski*, p. 40/ET: p. 46.
[33] Thurneysen, *Dostojewski*, pp. 40-41/ET: p. 46.

PART FOUR
DOSTOEVSKY
AND
RÖMERBRIEF 2

'...he was the one who first put me on the trail of Blumhardt and Kutter, and then also Dostoevsky without whose discovery I would not have been able to write either the first or the second edition of the commentary on Romans.'

Barth commenting on Thurneysen's mediation of the works and theology of Dostoevsky in *Gottedienst-Menschendienst*, p.13

CHAPTER 12

Barth and *Der Römerbrief*

Barth-Thurneysen : The Period of The Rewriting of *Der Römerbrief*
We have seen briefly the importance of the correspondence exchanged between Barth and Thurneysen. It is important to look in more detail at this correspondence for the evidence it gives of the developing understanding they had of Dostoevsky, and how 'this Russian' influenced them and is used by them. We have seen already the evidence in a letter from Barth to Thurneysen about how important Dostoevsky was to him in 1915, how he was spending time reading *Crime and Punishment* and how he wanted to become well informed, wise, about Dostoevsky.[1] By 1918 Thurneysen is well under way with his study of Dostoevsky, and Barth has almost finished writing *Römerbrief 1*.

Correspondence 1919-1923

In April 1919 Barth wrote to Thurneysen about the *'Bolshevik evening in the worker's club'* where heated discussions about Lenin ensued - raising for Barth the issue of what he referred to as 'the Dostoevskian Russian Christ, the Elijah-Calvin-Cromwell problem of the kingdom of God!'[2] In the context of Dostoevsky both raised the question of whether the Bolshevik revolution in Russia was a manifestation of Christ's Kingdom coming on earth, but they were wise enough not to jump to easy conclusions about perceiving earthly powers as divine (hence their reading and understanding of the same problem as exhibited in the post English Civil War period).[3] The question of religious socialism had not diminished completely in their thinking, and at this time both could see the dangers of a Bolshevik/communist revolution portrayed prophetically by Dostoevsky in The Grand Inquisitor. A few weeks later Barth wrote of his uncle and an elderly friend by the name of Rutimeyer who argued out the pros and cons between Dostoevsky and the Swiss nineteenth-century

---

[1] Barth to Thurneysen, 18 August 1915, in Barth and Thurneysen, *Briefwechsel Band 1 1913-1921*, pp. 71-72.
[2] Barth to Thurneysen, 13 April 1919, in Barth and Thurneysen, *Briefwechsel Band 1 1913-1921*, pp. 324-325.
[3] Barth to Thurneysen, 13 April 1919, in Barth and Thurneysen, *Briefwechsel Band 1 1913-1921*, pp. 324-325.

writer Jeremias Gotthelf;[4] also of coverage about Dostoevsky and Kutter in the Ehrenburg paper.[5]

There is much discussion between Barth and Thurneysen about possible works to write - particularly as they discover other writers who complement the existential nature of their reading of the Gospel. For example, Ibsen, who, Barth writes, deserves an article in the periodical *Neue Werk*; then he speculates on writing a book, 'But perhaps it must happen in greater connection: in a work on Dostoevsky, Nietzsche and Ibsen, which would explain these very contemporaries. I am very glad that I can now read all these people rightly.'[6] In the summer of 1920 Barth writes of the frenetic pace of life, commitments, and yet he is reading Dostoevsky's *The Demons* at the same time.[7] In October 1920 Barth commented to Thurneysen about how Wolf Meyer saw him 'as some sort of form of Dostoevsky: human, sinful by nature, subject to all kinds of passions, indeed the utmost depths and recesses of passion, yet no stranger to prayer ... taking on its full shape, without the pseudo-eschatological claims of the Patmos brother, without the idealist-Christian illusions of the "*Neue-Werk*-People"...'[8] There is much in this quotation that informs of the importance of Dostoevsky in Barth and Thurneysen's thinking, their understanding of the passion in Dostoevsky's characters, the fallenness, the fleshly all-too-real-nature of them, yet also their prayerfulness and the acknowledgement by some of the characters of their overwhelming need for the grace and forgiveness of God. But Barth is all too aware of the dangers of theological insight breeding a conceit or pride: for example, 'too a great theological wisdom and its peculiar danger of hubris'[9]

Later in the same year Thurneysen writes about the opportunity of lecturing on Dostoevsky at the Aarauer Studentenkonferenz the following spring - 'Hopefully I have to lead out! One thing to say is quite clear. Your letter has given me courage.'[10] Barth continued to comment on those theologians, writers and pastors who, like themselves, could read Dostoevsky with ease.[11] Indeed, it

---

[4] Barth to Thurneysen, 11 May 1919, in Barth and Thurneysen, *Briefwechsel Band 1 1913-1921*, pp. 326-327.
[5] Barth to Thurneysen, 14 December 1919, in Barth and Thurneysen, *Briefwechsel Band 1 1913-1921*, pp. 326-327.
[6] Barth to Thurneysen, 4 July 1920, in Barth and Thurneysen, *Briefwechsel Band 1 1913-1921*, pp. 403-405.
[7] Barth to Thurneysen, 19 July 1920, in Barth and Thurneysen, *Briefwechsel Band 1 1913-1921*, pp. 413-415.
[8] Barth to Thurneysen, 14 October 1920, in Barth and Thurneysen, *Briefwechsel Band 1 1913-1921*, pp. 432-434.
[9] Barth to Thurneysen, 14 October 1920, in Barth and Thurneysen, *Briefwechsel Band 1 1913-1921*, pp. 432-434.
[10] Thurneysen to Barth, 28 October 1920, in Barth and Thurneysen, *Briefwechsel Band 1 1913-1921*, pp. 436-437.
[11] Barth to Thurneysen, 17 November 1920, in Barth and Thurneysen, *Briefwechsel Band 1 1913-1921*, pp. 442-444.

is through their correspondence that both developed their understanding of Dostoevsky further. For example, Thurneysen in December 1920 wrote:

> Your suggestion about the *satisfactio vicaria* hit the point I had been forced to by all sorts of thoughts I had had about Dostoevsky. With him it is expressed by that wonderfully gracious, almost completely transcendent light, that falls on the world. I also did not miss the thoughtful shake of the head that we stand under.[12]

In reply, Barth wrote in the context of criticism Thurneysen received from a publisher in Zürich,

> Of course you will now have had first of all to leave alone the tombs with your *Dostojewski*. Perhaps you were not able to make the psychological phenomenon clear (even in some way) to the head-shaking man of letters in Zürich... That you have had to receive and endure this blow makes it all the more necessary to complete the new *Römerbrief* of mine in the summer, unless some miracle occurs.[13]

By the new year the problem of adverse criticism from the publishing establishment in Zürich ('the tombs') towards Thurneysen's work on Dostoevsky had passed and Thurneysen was able to reflect when writing to Barth on the peaceful Christmas that had passed and the amount of reading he had done: 'I received a few good books: Kierkegaard, Nietzsche, Gotthelf and Dostoevsky, quite an intellectual lot'[14] Again, in reply, Barth was to write on the impact Dostoevsky and Kierkegaard were having on his thinking as he wrestled with the fifth chapter of *Römerbrief 2*: 'I can approach the fifth chapter only by elaborately clearing my throat, spitting into my hands, and reading *The Brothers Karamazov* and *The Philosophical Fragments*'[15] A month later when Barth again wrote on the struggle to push forward with writing *Römerbrief 2* he commented, 'You really must come, Dostoevsky everywhere. I am taking the Karamazovs with me on my trip and would really

---

[12] Thurneysen to Barth, 20 December 1920, in Barth and Thurneysen, *Briefwechsel Band 1 1913-1921*, p. 453; regarding *satisfactio vicaria* (vicarious satisfaction), that element of Christ's atonement that is considered propitiation and expiation for the sake of believers and *in their place*. It can be seen from the consideration of sin and grace in the influence of Dostoevsky on Barth in 1915 that was examined earlier in chapters 3 to 6 that this was an element which was understated as not having been fully explored in Barth's understanding of sin and grace gleaned from his reading of *Crime and Punishment* in 1915. It is clear, therefore, that this element was being deliberated here in 1920 with Thurneysen.

[13] Barth to Thurneysen, 28 December 1920, in Barth and Thurneysen, *Briefwechsel Band 1 1913-1921*, pp. 455-458.

[14] Thurneysen to Barth, 8 January 1921, in Barth and Thurneysen, *Briefwechsel Band 1 1913-1921*, pp. 460-461.

[15] Barth to Thurneysen, 22 January 1921, in Barth and Thurneysen, *Briefwechsel Band 1 1913-1921*, p. 461.

like you to clear a few things up for me...';[16] he was clearly wanting Thurneysen's advice on interpreting much of the theological polemic in *The Brothers Karamazov* prior to his use of Dostoevsky's ideas in *Römerbrief 2*. We have noted already the influence of Stefan Zweig on the structure of Thurneysen's *Dostojewski* and the inspiration this writer was for the opening chapter. Thurneysen commented further to Barth on the importance of Zweig:

> My reading was a good book of Stephan Zweig on Balzac-Dickens-Dostoevsky, everything they say about this book is good as well as intelligent and sparkling. Such artists as Zweig with their inner efforts are our nearest neighbours! ... The festive days are coming and I must put the *Dostojewski* to one side again as you do your *Römerbrief* and try to say to a full church what still remains at best a secret conversation between us both. Sometimes I seem to myself to be so uninvolved (in a bad way) in the broader activity of the church, sitting daily on my own, reading, writing and - without intending it — a somewhat esoteric sphere is forming with the reservation that people as such are not a matter of indifference for me. It actually helps me to understand Dostoevsky.[17]

Thurneysen's comment was not uncommon between Barth and himself, that is, the secret conversation between them. It is important to remember that at this point there is only *Römerbrief 1* (1919) published by Barth, and the first joint volume of sermons - *Suchet Gott, so werdet ihr leben!* (1917)[18] - available for others to read; apart from the memory of Barth's addresses from 1916 that had exerted a profound impact. Their understanding of Dostoevsky was as yet unavailable to a wider audience, however, they acknowledged in their correspondence that both of them were being *fêted* in Germany as religious personalities. Writing on this in March 1921 Barth commented that 'The fear I expressed to you in Munich that we may have to do penance for the adulation we are so freely accorded in Germany for being religious personalities is being realized, so much so that I find it embarrassing.'[19]

With the date for the Aarauer Studentenkonferenz approaching Thurneysen wrote in March 1921 about his aims and hopes:

> In my lecture on Dostoevsky I will deal with remarks on human love as love for the individual, earthly human. In Dostoevsky, because of his elevation of the human being, there occurs a remarkable turn to the human itself and not only to the idea of humanity, but to the empirical, concrete human. His whole *oeuvre*

---

[16] Barth to Thurneysen, 22 February 1921, in Barth and Thurneysen, *Briefwechsel Band 1 1913-1921*, p. 472.

[17] Thurneysen to Barth, 16 March 1921, in Barth and Thurneysen, *Briefwechsel Band 1 1913-1921*, pp. 476-477. Thurneysen is referring to Zweig, *Drei Meistes*.

[18] Karl Barth and Eduard Thurneysen, *Suchet Gott, so werdet ihr Leben*.

[19] Barth to Thurneysen, 18 March 1921, in Barth and Thurneysen, *Briefwechsel Band 1 1913-1921*, pp. 477-479. See comments by Thurneysen to Barth two days earlier on how 'in an avowedly Lutheran church newspaper I am heralded a "famous leader"'. Thurneysen to Barth 16 March 1921, in Barth and Thurneysen, *Briefwechsel Band 1 1913-1921*, pp. 476-477.

testifies to this, a gigantic turn of all the furthest points of the universe, both heavenly and hellish, to earth - but under the sign of the resurrection. [20]

Writing again a few days later, Thurneysen commented further about the writing of the Aarau lecture and the importance to both of them of a sound understanding of Ivan Karamazov and The Grand Inquisitor and how this related to Barth's manuscript for *Römerbrief 2* - proofs for chapters six and seven of *Römerbrief 2* were returned by Thurneysen whilst still working on his Aarau lecture. Their thinking for both *Dostojewski* and *Römerbrief 2* was closely shared, so much that Thurneysen was able to comment confidently that their thinking was beginning to yield original results:

> ...I am getting stuck in some crevices right beneath the summit: in The Grand Inquisitor and the speeches of Ivan Karamazov with the Devil. I will be very glad for your presence in the fight, our thinking is yielding even in Dostoevsky a new exegesis that nobody else is doing as well as some astounding insights into the situation in general. I have read the *Römerbrief* manuscript and find it all in perfect order, and the shocking turn and new direction is expressed with great power. Have a read some time in Dostoevsky's political writings, as there Christ is invoked in the remarks on Russian power politics and the associated chiliastic expectations that can only be understood in terms of 'Second Coming', even though it is never pronounced as such. In Dostoevsky, as in Kutter, there is an emphasis on the real, a grasping beyond everything distant, that I find more comprehensible and attractive than all cleverness of the *Neue Wege*. [21]

We find here the link still present in their thinking between Kutter and Dostoevsky, a link that was there six years earlier in 1915 and how this contrasted with the position generally of Swiss Reformed and German Lutheran theology. There are important points here to do with Christ and political aspirations in Russia, not least how Barth and Thurneysen approached the Bolshevik revolution in the light of their reading of The Grand Inquisitor likewise the character of Ivan Karamazov and so forth. By early April, Barth is writing, 'I am on tenterhooks to see what comes of your Dostoevsky. Don't let it slip away. It really must not disappear like all the other Aarau lectures.' [22]

After Thurneysen's Aarau lecture, Barth wrote, 'Is Dostoevsky ready? I repeat, the whole educated world is waiting for it and since the Aarauer Studentenkonferenz three months have past...You are fearsome in this matter. See how I am wading knee-deep in ink - you should follow my example.' [23] By return Thurneysen commented that he was still struggling with Ivan Karamazov

---

[20] Thurneysen to Barth, 21 March 1921, in Barth and Thurneysen, *Briefwechsel Band 1 1913-1921*, p. 479.

[21] Thurneysen to Barth, 29 March 1921, in Barth and Thurneysen, *Briefwechsel Band 1 1913-1921*, pp. 480-481.

[22] Barth to Thurneysen, 7 April 1921, in Barth and Thurneysen, *Briefwechsel Band 1 1913-1921*, pp. 481-482.

[23] Barth to Thurneysen, 20 June 1921, in Barth and Thurneysen, *Briefwechsel Band 1 1913-1921*, p. 496.

and The Grand Inquisitor but also explained how he saw his work relating to *Römerbrief 2*:

> I'm now dealing with the heated battles with The Grand Inquisitor and the problems concerning Ivan Karamazov. I really have been doing nothing else night and day, and have got a strategy for writing the whole thing, and can now set the whole thing in motion with a quiet heart. For the most part it will serve as an illustration of your exegesis of Romans. [24]

Writing again early in July Thurneysen has completed *Dostojewski* and is still proofreading *Römerbrief 2* for Barth, assessing how it fits in with their thinking:

> I am returning chapter eight. I find it all amazing, sentence-by-sentence, densely expressed, no redundant expression, all rather terse, but that is no criticism. If the reader has followed you in the previous seven chapters, he cannot disagree with anything at all in the eighth. It underlines everything that precedes it, and is a final, imposing summation. [25]

By late July Thurneysen writes of his joy that *Dostojewski* was published so promptly.[26] In early August Barth wrote:

> This hot summer ... I amble like a drunk man back and forth between writing desk, dining table, and bed ... I think regretfully of the close of the second section of Romans 10; there was something there that, between two and three in the morning, would not come out right. Besides, your Dostojewski provided me with steam for the whole section as well as a quotation. [27]

By October Barth had completed *Römerbrief 2*.

From November 1921 the emphasis on the influence and use of Dostoevsky changes. Thurneysen reports that shops are displaying his book; Barth notes that his mother is even reading Thurneysen's *Dostojewski*.[28] Barth also writes of publishing plans for their addresses and lectures[29], then later in the month, writing from Göttingen, comments that lots of people around him are reading Thurneysen's *Dostojewski*, and it 'works like "worm powder," to use Schäidelin's language;' later in December, he congratulates Thurneysen on the

---

[24] Thurneysen to Barth, 24 June 1921, in Barth and Thurneysen, *Briefwechsel Band 1 1913-1921*, pp. 498-499.

[25] Thurneysen to Barth, 1 July 1921, in Barth and Thurneysen, *Briefwechsel Band 1 1913-1921*, p. 499.

[26] Thurneysen to Barth, 22 July 1921, in Barth and Thurneysen, *Briefwechsel Band 1 1913-1921*, pp. 505-506.

[27] Barth to Thurneysen, 3 August 1921, in Barth and Thurneysen, *Briefwechsel Band 1 1913-1921*, p. 508.

[28] Thurneysen to Barth, 5 November 1921, and Barth to Thurneysen, 6 November 1921, in Barth and Thurneysen, *Briefwechsel Band II 1921-1930*, pp. 3-4 and 4-7.

[29] Barth to Thurneysen, 27 November 1921, in Barth and Thurneysen, *Briefwechsel Band II 1921-1930*, pp. 12-15.

success of *Dostojewski* with the book companies.[30] In a circular letter in early January Barth comments, 'Your Dostoevsky, Eduard, commends itself as an extraordinarily good book. Many of my hearers eat it up in quiet moments, with the result that they are gradually becoming more sheepish and withdrawn.'[31] However, Barth does note that they are not, theologically, having it all their own way and that there are some disapproving reviews of Thurneysen's work.[32]

In a long letter dated 9 May 1922 Barth continues to note the spread of interest in Dostoevsky amongst German theological circles and the impact they are both having:

> One of them was a cheerful old gentleman ... who has moved on from Ritschl and who presented himself to me as a downright enthusiastic reader, first of Eduard's *Dostojewski* (and of Dostoevsky himself), then, what is more, of *Römerbrief*, and he flourished a recently purchased copy of *On the Inner Situation* fervently in the spring sunshine... Besides, even old Heilmann wants now to get into Dostoevsky! (Eduard, it is time for us to move on from there to another place, is it not? We must keep a length ahead!!)[33]

This last remark is very important: 'it is time for us to move on', because it delineates the limit, for Barth, of the influence and importance of Dostoevsky. Barth fears that much of the German theological establishment is now focussing on the existential Gospel that he and Thurneysen have highlighted in the works of Dostoevsky; this is better than the liberal humanism of nineteenth-century German neo-Protestantism, but they are still focussing on a human response (theological existentialism being about the *human* relationship with God). That is why the works of Dostoevsky are, in their interpretation, truer to the Gospel but they must move on. Dostoevsky has been an important stepping-stone for Barth, as we have seen from the influence initially of *Crime and Punishment* in 1915 (seven years earlier!), but they are still focussing on the human reaction to the critically realistic God, and not completely on God and the revelation in Jesus Christ - *deus dixit*. The references in the correspondence therefore reflect Barth's changed interests - references to Dostoevsky tail-off. It is important to note comments by Thurneysen in this context, from 1956, that both realized that existentialism could work against the *deus dixit* - '...the profound loss of substance that is inevitable in a theology that tries to base itself upon existentialism. Its failure is already to be seen. It carries through the

---

[30] Barth to Thurneysen, 11 and 15 December 1921, in Barth and Thurneysen, *Briefwechsel Band II 1921-1930*, pp. 21 and 24-25.
[31] Barth to Thurneysen, 22 January 1922, in Barth and Thurneysen, *Briefwechsel Band II 1921-1930*, pp. 27-34.
[32] Barth to Thurneysen, 26 February 1922, in Barth and Thurneysen, *Briefwechsel Band II 1921-1930*, pp. 41-54.
[33] Barth to Thurneysen, 9 May 1922, in Barth and Thurneysen, *Briefwechsel Band II 1921-1930*, pp. 69-76.

process of demythologizing (Entmythologisierungsthese) consistently until it becomes dekerygmatizing (Entkerygmatisierung).'[34]

Regarding Luther, Barth comments that 'I am reading extensively in his letters and am astonished - he is to be placed together with Dostoevsky, only as Overbeck is with Blumhardt!!'[35] It is interesting that Barth is still discovering aspects of Dostoevsky's thought in the work of the Reformers. Thurneysen, in February 1923 notes the influence of Dostoevsky on The Kant Society in Basel, '...where Natorp (from Marburg) spoke about Dostoevsky ... and made Dostoevsky a new-Kantian in an unenlightening way, but in marvellously transfigured words. Joel, who was presiding, discovered me in the audience, and at his request I had to give a response, although I was not keen on the idea and had been quite startled by Natorp's interpretation.'[36] This comment seems to confirm Barth's concerns echoed almost a year earlier with regard to delineating the limits of the influence and uses of Dostoevsky; however, Barth still quotes Dostoevsky illustratively.[37] Thurneysen discusses an essay to be published on the diary of Dostoevsky,[38] Barth commenting in reply in a circular letter from October 1923 wrote, 'The new issue of *Zwischen den Zeiten* looks very good; you will like it more than the last one!! The bit on Dostoevsky is first rate.'[39] Later, in November 1923, Barth observes that 'Last Tuesday at the open evening (forty participators) we talked of The Grand Inquisitor and you were honourably remembered.'[40] With this the topic of Dostoevsky tails off. Within a year Barth is about to give the lecture series later published as *The Göttingen Dogmatics,* and although as we shall see the imprint of Dostoevsky to a small degree in these lectures, this marks the end of a conscious influence of Dostoevsky. Indeed from the autumn of 1921 Barth conducted evening seminars in his house at Göttingen for some of the students for 'pressing discussions' following the 'catastrophe of the First World War.' These discussions were always linked to a text: sermons by Blumhardt and Kutter; Thurneysen's book *Dostojewski*; plays by George Bernard Shaw; novels by

---

[34] Thurneysen, 'die Anfänge', p. 834.
[35] Barth to Thurneysen, 18 May 1922, in Barth and Thurneysen, *Briefwechsel Band II 1921-1930*, pp. 120-129.
[36] Thurneysen to Barth, 12 February 1923, in Barth and Thurneysen, *Briefwechsel Band II 1921-1930*, pp. 138-143.
[37] Barth to Thurneysen, 28 February 1923, in Barth and Thurneysen, *Briefwechsel Band II 1921-1930*, pp. 149-155.
[38] Thurneysen to Barth, 6 June 1923, in Barth and Thurneysen, *Briefwechsel Band II 1921-1930*, pp. 174-175, referring to E. Thurneysen, 'Der Schritt zur Kultur. Eine Bemerkung zu Dostojewskis Tagebuch eines Schrifstellers', *Zwischen den Zeiten* IV (1923), pp. 70-77.
[39] Barth to Thurneysen, October 1923 (no specific date), in Barth and Thurneysen, *Briefwechsel Band II 1921-1930*, p. 191.
[40] Barth to Thurneysen, 19 November 1923, in Barth and Thurneysen, *Briefwechsel II 1921-1930*, pp. 198-200.

Thomas Mann; also some political autobiographies.[41] Fortunately he acknowledges this Russian writer five years later in 'Der römische Katholizismus als Frage an die protestantische Kirche' as the source of his understanding of sin and grace - a full thirteen years after their discovery of *Crime and Punishment* in the summer of 1915.

Römerbrief 1 (1916-18, Published 1919)

The primary influence on Barth in his writing of *Römerbrief 1* is, of course, the apostle Paul, then to a lesser extent Luther and Calvin (whom Dostoevsky had pointed Barth towards in terms of his understanding of sin). There is no explicit mention of Dostoevsky in *Römerbrief 1*. The imprint of Dostoevsky, however, is discerned in *Römerbrief 1* in the form of this doctrine of sin. It is important to remember that the offer of a teaching post at Göttingen in 1921, as well as the comment by Karl Adam (the bombshell on the playground of the theologians[42] - the wake up call, as such, to German theologians following the catastrophe of the First World War), came as a result of Barth's first commentary on Paul's Epistle to the Romans - *Römerbrief 1*. *Römerbrief 1* is a commentary, a biblical commentary, but it is also a theological treatise. Barth focuses on God's relations with the World, and the solution God forges to humanity's condition, fallen as it is. This is seen dialectically: humanity is fallen yet 'Christian'; fallen yet of faith; living in the old world yet for the new world. Direct experience/knowledge of God is no longer possible yet we are moulded, changed by the Holy Spirit. Dialectic points to a reality that is ultimate, concrete and universal; such dialectics include a dialectical criticism of religion. Von Balthasar[43] asserted that a dynamic eschatology seen as the irreversible movement from a fatally doomed world to a new living order filled with the life of God was the main thrust of *Römerbrief 1*; this was the restoration (in the form of ἀποκατάστασις) of the original ideal creation in God. This condemned world cannot return to the original state through its own strength or will, though it still has some intimation of its true origin. Ἀποκατάστασις will be entirely achieved through the graciousness of Christ. Von Balthasar correctly identifies the influence of Origen here, but these passages also give the impression of being influenced by Barth and Thurneysen's reading of Dostoevsky's *The Dream of the Ridiculous Man*.

Römerbrief 1 owes much of its conceptual framework to Plato, as mediated by Barth's brother Heinrich. McCormack[44] has quite rightly shown that

---

[41] Noted in Busch, *Karl Barths Lebenslauf*, p. 144/ET: pp. 129-130. See Barth and Thurneysen, *Briefwechsel Band II 1921-1930*, pp. 164, 252 and 329.
[42] Karl Adam, 'Die Theologie der Krisis', *Hochland* XXIII (1926), pp. 271-286 (comment on pp. 276-277).
[43] Von Balthasar, *The Theology of Karl Barth*, p. 64.
[44] McCormack, *Karl Barth's Critically Realistic Dialectical Theology*, p. 139.

Römerbrief 1 was as expressionistic as *Römerbrief 2*, the main difference being emphases. Like the expressionist painters and writers, and also concurring with the way Thurneysen was to invoke expressionistic concepts in *Dostojewski*, Barth sought to get to the reality that underpinned mere outward appearance - in this case to get behind religion to the truth of the Gospel:

> ...it was precisely this conviction that the truly real lies hidden beneath the surface of so-called reality which everywhere governed *Römerbrief* 1. In the light of this conviction, *Römerbrief 1* is rightly understood as an attempt to engage in a thoroughgoing criticism of the reality which lies ready to hand in an effort to create an open space for the emergence of the 'real reality' (i.e. God or the Kingdom of God).[45]

This ready-to-hand reality was all too often, for Barth, religion. Barth was attacking, as McCormack correctly shows, liberal Pietism, idealistic epistemology and ethics, the positive (i.e. kataphatic) elements in church and religion (hence the predominance of apophatic language) and religious socialism (especially in the light of the Bolshevik revolution in Russia in 1917). Individualism is decried, the communal elevated, that is, the communal in the context of Christ unifying people, the body of Christ. Eschatology and history is a major theme in *Römerbrief 1*. Whilst refuting much nineteenth-century German theology and philosophy on the subject of history and eschatology, Barth does seek to show how the two realities of *welt* and *Gott* can come together - this is objective soteriology. Walker sees Barth's criticism focused on two idolatrous groups: idealism (Hegel) and romanticism (Schleiermacher).[46] Knowledge of God by contrast is treated as subjective soteriology. *Römerbrief 1* is heavily dialectical, as both Michael Beintker and Bruce McCormack have shown,[47] and there is much interesting speculation by these scholars along with Herbert Anzinger,[48] as to the precise nature of Barth's dialectic here and how it relates to Hegelian and Socratic dialectic. *Römerbrief 1* is important in Barth's development away from theological liberalism. Therefore it is worth examining sin in *Römerbrief 1*.

For example, in Chapter Five 'Der Tag' (The Day), of *Römerbrief 1*, Barth invokes the concept again of *eritis sicut deus,* that we saw earlier that came essentially from reading *Crime and Punishment*. In the sub-section dealing with Romans 5:12-21, 'Der Sieg des Lebens' (The Victory of Life), Barth writes:

---

[45] McCormack, *Karl Barth's Critically Realistic Dialectical Theology*, p. 140.
[46] James Silas Walker, 'The Development of Karl Barth's Theology from the first edition of *Der Römerbrief* through to the second edition of *Der Römerbrief*' (PhD, Claremont Graduate School, 1963; University Microfilms Inc, Ann Arbor, Michigan, 1963).
[47] See Beintker, *Die Dialektik in der 'dialektischen Theologie' Karl Barths*. and McCormack, *Karl Barth's Critically Realistic Dialectical Theology*, p. 162.
[48] Anzinger, *Glaube und kommunikative Praxis*.

The sin: here we stand before the pathogen of the 'sickness unto death.' There is only one sin: the Seibständigseinwollen (the want, or desire, to be autonomous, independent) of the person over against God.[49]

Over the page Barth continues on the rebellious character (reminiscent of Raskolnikov),

> ...He transfers the characteristics and functions of God to himself. He wanted to be like God (Genesis 3:5): a being for himself, resting in its own importance. He becomes clever. He begins to analyze. He gets evil, pricking, piercing - yet blind - eyes. He views himself through 'knowledge of humankind', 'experience', 'psychology', 'historical' thinking - all of which is possible only outside of God.[50]

McCormack comments in the context of this sub-section of *Römerbrief 1* (Barth on Romans 1:18-21) that 'The Fall was the consequence of Adam's desire for independence from God, for self determination, or autonomy.'[51] Barth on Romans 1:19: 'In truth, we left our homeland in God, it was not that we had no other possibility...'[52] Barth is talking about Adam, the Fall, and the desire for autonomy that fed the actions of 'Eve' and 'Adam'. But he also has in mind Raskolnikov - transferring the functions of God to himself, the piercing, rational analysing eyes, but which are blind. This attempt at justification is pursued, according to Barth's criticism, through human experience, psychology and the sort of thinking about history that was common amongst nineteenth-century German philosophers such as Hegel; all of this was for Barth outside of God or the possibility of God. Von Balthasar commented on Barth's treatment of the Fall in *Römerbrief 1*, 'What then does the Fall consist in? 'There is only one sin: man's desire to set himself up against God. Man falls from the immediacy of being with God. He "resents living directly, simply, purely in the Spirit like a child ... He would like to be like God is: self-subsistent and self-important in his own right."'[53] There is more than an echo here of Raskolnikov, but also of the *prelapsarian* condition of the people in Dostoevsky's *The Dream of the Ridiculous Man*.

Often in *Römerbrief 1* it is hard to discern whether Barth is speaking as himself or as Paul, what is important is that he is attempting to apply Paul's words to contemporary problems. Hence in the preface to *Römerbrief 1* we find:

---

[49] Barth, *Römerbrief 1*, p. 177.
[50] Barth, *Römerbrief 1*, p. 178.
[51] McCormack, *Karl Barth's Critically Realistic Dialectical Theology*, p. 150. See Barth, *Römerbrief 1*, 1 Kapitel *Die Nacht* 1:18-21 'Der Abfall', pp. 24-31.
[52] Barth, *Römerbrief 1*, 1 Kapitel *Die* Nacht Romans 1:18-21 'Der Abfall', p. 30.
[53] Von Balthasar, *The Theology of Karl Barth*, p. 65, on Barth, *Römerbrief 1*, 4 Kapitel 'Die Stimme und der Bibel' on Romans 4:13-22 'Die Gerechtigkeit und die Moral', p. 128.

Paul, as a child of his age, addressed his contemporaries. It is, however, far more important that, as Prophet and Apostle of the Kingdom of God, he veritably speaks to all - of every age ... If we rightly understand ourselves, our problems are the problems of Paul; and if we be enlightened, by the brightness of his answers, those answers must be ours:

> 'Long, long ago the Truth was found,
> A company of men it bound.
> Grasp firmly then - that ancient Truth!'[54]

For Barth the central message of Paul's Epistle to the Romans is that God has established a new world in Christ in which all can participate. It is an objective reality that is known only dialectically, hence the overarching importance of the *denkform* of dialectic - confirmed by McCormack, Beintker and Anzinger.[55]

Barth and Thurneysen invoke dialectic in the contrast between this world and the *real* reality that permeates all of *Römerbrief 1*. Barth, like Thurneysen in *Dostojewski*, uses a *Diesseits-Jenseits* dialectic ('on this side of' - 'on the other side of, beyond'). For example, Barth: 'We are no longer the same. We have been placed into the process which reaches from *jenseits* into *diesseits*.'[56] Why? 'With the breakthrough - Immanuel! God with us! which has taken place in the present time in the messianic present, in the decisive turn of the aeons in heaven'.[57] Barth is saying that the possibility of the new world is with God only, for it is the reality that is *jenseits* and inaccessible to us.[58] This is a platonic use of *Diesseits-Jenseits*. Thurneysen: 'Only now is it clear that this world is this world (*Diesseits*), and the beyond is the beyond (*Jenseits*), that humanity is humanity and God is God.'[59] Seen from above, the world is still the world and God is still God - transcendent and other. This understanding is fundamental to Thurneysen's study *Dostojewski*, and to Barth's Platonism in *Römerbrief 1*. For Barth and Thurneysen this was the basis of the theology underpinning Dostoevsky's novels. This realization, this *diastasis*, was of great importance to them at this juncture in their development. God was not to be seen as infused through history and human events (Hegelian like); but human events *diesseits* were, as we see here in *Römerbrief 1*, moving, being pulled into, towards *jenseits*:

---

[54] Barth, *Römerbrief 1*, 'Vorwort', pp. 3-4.
[55] See McCormack, *Karl Barth's Critically Realistic Dialectical Theology*; Beintker, *Die Dialektik in der 'dialektischen Theologie' Karl Barths* and Anzinger, *Glaube und kommunikative Praxis*.
[56] Barth, *Römerbrief 1*, p. 167.
[57] Barth, *Römerbrief 1*, p. 167.
[58] Barth, *Römerbrief 1*, p. 167. See 3 Kapitel 'Die Gerechtigkeit Gottes' on Romans 3:21-25 'Die Offenbarung', p. 83; also Barth, *Römerbrief 1*, 7 Kapitel 'Die Freiheit' on Romans 7:1-6 'Das neue Wesen', p. 250.
[59] Thurneysen, *Dostojewski*, p. 67/ET: p. 62.

12. Barth and Der Römerbrief

> Again we see the attempt, by turning the God who is other-worldly and unknown into one who is this-worldly and known, to escape that deeply problematical feature of life, in which alone the God who is beyond can and will attest himself to man.[60]

The *Ursprung* is for Barth a category of the primal source of all that is ultimately connected with God and creation. We have noted already the origin of this phrase in the work of Barth's brother Heinrich who wrote, 'Divinity and soul are in the Ursprung (Ursprung ist also die Gottheit und Ursprung ist die Seele).'[61] Barth uses *Ursprung* to refer to the world from which humanity has fallen, and to which all will return, the present sinful world having lost contact with this *Ursprung* but it will be restored by the Christ, in the resurrection.[62] The reality of God will prevail over all - a solution to the antinomy between salvation or damnation can only be in the eschaton; the eschaton closes the dialectic, not a Hegelian synthesis. However, some scholars consider that there is too great a tension in Barth's eschatological dialectics. The problem is how to maintain the wholly otherness of God, whilst asserting the direct movement of the old fallen world towards this new world through an organic understanding of Heilsgeschichte. Walker:

> God's history plus man's history equals Heilsgeschichte. It is in this area - the history, organism, eternity, synergism, and related themes that Barth's basic difficulties and inconsistencies occur. In his great interest in Beck and the other Biblicists, Blumhardt, and Kutter, Barth has found much of value to him, but also his biggest problem in the first edition. It is the problem of maintaining the supracosmic reality of God and his new world while still retaining the direct movement of the old world into the new by way of organic Heilsgeschichte. The burden is greater than dialectic can carry.[63]

Dialectic may allow for this juxtaposition but it also denies the movement - only in the eschaton can there be a closure of this antinomy. That we can glimpse the first fruits of this now is a paradox (closely related in philosophical conceptual terms to dialectic). If *Römerbrief 1* was a harsh criticism of the world of humanity and human cultural aspiration, even more so by setting off this Tower of Babel against the reality of the supreme, transcendent other-worldly God, then this critique posited a real objective solution to the problem, this irreconcilable antinomy of 'God-humanity' in the form of faith in Jesus Christ universally open to all. But again, this effectively makes redundant the organic movement of Heilsgeschichte. By the time of publication in the autumn

---

[60] Thurneysen, *Dostojewski*, p. 45/ET: p. 51.
[61] Heinrich Barth, *Das Problem des Ursprungs in der platonischen Philosophie* (Munich: Christian Kaiser Verlag, 1921), p. 19.
[62] See Barth, *Römerbrief 1*, 1 Kapitel 'Die Nacht' on Romans 1:18-21 'Der Abfall', pp. 24-31.
[63] Walker, 'The Development of Karl Barth's Theology', pp. 75-76.

of 1919 Barth was sufficiently dissatisfied to want to initiate a wholesale rewrite and revision - hence, *Römerbrief 2*.

Römerbrief 2 (1920-21, Published 1922)

During the second half of 1919 we can discern Barth's dissatisfaction with the first edition of *Der Römerbrief* from his correspondence with Thurneysen. This dissatisfaction came to a head in the late summer of 1920. During October 1920, the year following the publication of *Römerbrief 1*, Barth set about the task not just of revising or even redrafting this work, but wholly rewriting - '...the original has been so completely rewritten that it may be claimed that no stone remains in its old place.' [64] The process of rewriting was completed in September 1921. Published in September 1922 this second edition had as profound an impact on the German theological establishment as the first edition had. Why did Barth rewrite *Der Römerbrief*? Both Walker (1963) and McCormack (1995) in examining the reviews of *Römerbrief 1* have shown that the reactions were mostly negative. The reviewers criticized Barth's work for not being in the tradition of an historical-critical commentary, 'still others, shocked by Barth's polemic against religion and the church and repelled by his "pneumatic" exegetical method, brushed the book aside as heretical.' [65] He was criticized for ignoring the work by many German scholars on the historical Jesus - '...Barth speaks of "the Christ", not "Jesus of Nazareth" and says that this is he whom Abraham saw and Plato discussed. Barth was preoccupied with the future, and, like most anti-liberals, uses many biblical terms.' [66] More, they complained that Barth was guilty of tearing down more than building up. Barth was forced to conclude from the reviews that his essential message had been misunderstood. In Barth's own mind the second edition was intended to answer these objections. Rewriting was in order to clarify the essential points he was trying to make. And so in October 1920 Barth commenced the rewriting of his commentary on Paul's Epistle to the Romans.

From our perspective what is important about the period August 1918 (the completion of *Römerbrief 1*) to Autumn 1921 (the completion of the rewrite) is that he read widely, not just theologians and philosophers but the work of artists, novelists, writers who were on the fringe of the church - or who were even atheistic and in opposition to the church. These writers assisted him in forming new ways of expressing his aims better. In this context Von Balthasar commented on *Römerbrief 2* that,

> In the fire of Overbeck, Nietzsche, Dostoevsky and Kierkegaard (and the Reformers...), the gunpowder has been ignited... The second edition is like

---

[64] Barth, *Römerbrief 2*, p. XII/ET: p. 2.
[65] Walker, 'The Development of Karl Barth's Theology', p. 77.
[66] Wilhelm Lowe, 'Noch einmal Barths *Römerbrief*', *Die Christliche Welt* XXXIV (1920), pp. 585-587.

'dynamite' (p.238) coming dangerously close to Nietzsche; it 'revolutionizes religion' (p.237), it is the 'cry and the silence' (p.238). We have now truly fallen into the 'hell of religion' (p.239). We must smell 'the stench of death to the point of death that is wafted from the summits of religion' (p.259). [67]

McCormack:

What makes the style of Romans II distinctive is the tone of anger with which it is written... In later years Barth himself would criticize the theology which he wrote in this phase for its powerful one-sidedness and the almost catastrophic opposition of God and the world, God and humanity, God and the Church. [68]

Der Christ in der Gesellschaft (1919)

The consistent eschatology of *Römerbrief 2*, the use of a plethora of writers to promote in the form of illustrations, can be perceived in an important address from 1919 two years before he completes the rewrite: 'Der Christ in der Gesellschaft' ('The Christian in Society' - hereafter referred to as The Tambach Lecture).[69] In the collapse of conventional politics after the First World War, various political or religious-political groups emerged. In the spring of 1919 a new journal dedicated to the Christian Democrats was formed; likewise a new society was also formed to promote the principles of Christian democracy.[70] The first conference was planned for the autumn of 1919 at Tambach, in Thuringia. The one factor that united the disparate people at the conference was an interest in religious socialism. 'The Christian in Society' was the title that was given to Barth by those organising the conference, however, he challenged them by asserting that we are not the Christian in society - it is Christ that is. Christ is different from us, but is Christ in us? This question recurs consistently throughout the lecture. In many ways Barth is attempting to secularize Christ. Barth asserts (reasserts) the realism of God, the utter difference between humanity and God; further that God cannot be used for human purposes. Therefore he criticizes as vain such concepts as religious socialism.[71] So what was the role of a Christian in society? In part, says Barth, the role is to seek to discern the movements of God in society, to find the meaning hidden beneath

---

[67] Von Balthasar, *The Theology of Karl Barth*, p. 68. The page numbers in parentheses are Von Balthasar referring to Barth, *Römerbrief 2*.

[68] McCormack, *Karl Barth's Critically Realistic Dialectical Theology*, p. 244.

[69] 'Der Christ in der Gesellschaft' (often referred to as The Tambach Lecture) address written and delivered at *Die religiös-soziale Konferenz* (The Conference on Religion and Social Relations) held at Tambach on the 25 September 1919: Karl Barth, 'Der Christ in der Gesellschaft', in Barth, *Das Wort Gottes und die Theologie*, pp. 33-69; ET: Karl Barth, 'The Christian in Society', in Barth, *The Word of God and the Word of Man*, pp. 272-327.

[70] The journal *Die christliche Demokrat: Wochenblatt für das evangelische Haus* founded by Otto Herpel, was first issued on 6 April 1919.

[71] Barth, 'Der Christ in der Gesellschaft', pp. 35-36/ET: p. 276. Barth refers to 'christliche-soziale', ' evangelisch-soziale' and ' religiös-soziale'.

the surface. Barth is tempted to assert that the social democrat movement is the parable of the kingdom of God. McCormack:

> Judged from the standpoint of its significance for an understanding of Barth's theological development, the Tambach lecture showed that Barth's thought was in transition, though he had clearly not yet departed from the conception of eschatology which had governed Romans I.
>
> What is new is the greater emphasis on the notion of analogy, which testifies to the fact that Barth's realism is by now making itself felt in a more consistent way in his ethics. Gone is the appeal to idealistic ethics in the 'confused situation' [72]

In The Tambach Lecture we have the first real use of Barth quoting relatively secular writers to support what he is arguing - illustratively. This is an indication of how his thinking is developing, but also of his openness to a wide range of sources.

Dostoevsky is one of a group of writers used. Compared to what we will see later in *Römerbrief 2*, this is a relatively small group of major sources: Friedrich Naumann features prominently because Barth is writing only a matter of weeks after discovering the writings of this religious socialist.[73] Socrates provides much for his critique of the pretensions and self-importance of religious socialism. Plato is important much in the same way that Platonism featured in *Römerbrief 1*. Tolstoy is used negatively, that is, to give an example of what he considers something should not be; these comments are entirely critical of the writer - however, this has the effect of pushing Barth's thinking in a particular direction (Goethe is used predominantly in the same manner). Then we find Dostoevsky used critically (that is, some references favourably, one not); likewise Hermann Kutter. Nietzsche continues to figure in his thinking because of Barth's respect for the man's honesty and how Nietzsche could cut through much of the cultural accretions of nineteenth-century German liberal neo-Protestantism to focus on the essence, as Barth saw it, of the Gospel. Kierkegaard has a brief mention - it is important to remember that it is at this time, 1919, Barth is beginning to discover Kierkegaard. Kant relates to Barth's use of Plato, but there is one other name - the Norwegian playwright, Ibsen - that crops up again in Barth's thinking at the time of the writing of *Römerbrief 2*. What does Barth have to say about Dostoevsky, and what does this tell us about his developing understanding? There are three main references/uses of Dostoevsky. In the first reference, Barth comments about the nature of the parables in the synoptic Gospels and how they are simply set in the real world, the accustomed earthly life that ordinary, everyday people live -

---

[72] McCormack, *Karl Barth's Critically Realistic Dialectical Theology*, p. 201.
[73] Barth published an article about Friedrich Naumann and Christoph Blumhardt both of whom died in the summer of 1919: Karl Barth, 'Vergangenheit und Zukunft (Friedrich Naumann und Christoph Blumhardt)', *Neuer Freier Aargauer* (1919), pp. 204-205.

unlike the religious myths of India, or Aesop's fables. Barth then continues,

> ...and then follows regularly a picture of social life which in itself discloses nothing heavenly whatever. Not the moral world, nor the Christian, nor any theoretical and postulated world is described, but simply the world as one finds it ...It is all so commonplace ... just like the actual life of people, and for that very reason brimful of eschatology! For this is not storyteller's technique nor literary form, but content itself, full of meaning, with a form which issues from an inner necessity. Here we have the same free survey and understanding and representation of the actual life of society that distinguishes the novels of Dostoevsky, for example, from the kind in which, as in most of Tolstoy's, we feel ourselves directly preached to.[74]

Barth is using Dostoevsky here to illustrate a criticism of moral, pious religion, even the need to be 'religious', 'mythological' or 'fantastical'. The world in Dostoevsky's novels is not romantic or conventionally religious, like the world of the Gospel parables it is distinguished by its very ordinariness. Barth quotes examples from the Gospel parables at length so as to draw the comparison: 'it is all so commonplace'. Barth also criticizes Tolstoy in comparison to Dostoevsky because the former is portraying a moral message. As we saw earlier, Sonya does not preach to Raskolnikov, she simply bears witness to the Gospel truth through the story of Lazarus' resurrection. She exerts pressure on Raskolnikov through this witness, she requests that he publicly confess his crime, but she does not preach to him. For Dostoevsky, an existential Gospel can best be seen in a secular context; this Barth identifies with.

In the second reference we have a warning from Barth about the potential of dualism in Dostoevsky's work. This is a relatively small aside and Barth does not try to justify his accusation, merely throws it out, so to speak, as a way of warning about denying life:

> We shall do better to keep quietly to this Biblical perception of life than to call, or at any rate to call too loudly, for Platonic philosophy or German idealism. This will save us from allowing the denial of life to become a theme in its own right - an error made by some Russian and many Oriental thinkers. We shall not again go back to the fundamental dualism of Dostoevsky.[75]

This third reference focuses on a constant theme in both Thurneysen and Barth's thinking at the time of the writing of *Römerbrief 2*: the paradox of Christlikeness. Barth seriously asked those assembled, whether they truly understood the paradox represented by Prince Myshkin in Dostoevsky's *The Idiot* and how this related to their idea of the Christian in society. That is,

> Why can we work up no indignation against Dostoevsky's daring to make Christ

---

[74] Barth, 'Der Christ in der Gesellschaft', pp. 53-55/ET: p. 305.
[75] Barth, 'Der Christ in der Gesellschaft', p. 58/ET: p. 310.

pass as an idiot in society and the real understanding of him begin with the murderer and the harlot?[76]

This is more than merely illustrative. It represents an element in Barth's thinking that will appear in *Römerbrief 2*. But here in the context of The Tambach Lecture Barth is raising up the downtrodden, the marginalized, the innocent, those who would in all probability be passed over by the religious socialist, the Christian democrats, eager for political and worldly success; and most probably snubbed, avoided, by the religiously pietistic bourgeoisie. What is more, it is the sinners who truly know their plight and recognize this: as do Nastasya and Rogozhin - 'the murderer and the harlot' -in *The Idiot*. The subtlety of this was probably lost on most assembled to hear Barth.

By and large Barth is using Dostoevsky, along with Tolstoy, Nietzsche, Ibsen and Kierkegaard illustratively. This technique continues as the main thrust of his thinking moved towards the rewriting of *Der Römerbrief*.

---

[76] Barth, 'Der Christ in der Gesellschaft', p. 61/ET: p. 315.

CHAPTER 13

Kierkegaard and Dostoevsky

Influences on the Rewriting of *Römerbrief 2*

That theological ideas and reflections, stories and models by Dostoevsky are used by Barth in the rewriting of *Der Römerbrief* is not disputed. Many scholars acknowledge that Dostoevsky's understanding of the *surd*-like nature of sin is important to Barth during the period of the rewrite.[1] We have already established that Dostoevsky influenced Barth's developing understanding of sin and grace in 1915-16. But what are the influences on *Römerbrief 2*? Barth wrote:

> First, and most important: the continued study of Paul himself. My manner of working has enabled me to deal only with portions of the rest of the Pauline literature, but each fresh piece of work has brought with it new light upon the Epistle to the Romans. Secondly: the man Overbeck. Elsewhere, Edward Thurneysen and I have drawn attention, at some length, to the warning addressed by Overbeck to all theologians... Thirdly: closer acquaintance with Plato and Kant. The writings of my brother Heinrich Barth have led me to recognize the importance of these philosophers. I have also paid more attention to what may be culled from the writings of Kierkegaard and Dostoevsky that is of importance for the interpretation of the New Testament. The latter I owe more particularly to hints given me by Edward Thurneysen...[2]

The overarching influence on *Römerbrief 2* is, naturally, the apostle Paul; second is Barth's discovery of Franz Overbeck; thirdly, Barth cites Plato and Kant, then Kierkegaard and Dostoevsky; fourthly, his response to the critical acclaim generated by the first edition (1919). Also, McCormack has shown

---

[1] See Nicolaas Tjepko Bakker, *Der Krisis in der Offenbarung - Karl Barths Hermeneutik, dargestellt an seiner Römerbrief-Auslegung* (Neukirchen-Vluyn: Neukirchener Verlag, 1974), pp. 25-26, 44-45, 73, 77, 104, 108, 128 and 174; see specifically in Bakker's work II. 'Die Zerstörung von Ontologie und Metaphysik, B. Philosophische und theologische Einflüsse, Dostojewski', pp. 100-103. See also Von Balthasar, *The Theology of Karl Barth*, p. 375, and Richard Birch Hoyle, *The Teaching of Karl Barth An Exposition* (London: SCM Press, 1930), p. 55. See on Barth's development and general use of Dostoevsky, McDowell, *Barth's Eschatology Interrogation and Transformations Beyond Tragedy*, pp. 77, 79 n. 90 and 221, and T.F. Torrance, *Karl Barth Biblical and Evangelical Theologian* (Edinburgh: T&T Clark, 1990), p. 10.
[2] Barth, *Römerbrief 2*, pp. XIII-XIV/ET: pp. 3-4.

how Barth understood these influences: 'Careful study of all the possible influences on Barth in this phase (political, cultural and theological) has convinced me that Barth understood himself quite well.'[3] McCormack also notes that although in the English-speaking world the influence of Kierkegaard is considered pre-emptive in the changes leading to *Römerbrief 2* the importance of Kierkegaard is considered somewhat over inflated in European circles.[4] Whether McCormack, Beintker or others are correct is not the point here - that Plato and Kant are more important than Kierkegaard or for that matter Dostoevsky, is correct.

In 1919-20 Barth discovered Overbeck, more pertinently Overbeck's criticism of religion; this is well documented not only by the scholarly tradition but also by Barth himself. Unlike the influence of Kierkegaard or Dostoevsky, Barth did in the case of Overbeck write an essay about his understanding of the man and how his writings had influenced him.[5] Overbeck as an atheist Church historian came to the understanding that Christianity was eschatological or it was nothing - as he was an atheist then it could not be eschatological so, for him, it was nothing (Albert Schweitzer's realization of an eschatological dimension to Christology, from the early years of the twentieth-century also pressed on Barth). Barth admired Overbeck, in particular his intellectual bite, despite the man's atheism. Barth could see that Overbeck had cut through the muddle and the compromise that was inherent in the nineteenth-century Liberal neo-Protestant approach: Overbeck could see that Christianity was not primarily a religion. Therefore Barth's dialectical criticism of religion received an important added input from Overbeck's anti-bourgeois approach.[6] At the

---

[3] McCormack, *Karl Barth's Critically Realistic Dialectical Theology*, p. 216.

[4] McCormack, *Karl Barth's Critically Realistic Dialectical Theology*, pp. 216-217. McCormack is referring to Michael Beitker's assertion that the order of influences cited by Barth in the preface to *Römerbrief 2* is not accidental: the priority is of Plato and Kant over Kierkegaard and Dostoevsky. See Beintker, *Die Dialektik in der 'dialektischen Theologie' Karl Barths*, pp. 222-238; and Spieckermann, *Gotteskenntnis: Ein Beitrag zur Grundfrage der neun Theologie Karl Barths*, p. 109. Questioning the influence of Kierkegaard is Henri Bouillard, *Karl Barth i. Genèse et évolution de la théologie dialectique* (Aubier: Editions Montaigne, 1957), p. 107, and Gerhard Sauter, 'Die "dialektische Theologie" und das Problem der Dialektik in der Theologie', in Gerhard Sauter, *Erwartung und Erfahrung - Predigten, Vortrage und Aufsatze* (Munich: Christian Kaiser Verlag, 1972), p. 126.

[5] Karl Barth, 'Unerledigte Anfragen an die heitige Theologie', in Barth, *Die Theoligie und die Kirche*, pp. 1-26; ET: Karl Barth, 'Unsettled Questions for Theology Today', in Barth, *Theology and Church: Shorter Writings 1920-1928*, pp. 55-73. The posthumous writings of Franz Overbeck (1837-1905), Professor of New Testament and Early Church History University of Basle 1870-1897, were published in 1919 edited from his papers: Franz Overbeck, *Christianity and Culture: Thoughts and Observations on Modern Theology* (ed. Carl Albrecht Bernoulli; Basel: Benno Schwabe, 1919).

[6] See McCormack, *Karl Barth's Critically Realistic Dialectical Theology*, pp. 226-235.

time of writing soon after he had discovered Overbeck's work Barth cites the influence of Overbeck above even that of Plato and Kant, and certainly greater than Kierkegaard and Dostoevsky. But then if he had written an essay on Dostoevsky in 1915/16 he would probably have rated the Russian over all other influences at that time. However, what we do need to look at is the use and influence of Dostoevsky in the rewriting of *Der Römerbrief*, more pertinently the relationship between Kierkegaard and Dostoevsky in *Römerbrief 2*.

Kierkegaard or Dostoevsky

Commenting at his reception of the Sonning Prize in Copenhagen, 19 April 1963, Barth asserted that he discovered Kierkegaard in 1919. He explained that the first book of Kierkegaard he owned was *The Instant*, purchased in 1909 - but he did not remember reading it; he continued, 'He entered my thinking to a more serious and large extent only about 1919, at the critical juncture between the first and second editions of my commentary on Romans, and from that time onwards he appeared in an important role in my literary utterances.'[7] We can identify the novels of Dostoevsky that Barth and Thurneysen read and studied from their correspondence and writings. The same cannot be said with the same degree of certainty for Kierkegaard; this is in part because Barth does not cite works by Kierkegaard to the same degree as he does with Dostoevsky, indeed what we have in Barth's work are phrases from Kierkegaard. McCormack has identified many of these phrases in *Römerbrief 2* and located them in Kierkegaard's work: essentially, Kierkegaard's journals, *Training in Christianity* and *The Moment*. It is difficult to tell whether Barth read other works or not. McCormack comments that, 'Virtually all of the concepts and phrases which assumed an importance in Romans II can be found in *Training in Christianity*: Christ as the paradox; the problem of contemporaneity with Christ; the infinite qualitative distinction; the incarnation as the divine incognito; and the impossibility of direct communication.'[8]

---

[7] Karl Barth, 'Dank und Reverenz', *Evangelische Theologie* 23.7 (1963), p. 339; ET: Karl Barth, 'A Thank You and a Bow: Kierkegaard's Reveille', *Canadian Journal of Theology* 11.1 (1965), p. 4.
[8] McCormack, *Karl Barth's Critically Realistic Dialectical Theology*, p.236 n. 93. See sub-section on Kierkegaard pp. 235-240, referring to Søren Kierkegaard, *Einübung in Christentum* (Erste Fassung; Halle: Fricke, 1878), the first German edition Barth was working from. McCormack: Christ as 'the paradox' (pp. 20, 25 and 57); the problem of 'contemporaneity' with Christ (pp. 56-60); the 'infinite qualitative distinction' (p. 124); the incarnation as the divine 'incognito' (p. 112); and the impossibility of 'direct communication' (pp. 121-128); McCormack's references are to the second German edition: Søren Kierkegaard, *Einübung in Christentum* (Zweite Fassung; Jena: Eugen Diederichs, 1924).

Infinite Qualitative Distinction

Barth commented often that in his mature work that he kept Kierkegaard's phrase infinite qualitative distinction before him always. Indeed, in the preface to *Römerbrief 2* he commented that a prime requirement in terms of method was to identify 'the "inner dialectic of the matter" (innere dialektik der Sache) in the actual words of the text' [9] therefore when accused of imposing his own system on the text (in this case of *Römerbrief 1*, by his critics) he continued, 'My reply is that if I have a system, it is limited to a recognition of what Kierkegaard called the "infinite qualitative distinction" (unendlichen qualitativen Unterschied) between time and eternity, and to my regarding this as possessing negative as well as positive significances.' [10] The influence of the Danish philosopher Søren Kierkegaard on Barth is philosophical. For example, this use of the phrase inner dialectic of the matter or comments about a dialectic of antinomies that stand over and against each other, unresolved; or Kierkegaard's use of *eristis*, that is, a dialectic of existence.[11] This influence is well established and accepted by the Barthian scholarly tradition, as is the appropriation of Kierkegaard's phrase infinite qualitative distinction between humanity and God to assert the wholly otherness of God. For example, in terms of the phrase, infinite qualitative difference/distinction, the first English translation by Walter Lowrie[12] offers the following: '...endless yawning difference...';[13] '...qualitative infinite emphasis...';[14] '...it is the false invention of human sympathy which forgets the infinite difference between God and man...';[15] 'As God-man he is qualitatively different from every other man...';[16] '...infinite yawning difference which he posits between God and the emperor';[17] '...infinite distinction...'.[18] However, Barth spoke of this wholly otherness of God as early as 1915. Therefore this concept is not uniquely the result of the influence of Kierkegaard. A reading of Kierkegaard sharpened up this concept/theme; Barth may have appropriated the phrase infinite qualitative difference from Kierkegaard, but the concept is traceable, as we saw earlier, in Barth's thinking to as early as 1915 in his address 'Kriegszeit und Gottesreich': 'Welt bleibt Welt ... Daß Gott Gott ist'. From what we have seen already of the

---

[9] Barth, *Römerbrief 2*, p. 12/ET: p. 10.
[10] Barth, *Römerbrief 2*, p. 12/ET: p. 10.
[11] See Terry L. Cross, *Dialectic in Karl Barth's Doctrine of God* (Issues in Systematic Theology 7; New York and Washington: Peter Lang, 2001), p. 70, and McCormack, *Karl Barth's Critically Realistic Dialectical Theology*, p. 235.
[12] Søren Kierkegaard, *Training in Christianity* (trans. Walter Lowrie; London: Oxford University Press, 1941).
[13] Kierkegaard, *Training in Christianity*, p. 67.
[14] Kierkegaard, *Training in Christianity*, p. 72.
[15] Kierkegaard, *Training in Christianity*, p. 139.
[16] Kierkegaard, *Training in Christianity*, p. 142.
[17] Kierkegaard, *Training in Christianity*, p. 169.
[18] Kierkegaard, *Training in Christianity*, p. 170.

novels and theology of Dostoevsky, we can actually assert that there is something of an infinite qualitative distinction or difference between humanity and God. This was clear in the theological anthropology of Raskolnikov, the importance of faith in Sonya, but also in the fallen people in *The Dream of the Ridiculous Man*. Dostoevsky across all his middle period and mature novels paints a picture of this infinite qualitative distinction/difference between humanity and God. But when Barth discovers Kierkegaard (in 1919) he finds a Christian philosopher who expresses succinctly and with brevity in only three words, infinite qualitative distinction, what Dostoevsky does using over one million words in his novels: a distinction that is infinite in its qualification, but not said in so few words as Kierkegaard.

An example of this is given in *Römerbrief 2* when Barth is commenting on Romans 9:19-20. Barth is dealing once again with the rebellion characterized by *eritis sicut deus*, the arrogance at the heart of sin. Barth opens with the observation that the rebel overlooks the infinite qualitative distinction between God and humanity ('unendlichen qualitativen Unterschied zwischen Gott und Mensch'[19]); such a rebel believes that humanity can argue with God, define the good better than God, Human will in this instance regards itself the near equal of God, if God exists. The rebel is therefore the objector:

> The objector overlooks the infinite qualitative distinction between God and humanity. He proceeds as though God and humanity were two things. He speaks of humanity as though they were God's partners, junior partners perhaps, but nevertheless competent to conduct an argument with Him. ...But this is preposterous.[20]

It is God's *aseity* that confronts; thus Barth continues:

> Between human responsibility and the freedom of God there is no direct observable relation, but only the indirect, underivable, unexecutable relation between time and eternity, between the creature and the Creator. The freedom of God confronts humanity neither as a mechanism imposed upon them from outside nor as their own active and creative life. The freedom of God is the pure and primal Ursprung of all ... the Decision, by which they stand or fall.[21]

The turning from this Promethean rebellion is then stated illustratively and explicitly in the character of Rodion Romanovich Raskolnikov - the turning to fear God once again. If not, the path as shown by Dostoevsky is all to clear:

> It is precisely the one who respects God as God who will have no occasion to object, for he will neither fear nor desire the dissolution of his responsibility: such a man will become NOT insane, NOT immoral, NOT a criminal, NOT a suicide. ... rather, like the murderer Raskolnikov in Dostoevsky's novel, will take it as a warning monument to the possibility of a final misunderstanding of the command

---

[19] Barth, *Römerbrief 2*, p. 371/ET: p. 355, on Romans 9 'The Tribulation of the Church', Romans 9:14-29, 'The God of Esau'.
[20] Barth, *Römerbrief 2*, pp. 371-372/ET: pp. 355-356.
[21] Barth, *Römerbrief 2*, p. 372/ET: p. 356.

that humanity should fear and love God above all things.[22] (Barth's emphasis)

Barth therefore starts with the Kierkegaardian phrase, infinite qualitative distinction, which causes the tribulation in humanity; he then outlines the psychology of this, drawing further into Dostoevsky's theological anthropology, then to conclude explicitly with Raskolnikov as an illustration. God's *aseity* and the forgiveness of sins proffered through Christ do not absolve Raskolnikov of individual responsibility. The Krisis that bedevilled Raskolnikov was caused by his promethean rebellion in the face of this Kierkegaardian infinite qualitative distinction. Thus the discovery of Kierkegaard sharpened up Barth's realization of this distinction or difference (Unterschied), seen in the biblically charged world of *Crime and Punishment*.

Dialectic and an Interpretation of the New Testament

The assumption often is that the influence of Kierkegaard has been categorically identified, itemized and laid out. For instance, although Barthian dialectic predominates as a method in *Römerbrief 2* and this is often attributed essentially to Kierkegaard, if we press the tradition (Cross, McCormack, Torrance, etc.) the following comment is typical: '...Kierkegaard's influence is scattered all over the second edition ... Kierkegaard is a major factor in Barth's change.'[23] What does McCormack have to say on the influence of Kierkegaard?

> It is beyond question that Kierkegaardian language and concepts play such a significant role in Romans II. But what does such usage tell us about the degree of Kierkegaard's influence on Barth? The truth is ... most of the building blocks needed to produce the characteristic shape of dialectic in Romans II were already in place before the encounter with Kierkegaard...[24]

McCormack is supported in this by the German scholar Michael Beintker.[25] McCormack goes on to show successfully that the root influence on Barth's use of dialectic lay in the *Ursprungsphilosophie* of his brother, Heinrich.

> ...The *diastasis* motif, giving rise as it does in Heinrich Barth's philosophy to the idea that the Ursprung grounds human knowledge precisely by negating its prior attainments, goes a long way in explaining the predominance in the second Romans of those 'complementary dialectics' in which two members stand over against one another in a relation of contradiction or antithesis. The reception of Kierkegaard thus fell on already prepared soil...[26]

It is not without significance that in the preface to *Römerbrief 2* Barth treats

---

[22] Barth, *Römerbrief 2*, pp. 371-372/ET: pp. 355-356.
[23] Cross, *Dialectic in Karl Barth's Doctrine of God*, p. 71.
[24] McCormack, *Karl Barth's Critically Realistic Dialectical Theology*, p. 237.
[25] Beintker, *Die Dialektik in der 'dialektischen Theologie' Karl Barths*, p. 233.
[26] Thurneysen to Barth, 28 October 1920, Barth and Thurneysen, *Briefwechsel Band 1 1913-1921*, p. 237.

13. Kierkegaard and Dostoevsky

Kierkegaard and Dostoevsky equally; but further, that the nature of their influence is not necessarily in terms of the philosophical idealism of Plato or Kant; no, the influence, according to Barth's own words was in their '...importance for the interpretation of the New Testament.'[27] And *Der Römerbrief* was in the final analysis about the interpretation of a New Testament book. Barth also comments in a late essay, from 1956, about how Kierkegaard and Dostoevsky were read by him and Thurneysen as a commentary on the message of the Kingdom of God, initially learned from the Blumhardts.[28] Kierkegaard and Dostoevsky were to provide an example of the life of the Gospel. Not a philosophical analysis - but an illustration of human existence under the Gospel (though there is still a philosophical influence - in the form of existentialism). There is what we may call a comparative analogy of ideas with regard to the influence of the novels and theology of Dostoevsky, and the writings of Kierkegaard. Likewise, the influence of Kierkegaard and Dostoevsky permeates the entire reworking that resulted in *Römerbrief 2* - for example, the influence that Dostoevsky's critique of religion had on Barth's 'interpretation of the New Testament'.[29] It is important to distinguish from the standpoint of theological methodology between a general and specific (or primary) influence from Dostoevsky at this time (the primary influence of Dostoevsky on Barth's doctrine of sin is traceable, as we have seen to 1915-16). For example, it may be possible to conclude that there is a general influence from Dostoevsky that is scattered all over the second edition of *Der Römerbrief*, an influence that permeates Barth's thinking in the same way that Kierkegaard's philosophical writings permeated his thought. This is borne out by the fact that Barth places the two of them together in the same sentence in his preface to the second edition. Then there are specific examples of where Barth cites Dostoevsky in *Römerbrief 2*. For example, general references to Dostoevsky[30] as distinct from specific references to the novels[31]. There are then specific references to characters and events within novels, where Dostoevsky is used as a vehicle for the transmission of Barth's theological beliefs.[32]

---

[27] Thurneysen to Barth, 28 October 1920, Barth and Thurneysen, *Briefwechsel Band 1 1913-1921*, p. 237.
[28] Barth, 'Die Menschlichkeit Gottes', p. 6/ET: pp. 40-41.
[29] Barth, *Römerbrief 2*, pp. XIII-XIV/ET: pp. 3-4.
[30] See Barth, *Römerbrief 2*, p. 46/ET: p. 67, p. 101/ET: p. 117, p. 106/ET: p. 122, p. 128/ET: p. 141, pp. 219-220/ET: p. 220, p. 240/ET: p. 238, p. 255/ET: p. 252, p. 452/ET: p. 428 and p. 532/ET: p. 505.
[31] See Barth, *Römerbrief 2*, pp. 528-529/ET: pp. 501-502 (on *The Brothers Karamazov*), p. 370/ET: p. 354 (on *The Idiot*) and p. 372/ ET: p. 356 (on *Crime and Punishment*).
[32] See Barth, *Römerbrief 2*, p. 309/ET: p. 300 (Ivan Karamazov), p. 256/ET: p. 253 (Ivan Karamazov, Luther and the devil), p. 346/ET: p. 332, p. 412/ET: p. 393, p. 504/ET: p. 479, pp. 532-533/ET: pp. 504-595, p. 548/ET: p. 520 (The Legend of the Grand Inquisitor) and p. 372/ET: p. 356 (Rodion Romanovich Raskolnikov).

A Criticism of Religion in the Service of the Gospel

A critique of religion leading to an orthodox understanding of sin and grace was the primary influence of Dostoevsky on Barth from 1915. This influence is also dialectical. Barth develops this criticism of religion in the service of the Gospel further during his reading in 1918-1921. To Dostoevsky is added Kierkegaard's criticism of institutionalized Christianity, then as we have seen, his discovery of the posthumously published work of Overbeck. The use of negation, apophatic theology, in *Römerbrief 2* continues on from the first edition but is much more acerbic.

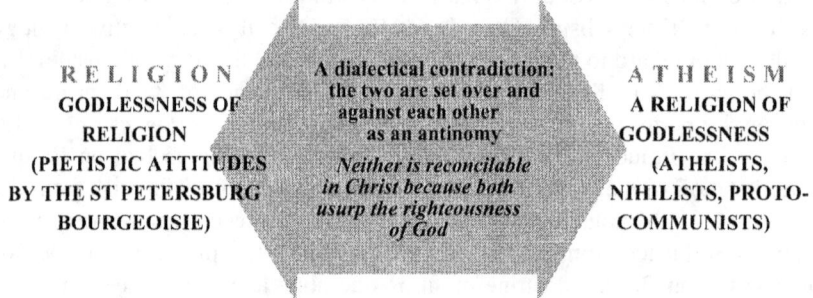

Figure 5 A Religion-Atheism Dialectic

A powerful dialectical criticism of religion occurs in *Crime and Punishment* and *The Idiot* between the godlessness of religion manifested in the church attendance by the St Petersburg bourgeoisie and a religion of godlessness in the form of atheists, nihilists, proto-communists (see Figure 5 A Religion-Atheism Dialectic, above). For example, in *Crime and Punishment*, Pulkheria Alexandrovna (Raskolnikov's mother) balks at Sonya who is forced to prostitute herself so as to feed her younger brothers and sisters, yet is happy for her daughter, Dunya, to marry the middle-aged Luzhin where there is no love, but simply lust, vanity and status on the part of Luzhin - and money for Pulkheria Alexandrovna who is poor after her husband's premature death. At least Sonya is honest about her plight as a prostitute - forced into the role through abject poverty and destitution.

Madame Yepanchina (in *The Idiot*) represents for Dostoevsky the hypocrisy of institutionalized religion. Here a dialectic is set up between the proud piety of, Elizaveta Prokofievna Yepanchina (the wife of General Ivan Fyodorovich Yepanchin), and the unconscious relatively innocent holiness of the actions of Prince Myshkin. For example, when a group of nihilistic proto-communist atheists descend on the Yepanchin's country villa, where Myshkin is recovering from an epileptic seizure, Elizaveta Prokofievna is disgraced by them - but also by Myshkin's refusal to reject them, expel them; worse, he gives in to the demands for money from one of them who claims he is vaguely related to

Myshkin. Myshkin successfully disproves the claim of kinship but still gives him some money. The entire scene is reminiscent of the story in Luke's Gospel of the Pharisee who invited Jesus to eat with him in his house.[33] Whilst Jesus is eating with the Pharisee - a meal not given out of generosity but to try to find out what this man Jesus was about - a woman who is reputed to be a prostitute enters, '...she stood behind him at his feet, weeping, and began to bathe his feet with her tears and to dry them with her hair. Then she continued kissing his feet and anointing them'. The Pharisee is outraged - but Jesus answers with a parable that exposes the self-righteousness of the Pharisee and how great repentance and humility will receive great forgiveness. Jesus does not rebuke her and send her away - he forgives her sins, which has the Pharisee's guests falling around in shock at the audacity of this man Jesus. In Dostoevsky's Russian New Testament Luke 7:47 is marked with a pencil in the margin and the last sentence is marked 'N.B.' (shown here italicized): 'Therefore, I tell you, her sins, which were many, have been forgiven; hence she has shown great love. *But the one to whom little is forgiven, loves little.*'

The self-righteous indignation of the Pharisee is analogous with Madame Yepanchina's vocal criticism of both the nihilists who have visited and Myshkin for not rejecting them.[34] There is, therefore, a dialectical tension between the nihilists and Madame Yepanchina; both have elements of truth but are a long way from God - this dialectical tension can only be resolved in God. Myshkin tries, but fails because he is human and not divine; he may be Christlike but he is not the Christ. The subtlety of this criticism was not lost on Barth and Thurneysen. Dostoevsky saw God and faith as the solution - applying a healthy scepticism in the form of a *yes-no* dialectic to the church. He suspected the power and authority of the church but saw the value of the church, that is, its temporal necessity. However, both Barth and Thurneysen saw Dostoevsky's most fearsome attack on the church and religion in the form of the demonic creation Ivan Karamazov and his prose poem The Grand Inquisitor, which we will examined in the chapter 16.

It is important to remember that Kierkegaard was also criticising religion in the form of institutionalized Christianity in Denmark around the same time that Dostoevsky was languishing in a Siberian prison camp in the middle years of the nineteenth-century (though they were unknown to each other). Kierkegaard wrote to show what it meant to be a Christian, which he saw as being very different from a 'name-Christian' in the Danish state church. In theological terms he rejected an over-intellectualist understanding of faith (indeed much of his agenda was to contradict Hegelian philosophy/theology) focussing on the role of ethical decisions, and the point at which faith transcends human culture. His most profound attack on the established church centred on the way it had

---

[33] Luke 7:36-50.
[34] Dostoevsky, *The Idiot*, pt. 2 chps. 7-9, pp. 76-111.

sought to accommodate revelation to human desires: he attacked this interpretation of Christianity as 'the system', particularly in *The Philosophical Fragments* (1844) and *Concluding Unscientific Postscript* (1846). In *Training in Christianity* (1850) Kierkegaard's criticism of institutionalized Christianity is predominantly dialectical; a dialectic that is often seen as Socratic, relying on an indirect question and answer dialogue.[35] Such a dialectic does not in itself recognize the absolute (God), but it does point the way for faith and worship, and as such does serve to criticize religion when it fails to focus on the supreme transcendent God in faith. There is a strong religion-atheism dialectic in the work of Dostoevsky, also perceivable in the theological thinking of Barth and Thurneysen in the immediate post-First World War period: this is a dialectical contradiction, the two are set over and against each other as an antinomy, neither is reconcilable in Christ because both usurp God's righteousness.

The Nature of the Influence of Kierkegaard and Dostoevsky

A criticism of religion in the service of the Gospel is therefore the leading influence of Dostoevsky at the time of the rewriting of *Der Römerbrief*. But then we may also assert that whereas the leading influence from Kierkegaard is to be seen in the particularly Barthian *denkform* of dialectic used at the time of the rewriting of *Der Römerbrief* there is also a critique of religion in Kierkegaard's writings that influences Barth. The influence of Kierkegaard and Dostoevsky is not as one sided as most scholars have assumed. If we are to examine the general and specific influences of Dostoevsky on Barth we must also take into account the influence of Kierkegaard.

Primarily Kierkegaard's influence is in a specific form of dialectic, which subtly alters the already emerging denkform of dialectic in Barth's theology (as evidenced by *Römerbrief 1*) and the early sermons/lectures, but there is also an influence from Kierkegaard's criticism of religion (in the form of institutionalized Christianity). This criticism of religion is at the heart of the influence of Dostoevsky, but it is also fair to assert that there is a dialectical influence here as well - in the form of a dialectic of 'dynamic tension' that we have seen already in Dostoevsky's work. Although there is mention of specific Dostoevsky novels as well as specific characters by Barth in *Römerbrief 2* and likewise Barth makes use of the theology that surrounds the belief system of such protagonists as Ivan Fyodorovich Karamazov there are also general theological themes to be analysed. The influence/effect of Kierkegaard is well researched by Barthian scholars and although it is Dostoevsky that is the object

---

[35] Kierkegaard, *Training in Christianity*, pp. 67-72, 139-142 and 169-173. See also Søren Kierkegaard, *Philosophical Fragments: Johannes Climacus* (trans. Howard V. Hong and Edna H. Kong; New York: Princeton University Press, 1985), and Søren Kierkegaard, *Concluding Unscientific Postscript to Philosophical Fragments* (trans. Howard V. Hong and Edna H. Kong; New York: Princeton University Press, 1992).

of this book (or more pertinently the effect of the encounter with the work of Dostoevsky on Barth), it is not really possible to separate the two: Barth did, in the final analysis, place Kierkegaard and Dostoevsky together in the same phrase in the preface to *Römerbrief 2*.

What does this tell us about Barth's relationship with Kierkegaard and Dostoevsky? None of this denies the effect, illustrative or otherwise, of the encounter with Kierkegaard in the period 1919-21. But we need to note three important points:

First: that the *denkform* of dialectic was already well established in Barth (primarily from the influence of his brother, Heinrich) prior to the encounter with Kierkegaard; and that in the same way that Kierkegaard sees an acceptance of the paradoxical antinomies of the Gospel as a necessary step to faith, likewise Barth moves from the critically realistic dialectical theology (characterized by an acceptance of paradox, dialectic, negation, the *via dialectica* that establishes him as a theologian of rank) to the mature work of *The Church Dogmatics* based on the *analogia fidei* (but still dialectical to a degree). Barth moves on from the *via dialectica* in the same way that Kierkegaard expected someone to move beyond the acceptance of paradox and logical contradiction to faith, a faith that absolved, to a degree, these antinomies.[36]

Second: Kierkegaard's effect on Barth was to a degree illustrative. Kierkegaard's writings provided him, as did those of Dostoevsky, with an illustration of life under the Gospel - an existential life characterized by movement, movement either towards God or (as is the case of many of the fallen and evil characters in Dostoevsky's writings) away from God. As the individual moved towards God, being reconciled by Christ, s/he encountered seemingly paradoxical contradictions in the Gospel and in their own belief system (again this is very true in Dostoevsky's novels). This will seem paradoxical, an apparent contradiction, because a paradox is the result of an encounter with a reality, which the conceptual structure of our minds are inadequate to deal with. Paradoxes are to a degree an illustration of human epistemic limitation.

Third: these conclusions imply that any hard and fast, definitive definitions of the influence of Kierkegaard must now be seen as relative. Both Kierkegaard and Dostoevsky provided an illustration of life under the Gospel and as such were an aid to Barth in the interpretation of the New Testament. The influence of Kierkegaard cannot be seen as categorically identified, itemized and laid out, in effect unique from other influences on Barth during the rewriting of *Der Römerbrief*.

---

[36] See Alastair McKinnon, 'Barth's Relation to Kierkegaard: Some Further Light', *Canadian Journal of Theology* 13.1 (1967), pp. 31-41, and Cornelio Fabro, 'Faith and Reason in Kierkegaard's Dialectic', in H. A. Johnson and N. Thulstrup (eds.), *A Kierkegaard Critique* (New York: Harper and Brothers, 1962), p. 182.

To summarize: Barth's criticism of religion in the service of the Gospel received impetus from Dostoevsky (1915 on), then from Kierkegaard (1919 on), but the overarching influence on the acerbic critique of religion in *Römerbrief 2* is Overbeck (early 1920 on): hence the illustrative nature of the use of Dostoevsky and Kierkegaard in *Römerbrief 2*. Barth did not rely slavishly upon Kierkegaard; neither was he the original source of much of Barth's dialectic/paradoxical language. Barth used Kierkegaardian terminology because his dialectical method was close enough to Barth's own developing *via dialectica* to be supported, reinforced by Kierkegaard above all in the phrase, infinite qualitative distinction. What is of particular importance is that Kierkegaard's method opposed Hegel's - and so did Barth's. This is particularly so as Barth's own dialectic (rooted as it was in the influence of his brother, Heinrich), was, relatively, a pre-enlightenment dialectic - that is, distinct from Kant and Hegel, essentially in the Socratic mould. Kierkegaard's conception of an infinite qualitative difference between time and eternity, between humanity and God was in many ways similar to Barth's understanding of old history and new history in *Römerbrief 1*; and also Kierkegaardian talk of an existential leap of faith, the risk of making a decision to live for God, resonated with the polemic that was emerging in *Römerbrief 1* and was to be clearer in *Römerbrief 2*. Along with the use of paradox when referring to the incarnation was talk of God as incognito in Jesus Christ - all this essentially fitted in with Barth's own developing theological position. Barth at this time was still seeking a way forward, distancing himself from the liberal theological heritage he had been trained in. *Römerbrief 1* was receiving critical acclaim but he was still seeking a way forward with theological method. Kierkegaard (and also, as we shall see, Dostoevsky) pointed the way to a great extent because they were outsiders - outside of the cultural norms of nineteenth-century institutionalized Christianity. This outsiderness was to be important in his reforming of theological method.

CHAPTER 14

Dostoevsky and *Römerbrief 2*

The Nature of the Evidence

The sources and influences in *Römerbrief 2* represent a wide variety of sources both ecclesial and secular. We have seen an example of this method already in The Tambach Lecture. These sources were by and large illustrative - Dostoevsky amongst others. There are, as we have encountered, many references to Dostoevsky not only in correspondence but also in essays/addresses and of course in *Der Römerbrief*. During the period 1915 to 1925 these references point to a formative influence - that is the period of Barth and Thurneysen's theological *Wendung und Retraktation*, through to the lecture series delivered at Göttingen. During this period we have seen how both Barth and Thurneysen are receptive not only to the influence of Dostoevsky but other sources as well. From 1922 Barth starts to distance himself from Dostoevsky as he reads in-depth in the Reformed tradition and the Reformed Confessions. Therefore, by contrast, from the mid-1920s Barth speaks/writes reflectively about the influence of Dostoevsky (as in 'Der römische Katholizismus als Frage an die protestantische Kirche', 1928). Such evidence is as important as, for instance, the correspondence from August 1915. We have also drawn on reflective comments from, for example, the 1956 essay *Die Menschlichkeit Gottes*[1] and the crucial comments both Barth and Thurneysen made about the influence of Dostoevsky (amongst others) in the seventieth birthday volumes that each produced for the other in the late 1950s.[2] Both these formative and reflective comments were important pieces of evidence in the identification of the year August 1915 to August 1916 as the point of primary influence of Dostoevsky on Barth.

The Content and Spread of the References to Dostoevsky and Others in *Römerbrief 2*: Sources Secular and Ecclesial

If we analyse the sources/references in *Römerbrief 2*, that is, arrive at statistics representing the various sources used by Barth in support of his aims in *Römerbrief 2*, we find much that affects how we perceive the influence of

---

[1] Barth, 'Die Menschlichkeit Gottes', pp. 40-41.
[2] Thurneysen, *Antwort - Festschrift zum 70 Geburtstag von Karl Barth*.

Dostoevsky and others. In all there are over one hundred significant references by Barth to writers whom he uses illustratively; these references also show evidence that even when the illustration/use is negative, this writer or artist has the effect of subtly pushing Barth's thinking in a particular direction. Broadly speaking, these sources/references are in two groups: artists, writers and philosophers in one group, references to theologians, church historians and pastors in the other. The first group is representative of people who are secular, or are considered the laity; the second group, ecclesial (though in the first group we find a Christian philosopher, whereas in the second an atheist church historian!) The dividing principle across the two groups is essentially that the first group are people who are not employed as religious professionals; in the second group we find religious professionals, ecclesially employed in either a specific or general sense. The first group represents 61 references to people who are secular or laity; the second group represents 42 references to people who are religious professionals (see Figure 6 The Content and Spread of the References to Dostoevsky and Others in *Römerbrief 2* - Sources Secular and Ecclesial, opposite).

It is of no surprise considering the criticism of religion that has, in many ways, driven Barth's theological *Wendung und Retraktation* over the previous seven to eight years, that the majority of sources/references are in this first group. It is also of no surprise that considering Barth's stated aim that the church and theologians, especially in Germany, had misunderstood his aim in writing *Römerbrief 1* and therefore he wanted to speak louder and more forcefully in the second edition, that he should, therefore, draw to a greater extent from this first group - those who were not religious professionals. This reflects what we found had impressed Barth from Hermann Kutter, that 'the sphere of God's power really is greater than the sphere of the church and that from time to time it has pleased God, and still pleases him, to warn and to comfort his church through the figures and the events of secular world history.'[3]

In the first group the majority of people are from the late eighteenth- through nineteenth-centuries (Dostoevsky, Kierkegaard, Nietzsche, Kant, Tolstoy, Rousseau and Schiller); the remaining references are to people from the fifteenth- and sixteenth-centuries (Grünewald and Michelangelo) or from Greek philosophy (Plato and Socrates). This does not necessarily show the true level of influence that can be attributed to Plato - or more pertinently, Platonism, or platonic concepts, in *Römerbrief 2*. In the second group again we find the majority of sources are nineteenth/early twentieth-century (Overbeck, the Blumhardts, Kutter, Schleiermacher, Feuerbach, Strauss and Tröltsch), then four leading writers from the Reformation (Luther, Erasmus, Calvin, Zwingli);

---

[3] Barth speaking in an interview with H. Fischer-Barnicol in 1964, quoted in Busch, *Karl Barths Lebenslauf*, p. 88/ET: p. 76.

14. *Dostoevsky and Römerbrief 2* 173

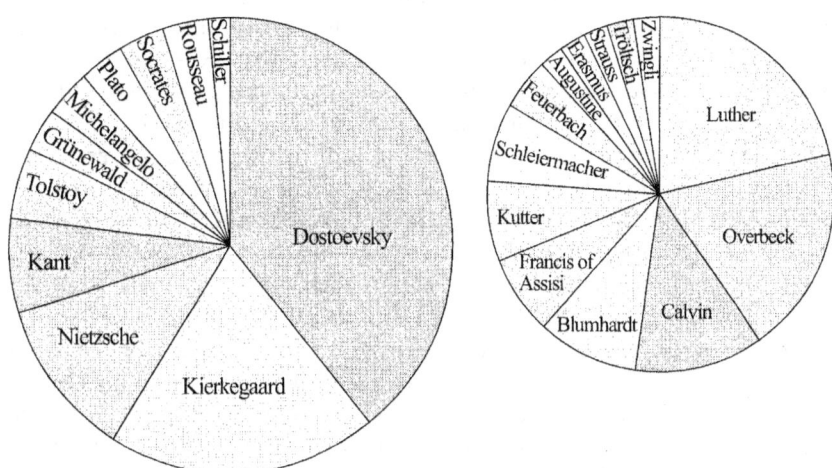

References to artists, writers and philosophers in *Römerbrief 2* : 61 references		References to theologians, church historians and pastors in *Römerbrief 2* : 42 references	
Dostoevsky	24 references	Luther	9 references
Kierkegaard	12 references	Overbeck	8 references
Nietzsche	7 references	Calvin	5 references
Kant	4 references	Blumhardt	4 references
Tolstoy	3 references	Francis of Assisi	3 references
Grünewald	2 references	Kutter	3 references
Michelangelo	2 references	Schleiermacher	3 references
Plato	2 references	Feuerbach	2 references
Socrates	2 references	Augustine	1 reference
Rousseau	2 references	Erasmus	1 reference
Schiller	1 references	Strauss	1 reference
		Tröltsch	1 reference
		Zwingli	1 reference

Figure 6 The Content and Spread of the References to Dostoevsky and Others in *Römerbrief 2* - Sources Secular and Ecclesial

In the second edition of *Der Römerbrief* (1922) there are over 100 references to other writers. These references are sometimes illustrative but behind the inference is an idea that changed Barth's thinking or illustrated a point he was making. These works press on Barth's thinking during the period of the rewriting of *Der Römerbrief* and are represented in the text of *Römerbrief 2*. These sources/references are in two groups: artists, writers and philosophers in the first group (people who are secular/lay); theologians, church historians and pastors in the second group (ecclesially employed - i.e. religious professionals). The two pie charts above show graphically the relationship between these two groups and the sub-division of sources within; these are shown proportionately: the first of the two pie charts is mathematically relative to the second, as 61 is to 42.

then we find Augustine and Francis of Assisi (essentially, Patristic and Medieval). Although Barth in his theological *Wendung und Retraktation* was essentially working against and away from nineteenth-century theology and philosophy, in order to refute nineteenth-century liberal neo-Protestantism he draws, in the main, from eighteenth- and nineteenth-century writers. Whether Christian or atheist these individuals are valuable to Barth because they were either prophets outside of the bourgeois control of the church (Kierkegaard, Dostoevsky, and to a degree, Kant); or they were self-confessed atheists who could cut through the pretence of liberal neo-Protestant theology/ecclesiology (Nietzsche, Feuerbach, Overbeck). Barth's genius is to use these writers, take what they have said and use it to refute experiential-based religion, or the stifling hypocrisy, as Barth and Thurneysen saw it, of the church of their day. Almost a quarter of these references to artists, writers and philosophers, also theologians, church historians and pastors, are to Dostoevsky - twenty-four out of one hundred and three references ($^{24}/_{103}$ - this does not include general allusions say to a character or theme from a novel that does not then use the reference to make a point). Dostoevsky is used explicitly to a greater extent than Kierkegaard or any other writer/artist. Likewise the number of explicit references to material from Dostoevsky far exceeds those to Luther, and Calvin. Indeed, over one-third of these references/sources are to, and drawn from, Dostoevsky and Kierkegaard.

In *Römerbrief 2* there are some twenty-four references to Dostoevsky the man, his novels or characters within the books, or the theological beliefs represented by his stories. These references are sometimes illustrative but behind the inference is an idea that changed Barth's thinking - by and large, this influence is on the development of his theological anthropology underpinning his understanding of the relationship of sin and grace between humanity and God; but there is also his realization of the dangers of socialism/communism. These two categories are from the dialectical critique of religion that is evident in Dostoevsky's work, and as such complement Barth's own criticism of religion. These references to Dostoevsky can be divided into three sub-groups that will form the remaining chapters: chapter fifteen theological anthropology; chapter sixteen a criticism of church-religion; chapter seventeen the paradox of Christlikeness.

With regard to the references to Dostoevsky in *Römerbrief 2* (see Figure 7 Dostoevsky and *Römerbrief 2*, opposite), half refer to Dostoevsky's last novel, *The Brothers Karamazov*. A third, approximately, of the remaining sources refer to Dostoevsky generally. Globally, of the references to Dostoevsky and his writings, over a quarter of them refer to the prose poem, The Grand Inquisitor from *The Brothers Karamazov*. Ivan Karamazov figures prominently in the references to Dostoevsky in *Römerbrief 2* not only in this prose poem, The Grand Inquisitor, but also the nightmare/hallucinatory visit from the devil as well as other general references to Ivan. Approximately one third

14. Dostoevsky and *Römerbrief 2*

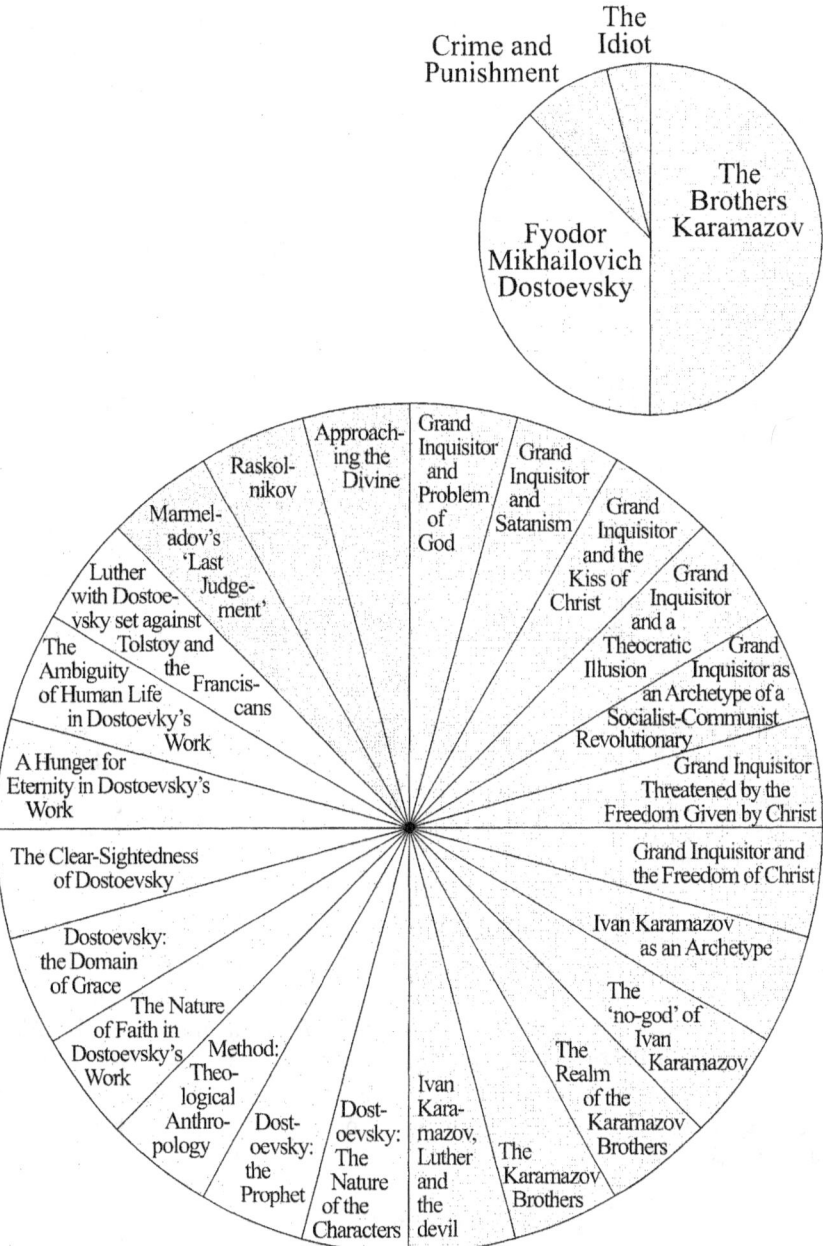

Figure 7 Dostoevsky and *Römerbrief 2*

A schematic breakdown of the references to Dostoevsky in *Römerbrief 2* showing the proportion and the nature of the use of these sources by Barth; for full page references see the tables at the opening of chapters 15, 16 and 17.

of the total references are generally to Dostoevsky, though it is important to remember that these refer to various topics within his work. The references to *Crime and Punishment* are split equally between specific references to the character of Rodion Romanovich Raskolnikov and references to Marmeladov (Sonya's step-father). References to *The Idiot* are small in *Römerbrief 2* yet the work gets a better mention/citation in The Tambach Lecture.

The general references to Dostoevsky, the man, his beliefs and work, are indicative of Barth (and Thurneysen's) concerns. For example, Barth comments on the religious/secular nature of Dostoevsky's characters[4] (similar to Barth's perceptions that we encountered in The Tambach Lecture). In addition, Dostoevsky is seen as a prophet (similar in many ways to Kierkegaard, and his role in Copenhagen society).[5] Method in Dostoevsky's theological anthropology is another concern: for example, in the context of Romans 4:5, the righteousness granted to Abraham, and in comparing the work of Dostoevsky with the Book of Genesis.[6] Again, regarding Abraham's faith, Barth comments 'a similar faith appears on the borderland of the philosophy of Plato, of the art of Grünewald and Dostoevsky, and of the religion of Luther.'[7] When attempting to identify a domain of grace, Barth categorically refutes that such a thing is possible - grace is not the property of this or that person, neither is it owned by 'children, or socialists, or to the Russian nation or to the German people, or to Dostoevsky! or to Kutter!'[8] Barth comments on the clear-sightedness of Dostoevsky - a perception, like Kierkegaard's, or for that matter Overbeck's and Nietzsche's, uncluttered by human religious needs, which cuts through human vanity to lay bare deceit and pretentiousness: for example,

> ...people cling to religion with a bourgeois tenacity ... but religion must die. In God we are rid of it ... like all clear-sighted-people from Job to Dostoevsky, we are compelled to recognize, whether we acknowledge it or not, that our concrete status in the world of time and men and of things lies under the shadow of death.[9]

Both Barth and Thurneysen perceived in Dostoevsky's characters a hunger for eternity (*Ewigkeitshunger*) that either drives people to God or into the mental breakdown of Ivan Karamazov (*The Brothers Karamazov*) or the suicidal insanity of Smerdyakov (*The Brothers Karamazov*) and Svidrigailov (*Crime and Punishment*): for example, commenting on Romans 7:10-11, in the context of freedom and the meaning of religion, Barth comments critically of the dangers of religion and the example of prophets such as Kierkegaard and Dostoevsky:

---

[4] Barth, *Römerbrief 2*, p. 46/ET: p. 67.
[5] Barth, *Römerbrief 2*, p. 101/ET: p. 117.
[6] Barth, *Römerbrief 2*, p. 106/ET: p. 122.
[7] Barth, *Römerbrief 2*, p. 128/ET: p. 141.
[8] Barth, *Römerbrief 2*, p. 220/ET: p. 220.
[9] Barth, *Römerbrief 2*, p. 240/ET: p. 238.

14. Dostoevsky and Römerbrief 2

> There is for us no honourable alternative but to be religious, repenting in dust and ashes, wrestling in fear and trembling, that we may be blessed; and, since we must take up a position, adopting the attitude of adoration. To all this we are urged by the commandment which directs us unto life. Knowing, then, that we have no alternative, knowing also what that alternative involves, ought we to shrink from advancing to take up our position on the very outermost edge of the precipice, on the very brink of the possibility of religion? We may, however, judge the relentlessness of Calvin, the dialectical audacity of Kierkegaard, Overbeck's sense of awe, Dostoevsky's hunger for eternity, Blumhardt's optimism, too risky and too dangerous for us. We may therefore content ourselves with some lesser, more feeble possibility of religion. We may fall.[10]

This hunger for eternity was something that Karl Adam lighted upon as an important influence of Dostoevsky on Barth when he was writing in 1926.[11] Adam, who had worked to a degree with Barth in the late 1920s, understood the influences on Barth's emerging theology of Krisis in the period 1918-22. Adam and Erich Przywara (whom we encountered in chapter 5) had intimate knowledge of Barth's development from having discussed these issues with him! For example:

> In the close connection with Kierkegaard, that of dialectics corroding, probing the endless qualitative difference between God and humanity, creator and cosmos, eternity and time is always newly striking out at the rudiments but does not lay bare; and is unaffected by the older Blumhardt, of the serious repentance and preaching of the kingdom of God from Bad Boll; there were touches also, of the hunger for eternity of Dostoevsky and the respect for Overbeck; all this moves the theology of *Krisis*, the *deus absconditus*, of protestant predestination to all.[12]

Adam, who was writing in 1926, four years after the publication of *Römerbrief 2*, understood the importance of Dostoevsky in Barth's development, likewise Kierkegaard, Blumhardt and Overbeck, but also the complicated web of influences/sources that had generated Barth's *Wendung und Retraktation*.

We also find two related illustrative uses of Dostoevsky in the nature of grace and the ambiguity of human life,

> Grace means not judging, because the judgement has already taken place. Grace means the recognition that a bad conscience must be assumed in the daily routine of an evil world. But precisely for this reason grace means also the possibility, not of a 'good' (!) conscience, but of a consoled conscience. If then - in agreement with Luther and Dostoevsky against Tolstoy and the Franciscans - exhortation be the exposition of the validity of grace, it involves a perception of the pre-supposition of grace in all concrete phenomena.[13]

This ambiguity is seen in the bestowing of grace, not on good moral

---

[10] Barth, *Römerbrief 2*, p. 255/ET: p. 252.
[11] Adam, 'Die Theologie der Krisis', pp. 271-286.
[12] Adam, 'Die Theologie der Krisis', p. 271.
[13] Barth, *Römerbrief 2*, p. 452/ET: p. 428.

religious people but in the acceptance of grace by one who is fallen and in an evil world (as we have seen in the work of Dostoevsky). Barth therefore sets Dostoevsky and Luther apart, against Tolstoy and the Franciscans. This relates to the ambiguity of human life at the end of Dostoevsky's work and also at the conclusion of Paul's Epistle to the Romans: Barth writes of the importance of Krisis in people's lives, of judgement balanced by grace, the grace given freely to the one imprisoned by God. This freedom leads Barth to comment, on the ambiguity in this, the Krisis of human freedom characterized by the great disturbance, he finds in Romans 14:

> If the Krisis be not pressed home to the end, all would be but sounding brass and a tinkling cymbal. Once again, therefore, at the end of the Epistle to the Romans - just as at the end of the novels of Dostoevsky - there is presented to us the impenetrable ambiguity of human life - even of the life of the Christian and of the Christian Community. Once again, it is the fact of the existence of our fellow men - the ethical problem - by which we are brought face to face with the great disturbance.[14]

Göttingen - a Reformed position

Barth eventually left the work of a Reformed minister at Safenwil in the autumn of 1921 to take up a teaching post as Honorary Professor of Reformed Theology at the University of Göttingen. Between 1924 and 1926 he presented a series of lectures, his first foray into dogmatics, entitled *Unterricht in der christlichen Religion*. Barth has to leave the role of an Old Testament type prophet, secure in his Swiss parish, to teach theology and dogmatics in Germany. This lecture cycle has been published in three volumes;[15] it features many of the sources we have seen in *Römerbrief 2*, but such sources are used to a much lesser extent. There are three explicit references to Dostoevsky; in addition two sections owe much to Thurneysen's *Dostojewski*. For example, Chapter 1, 'The Word of God as Revelation', §4 'Humanity and its Question', which reflects the theological anthropology in chapter III 'Dostoevsky's

---

[14] Barth, *Römerbrief 2*, p. 532/ET: p. 505.
[15] Karl Barth, *Unterricht in der christlichen Religion 1, Erster Band: Prolegomena 1924* (Gesamtausgabe 17; Zürich: Theologischer Verlag Zürich, 1985); *Unterricht in der christlichen Religion 2, Zweite Band: Die Lehre von Gott/Die Lehre vom Menschen* (Gesamtausgabe 20; Zürich: Theologischer Verlag Zürich, 1990); *Unterricht in der christlichen Religion 3, Dritter Band: Die Lehre von der Versöhnung/Die Lehre von der Erlösung (Eschatologie) 1925/1926* (Gesamtausgabe 38; Zürich: Theologischer Verlag Zürich, 2003); Vol. 1 (§. 1-13) and half of vol. 2 (§. 14-18) are published in English: Karl Barth, *Göttingen Dogmatics - Instruction in the Christian Religion vol. 1* (trans. G.W. Bromiley; Grand Rapids, MI: Eerdmans, 1990).

Perspective' in *Dostojewski* (a point acknowledged by Barth in a footnote);[16] and Chapter 4 'The Doctrine of God', §15 'The Knowability of God', which reflects the theological epistemology in chapter IV 'Ivan Karamazov, The Grand Inquisitor, and the Devil' in *Dostojewski,* and Dostoevsky's *The Brothers Karamazov* (Book V Pro and Contra, Chapter 3 The Brothers Make Friends, Chapter 4 Rebellion, Chapter 5 The Grand Inquisitor) - again, acknowledged by Barth in a footnote.[17] What Barth actually has to say here is relevant to the question of humanity in chapter fifteen, theological anthropology, and the knowability of God in chapter seventeen, the paradox of Christlikeness, and will be dealt with there. Despite the comments by Barth evidenced in his correspondence with Thurneysen in 1922, that it was time to move on from Dostoevsky, the Russian writer still has a small but as we shall see significant role in many ways to play, in what is today known as the *Göttingen Dogmatics* - in Barth's theological anthropology and his theological epistemology.

---

[16] Barth, *Unterricht in der christlichen Religion 1, Erster Band: Prolegomena 1924*, p. 104/ET: p. 86 n. 21.
[17] Barth, *Unterricht in der christlichen Religion 2, Zweite Band: Die Lehre von Gott/Die Lehre vom Menschen*, p. 46/ET: p. 350 n. 68.

CHAPTER 15

Theological Anthropology

Theological Anthropology: The Human Condition and the Nature of the Relationship of Sin and Grace between Humanity and God

p. 46/ET: p. 67 : The religious/secular nature of Dostoevsky's characters.
p. 106/ET: p. 122 : Method in Dostoevsky's theological anthropology.
p. 220/ET: p. 220 : The domain of grace in Dostoevsky's work.
p. 255/ET: p. 252 : A hunger for eternity in Dostoevsky's work.
p. 300/ET: p. 292 : Marmeladov and The Last Judgement.
p. 346/ET: p. 332 : The problem as represented by the Grand Inquisitor - cannot live with God, cannot live without God.
p. 370/ET: p. 354 : Problems of approaching the divine.
p. 372/ET: p. 356 : Rodion Romanovich Raskolnikov.
p. 412/ET: p. 393 : Dostoevsky's answer to the Grand Inquisitor: the kiss of Christ.
p. 452/ET: p. 428 : The ambiguity of human life at the end of the novels and also at the conclusion of Paul's Epistle to the Romans.
p. 532/ET: p. 504 : The freedom given by Christ seen as a threat to the Grand Inquisitor.
p. 532/ET: p. 505 : Dostoevsky and Luther set against Tolstoy and the Franciscans.

Theological anthropology and the human condition before God : key references/influences acknowledged in 'Der römische Katholizismus als Frage...' (1928) and in §4 of the *Göttingen Dogmatics* (1985-2003 [1924-1926]), key reference pp. 103-4/ET: p. 86; the latter also acknowledging chapter 3 of Thurneysen's *Dostojewski* (1921) as an influence.

Figure 8 *Römerbrief 2* **Dostoevsky and Theological Anthropology - Evidence**

Underpinning the emerging doctrine of sin in Barth's addresses, essays, and the two commentaries *Römerbrief 1* and *Römerbrief 2*, is his theological anthropology - Barth's understanding of humanity before God. Humanity as such is fallen, corrupt, a depravity that is self-inflicted: we have seen how Dostoevsky's theological anthropology affected Barth and Thurneysen not only through *Crime and Punishment* and *The Dream of the Ridiculous Man*, but also from *The Brothers Karamazov*. It is worth seeing how Barth uses Dostoevsky, to a degree illustratively, in *Römerbrief 2*.

Theological Anthropology in *Römerbrief 2*

Barth's theological anthropology reflects that which characterized Dostoevsky's mature period of writing. Yes, the main person behind Barth's understanding of humanity is Luther, but it is important to remember that it was

Dostoevsky that led Barth to Luther and Calvin, their doctrine of sin and their theological anthropology. This understanding is rooted in the Fall - that humanity cannot save itself. The effectiveness of Dostoevsky's beliefs as projected into his novels revolves around this theological anthropology. Within this there is one central question: how much good is there remaining in humanity? The answer for Dostoevsky revolved around the condition of humanity. Concurring with Calvin, original sin is the cause of humanity's condition: it has led to hereditary depravity and the corruption of our nature.[1] Adam's sin has been transmitted to all. Dostoevsky's theological anthropology pivots on the inner conflict presented in Romans 7:14-20 - try as hard as we can, we mere humans are weighed down and fail to do the good we wish to; our good intentions are always compromised by the weight of a corrupt will. This was not just mere selfishness, there was for Dostoevsky, as with Calvin, a strong element of evil for its own sake in the human condition. Dostoevsky saw evil as a noun - something real, tangible, outside ourselves that infiltrated and infected, so to speak, the human soul, causing it to move further and further away from God, becoming ever more immune to the depravity of human actions. To Dostoevsky the nature of humanity before God was fundamental: his theological anthropology develops from the naivety of his early novellas and short stories through the pessimism of his understanding of the human condition in the middle years following the return from Siberia, culminating in the more balanced approach to the human predicament in his mature years (as we saw in chapter 3). Dostoevsky's early writings were characterized by optimism in the inherent goodness of humanity (late 1840s); the years in Siberia and immediately following his return to European Russia (late 1850s and 1860s) were the pessimistic years (characterized by *Crime and Punishment*): without God humanity is corrupt, depraved, with virtually no good left in people, the *imago dei* is totally obscured by a corrupt will. By the late 1870s, we find in *The Brothers Karamazov* a more balanced approach between good and evil in people. It is this later period that influences Barth's understanding of humanity in *Römerbrief 2*.

The Human Condition before God

We have seen much already of this concept of the human condition before God in Barth's understanding of sin and grace from his reading of *Crime and Punishment* in 1915 - the full depravity and delusions that sin brings can only be fully understood in the light of the grace of God in the forgiveness proffered

---

[1] 'Original sin, therefore, seems to be an hereditary depravity and corruption of our nature, diffused into all parts of the soul, which first makes us liable to God's wrath, then also brings forth in us those works which Scripture calls "works of the flesh" (Galatians 5:19). And that is properly what Paul often calls sin.' Calvin, *Institutes of the Christian Religion*, bk. 2 chp. 1, §. 8, p. 251.

by Jesus Christ. We have seen an important example already (chapter 13, Kierkegaard and Dostoevsky, commenting on Romans 9:19-20) of Barth's theological anthropology in *Römerbrief 2* where he outlined the demonic depths of the Fall as manifested in the self-centred narcissistic decisions of people of whatever era, then invoking Raskolnikov as the ultimate example to drive his point home.² This understanding of theological anthropology is spread throughout *Römerbrief 2* and draws much on Dostoevsky (see Figure 8 *Römerbrief 2* Dostoevsky and Theological Anthropology - Evidence, on page 181). In this context Barth wrote in the *Göttingen Dogmatics*: 'What must humanity be, because revelation is?'³ Without this saving grace any full understanding of the brokenness and delusions of the human condition leads, for Dostoevsky, to insanity. We can find this theological anthropology in *Römerbrief 2*, for example it is generally stated in Barth's presentation of sin and grace in his commentary on Romans 1:18-21, under the title of 'The Night'.⁴ Humanity holds the truth imprisoned in unrighteousness:

> People fall a prey to themselves and then to the 'No-God'. First is heard the promise - ye shall be as God (Ihr werdet sein wie Gott!) - and then men lose the sense for eternity. First humanity is exalted, and then people obscure the distance between God and humanity.⁵

This is what we discovered earlier of the root of Barth's understanding of sin: Raskolnikov - *eritis sicut deus*. In the context of general comments on Dostoevsky's theological anthropology it is important to note Barth's comments in the lecture series *Unterricht in der christlichen Religion* he presented at Göttingen within two years of the publication of *Römerbrief 2*.⁶ In the first chapter on the word of God as revelation, we find comments at the end of the section on humanity and its question, which draws what has been said together in the context of Dostoevsky's theological anthropology:

> Humanity should recall once again that on earth it has no continuing city (Hebrews 13:14), that it is a sinner (Romans 3:23), and that it must die (Psalm 90:12). Humanity must be made afraid again of what it means to be human. Humanity must note how truly uprooted it is. Why? because it reads this in Dostoevsky.⁷

In specific terms the use illustratively and the influence of Dostoevsky on

---

² Barth, *Römerbrief 2*, p. 371/ET: p. 355, on Romans 9 'The Tribulation of the Church', and Romans 9:14-29 'The God of Esau'.
³ Barth, *Unterricht in der christlichen Religion 1, Erster Band: Prolegomena 1924*, p. 87/ET: p. 72.
⁴ Barth, *Römerbrief 2*, p. 19/ET: p. 42, 'Die Nacht - Ursache' ('The Night - its Cause').
⁵ Barth, *Römerbrief 2*, p. 21/ET: p. 44.
⁶ Barth, *Unterricht in der christlichen Religion 1, Erster Band: Prolegomena 1924*, pp. 53-244/ET: pp. 43-198.
⁷ Barth, *Unterricht in der christlichen Religion 1, Erster Band: Prolegomena 1924*, pp. 103-104/ET: p. 86.

Barth's theological anthropology can be found in several places in *Römerbrief 2* (see table at the beginning of this chapter). For example, the religious/secular dialectic seen in the nature of Dostoevsky's characters - 'But who will deny what God alone can deny? The religion and the experiences of the characters in the novels of Dostoevsky have presumably their counterparts in many other forms of religion and of experience'.[8] Or Barth's understanding of method in Dostoevsky's theological anthropology, the method of assessing human worth that Barth identified in both the work of Dostoevsky and the Book of Genesis:

> (There is a) method of assessing human worth: a method employed, for example, both in the book of Genesis and by Dostoevsky. This method of reckoning is not concerned to give honour where honour is due. It is not busied with proving the righteousness of men. It does not over-look or forget the final question, by which the whole procedure is conditioned. It does not think only of wage-books, but remembers that there is a Book of Life in which is recorded the secrets of all, which can become known. It is not pre-occupied with what may be reckoned to men as of debt, but with that which is of grace. It runs little risk of confusing the judgements of men with the judgements of God...[9]

There is therefore not the morality of Tolstoy that we saw Barth criticising in the context of Dostoevsky in The Tambach Lecture. But warns Barth, this domain of grace is not a form of property, 'it is not the property of this or that man; that it does not belong to children or to socialists or to the Russian Nation or to the German People, or to Dostoevsky! or to Kutter!'[10] That humanity cannot own God's righteousness is seen in the hunger for eternity in Dostoevsky's characters.[11] Further,

> It is what Dostoevsky's perplexing, doubtful characters, deep in their swamp, remember of the Lord: that He will one day say to those debauched, weak-willed, shameless creatures - 'Come unto Me, though ye be swine and like unto beasts.' It is also what enables Luther to die with those unedifying words on his lips: 'Beggars we are'.[12]

This is seen in the proposition of Dostoevsky, Barth and Thurneysen, that humanity - 'cannot live with the Living God, and yet cannot live without God (The Grand Inquisitor!).'[13] Furthermore, Barth commented about the nature of humanity before eternity, before God,

---

[8] Barth, *Römerbrief 2*, p. 46/ET: p. 67.
[9] Barth, *Römerbrief 2*, p. 106/ ET: p. 122.
[10] Barth, *Römerbrief 2*, p. 220/ET: p. 220.
[11] Barth, *Römerbrief 2*, p. 255/ ET: p. 252.
[12] Barth, *Römerbrief 2*, p. 300/ ET: p. 292. Barth is also quoting from the paraphrase by Marmeladov (Sonya's step-father) of the Last Judgement (Matthew 25) that we saw earlier in chapter 6: Dostoevsky, *Crime and Punishment*, bk. 1 chp. 2, p. 23.
[13] Barth, *Römerbrief 2*, p. 346/ET: p. 332, on Romans 9:1-5 'The Tribulation of the Church - Solidarity'.

The conclusion of Dostoevsky's *The Idiot*, the end of men like Hölderlin and Nietzsche ... make it only too clear that, in spite of its supposed richness and healthiness and righteousness, humanity has no alternative but death when confronted by the Truth.[14]

The sickness, the contagion, that is sin, makes approaching directly and comprehendingly the divine impossible, even for the most innocent and sanctified. This is of course seen for Barth and Thurneysen in the figure of Raskolnikov.[15] (We have noted already how Barth saw this in the ambiguity of human life at the end of the novels and also at the conclusion of Paul's Epistle to the Romans.[16])

The hopelessness of the human condition as Barth and Thurneysen read in Dostoevsky was balanced by the grace given in judgement; therefore the initial point of gracious forgiveness had to be forensic/legalistic, leading to sanctification. This is seen in the God-given freedom of the one imprisoned by God, owned by Christ for whom judgement has sanctified - Barth and Thurneysen perceived how this freedom and the knowledge of the grace of God was seen as a threat to the religious monopoly of the Church.

---

[14] Barth, *Römerbrief 2*, p. 370/ET: p. 354, on Romans 9:1-5 'The Tribulation of the Church - The Problem of Approaching the Divine'.
[15] Barth, *Römerbrief 2*, p. 372/ET: p. 356.
[16] Barth, *Römerbrief 2*, p. 452/ET: p. 428.

CHAPTER 16

A Criticism of Church-Religion

A Criticism of Church-Religion : The Grand Inquisitor, Roman Catholicism, Socialism and Atheism

Hebrew Religion and the Church seen as Synonymous

See *Römerbrief 2*, chp 10 § 10:4-21, p. 128/ET: pp. 340-390, the guilt as the tribulation of church-religion (Hebrew or Christian) for failing to speak for God (see, Barth to Thurneysen letter, 3 August 1921, acknowledging the use of and influence of Thurneysen's *Dostojewski* on the second section of chapter 10 of *Römerbrief 2*).

Dialectic of *Faith-Religion* and *Atheism-Theism*

p. 101/ET: p. 117	:	Dostoevsky as a prophet.
p. 128/ET: p. 141	:	The nature of faith in Dostoevsky's work.
p. 240/ET: p. 238	:	The clear-sightedness of Dostoevsky.
p. 256/ET: p. 253	:	Ivan Karamazov, Luther and the devil.
p. 309/ET: p. 300	:	Ivan Karamazov as an archetype.
p. 312/ET: p. 303	:	Ivan Karamazov's 'No-God'.
p. 409/ET: p. 391	:	Satanism in the Grand Inquisitor.
p. 412/ET: p. 393	:	Dostoevsky's answer to the Grand Inquisitor: the kiss of Christ.
p. 504/ET: p. 479	:	The Grand Inquisitor as the culmination of the theocratic illusion.
p. 528/ET: p. 501	:	The realm of the Karamazov brothers.
p. 529/ET: p. 502	:	The Karamazov brothers.
p. 532/ET: p. 504	:	The freedom given by Christ seen as a threat to the Grand Inquisitor.
p. 548/ET: p. 520	:	The freedom of Christ.

Criticism of the Pseudo-Religious Archetype of a Socialist/Communist Revolutionary

p. 409/ET: p. 391	:	Satanism in the Grand Inquisitor.
p. 412/ET: p. 393	:	Dostoevsky's answer to the Grand Inquisitor: the kiss of Christ.
p. 504/ET: p. 479	:	The Grand Inquisitor as the culmination of the theocratic illusion.
p. 505/ET: p. 480	:	The Grand Inquisitor as an archetype of socialist/communist revolutionaries.
p. 532/ET: p. 504	:	The freedom given by Christ seen as a threat to the Grand Inquisitor.

Figure 9 *Römerbrief 2* **Dostoevsky and a Criticism of Church-Religion - Evidence**

The main issue relating to sin and grace in *Römerbrief 2* is the role of church-religion. This is where Barth's criticism of religion in the service of the Gospel comes to the fore. Church-religion has failed to convey to people the forgiveness and grace of the one supreme, transcendent God, who comes to us in humility in Christ Jesus, granting us the freedom of forgiveness and the grace of the Holy Spirit to sanctify. Church-Religion is seen as self-serving, it has turned the eschatology of the Gospel into human-centred religion - a religion that is self-perpetuating and self-promoting. Behind this, as we have noted already, is the influence of Franz Overbeck. However, Dostoevsky figures in this strongly (see Figure 9 *Römerbrief 2* Dostoevsky and a Criticism of Church-Religion - Evidence, on page 187). We have noted Thurneysen's comment already that the most fearsome attack Dostoevsky led against the church and religion was in the form of Ivan Karamazov and his prose poem, The Grand Inquisitor. But who was this Ivan Karamazov.

The Brothers Karamazov, Ivan Karamazov and The Legend of The Grand Inquisitor

The Brothers Karamazov, Dostoevsky's last and to many his greatest work, is about a father, Fyodor Karamazov and his four sons - Ivan, Dmitri and Alyosha, and the illegitimate Smerdyakov. Ivan, in his mid-twenties, is highly intelligent, and has already published. Dmitri is sensual, a womanizer and is all too fond of drink. Alyosha, the youngest, is in the noviciate at the local Russian Orthodox monastery. Fyodor's two wives both died, as did the servant woman, Lizaveta, that bore Smerdyakov - this fourth son working for his father as manservant. Both Fyodor and Dmitri are trying to seduce a young woman by the name of Grushenka. Against this backdrop is Father Zossima, a Starets at Alyosha's monastery, along with Rakitin, a seminarian and religious atheist. Half way through the story Fyodor is brutally murdered - suspicion and arrest fall on Dmitri because of the rivalry for Grushenka, and because of money stolen from Fyodor. Dmitri is convicted of the murder even though Smerdyakov has confessed to Ivan of his guilt. Against this story are several very long theological polemics - but not moralistic teaching. There are several scenes at the monastery contrasting the holiness of Father Zossima with the worldly ambitions of Rakitin (including several long chapters about the life and theological beliefs of Father Zossima recounted after his death); the faith of the Russian peasants is extolled, likewise the all-too-fleshly worldly desires and obsessions of Fyodor and his son Dmitri are exposed, as is the scheming of Grushenka who is honest about her whoring life as compared to the hypocrisy of more respectable women. Then we have the character of Ivan Karamazov who is not prone to the sins of the flesh, so to speak, but to the titanic intellectual sins of the mind - *eritis sicut deus*. When Ivan meets up with Alyosha, having returned home after many years away in Moscow and St Petersburg we have three long chapters where they become reacquainted.[1] In the chapter entitled Rebellion Ivan off-loads all his atheistic philosophy onto Alyosha the seventeen-year-old novice monk, then recounts the prose poem he

---

[1] Dostoevsky, *The Brothers Karamazov*, pt. 2 bk. 5 'Pro and Contra' chp. 3 'The Brothers get Aquainted', pp. 228-235, chp. 4 'Rebellion' pp. 236-245, and chp. 5 'The Grand Inquisitor', pp. 246-264.

has created entitled The Legend of The Grand Inquisitor. Later, as Ivan's mind becomes more and more unhinged due to his rebellious belief system, that is his denial of everything except his own ego, Dostoevsky presents the nightmare hallucinatory conversation Ivan has with the devil. By the time of Dmitri's trial and wrongful conviction for the murder of their father Fyodor, Ivan appears to have succumbed to a mental breakdown and his testimony before the court that Smerdyakov confessed to the murder of Fyodor before he committed suicide is ruled inadmissible. The story ends with Alyosha leaving the monastery (having been advised by Father Zossima before his death, that he should serve Christ in the world); Dmitri is transported to Siberia to serve his sentence, Grushenka announcing she will follow and wait for him. In *The Brothers Karamazov* Dostoevsky poured all his skill and talent as a writer, producing a massive book nearly a thousand pages in length (approximately 350,000 words), illustrating the fallenness, the brokenness of humanity, depraved and egocentric; but this is balanced by the theology in the work, and the proposition from Christian soteriology - repent and be forgiven, face sin in all its depth, and thereby accept God's forgiveness. Ivan does not - and loses his mind; Dmitri does and lives. Alyosha, still only a naive seventeen-year-old has to face coming to terms with the world, whilst retaining his faith. Sin therefore is gargantuan, manifold, highly deceptive, possessing, deceiving, deluding - but forgiveness and grace are always available. Sin and grace are forensic - repentance being the only path to life. This was Dostoevsky's doctrine, as such, of Christian soteriology in *The Brothers Karamazov*.

The Influence of Ivan Karamazov on Barth and Thurneysen

The influence of Ivan Karamazov on Barth and Thurneysen is profound. Just fewer than half the references to Dostoevsky in *Römerbrief 2* are to Ivan Karamazov. This is seen in three episodes from the novel: Ivan's conversation with Alyosha (Rebellion and The Grand Inquisitor) and Ivan's nightmare conversation with the devil.

The chapter entitled Rebellion is amongst the most profound pieces of theological polemic ever written. Ivan focuses on the antinomy between an omnipotent and merciful God and the cruel, bleak reality of relatively innocent suffering (relative that is to the Fall); this can also be seen as the *diastasis* between divine mercy and suffering. Dostoevsky's dialectics are rooted in theodicy: *si deus iustus - unde malum?*: if God is righteous, good and omnipotent, then why is there evil and the suffering that flows from it? Ivan speculates that if the suffering and death of an innocent child could solve this paradox, close the antinomy, then it would never be acceptable. Ivan refuses to accept that the sufferings here on earth can be assuaged, dismissed - as the persecuted and persecutor are reconciled by God. At this juncture in the story Ivan is not a logical atheist, he does not examine everything in life in terms of a denial of the existence of God and a denial of any meaning in life. It is his perception of suffering in the world that causes him not to deny the existence of God but to refuse to acknowledge God or God's creation. Rebellion is a long chapter and into Ivan's polemic Dostoevsky pours all the myriad arguments that he had encountered amongst the liberal atheists that influenced him in his youth. Ivan's rebellion is therefore against God, but this is not primarily to prove the non-existence of God. For Dostoevsky, the problem of humanity is the man-god, characterized by a rebellion against the limitations of humanity; the infinite pretensions of the human self are summarized by the determination of men and women to be God. Escape from the human condition, that is, salvation lies not in the man-god but in the God-man: Christ Jesus.

Of equal length and stature to Rebellion is The Legend of The Grand Inquisitor. Set in sixteenth-century Seville, The Grand Inquisitor, having supervised an *auto da fé* of over one hundred heretics, is then confronted by another heretic: Christ, arrested having returned. His crime? - to have healed a little girl. Confronted by the Inquisitor in his cell Christ says nothing, is silent. After a long monologue spoken by the Inquisitor (in the course of which he reveals himself to be a religious atheist) looking at the temptations of Jesus in the wilderness, the nature of the devil that tempted him, the role of miracle, mystery and authority, further the authority of the church (Peter's rock), the Inquisitor's objection is that Christ should not have returned, that all power and authority had been handed over, and could not be drawn back, that Christ had no right to interfere with the church. Furthermore they, the Roman Church, has taken the power to forgive people their sins, make them happy - by contrast Jesus Christ's expectations of humanity are too great, too unattainable: the burden of freedom is too much for them. Ivan speculates through the Inquisitor as to whether the Roman Church has been run for centuries by a secret fellowship of compassionate atheists as Dostoevsky terms them. Christ does not speak a word in his defence, merely sits and listens; however, at the end he rises and places a kiss, gently on the Inquisitor's bloodless lips as if to say 'I forgive you.' The Inquisitor, instead of holding Christ to be burnt alive at the stake the next morning, opens the door and orders him to go, and not to return. We are left suspended at the end of the story with The Grand Inquisitor tormented by the kiss of Christ. After Ivan has finished recounting his prose poem, convinced he has won whatever polemical battle he was engaged in with his younger brother, Alyosha simply stands, kisses him softly - to which Ivan angrily responds, 'That's plagiarism ... You stole that from my poem.'

Dostoevsky is not so naive as to aim this criticism only at Rome. His polemic is aimed at two groups: first, the liberal humanist atheists that had influenced him in his youth (the proto-socialist sympathizers with the French evolution) and, second, the Roman Catholic Church. Indeed he saw socialism as the illegitimate offspring of the Roman church; but he is also criticizing any

16. A Criticism of Church-Religion

dictatorial authority claiming to act *as if* God (again, *eritis sicut deus*).[2] The Grand Inquisitor refers to the anthill for humanity and The Tower of Babel for the role of the church, though Dostoevsky also used these metaphors for a denunciation of atheistic socialism.[3] He is writing a few years after the first Vatican Council that declared infallibility for the papacy, therefore, in the context of Roman oppression and attacks on the Russian Orthodox Church over the previous eight hundred years it is easy to see why Dostoevsky takes this stand. The Grand Inquisitor is characterized by a dialectic between the freedom of Christ and religious oppression: something that appealed to Barth at this juncture in his thinking with Thurneysen. Dostoevsky is also tackling the subject of atheism - again in the form of a dialectic between theism-atheism. For Dostoevsky atheism may be of value. This is atheism seen as a negation and a paradox: for instance, the clearing away of all human conceptions and preconceptions. For example, Dostoevsky knew only too well that atheists might often have a better grasp of the truth of God than bourgeois Christians immersed in the religious culture of polite society in St Petersburg. And of course Dostoevsky, Barth and Thurneysen saw varying degrees and forms of atheism/atheists with varying degrees and characteristics of negation, dialectic and paradox. Within this is Dostoevsky's respect for atheists as voiced by his Orthodox Starets, Father Zossima in *The Brothers Karamazov*:

> Hate not those who reject you, who insult you, who abuse and slander you. Hate not the atheists, the teachers of evil, the materialists - and I mean not only the good ones - for there are many good ones among them, especially in our day - hate not even the wicked ones. Remember them in your prayers thus: Save, O Lord, all those who have none to pray for them, save too all those who will not pray. And add: it is not in pride that I make this prayer, O Lord, for I am lower than all men.... Love God's people, let not strangers draw away the flock.[4]

Such atheism may clear away the accumulations of religious culture and may be of value provided that the individual returns to a truer faith. Thurneysen notes how Ivan's atheism is dialectical and develops in three stages: first, Ivan's passionate protest against the reconciliation of the riddles and torments of life within the divine order of the world that is asserted by the Gospel (that the immeasurable suffering of a child is tolerable when measured against the joy of the life to come); second, Ivan then moves from this dialectical-animated atheism to a rigid-satanic atheism (he systematically attacks and denounces anything to do with the church and/or religion); third, in consequence Ivan

---

[2] The relations and history between Rome and the Russian Orthodox Church are well presented in Dirscherl, *Dostoevsky and the Catholic Church*, pt. 3 'Dostoevsky and the Catholic *Pax Romana*', pp. 79-125.

[3] Dostoevsky, *The Diary of a Writer vol. II*, March 1877, chp. 1 '2 The Russian People', pp. 628-630.

[4] Dostoevsky, *The Brothers Karamazov*, pt. 2 bk. 4 'Lacerations' chp. 1 'Father Ferapont', pp. 163-171.

moves from rigid-satanic atheism to demonic-satanic atheism (the stage at which he begins to lose his mind): The Grand Inquisitor is in the role of the devil, Ivan Karamazov is The Grand Inquisitor - he projects his rebellion into his creation of The Grand Inquisitor - therefore Ivan Karamazov is the devil.[5]

Ivan's theological counterpart is his illegitimate brother Smerdyakov. It is through Smerdyakov that Dostoevsky voices again the central ethic that we established earlier in 'The Idea' in chapter 3 - that if there is no God then there are no limits on human behaviour, human depravity. Michael V. Jones comments that there are,

> ...four, or possibly five, stages in Ivan's thought ... they span the period between his eighteenth and twenty-fourth year: they are the legend of the philosopher who refused to believe in paradise, the story of The Grand Inquisitor, the article on the ecclesiastical courts, the conversation with Alyosha on rebellion and the theory of 'geological upheaval' set forth by Ivan's hallucinatory devil. Each of them represents a stage in Ivan's wrestling with questions of theodicy, God and the world-order. And they feed back into the plot through the axiom which so impresses Smerdyakov, that 'if there is no God there is no morality'.[6]

Dostoevsky foresaw and prophesised through Ivan the chaos and nihilism of twentieth-century Western history. Hermann Hesse, studying Dostoevsky contemporaneous with Thurneysen and Barth, wrote:

> Humanity is now on the point of realizing this. Already half Europe, at all events half Eastern Europe, is on the road to chaos. In a state of drunken illusion she is reeling into the abyss and, as she reels, she sings a drunken hymn such as Dmitri Karamazov sang. The insulted citizen laughs that song to scorn, the saint and seer hear it with tears.[7]

So what did Barth make of all this? In *Römerbrief 2* the use of Dostoevsky's *The Brothers Karamazov* can be categorized thematically: see table at the beginning of this chapter.

Hebrew Religion and the Church seen as Synonymous

The focus of Barth's criticism of the church is very much in chapters nine through to eleven of *Römerbrief 2* (The Tribulation of The Church; The Guilt of The Church; and The Hope of The Church. It is in this context that Barth wrote to Thurneysen on 3 August 1921, commenting that,

> I think regretfully of the close of the second section of Romans 10; there was something there that, between two and three in the morning, would not come out

---

[5] Thurneysen, *Dostojewski*, pp. 45-46/ET: p. 51.
[6] Michael V. Jones, 'Introduction', in Dostoevsky, *The Brothers Karamazov*, pp. ix-xxv.
[7] Hesse, 'Die Brüder Karamasow', ET: pp. 607-618.

right. Besides, your Dostojewski provided me with steam for the whole section as well as a quotation.[8]

There is no explicit quotation from Thurneysen in chapter ten, whatever Barth alludes to may have been removed at a later stage of proof reading, but the whole chapter does bear witness to the criticism of religion that Thurneysen identifies in *The Brothers Karamazov* and the dangers of the misuse of religion. It is not surprising therefore that Barth draws illustratively on The Grand Inquisitor in several places. For example, the problem as represented by The Grand Inquisitor: that he cannot live with God, nor can he live without God;[9] the problems of encountering/approaching the divine;[10] the dangers associated with Rodion Romanovich Raskolnikov;[11] satanism in the stance of The Grand Inquisitor;[12] also the confrontation between Christ and The Grand Inquisitor.[13] This criticism of religion is reinforced by Barth aligning the church with Hebrew religion, indeed the two are seen as synonymous.

Dialectic of Faith-Religion and Theism-Atheism

Barth refers to the character of Ivan on several occasions: the beguiling 'demons appear (Ivan Karamazov and Luther!). There the old enemy of man is strangely near. There sin deceives.'[14] For Barth Ivan is something of an archetype. He is the man who has seen by some superior and detached academic power of perception that,

> ...existentially, earnestly, unavoidably, unescapably, unambiguously, with the ears and eyes of an Ivan Karamazov! himself burnt up, thrown from the saddle - such a man questions no more, but hears and sees-what? - himself as believing and loving and hoping? 'No', a thousand times 'No'; he hears and sees himself confronted by the wholly impossible, by the absolute contradiction, by that which can never be justified and can never be enthroned in any 'concept of God'.[15]

Why? - by 'observing with the eyes of an Ivan Karamazov - "No-God", the god of this world, fashioned after our image.'[16] Ivan is therefore the archetype

---

[8] Barth to Thurneysen, 3 August 1921, Barth and Thurneysen, *Briefwechsel Band 1 1913-1921*, p. 508.
[9] Barth, *Römerbrief 2*, p. 346/ET: p. 332.
[10] Barth, *Römerbrief 2*, p. 370/ET: p. 354.
[11] Barth, *Römerbrief 2*, p. 372/ET: p. 356.
[12] Barth, *Römerbrief 2*, p. 409/ET: p. 391.
[13] Barth, *Römerbrief 2*, p. 412/ET: p. 393.
[14] Barth, *Römerbrief 2*, p. 256/ET: p. 253. Barth is here drawing on the long hallucinatory conversation that Ivan has with the devil, psychologically reminiscent of schizophrenia, as Ivan falls further and further towards a mental breakdown.
[15] Barth, *Römerbrief 2*, p. 309/ET: p. 300.
[16] Barth, *Römerbrief 2*, p. 312/ET: p. 303. See also 'Dostoevsky as a prophet', p. 101/ET: p. 117, 'The nature of faith in Dostoevsky's work', p. 128/ET: p. 141, and 'The clear-sightedness of Dostoevsky' p. 240/ET: p. 238.

for Barth of *faith-religion*, *theism-atheism*. There is value in his piercing observations, as there were for Barth and Thurneysen in Nietzsche, Feuerbach, Overbeck, and so forth.

Barth writes of this as the culmination of the theocratic illusion that characterizes institutionalized religion, seen in The Grand Inquisitor: 'This theocratic dream comes abruptly to an end, of course, when we discover that it is the Devil who approaches Jesus and offers Him all the kingdoms of this world. It ends also with Dostoevsky's picture of The Grand Inquisitor.' [17] For, 'do we not also stand in the realm of the 'Brothers Karamazov' where all these evil things are possible?' [18] However much humanity, religious humanity, may want to escape the archetype of Ivan Karamazov, the taint of sin is always there: 'Questionable at all times is human conduct ... even the saints have not rid themselves of the possibilities of a Karamazov.'[19]

Religion-church in the form of The Grand Inquisitor is satanic,[20] this is the hell of religion. But the answer for Barth lies in the kiss that Christ gave to The Grand Inquisitor after the long diatribe that concludes in condemning Christ:

> If God really does spread forth His hands to us, what are we to make of our disobedient gainsaying, even though it be utterly satanic? What of the death, which is our end? What of that murder and burial, which is the prelude to our hope? What of our betrayal of Christ? Well, He kissed The Grand Inquisitor "upon his old and bloodless lips - and this was His complete and only answer". But it is just this "complete and only answer" which is the hope of the Church; for, established in God only, mercy is eternal, unconditional, unfathomable, it passes all understanding. We are not saved by our knowledge of God.[21]

It is in this context that we find Barth talking of the freedom given by God to those who have turned to Him: the freedom of the one imprisoned to God, that we saw in the context of Barth's comments from 'Der römische Katholizismus als Frage...', the freedom given by Christ that is seen as a threat to The Grand Inquisitor:

> Those who, overlooking the clarion call of its demand 'Thou art the man! Thou shalt!', treat it merely as a diatribe of theological philosophy - which assuredly it is - have woefully misunderstood it. It is true, also, that freedom is the essential meaning of the manner of life which is here required: the freedom which was bought by Christ and which The Grand Inquisitors of all ages have found so

---

[17] Barth, *Römerbrief 2*, p. 504/ET: p. 479. See also Barth, *Römerbrief 2*, 'The Great Negative Possibility' on Romans 12:21-13:7, pp. 478-481.
[18] Barth, *Römerbrief 2*, p. 528/ET: p. 501.
[19] Barth, *Römerbrief 2*, p. 529/ET: p. 502.
[20] Barth, *Römerbrief 2*, p. 409/ET: p. 391.
[21] 'Auf seine blutleeren neunzigjährigen Lippen ... Das war seine ganze Antwort', Barth, *Römerbrief 2*, p. 412/ET: p. 393. Barth is here quoting exactly from an early German translation: Fjodor Michailowitsch Dostojewski, *Die Brüder Karamasoff* (trans. E K Rahsin; München: R. Piper Verlag, 1906).

awkward and so dangerous - the freedom of the prisoner of God. But the freedom in this freedom is the Freedom of God. [22]

Barth elaborates: 'How right also was The Grand Inquisitor when he declared that the freedom which Christ brought was open to the very gravest objection!', he then goes on to criticize the vast armies of moralists and upright religious persons (reminiscent of the comments we encountered in 'Der Gerechtigkeit Gottes'). [23]

Criticism of the Pseudo-Religious Archetype of a Socialist-Communist Revolutionary

So, Barth balances the demonic satanism[24] of corrupt, self-serving religion seen in The Grand Inquisitor of all ages with the kiss of Christ given to the bloodless lips of the Roman Catholic Cardinal before him. [25] Despite the demonic agenda of this man, Christ still loves him and offers unconditional forgiveness. This applies specifically to the character in Ivan's prose poem but both Barth and Thurneysen saw this character, this Inquisitor as representative of the human desire to build The Tower of Babel, to rule, to judge in place of God. It is of no surprise considering the disillusionment with which Barth now greeted religious socialism, that he should see this archetype of The Grand Inquisitor not just as the epitome of religious control over God's salvation but also as an archetype of socialist-communist revolutionaries. The manner in which the Bolsheviks had passed judgement and were beginning to define truth in their own image was analogous with the theocratic illusion[26] of Roman authority as condemned by Dostoevsky in The Grand Inquisitor.

Commenting on Romans 12 Barth deals with the criticism of Religious Socialism and the Bolsheviks in Russia in a chapter of his commentary entitled 'The Great Disturbance' (see, 'The Great Negative Possibility' on Romans 12:21-13:7): the socialist-communist revolutionary as a pseudo-religious archetype. Barth wrote about how easy it was for people to see the evil that lay behind all governments: the revolutionary 'determines to remove the existing ordinances, in order that he may erect in their place the new right.' This seems a justifiable course of action before the world, but it is born of resentment that feeds on *eritis sicut deus*, 'harbouring a certain secret poisonous resentment against the existing order.' That this is born of oppression is not wrong but the

---

[22] Barth, *Römerbrief 2*, p. 532/ET: p. 504, on *Romans* 14:1-15:13. Note, Hoskyns translates 'Die Freiheit in der Gefangenschaft Gottes' as 'the freedom of the prisoner of God'; this should more accurately be rendered 'the freedom of the imprisonment from God'.
[23] Barth, *Römerbrief 2*, p. 548/ET: p. 520, on Romans 14:16-18 'The freedom of Christ'. See also Barth, *Römerbrief 2*, pp. 519-520, on Romans 14:1-15:13.
[24] Barth, *Römerbrief 2*, p. 409/ET: p. 391.
[25] Barth, *Römerbrief 2*, p. 412/ET: p. 393.
[26] Barth, *Römerbrief 2*, p. 504/ET: p. 479.

taking of action in the form of revolution is. Why? - for Barth the entire socialist-communist agenda is a delusion similar to that of the Courts of the Inquisition:

> The revolutionary must, however, own that in adopting his plan he allows himself to be overcome by evil. He forgets that he is not the One, that he is not the subject of the freedom, which he so earnestly desires, that, for all the strange brightness of his eyes, he is not the Christ who stands before The Grand Inquisitor, but is, contrariwise, The Grand Inquisitor encountered by the Christ. He too is claiming what no man can claim. He too is making of the right a thing. He too confronts other men with his supposed right. He too usurps a position which is not due to him, a legality which is fundamentally illegal, an authority which - as we have grimly experienced in Bolshevism, but also in the behaviour of far more delicate-minded innovators! - soon displays its essential tyranny.[27]

Therefore the revolutionary is deluded by his/her ambitions into believing that s/he has the right, for righteousness lies with God alone, and when standing before an oppressive government, when killing and maiming in the name of freedom, revolutionaries are, for Barth, actually denying that freedom, the freedom given by Christ and they are also foreshadowing the eschaton in a demonic manner: for Christ's right is seen in the eschaton not in the revolutionary.[28] Barth states explicitly that such a bright-eyed revolutionary is not the suffering Christ before The Grand Inquisitor, but is contrawise The Grand Inquisitor[29] who has taken the righteousness of God and is usurping - hence *eritis sicut deus*. This is the human delusion that Barth dealt with when looking at Romans 7. Gone now is Barth's naive and seemingly innocent involvement with the religious socialists. In this context and dealing with the guilt of the church Barth argues that the church often acts with the zeal and judgement of the socialist-communist revolutionary even when its politics may be diametric: 'The Church needs to be continually reminded of the most serious of symptoms - it was the Church not the world that Crucified Christ.'[30]

---

[27] Barth, *Römerbrief 2*, p. 505/ET: p. 480.
[28] Barth, *Römerbrief 2*, p. 532/ET: p. 504.
[29] '...nicht der Christus, der dem Großinquisitor gegenübersteht, sondern umgekehrt immer noch und erst recht der Großinquisitor, der Christus gegenübersteht.' Barth, *Römerbrief 2*, p. 505/ET: p. 480.
[30] Barth, *Römerbrief 2*, p. 407/ET: p. 389. Barth's remarks are reminiscent of the Congregationalist minister and theologian P. T. Forsyth: 'It was the national church that slew the universal Christ. You will note that it is one thing to have a church established in law and another thing to have religion established in a nation's heart'. P.T. Forsyth, *The Charter of the Church* (London: Alexander and Shepherd, 1896), p. 32.

CHAPTER 17

The Paradox of Christlikeness

The Paradox of Christlikeness:
The Parables of Jesus and the Characters of Dostoevsky

p. 46/ET: p. 67 : The religious/secular nature of Dostoevsky's characters.
p. 101/ET: p. 117 : Dostoevsky as a prophet.
p. 128/ET: p. 141 : The nature of faith in Dostoevsky's work.
p. 240/ET: p. 238 : The clear-sightedness of Dostoevsky.
p. 370/ET: p. 354 : Problems of approaching the divine.
p. 548/ET: p. 520 : The freedom of Christ.

The Paradox of Christlikeness: key reference also in *The Tambach Lecture* (p. 61/ET: p. 315) and *The Göttingen Dogmatics* (p.46/ET: p. 350).

Figure 10 *Römerbrief 2* Dostoevsky and the Paradox of Christlikeness - Evidence

We have noted already Barth's comments in The Tambach Lecture from 1919 about the similarity between the ordinariness, the secularity of the characters in the parables of Jesus and the people in Dostoevsky's novels ('Here we have the same free survey and understanding and representation of the actual life of society that distinguishes the novels of Dostoevsky, for example, from the kind in which, as in most of Tolstoy's, we feel ourselves directly preached to' [1]). Barth developed this idea further at the time of the writing of *Römerbrief 2* and into the period of the lectures at Göttingen. What we find in the quotations/evidence considered in this chapter (see Figure 10 Römerbrief 2 Dostoevsky and the Paradox of Christlikeness - Evidence, above) may be surprising to many Barthian scholars who place a heavy emphasis on the intellectual strength of Barth's mature work, work that relied so much on a systematic theological solution to understanding life and salvation. However, what we have here is the *answer*, as Barth and Thurneysen saw it, as *no-answer*.

This criticism of Tolstoy as moralistic preaching that Barth voiced in The Tambach Lecture was taken further in Thurneysen's *Dostojewski* and this is probably the source for Barth of many of the concepts in this final chapter.[2]

---

[1] Barth, 'Der Christ in der Gesellschaft', pp. 53-55/ET: pp. 305.
[2] Thurneysen, *Dostojewski*, V, 'The Knowledge of God', pp. 62-66/ET: pp. 69-73.

Quoting the Russian Orthodox Starets, Father Zossima, from *The Brothers Karamazov*, Thurneysen comments,

> 'Brethren, do not be repelled by the sin of man; love man even in his sin, for that is the image of the divine love.' Herein lies the deep difference between Dostoevsky and Leo Tolstoy, who throughout his whole life never progressed beyond this tragedy.' [3]

That Thurneysen places these observations in his final chapter on the knowledge of God is no coincidence. Tolstoy's characters and stories are regarded as religious-moralistic teaching; worse for Barth, pietistic: 'they appear almost without exception as the highest ultimate religious-moral accomplishments'; by contrast, 'In Dostoevsky, on the other hand, there is something which, though not without conflict, is not convulsive, something free, almost rejoicing in the worldly aspects of these "conversions" ... They remind us of the conversions of publicans and sinners in the Gospels' whereas Tolstoy concentrates on 'pietistic struggles of penitence.' [4]

Why is this important? - because Barth shares many of these ideas in relationship to theological epistemology with Thurneysen and develops them in *Römerbrief 2*. Knowledge of God is related to approaching the divine - if only with our cognition - and as such is wrought with all sorts of problems. In *Römerbrief 2* Barth wrote that Nietzsche was an example of the axiom that approaching this truth was intolerable: 'For such disturbances show that, when mankind and the world approach the ordering of God too nearly, they are thrown out of gear' Barth continues that this was seen in 'the conclusion of Dostoevsky's *The Idiot.*' [5] Any attempt at Christlikeness would fail because we are mere mortals, as happens to Prince Myshkin in *The Idiot*. This is paradoxical considering how we are called to follow Christ. Barth had elaborated on this understanding in The Tambach Lecture:

> 'Why can we work up no indignation against Dostoevsky's daring to make Christ pass as an idiot in society and the real understanding of him begin with the murderer and the harlot?' [6]

Dostoevsky's *The Idiot,* as we have seen already, is a parable about Christlikeness, how the unworldly Myshkin who always unnervingly speaks the truth and never partakes in the games of status, power and sexual politics that other people do, eventually returns to the asylum as the result of *status epilepticus* (continuous epileptic seizures) having effectively been destroyed by the people he was trying to save. Myshkin is only understood truly for what he is - Christlike - by, as Barth terms it, a harlot (Nastasya) and a murderer

---

[3] Thurneysen, *Dostojewski*, p. 63/ET: pp. 69-70. See also Barth, *Römerbrief 2*, p. 46/ET: p. 67.
[4] Thurneysen, *Dostojewski*, pp. 71-72/ET: p. 78.
[5] Barth, *Römerbrief 2*, p. 370/ET: p. 354.
[6] Barth, 'Der Christ in der Gesellschaft', p. 61.

(Rogozhin). What does this tell us about the knowledge of God? - that we will not know and understand God in our haltingly human manner through the understanding gained solely from this world. Barth developed this further for the lecture cycle, *The Göttingen Dogmatics*. In the section on the knowability of God he comments that whatever Kant observed/discovered in relation to astronomy[7] only highlighted 'the depth of ignorance which human reason could never have imagined to be so great.' Barth continued:

> And do not regard it merely as a literary flourish if I say that Dostoevsky, by confronting the unteachable atheist Ivan Karamazov with the pure fool Alyosha, who has no arguments against his revolt, has perhaps done more for a real proof of God than Anselm and Thomas, Schleiermacher and Ritschl. If in the Book of Job it is the questioning Job who is in the right and not his friends (Job 42:7), this probably means that if there is any pointer to God or proof of God for us at all, it will be found where we come up against the mystery of God.[8]

Myshkin and Alyosha - Christlike Archetypes

Therefore, Myshkin and Alyosha are seen as Christlike archetypes in relation to theological epistemology. Why? - because in not being able to answer or refute his brother's rebellious atheistic theologoumena Alyosha is not failing. Neither does Myshkin fail when he does not save the St Petersburg bourgeoisie from themselves. Likewise Job is righteous before God because of his honesty, but also through his acceptance of the mystery of God and theodicy as compared to his so-called comforters (!). No amount of systematization in theology and philosophy will close the antinomies between God and humanity, between suffering in this life and the resolution, reconciliation to come. We saw this was central to Dostoevsky's work, especially as theodicial objections are central to Ivan Karamazov's rebellion. For Barth this is about 'determining the final purpose of the use of reason.' These comments come at the conclusion of the section on the knowability of God, which for Barth and Thurneysen lay at this juncture in their thinking in a negative mystery: Myshkin and Alyosha being an example of it. The *answ*er therefore was *no-answer*. Alyosha bears witness to the futility of Ivan's assertions by merely standing for what he knows to be the way of truth: the naive and halting way he mimics Christ from the end of Ivan's prose poem about The Grand Inquisitor by offering Ivan the same kiss of forgiveness. Both Alyosha and Myshkin, and importantly Marie from *The Idiot* that we mentioned in chapter 3, are representative of the юродивый (*iurodivyi* - holy fool, or God's fool), who exhibit юродство (foolishness in Christ) as found in Russian Orthodox thinking, people that transcended the cognitive

---

[7] Barth is here referring to Immanel Kant, *Critique of Practical Reason* (ed. Mary J. Gregor, Cambridge Texts in the History of Philosophy; Cambridge: Cambridge University Press, 1990), p. 354.

[8] Barth, *Unterricht in der christlichen Religion 2, Zweite Band: Die Lehre von Gott/Die Lehre vom Menschen*, p. 46/ET: p. 350.

limits of theological epistemology, and thereby witness to God's forgiveness through altruistic love. This concept affects Barth and Thurneysen from their reading of Dostoevsky's work, though to be fair, this thinking was more explicit in Thurneysen than Barth. Marie in particular is presented by Dostoevsky as an example of юродивый (*iurodivyi*) characterised by смирение (*smirenie* - a form of humility, meekness, often deeply submerged, characterized by, above all else, restraint - that which Christ exhibited at the hands of his tormentors at his trial and execution). Marie dies as a consumptive outcast, rejected by the mean-spirited, self-righteous, pietistic moralising of the village minister and his congregation. Dostoevsky in the notebooks for *The Idiot* comments that Marie was crucial for understanding the story[9] - that like Mitya in *The Brothers Karamazov* it is not primarily licentiousness in itself which destroys people, but bad ideas. And the dialectical antithesis of юродивый (*iurodivyi*) characterised by смирение (*smirenie*) is the assertive human-centred religion of Raskolnikov, Ivan Karamazov, etc. At no point does Marie answer her persecutors back or challenge their prejudiced beliefs, such is her restraint, her submerged humility (смирение - *smirenie*). In the story of Marie Dostoevsky is dialectically setting-off holiness/sanctification against formal self-righteous religion. We noted earlier in chapter 10 on Thurneysen and Barth's understanding of Dostoevsky how it was asserted by them that the meaning of life is concealed so that the wise and the proud and powerful will never find it because the one who does understand sees it as a denial before God, and is regarded as foolish and weak.[10] Hence юродивый (*iurodivyi*) characterised by смирение (*smirenie*), which were traditional marks of saintliness and Christlikeness in Russian Orthodox thinking. In many ways this is a Christian tragedy - but we are wrong to interpret such Christlike worldly failure as wrong before God in Christ, for was not Christ himself forced outside of the formal respectable religion of his day? Boyce Gibson notes how,

> Myshkin is physically and psychologically unequal to the task ... If Myshkin had been physically more robust and normal, and less of an *iurodivyi*, a God's fool... Myshkin is anthropologically Christian, but shows no sign anywhere of corporate affiliations. The tragedy of *The Idiot* is the tragedy of a natural-born but

---

[9] Fyodor Mikhailovich Dostoevsky, *The Notebooks for The Idiot* (trans. Edward Wasiolek; Chicago, IL: University of Chicago Press, 1967), pp. 97, 107, 172, 193, 203. Dostoevsky wrote in these notebooks how, 'смирение (*smirenie* - humility) is a great force', p. 172, and 'смирение (*smirenie* - humility) is the most terrible force that can ever exist in the world!', p. 193. He also noted the importance of 1 Corinthians 4:10 - how we are to be fools for Christ, how our discipleship should be characterized by a foolishness in Christ - юродство (*iurodstvo* - a holy foolishness for Christ's sake, a concept commonly found in Russian Orthodox hagiography). See also Boyce Gibson, *The Religion of Dostoevsky*, pp. 105, 114, 122 and 177.

[10] Thurneysen, *Dostojewski*, p. 23/ET: p. 27.

non-participating Christian. Human compassion needs roots to nourish it and affiliates to work with.[11]

Boyce Gibson continues noting that if Myshkin 'had had the support of an integrated religious community' then perhaps he would not have failed. For Dostoevsky perceiving such holy foolishness is not beyond the most demonic of fallen and wilful people: Svidrigailov perceives it in Sonya and her little sister Polenka (though it does not stop him exercising his predilection for little girls - though he is not without graceful acts of charity). Raskolnikov at the height of his paranoia curses the presence of these holy fools for Christ, and when visiting Sonya and demanding she read the raising of Lazarus to him and in realising how she had spent her evenings in bible study with Lizaveta complains that 'One might well become a holy fool [юродивый] oneself here! It's catching!'[12]

But perhaps it is the curse of saintliness that such people will always be outside of the religious norms, religion that draws its sustenance from this world, not from eternity. This brings in Barth's apophatic understanding that we encountered earlier in chapter 2: the importance and value of negation, provided it pointed ultimately to positive assertions about God, assertions that could only be validated by God - God can only be known by and through God (the *deus dixit*). Thurneysen summed up their love for the work of Dostoevsky in that such negativity clears the way for a more positive affirmation: writing about the novels and characters, 'It is for this that we love them, not for the radical nature of their negations but for their still greater affirmations, which arise from their denials.'[13] This paradox is evident for Barth and Thurneysen in the way love is presented in the New Testament, a form of love that characterized Zossima and Alyosha (*The Brothers Karamazov*), Sonya, Lizaveta and Polenka (*Crime and Punishment*), Myshkin and Marie (*The Idiot*), amongst others:

> This love is astonishingly negative and passive, different from all that we are otherwise accustomed to regard as love. Only in the great negations of 1 Corinthians 13 could it be adequately described: love does not envy; love does not vaunt itself, it is not puffed up, does not behave itself unseemly, seeks not her own, is not easily provoked, thinks no evil.[14]

For Barth this love is shown in the quiet way Alyosha and the Starets Father Zossima refute Ivan's rebellious atheism merely by standing and not by indulging in a Socratic dialogue in an attempt to disprove the other (again, юродивый - *iurodivyi*):[15]

---

[11] Boyce Gibson, *The Religion of Dostoevsky*, p. 122.
[12] Dostoevsky, *Crime and Punishment*, pt. 4 chp. 4, pp. 324-325.
[13] Thurneysen, *Dostojewski*, p. 10/ET: p. 14.
[14] Thurneysen, *Dostojewski*, p. 64/ET: pp. 71-72, referring to 1 Corinthians 13:4b-5.
[15] See Barth, *Römerbrief 2*, p. 128/ET: p. 141, p. 240/ET: p. 238, p. 370/ET: p. 354 and p. 548/ET: p. 520.

Therefore it remains thus. Dostoevsky does not have any final answer or solution to give to us. His solution is found in the great dissolution; his answer is a question, the one burning question of the being of man.[16]

That the *answer* is *no-answer* is exactly what happened when The Grand Inquisitor finishes haranguing Christ - the answer as such is the placing of a kiss of forgiveness on the Cardinal's bloodless lips. It is also *no-answer* as an *answer* that Ivan Karamazov receives at the end of his long theologoumena against a divine reconciliation of the antinomies of suffering in this life.

This theme of the limits to a noetic-logical explanation and closure of the dialectical antinomies of life is something that is consistent in Thurneysen and Barth's work, though in some ways it is a minor theme that is often hidden by Barth's more explicitly intellectual work. For example, Thurneysen comments that it is the children in *The Idiot* who seem to instinctively love and understand who Myshkin is (comments that relate, as Thurneysen asserts, to Kierkegaard's understanding of the *divine incognito*).[17] Barth also shared this understanding in writing to Thurneysen in March 1921, when he commented: 'Today I am collecting the final essays of my confirmation class, and it was such a disappointment. The best is when they say in unison that Christianity is something very complicated and you have to be 20 years old to understand it better. The poor souls, if only they knew!'[18] Such an understanding was still with Barth at the end of his life. In a correspondence with Eberhard Busch in 1968 they discussed this implicit understanding in children, like that shown by the people in Dostoevsky's *Dream of a Ridiculous man*, prior to their Fall. Further, that Christian education/instruction may be inappropriate for young children, as though only adults could truly believe: 'Who knows whether, occasionally, many a child in its 'primitiveness' has a better grasp of this than "we" (Dostoevsky, as you knew, had a special feeling, understanding, for this)!?'[19] Busch continued, 'Indeed is not the God who was in Christ better grasped, or as well, by children than adults?'[20]

---

[16] Thurneysen, *Dostojewski*, p. 10/ET: p. 14.
[17] Thurneysen, *Dostojewski*, pp. 25-26/ET: p. 29.
[18] Barth to Thurneysen, 18 March 1921, Barth and Thurneysen, *Briefwechsel Band 1 1913-1921*, p. 477.
[19] 'Wer Weiß, ob sich nicht gelegentlich herausstellen könnte (Dostojewski hatte bekanntlich ein besonders Gespür dafür), daß manch ein Kind - in seiner ganzen "Primitivität" - besser begreift, warum es geht, als "wir"?!' Eberhard Busch writing to Barth, in Karl Barth, *Briefe 1961-1968* (Gesamtausgabe 5; Zürich: Theologischer Verlag Zürich, 1979), p. 524.
[20] Busch also quotes Thurneysen's *Dostojewski* in support of the arguments cited.

Conclusion

The Marginalizing of Kierkegaard and Dostoevsky

From the mid-1920s on Barth's interest in Dostoevsky - indeed the impression this Russian writer's ideas had on Barth - fades. Indeed as with many other influences, such as Søren Kierkegaard's works, Barth actively distances his thinking from these formative influences and marginalizes their importance. For example, in an address given at his reception of the Sonning Prize in Copenhagen, in 1963 Barth actually marginalizes the importance of Kierkegaard and, in effect, argues against the Danish philosopher's work.[1] Likewise, although Barth did not write so critically on Dostoevsky long after the formative period we have been examining, he does cease to be interested, so to speak, in the Russian's theology - attested to in the scarcity of references to and place for Dostoevsky's ideas in *The Church Dogmatics*.[2] So what do we make of Barth and Dostoevsky in conclusion?

Influence or Illustration?

What role did Barth's reading of Dostoevsky play on his emerging, developing understanding of sin and grace (1915-16), this proto doctrine? How important is the rediscovery of his Reformed theological heritage in the 1920s - does it build on this influence from Dostoevsky, or supplant it? Indeed is it possible to assert categorically that such-and-such a person/work did influence another?' Even if we are sceptical about identifying and asserting influence in a person's work this study has placed Dostoevsky (and Thurneysen) back in with the group of theologians, writers, et cetera who press on Barth's development as a young pastor and theologian: a group which at present omits Dostoevsky to a greater or lesser degree.

---

[1] Karl Barth, 'Dank und Reverenz', pp. 337-342/ET: pp. 3-7.

[2] See Barth, *Church Dogmatics*: II/1, §. 26 'The Knowability of God - 1 The Readiness of God', p. 88; II/2, §. 36 'Ethics as a Task of the Doctrine of God - 1 The Command of God and the Ethical Problem', p. 542; III/4, §. 54 'Freedom in Fellowship - 1 Man and Woman', p. 139; III/4, §. 55 'Freedom for Life - 2 The Protection of Life', p. 413; III/4, §. 56 'Freedom in Limitation - 3 Honour', p. 676; IV/1, §. 61 'The Justification of Man - 3 Justification by Faith Alone', p. 609.

As we have examined Barth and Dostoevsky the question inevitably is raised, 'Is Barth influenced by Dostoevsky, or does he simply use the writer's ideas illustratively?' Between 1911 and 1922 Barth underwent many changes in his thinking, his theology and his beliefs as a Christian. This is essentially what we have referred to as his period of *Wendung* (a radical change of direction) *und Retraktation* (a revision, a reaffirming). It is important to remember that even at this early juncture (1915 on) in this *radikale Wendung* Barth discovers, critically assesses, then he distances and moves on. Influences come thick and fast: this is *Wendung und Retraktation*, according to Barth's usage. This process applied to the influence of Dostoevsky (as also, the effect of the Religious Socialism of Hermann Kutter and Leonhard Ragaz on Barth, also the eschatology of Johann Christoph and Christoph Friedrich Blumhardt, as well as the existentialism of Kierkegaard, Overbeck, Nietzsche, during this period of change).

An Understanding/Doctrine of Sin and Grace?

The purpose of this study was to show how Dostoevsky was an influence on Karl Barth in the period of his theological development, his *Wendung und Retraktation*. Looking at the assembled evidence generally, and at the specific evidence that pointed to the year August 1915 to August 1916 summarized at the end of chapter three, it is fair to say that Dostoevsky was an influence and was not simply used illustratively. So what value can be placed on this influence in the wider context of Barth's theology? How important was the influence of Dostoevsky?

First, it is important to remember that this influence has been marginalized and in some quarters denied. This study therefore re-establishes what was understood implicitly by, for example, Von Balthasar and T.F. Torrance in the mid twentieth-century, and by Barth's contemporaries in the 1920s. However, some of the responsibility lies with Barth - by the end of the 1920s his theology had moved on beyond the existentialism of Dostoevsky, and, as with Kierkegaard, Barth actively marginalized the influence.

Second, it is important to remember that the influence of Dostoevsky rightly belongs in the early period of Barth's *Wendung und Retraktation* - prior to the return to the Bible as the basis of theology in 1916 and subsequently the Reformers. The influence of Dostoevsky's understanding of sin and grace was one amongst many ideas/concepts: eschatology and the Kingdom of God (the Blumhardts and their ministry at Bad Boll); the utter transcendence, *aseity* and sovereignty of God (essentially from discussions with Hermann Kutter); also a criticism of religion and Swiss Religious Socialism. These influences were intense for a while, but Barth reassessed, reconsidered and moved on. They were then supplanted by the Bible and the Reformers as the ground, the foundational basis, (*Grund*) of his theology. In the case of Dostoevsky, this initial or primary understanding is short lived and is supplanted within the year by Paul's understanding of sin and grace in Romans, and a Reformed understanding from Luther and Calvin. But, it was Dostoevsky that gave this understanding to Barth in the first place:

> Where has there been preserved the insight that there is no other grace except the free pardon of criminals, grace in judgement? Is it not shameful that we needed to have this truth retold to us by the Russian Dostoevsky? If we have refused to hear it from our Reformers who really understood it better than Dostoevsky, are we then still Protestants?[3]

Third, it is important to give credit to the relationship between Barth and Thurneysen - that is, the theological relationship throughout their careers, the balance between the Johannine and the Pauline, which was not just in the 1910s and 1920s but something that characterized each man's theology right into their old age - therefore Barth's friend Eduard Thurneysen was also an influence on him (and not just in pointing Barth constantly towards Dostoevsky in the years 1915-1922); furthermore Thurneysen's preoccupation with Dostoevsky meant that the Russian writer's theological beliefs were always relatively fresh in Barth's mind. And we must not underestimate the influence of Barth on Thurneysen's writing of his theological study - *Dostojewski* (1921).

Fourth, it is important to remember that 'the driving forces seem to me to be the Bible and Reformed theology and confessions; other influences have their part, but it is more limited'[4] The importance of the Reformers cannot be overstated in Barth's development particularly in the 1920s when he is teaching theology as Professor of Reformed Theology at Göttingen. Busch, commenting on this period, asserts that the lectures on Calvin show that once Barth turned to the heritage of the Reformers this is his major preoccupation. In Safenwil he had still not really found a way into the Reformers. Barth on his time in Safenwil:

> Of course I also studied Luther and Calvin to some extent. But because I did so through the lenses of spectacles to which I had become accustomed over my years of study (liberal neo-Protestantism), that was not the time and place when I first sought and ... found access to them.[5]

Once he is teaching in Göttingen his priorities change. Barth now concluded that this previous theological understanding (early Safenwil, 1911-16) was grounded in what he termed a pre-Reformation position:

> Now, (writing in 1922) I study. Chiefly the Reformation and everything connected with it... The Calvin lecture for the summer gives me considerable

---

[3] Barth, 'Der römische Katholizismus', p. 357/ET: p. 328.
[4] Comments by Prof. John Webster (King's College, Aberdeen) in correspondence regarding this research, 11 December 2003.
[5] Busch, *Karl Barths Lebenslauf*, p. 156/ET: p. 143, quoting from unpublished notes/sketches towards an incomplete autobiography (*Selbsdarstellung*) by Barth from 1964.

trouble... Yes, dear Edward, we too have probably been there once already, and indeed, I suspect somehow at the corner along with nominalism, Augustinianism, mysticism, Wycliffe, etc. It was not itself the Reformation, but nevertheless the Reformation later sprang out of it. Your *Dostojewski*, Edward, maintains itself as an extraordinarily good book. It gnaws away in private at many of my hearers... [6]

This influence of Dostoevsky is cited by Barth as belonging to this pre-Reformation position in his understanding (but coming after his initial training in nineteenth-century Liberal neo-Protestantism) but nevertheless his passion with 'the Reformation later sprang out of it':

> Only now (Göttingen - early to mid-1920s) were my eyes properly open to the Reformers and their message of the justification and the sanctification of the sinner, of faith, of repentance and works, of the nature and the limits of the church, and so on. I had a great many new things to learn from them. (At that time) I swung into line with the Reformation, as they used to say, not uncritically, but certainly with special attention. [7]

And he was to reflect that this 'message of the justification and the sanctification of the sinner, of faith, of repentance' was initially taught to him by Dostoevsky ('Der römische Katholizismus als Frage...' 1928). The various influences - Blumhardt, Kutter, Dostoevsky, *et al* - during the year of the new starting point, 'led us, as it had to, to the Reformers' understanding of the Bible and of God. (But) what we had learnt on the detour ... was not forgotten' [8]

Fifth, it is important therefore not to over inflate the influence of Dostoevsky. Despite the use, illustratively, during the rewriting of *Der Römerbrief* (and the profound impression made by The Grand Inquisitor) Dostoevsky must be grouped with Christoph Blumhardt, Hermann Kutter, and Swiss Religious socialism in the pre-biblical turn of Barth's theological *Wendung und Retraktation* - specifically the year of the new starting point (1915). In the final analysis Dostoevsky is a stepping-stone, as much as a detour.

Sixth, Dostoevsky is to be seen as a major source in Barth's emerging understanding of sin and grace. Whilst working as assistant Minister at the German-speaking Church in Geneva, Barth's understanding of sin was in keeping with his teacher Wilhelm Herrmann, derived from nineteenth-century Liberal neo-Protestant theology generally. During his ministry in Geneva Barth's understanding of sin, as such, was sociological. With his arrival in Safenwil in 1911 Barth became heavily politicized: sin becomes very real. This

---

[6] Barth-Thurneysen 22 January 1922, Barth and Thurneysen, *Briefwechsel Band II 1921-1930*, p. 30.
[7] Busch, *Karl Barths Lebenslauf*, pp. 156-158/ET: pp. 143-145, quoting from unpublished notes/sketches towards an incomplete autobiography (*Selbsdarstellung*) by Barth from 1964.
[8] Busch, *Karl Barths Lebenslauf*, p. 143, quoting from Karl Barth, 'Rückblick' (a look back, a retrospective view), in Albert D. Schädelin, *Festschrift für Professor D. Albert Schädelin, Bern - Das Wort sie sollen lassen stahn* (Berne: Lang, 1950), p. 5.

was seen in the oppressive attitude of the bosses to the workers. Here we have the heavily political sermons, the involvement with trade unions, articles written against the bourgeois complacency of the wealthy classes, the involvement with Swiss Religious Socialism. Barth's understanding of sin was now political. Fortunately the arrival of Thurneysen in 1913 saves Barth from a secular political career change. In 1915 Thurneysen introduced Barth to the work of Dostoevsky; with this reading sin becomes theological - or more pertinently sin is defined by and in relation to God. Barth begins to develop a theological understanding of sin and grace centred on *eritis sicut deus*: sin and grace must be seen together, sin can only be understood in the light of grace, that is, what God has done to save humanity. This leads Barth into reading Luther and Calvin; and then into studying Reformed theology in-depth, which in turn feeds his developing doctrine of sin and grace. This doctrine was then sharpened up by Barth's encounter with Roman Catholic theologians and philosophers of Religion in the late 1920s. The same balance between sin and grace, the emphasis on *eritis sicut deus* as the ultimate form of sin is then found systematically laid out in Barth's mature work.[9]

The catalyst for Barth developing this doctrine of sin was in many ways his criticism of religion, which was triggered to a degree by his political observations soon after his arrival in Safenwil. There was little evidence of a serious concern with - or criticism of - religion when he was in Geneva. Barth's criticism of religion in the service of the Gospel was initially formed in the first year at Safenwil because of Barth's exposure to the appalling conditions of the poor and those working in factories. This critique was further developed by the influence of Hermann Kutter (1913/14 on). It then received theological impetus from Dostoevsky (1915 on), then from Kierkegaard (1919 on), but the overarching influence on the acerbic critique of religion in *Römerbrief 2* is Overbeck (early 1920 on). The development of Barth's understanding of sin is, like Luther's, built on this criticism of church-religion.

Conclusion - Barth and Dostoevsky

So how important was the influence of Dostoevsky? Yes, the influence of Dostoevsky is important, but as we have seen there were limits to an existential

---

[9] Barth, *Church Dogmatics*: II/2, chp. VII 'The Election of God' §. 33 'The Election of Jesus Christ', pp. 94-195; IV/1, chp. XIII 'The Subject-Matter and Problems of the Doctrine of Reconciliation' §. 58 'The Doctrine of Reconciliation (Survey)', pp.79-156; IV/1, chp. XIV 'Jesus Christ the Lord as Servant' §. 60 'The Pride and the Fall of Man', pp. 358-513; IV/1, chp. XIII 'The Subject Matter and Problems of the Doctrine of Reconciliation' §. 63 'The Holy Spirit and Christian Faith', pp. 740-816; IV/2, chp. XV 'Jesus Christ the Servant as Lord' §. 65 'The Sloth and Misery of Man', pp. 378-498; IV/2, chp. XV 'Jesus Christ the Servant as Lord' §. 66 'The Sanctification of Man', pp. 499-613; IV/3i, chp. XVI 'Jesus Christ the True Witness' §. 70 'The Falsehood and Condemnation of Man', pp. 368-480.

interpretation of the Gospel because it focused on the human side of salvation, not completely on God, or more pertinently it did not focus fully on God's revelation, the *deus dixit* in Christ Jesus. Within Barth's theological *Wendung und Retraktation* there was much apophatic theology - such negative theology can be of importance if it leads in the end to a positive affirmation, to a truer faith and a deeper understanding. The value of existentialism and apophatism is in its ultimate affirmation. Barth saw that the approach of Dostoevsky could under certain circumstances lead to a dualistic interpretation and we have noted his comments to Thurneysen in 1922: 'besides, even old Heilmann wants now to get into Dostoevsky! (Eduard, it is time for us to move on from there to another place, is it not? We must keep a length ahead!!)' [10] The influence of Dostoevsky is therefore on the origin of Barth's theological understanding of sin and grace. This is important but it leads to, and is supplanted by the Reformers.

---

[10] Barth to Thurneysen, 9 May 1922, Barth and Thurneysen, *Briefwechsel Band II 1921-1930*, pp. 69-76.

Bibliography

1. Karl Barth: Works — **210**
- KARL BARTH: PRIMARY SOURCES - BOOKS — 210
- KARL BARTH: PRIMARY SOURCES - ESSAYS, ARTICLES, PAPERS AND REVIEWS — 211
- KARL BARTH: SECONDARY SOURCES - BOOKS — 214
- KARL BARTH: SECONDARY SOURCES - ESSAYS, ARTICLES, PAPERS AND REVIEWS — 215

2. Eduard Thurneysen: Works — **217**
- EDUARD THURNEYSEN: PRIMARY SOURCES - BOOKS — 217
- EDUARD THURNEYSEN AND OTHERS: PRIMARY SOURCES - BOOKS — 218
- EDUARD THURNEYSEN: PRIMARY SOURCES - ESSAYS, ARTICLES, PAPERS AND REVIEWS — 218
- EDUARD THURNEYSEN: SECONDARY SOURCES - BOOKS — 219
- EDUARD THURNEYSEN: SECONDARY SOURCES - ESSAYS, ARTICLES, PAPERS AND REVIEWS — 219

3. Karl Barth and Eduard Thurneysen: Joint Works — **222**
- KARL BARTH AND EDUARD THURNEYSEN: PRIMARY SOURCES - BOOKS — 222

4. Fyodor Mikhailovich Dostoevsky: Works — **223**
- FYODOR MIKHAILOVICH DOSTOEVSKY: PRIMARY SOURCES - NOVELS AND SHORT STORIES — 223
- FYODOR MIKHAILOVICH DOSTOEVSKY: PRIMARY SOURCES - ONLINE RESOURCES — 224
- FYODOR MIKHAILOVICH DOSTOEVSKY: SECONDARY SOURCES - BOOKS — 224
- FYODOR MIKHAILOVICH DOSTOEVSKY: SECONDARY SOURCES - ESSAYS, ARTICLES, PAPERS AND REVIEWS — 225

5. General Sources — **229**
- GENERAL SOURCES: BOOKS — 229
- GENERAL SOURCES: ESSAYS, ARTICLES, PAPERS AND REVIEWS — 231

1. Karl Barth: Works

KARL BARTH: PRIMARY SOURCES - BOOKS

Barth, Karl, *A Letter to Great Britain from Switzerland* (London: Sheldon Press, 1941)
— *A Shorter Commentary on Romans* (London: SCM Press, 1959)
— *Against the Stream: Shorter Post-War Writings 1946-52* (London: SCM Press, 1954)
— *Briefe 1961-1968* (Gesamtausgabe 5; Zürich: Theologischer Verlag Zürich, 1979)
— *Christ and Adam: Man and Humanity in Romans 5* (trans. T.A. Smail; London: Oliver and Boyd, 1956)
— *Community State and Church - Three Essays* (intro. Will Herberg; Gloucester, Mass: P. Smith, 1968)
— *Credo: a Presentation of the Chief Problems of Dogmatics with Reference to the Apostles' Creed* (London: Hodder and Stoughton, 1936)
— *Der Römerbrief* (Erste Fassung; Zürich: Theologischer Verlag Zürich, 1985 [1919])
— *Der Römerbrief* (Zweite Fassung; Zürich: Theologischer Verlag Zürich, 1999 [1922])
— *Die Christliche Dogmatik im Entwurf - Erste Band Die Lehre vom Worte Gottes, Prolegomena zur christlichen Dogmatik 1927* (Gesamtausgabe 14; Zürich: Theologischer Verlag Zürich, 1982)
— *Die protestantische Theologie im 19 Jahrhundert* (Zürich: Theologie Verlag Zürich, 1947)
— *Dogmatics in Outline - lectures on the Creed* (trans. G.T. Thomson; London: SCM Press, 1949)
— *Dogmatik im Grundriß* (München: Christian Kaiser Verlag, 1947)
— *Ethics* (Edinburgh: T&T Clark, 1981)
— *Evangelical Theology* (trans. Grover Foley; London: Weidenfeld and Nicolson, 1963)
— *Fides quaerens intellectum - Anselms Beweis der Existenz Gottes im Zusammenhang seines theologischen Programms* (München, Christian Kaiser Verlag, 1931). ET: Karl Barth, *Anselm: Fides Quaerens Intellectum* (London: S.C.M. Press, 1960)
— *Fragments Grave and Gay*, (The Fontana Library of Theology and Philosophy; London: Collins, 1971)
— *God in Action - Theological Addresses by Karl Barth* (intro. Josias Friedli; Edinburgh: T&T Clark, 1936)
— *God, Grace and Gospel* (London: Oliver and Boyd, 1959)
— *Gottedienst-Menschendienst Eduard Thurneysen zum 70 Geburtstag am 10 July 1958* (Zollikon-Zürich: Evangelischer Verlag AG, 1958)
— *Göttingen Dogmatics - Instruction in the Christian Religion, vol. 1* (trans. G.W. Bromiley; Grand Rapids, MI: Eerdmans, 1990)
— *Karl Barth-Emil Brunner Briefwechsel 1916-1966* (Gesamtausgabe 33; Zürich: Theologischer Verlag Zürich, 2000)
— *Letters 1961-1968* (trans. G.W. Bromiley; Edinburgh: T&T Clark, 1981)
— *Natural Theology - Comprising 'Nature and Grace' by Professor Dr Emil Brunner and the reply 'No!' by Dr Karl Barth* (trans. John Baillie of *Nein!* a pamphlet originally published in 1934 by Barth and *Natur und Guade*, by Emil Brunner likewise a pamphlet from 1934; London: The Centenary Press, 1946)
— *Predigten 1913* (Gesamtausgabe 8; Zürich: Theologischer Verlag Zürich, 1994)
— *Predigten 1914* (Gesamtausgabe 5; Zürich: Theologischer Verlag Zürich, 1999)
— *Predigten 1915* (Gesamtausgabe 27; Zürich: Theologischer Verlag Zürich, 1996)
— *Predigten 1916* (Gesamtausgabe 29; Zürich: Theologischer Verlag Zürich, 1998)
— *Predigten 1917* (Gesamtausgabe 32; Zürich: Theologischer Verlag Zürich, 1999)

— *Predigten 1918* (Gesamtausgabe 37; Zürich: Theologischer Verlag Zürich, 2002)
— *Protestant Theology in the Nineteenth Century* (trans. Brian Cozens and John Bowden; London: SCM Press, 1959)
— *Service in Christ: Essays Presented to Karl Barth on his 80th birthday by J.L. McCord and T.H.L. Parker* (London: Epworth Press, 1966)
— *The Church Dogmatics* (14 vols., eds. G.W. Bromiley and T.F. Torrance; Edinburgh: T&T Clark, 1936-77)
— *The Epistle to the Romans* (trans. Edwyn Hoskyns; Oxford: Oxford University Press, 1933)
— *The Faith of the Church - a Commentary on the Apostles' Creed According to Calvin's Catechism* (ed. Jean-Louis Leuba, trans. Gabriel Vahanian; London: Collins, 1960)
— *The Heidelberg Catechism for Today* (London: Epworth Press, 1964)
— *The Holy Ghost and the Christian Life* (London: F. Muller, 1938)
— *The Humanity of God* (trans. John Newton Thomas; Louisville, KY: Westminster John Knox Press, 1960)
— *The knowledge of God and the Service of God According to the Teaching of the Reformation, Recalling the Scottish Confession of 1560* (London: Hodder and Stoughton, 1949)
— *The Resurrection of the Dead* (trans. H. J. Stenning; London: Hodder and Stoughton, 1933)
— *The Theology of Schleiermacher: Lectures at Göttingen, Winter Semester of 1923/24* (Edinburgh: T&T Clark, 1982)
— *Unterricht in der christlichen Religion 1, Erster Band: Prolegomena 1924*, (Gesamtausgabe 17; Zürich: Theologischer Verlag Zürich, 1985)
— *Unterricht in der christlichen Religion 2, Zweite Band: Die Lehre von Gott/Die Lehre vom Menschen* (Gesamtausgabe 20; Zürich: Theologischer Verlag Zürich, 1990)
— *Unterricht in der christlichen Religion 3, Dritter Band: Die Lehre von der Versöhnung/Die Lehre von der Erlösung (Eschatologie) 1925/1926* (Gesamtausgabe 38; Zürich: Theologischer Verlag Zürich, 2003)

KARL BARTH: PRIMARY SOURCES - ESSAYS, ARTICLES, PAPERS AND REVIEWS

Barth, Karl, 'Abschied', *Zwischen den Zeiten* 11 (1933), pp. 536-544
— 'Autobiographische Skizzen Karl Barths aus den Fakultätsalben der Evangelical Theologie Fakultät in Münster (1927)', in Karl Barth, *Karl Barth-Rudolf Bultmann, Briefwechsel 1922-1966* (Zürich: Theologischer Verlag Zürich, 1971), pp. 301-312. ET: Karl Barth, 'Autobiographic sketches of Karl Barth from the faculty album of the Evangelical theology Faculty in Münster (1927)', in Karl Barth, *Karl Barth-Rudolf Bultmann Letters 1922-1966* (trans. and ed. G.W. Bromiley; Edinburgh: T&T Clark, 1971), pp.150-158
— 'Biblische Fragen, Einsichten und Ausblicke', in Karl Barth, *Das Wort Gottes und die Theologie* (München: Christian Kaiser Verlag, 1924), pp. 70-98. ET: Karl Barth, 'Biblical Questions, Insights and Vistas', in Karl Barth, *The Word of God and the Word of Man*, (trans. Douglas Horton; London: Hodder and Stoughton, 1928), pp. 51-96
— 'Concluding Unscientific Postscript on Schleiermacher', in Karl Barth, *The Theology of Schleiermacher: Lectures at Göttingen, Winter Semester 1923-4* (trans. G.W. Bromiley; Grand Rapids, MI: Eerdmans, 1982)

— 'Dank und Reverenz', *Evangelische Theologie* 23.7 (July 1963), pp. 337-342. ET: Karl Barth, 'A Thank You and A Bow: Kierkegaard's Reveille', *Canadian Journal of Theology* 11.1 (1965), pp. 3-7

— 'Das Problem der Ethik in der Gegenwart', in Karl Barth, *Das Wort Gottes und die Theologie* (München: Christian Kaiser Verlag, 1924), pp. 125-155. ET: Karl Barth, 'The Problem of Ethics Today', in Karl Barth, *The Word of God and the Word of Man* (trans. Douglas Horton; London: Hodder and Stoughton, 1928), pp. 136-182

— 'Das Wort Gottes als Aufgabe der Theologie', in Karl Barth, *Das Wort Gottes und dieTheologie* (München: Christian Kaiser Verlag, 1924), pp. 156-178. ET: Karl Barth, 'The Word of God and the Task of Ministry', in Karl Barth, *The Word of God and the Word of Man* (trans. Douglas Horton; London: Hodder and Stoughton, 1928), pp. 183-217

— 'Der Begriff der Kirche', a lecture given at the University Association of the Centre Party in Münster on the 11 July 1927, in Karl Barth, *Die Theoligie und die Kirche* (Zollikon-Zürich: Evangelischer Verlag AG, 1928), pp. 364-391. ET: Karl Barth, 'The Concept of the Church', in Karl Barth, *Theology and Church: Shorter Writings 1920-1928* (ed. T.F. Torrance, trans. Louise Pettibone Smith; London: SCM Press, 1962), pp. 334-354

— 'Der Christ in der Gesellschaft', in Karl Barth, *Das Wort Gottes und die Theologie*, (München: Christian Kaiser Verlag, 1924), pp. 33-69. ET: Karl Barth, 'The Christian in Society', in Karl Barth, *The Word of God and the Word of Man* (trans. Douglas Horton; London: Hodder and Stoughton, 1928), pp. 272-327

— 'Der christliche Glaube und die Geschichte', *Schweizerische theologie Zeitschrift* 29 (1912), pp. 1-18 and 65-95

— 'Der Glaube an den persönlichen Gott', *Zeischrift für Theologie und Kirche* XXIV (1914), pp. 21-32 and pp. 65-95

— 'Der römische Katholizismus als Frage an die protestantische Kirche', in Karl Barth, *Die Theoligie und die Kirche* (Zollikon-Zürich: Evangelischer Verlag AG, 1928), pp. 329-363. ET: Karl Barth, 'Roman Catholicism: A Question To The Protestant Church', in Karl Barth, *Theology and Church: Shorter Writings 1920-1928* (ed. T.F. Torrance, trans. Louise Pettibone Smith; London: SCM Press, 1962), pp. 307-333

— 'Die Gerechtigkeit Gottes', in Karl Barth, *Das Wort Gottes und die Theologie* (München: Christian Kaiser Verlag, 1924), pp. 5-17. ET: Karl Barth, 'The Righteousness of God', in Karl Barth, *The Word of God and the Word of Man* (trans. Douglas Horton; London: Hodder and Stoughton, 1928), pp. 9-27

— 'Die Kirche und die Kulture', lecture delivered to the Congress of the Continental Association for Home Missions in Amsterdam on 1 June 1926 published in Karl Barth, *Die Theoligie und die Kirche* (Zollikon-Zürich: Evangelischer Verlag AG, 1928), pp. 364-391. ET: Karl Barth, 'Church and Culture', in Karl Barth, *Theology and Church: Shorter Writings 1920-1928* (ed. T.F. Torrance, trans. Louise Pettibone Smith; London: SCM Press, 1962), pp. 334-354

— 'Die Menschlichkeit Gottes', in Karl Barth, *Die Menschlichkeit Gottes* (Zollikon-Zürich: Evangelischer Verlag AG, 1956), pp. 6-7

— 'Die neue Welt in der Bibel', in Karl Barth, *Das Wort Gottes und die Theologie* (München: Christian Kaiser Verlag, 1924), pp. 18-32. ET: Karl Barth, 'The Strange New World in the Bible', in Karl Barth, *The Word of God and the Word of Man* (trans. Douglas Horton; London: Hodder and Stoughton), 1928, pp. 28-50

— 'Die Theologie und der heutige Mensch', *Zwischen den Zeiten* 8 (1930), pp. 374-396

— 'Der Glaube und die Geschichte', *Schweizerische Theologie Zeitschrift* 29 (1912), pp. 1-18 and 65-95

— 'Evangelical Theology in the nineteenth-century', in Karl Barth, *The Humanity of God* (trans. Thomas Weiser; Louisville, KY: Westminster John Knox Press, 1960), pp. 11-33

— 'Evangelische Theologie im 19 Jahrhundert', in Karl Barth, *Evangelische Theologie im 19 Jahrhundert* (Zollikon-Zürich: Evangelischer Verlag AG, 1956), p. 14

— 'Foreword', in Heinrich Heppe, *Reformed Dogmatics set out and Illustrated from the Sources* (trans. G.T. Thomson, ed. Ernst Bizer; London: Allen and Unwin, 1950. [1861])

— 'Geleitwort', in Eduard Thurneysen, *Das Wort Gottes und die Kirche* (München: Christian Kaiser Verlag, 1927), p. 227

— 'Jesus Christ and the Movement for Social Justice', in George Hunsinger (ed.) *Karl Barth and Radical Politics* (Philadelphia: The Westminster Press, 1976), pp. 19-37

— 'Jesus Christus und die soziale Bewegung', address to the Safenwil Workers' Association on the 17 December 1911, initially published in, *Der Freie Aargauer, Offizielles Organ der Arbeiterpartei des Kantons Aargau*, 6.153-156 (23, 26, 28 and 30 December 1911)

— 'Kirche und Theologie', an address given on the 7 October 1925 at the Göttingen Autumn Conference and on the 23 October 1925 at the Theological Week at Everfield, in Karl Barth, *Die Theoligie und die Kirche* (Zollikon-Zürich: Evangelischer Verlag AG, 1928). ET: Karl Barth, 'Church and Theology', in Karl Barth, *Theology and Church: Shorter Writings 1920-1928* (ed. T.F. Torrance, trans. Louise Pettibone Smith; London: SCM Press, 1962)

— 'Kriegszeit und Gottesreich', in Herbert Anzinger, *Glaube und kommunikative Praxis* (München: Christian Kaiser Verlag, 1991)

— 'Lebendige Vergangenheit', an essay in honour of Thurneysen, in Karl Barth (ed.), *Gottedienst-Menschendienst Eduard Thurneysen zum 70 Geburtstag am 10 July 1958*, (Zollikon-Zürich: Evangelischer Verlag AG, 1958), pp. 7-14

— 'Ludwig Feuerbach', an extract from lectures on the history of modern theology given at Münster in the summer of 1920, in Karl Barth, *Die Theoligie und die Kirche* (Zollikon-Zürich: Evangelischer Verlag AG, 1928). ET: Karl Barth, 'Ludwig Feuerbach', in Karl Barth, *Theology and Church: Shorter Writings 1920-1928* (ed. T.F. Torrance, trans. Louise Pettibone Smith; London: SCM Press, 1962)

— 'Moderne Theologie und Reichgottesarbeit', *Zeitschrift für Theologie und Kirche* XIX (1909), pp. 317-321

— 'Nachwort', in Karl Barth, *Schleiermacher-Auswahl* (series, Siebenstern Taschenbuch 113-14; München: Siebenstern Taschenbuch Verlag, 1968)

— 'Not und Verheißung der christlichen Verkündigung', in Karl Barth, *Das Wort Gottes und die Theologie* (München: Christian Kaiser Verlag, 1924), pp. 99-124. ET: Karl Barth, 'The Need and Promise of Christian Teaching', in Karl Barth, *The Word of God and the Word of Man* (trans. Douglas Horton; London: Hodder and Stoughton, 1928), pp. 97-135

— 'Reformierte Lehre, ihr Wesen und ihre Aufgabe', in Karl Barth, *Das Wort Gottes und die Theologie* (München: Christian Kaiser Verlag, 1924), pp. 179-212. ET: Karl Barth, 'The Doctrinal Task of the Reformed Churches', in Karl Barth, *The Word of God and the Word of Man* (trans. Douglas Horton; London: Hodder and Stoughton, 1928), pp. 218-271

— 'Rückblick', in Albert D. Schädelin, *Festschrift für Professor D. Albert Schädelin, Bern - Das Wort sie sollen lassen stahn* (with contributions from Heinrich Barth, Karl Barth, Robert Morgenthaler and Otto Erich Strasser; Bern: Lang, 1950)

— 'The Humanity of God', in Karl Barth, *The Humanity of God* (trans. John Newton Thomas; Louisville: Westminster: John Knox Press, 1960), pp. 40-41

— 'Unerledigte Anfragen an die heitige Theologie', in Karl Barth, *Die Theoligie und die Kirche* (Zollikon-Zürich: Evangelischer Verlag AG, 1928), pp. 1-26. ET: Karl Barth, 'Unsettled Questions for Theology Today', in Karl Barth, *Theology and Church: Shorter Writings 1920-1928* (ed. T.F. Torrance, trans. Louise Pettibone Smith; London: SCM Press, 1962), pp. 55-73

— 'Vergangenheit und Zukunft (Friedrich Naumann und Christoph Blumhardt)', *Neuer Freier Aargauer* (1919), pp. 204-205

KARL BARTH: SECONDARY SOURCES - BOOKS

Anzinger, Herbert, *Glaube und kommunikative Praxis* (München: Christian Kaiser Verlag, 1991)
Bakker, Nicolaas Tjepko, *Der Krisis in der Offenbarung - Karl Barths Hermeneutik, dargestellt an seiner Römerbrief-Auslegung* (Neukirchen-Vluyn: Neukirchener Verlag, 1974)
Balthasar, Hans Urs von, *Karl Barth, Darstellung und Deutung seiner Theologie* (Köln: Verlag Jakob Hegner, 1951)
— *The Theology of Karl Barth - Exposition and Interpretation* (trans. Edward T. Oates S.J.; San Francisco, CA: Ignatius Press, Communio Books, 1991)
Beintker, Michael, *Die Dialektik in der 'dialektischen Theologie' Karl Barths* (München: Christian Kaiser Verlag, 1987)
Bouillard, Henri. *Karl Barth vol. 1 Genèse et évolution de la théologie dialectique* (Aubier, Paris: Éditions Montaigne, 1957)
Brazier, P.H. ' "Die Freiheit in der Gefangenschaft Gottes" The Nature and Content of the Influence of Dostoevsky on Karl Barth 1915 to 1922' (PhD thesis, King's College London, September 2005)
Bromiley, G.W., *Introduction to the Theology of Karl Barth* (Edinburgh: T&T Clark, 1979)
Busch, Eberhard, *Karl Barth His Life from Letters and Autobiographical Texts* (trans. John Bowden; London: SCM Press, 1976)
— *Karl Barths Lebenslauf: nach seinem Briefen und autobiographischen Texten* (München: Christian Kaiser Verlag, 1975)
Coward, Harold and Toby Foshay (eds.), *Derrida and Negative Theology* (New York, NY: State University of New York Press, 1992)
Cross, Terry L., *Dialectic in Karl Barth's Doctrine of God* (series, Issues in Systematic Theology 7; New York, NY: Peter Lang, 2001)
Davis, Oliver and Denys Turner (eds.), *Silence and the Word Negative Theology and Incarnation* (Cambridge: Cambridge University Press, 2002)
Finke, Anne-Kathrin, *Karl Barth in Großbritannien Rezeption und Wirkungsgeschichte* (Neukirchen-Vluyn: Neukirchener, 1995)
Garnett, Paul E., *Karl Barth A Theological Legacy* (Philadelphia, PA: The Westminster Press, 1986)
Green, Clifford, *Karl Barth Theologian of Freedom* (London: Collins Liturgical Publications, 1989)
Gunton, Colin E., *The Barth Lectures* (ed. P.H. Brazier, foreword Christoph Schwöbel, intro. Stephen R. Holmes; London: T&T Clark, Continuum, 2007)
Hamer, Jerome, *Karl Barth - L'Occasionalisme Theologique de Karl Barth, Étude sur sa methode dogmatique* (Paris: Desclée de Brouwer, 1949)
Hoyle, Richard Birch, *The Teaching of Karl Barth An Exposition* (London: SCM Press, 1930)
Hunsinger, George, *Disruptive Grace - Studies in the Theology of Karl Barth* (Grand Rapids, MI: Eerdmans, 2000)
— *How to Read Karl Barth* (Oxford: Oxford University Press, 1991)
— *Karl Barth and Radical Politics* (Philadelphia, PA: The Westminster Press, 1976)
Jüngel, Eberhard, *Barth-Studien* (Zürich-Köln: Benziger Verlag, 1982)
Kooi, Cornelius Van der, *Anfängliche Theologie - Der Denkweg des jungen Karl Barth*

1909 bis 1927 (München: Christian Kaiser Verlag, 1987)

Küng, Hans, *Justification: the Doctrine of Karl Barth and a Catholic Reflection by Hans Küng with a Letter from Karl Barth* (London: Burns and Oates, 1964)

McCormack, Bruce, *Karl Barth's Critically Realistic Dialectical Theology: Its Genesis and Development 1909-1936* (Oxford: Oxford University Press, Clarendon Paperbacks, 1995)

McDowell, John C., *Barth's Eschatology: Interrogation and Transformations beyond Tragedy* (Aldershot: Ashgate, 2000)

Pfleiderer, Georg, *Karl Barths praktische Theologie: Zu Genese und Kontext eines paradignatischen Entwurfs systematischer Theologie im 20 Jahrhundert*, (series, Beiträge zur historischen Theologie 115; Tübingen: Mohr Siebeck, 2000)

Reardon, Bernard, (ed.) *Liberal Protestantism* (London: Adam and Charles Black, 1968)

Rumscheidt, Martin, *Revelation and theology - an analysis of the Barth-Harnack correspondence of 1923* (London: Cambridge University Press, 1972)

Rupp, George, *Culture-Protestantism: German Liberal Theology at the turn of the Twentieth Century* (American Academy of Religion Studies in Religion 15; Missoula, MT: Scholars Press, 1977)

Smith, Steven G., *The Argument to the Other - Reason Beyond Reason in the Thought of Karl Barth and Emmanuel Levinas* (American Academy of Religion, Academy series, no 42; Chico, CA: Scholars Press, 1983)

Spieckermann, Ingrid, *Gotteskenntnis: Ein Beitrag zur Grundfrage der neun Theologie Karl Barths* (München: Christian Kaiser Verlag, 1985)

Thorne, Phillip R., *Evangelicalism and Karl Barth his Reception and Influence in North American Evangelical Theology* (Pennsylvania, PA: Pickwick Publications, 1995)

Torrance, T.F., *Karl Barth An Introduction to his Early Theology 1910-1931* (Edinburgh: T&T Clark, 1962)

— *Karl Barth Biblical and Evangelical Theologian* (Edinburgh: T&T Clark, 1990)

Walker, James Silas, 'The Development of Karl Barth's Theology from the first edition of *Der Römerbrief* through to the second edition of *Der Römerbrief*' (PhD thesis, Claremont Graduate School, 1963; Ann Arbor, MI: University Microfilms Inc, 1963)

Webb, Stephen H., *Re-figuring Theology The Rhetoric of Karl Barth* (Albany, NY: University of New York Press, 1991)

Webster, John, *Barth* (series, Outstanding Christian Thinkers; London: Continuum, 2000)

Wingren, Gustaf, *Theology in Conflict* (Philadelphia, PA: Muhlenberg Press, 1958)

KARL BARTH: SECONDARY SOURCES - ESSAYS, ARTICLES, PAPERS AND REVIEWS

Adam, Karl, 'Die Theologie der Krisis', *Hochland XXIII* (1926), pp. 271-286

Brazier, P.H. 'Barth and Rome - II: Socialism, the Church and a Theocratic Illusion', *Downside Review*, 124.434 (January 2006), pp. 61-78

— 'Barth and Expressionism - Some Further Considerations', *Zeitschrift für dialektische Theologie*, 20.1 (Fall 2005), pp. 34-52

— 'Barth and Rome - a Critical Engagement', *Downside Review*, 123.431 (April 2005), pp. 137-152

— 'Barth's First Commentary on Romans (1919) - An Exercise in Apophatic Theology?', *The International Journal of Systematic Theology* 6.4 (2004), pp. 387-403

Busch, Eberhard, 'God is God: The Meaning of a Controversial Formula and the Fundamental Problem of Speaking about God', *Princeton Seminary Bulletin* 7.2

(1986), pp.101-113

Glick, Wayne G., 'Karl Barth and the Theology of the Word of God (Barth vs Harnack)', *Brethren Life and Thought*, 5 (Spring 1960), pp. 29-38

Gogarten, Friedrich, 'Karl Barths Dogmatik', *Theologische Runfschau* NF 1 (1929), pp. 60-80

Gunton, Colin E., 'One Mediator - the Man Jesus Christ', *Pro Ecclesia* 11.2 (Spring 2002), pp. 146-158

— 'The Triune God and the Freedom of the Creature', in Stephen W. Sykes (ed.), *Karl Barth - Centenary Essays* (Cambridge: Cambridge University Press, 1989)

Hart, Trevor, 'Revelation', in John Webster (ed.), *The Cambridge Companion to Karl Barth* (Cambridge: Cambridge University Press, 2000)

Heron, Alasdair, 'Karl Barth: a Personal Engagement', in John Webster (ed.), *The Cambridge Companion to Karl Barth* (Cambridge: Cambridge University Press, 2000)

Lowe, Wilhelm, 'Noch einmal Barths *Römerbrief*', *Die Christliche Welt*, XXXIV, (1920), pp. 585-587

McKinnon, Alastair, 'Barth's Relation to Kierkegaard: Some Further Light', *Canadian Journal of Theology* 13.1, (1967)

Neuser, Wilhelm, 'Karl Barth in Münster 1925 bis 1930', *Theologische Studien und Kritiken*, 130 (1985), pp. 37-40

Noordmans, Oepke, 'De Zwitserse Theologie (1926)', in Oepke Noordmans, *Geestelijke perspectieven* (Amsterdam: H.J. Paris, 1930)

Sauter, Gerhard, 'Die "dialektische Theologie" und das Problem der Dialektik in der Theologie', in Gerhard Sauter, *Erwartung und Erfahrung - Predigten, Vortrage und Aufsatze* (Munich: Christian Kaiser Verlag, 1972)

Sneller, Rico, 'Crisis in our Speaking about God: Derrida and Barth's Epistle to the Romans', in Isle N. Bulhof, and Laurens ten Kate, *Flight of the Gods - Philosophical Perspectives on Negative Theology* (New York, NY: Fordham University Press, 2000)

Webster, John, '"On the Frontiers of what is Observable": Barth's Römerbrief and Negative Theology', *Downside Review* 105 (July 1987), pp. 169-180

Wilson, John E., 'Der Briefwechsel zwischen Ida Overbeck-Rothpletz und Carl Albrecht Bernoulli über Frau Overbecks Gespräch mit Karl Barth im Jahre 1920', *Theologische Zeitschrift* 43.3 (1987), pp. 282-294

2. Eduard Thurneysen: Works

EDUARD THURNEYSEN: PRIMARY SOURCES - BOOKS

Thurneysen, Édouard, *Dostoïevski ou les confins de l'homme* (traduit de l'allemand par P. Maury; Paris: Éditions "Je sers", 1934)
— *A Theology of Pastoral Care* (trans. Jack A Worthington and Thomas Wieser; Richmond, VA: John Knox Press, 1962)
— *Antwort Festschrift zum 70 Geburtstag von Karl Barth* (Zollikon-Zürich: Evangelischer Verlag AG, 1956)
— *Christ und welt: fragen und antworten* (Basel: Reinhardt, 1950)
— *Christliche unterweisung* (Zürich: Gotthelf, 1948)
— *Christoph Blumhardt* (München: Christian Kaiser Verlag, 1926)
— *Das Wort Gottes und die Kirche* (München: Christian Kaiser Verlag, 1927)
— *Das Wort Gottes und die Kirche* (reissued with a 'Geleitwort' by Karl Barth; München: Christian Kaiser Verlag, 1971)
— *Der brief des Jakobus: ausgelegt für die gemeinde* (Basel: F. Reinhardt, 1941)
— *Der Brief des Paulus an die Philipper* (Basel: F. Reinhardt, 1943)
— *Der Mensch von heute und das Evangelium: ein Beitrag zur Praktischen Theologie in zwei Vorträgen über Seelsorge am Menschen von heute und Seelsorge am Seelsorger* (Zollikon-Zürich: Evangelischer Verlag AG, 1964)
— *Der Mensch von heute und die Kirche* (Berlin: Furche-Bücherei, 1936)
— *Die allgemein kirchliche verantwortung der Schweizer kirchen* (Zollikon-Zürich: Evangelischer Verlag AG, 1940)
— *Die Bergpredigt* (München: Christian Kaiser Verlag, 1963)
— *Die Fülle in Jesus Christus* (München: Christian Kaiser Verlag, 1935)
— *Die Gnade genügt! ein Wort zu zwei verwirrenden Geistesströmungen unserer Tage* (Basel: Verlag Bibelschule, 1950?)
— *Die Kirche in Luthers Auslegung des Glaubens* (München: Christian Kaiser Verlag, 1938)
— *Die Kraft der Geringen. Drei Predigten* (series, Theologische Existenz heute, Schriftenreihe 8; München: Christian Kaiser Verlag, 1934)
— *Die Lehre von der Seelsorge* (Zollikon-Zürich: Evangelische Verlag AG, 1946)
— *Die neue Zeit - Predigten 1913-1930* (Neukirchen-Vluyn: Neukirchener Verlag, 1982)
— *Die Verkündigung des Wortes Gottes in unserer Zeit: ein Beitrag zur erneuerung der Kirche* (Zollikon-Zürich: Evangelischer Verlag AG, 1941)
— *Dostoevsky - A Theological Study* (trans. Keith R. Crim; London: Epworth Press, 1964)
— *Dostojewski* (München: Christian Kaiser Verlag, 1921)
— *Dosutoefusukii kenkyu: benshoho shingaku yori mitaru. Dosutoefusuki kenkyu: igakuteki shinrigakuteki tachiba ni okeru* (trans. Thimoteus Segaloff, series Dosutoefusukii bunken shusei; Tokyo: Ozorasha, 1933)
— *In seinen Händen: Grabreden; ein Trostbuch* (Neukirchen-Vluyn: Neukirchener Verlag, 1978)
— *Karfreitag und Ostern - zwei predigten gehalten an Karfreitag und Ostern 1943* (Basel: Verlag Evangelische Buchhandlung, 1944)
— *Kreuz und Wiederkunft Christi: zwei Vorträge und ein Nachwort über Rechtgläubigkeit und Frömmigkeit* (München: Christian Kaiser Verlag, 1939)
— *Kriegszeit und Gotteswort - predigten* (Basel, Verlag Evangelische Buchhandlung, 1941?)

— *Lazarus und der reiche Mann: Lukas 16, 19-31, Predigt, gehalten am 26 Mai 1940 im Münster zu Basel* (Basel: Verlag Evangelische Buchhandlung, 1940)
— *Lebendige Gemeinde und Bekenntnis* (München: Christian Kaiser Verlag, 1935)
— *Praktische Seelsorge 2 Auflage* (Gütersloh: Verlagshaus Gerd Mohn, 1978)
— *Seelsorge im Vollzug* (Zollikon-Zürich: Evangelischer Verlag AG, 1968)
— *Seelsorge und Psychotherapie* (München: Christian Kaiser Verlag, 1950)
— *The Sermon on the Mount* (Richmond, VA: John Knox Press, 1964)
— *Unser Herr kommt!* (Basel: Reinhardt, 1965)
— *Warum mission heute?* (Basel: Basler missionsbuchhandlung, 1942)

EDUARD THURNEYSEN AND OTHERS: PRIMARY SOURCES - BOOKS

Thurneysen, Eduard and Max Geiger, *Karl Barth, Theologie und Sozialismus in den Briefen seiner Frühzeit* (Zürich: Theologischer Verlag Zürich, 1973)

Thurneysen, Eduard; Max Geiger and Rolf Eberhard, *Berner Splitter und Festtagsartikel* (Zollikon-Zürich: Evangelischer Verlag AG, 1967)

Thurneysen, Eduard and Walter Lüthi, *Abendmahl und Beichte: ein Wort an unsere Gemeinden* (Zollikon-Zürich: Evangelischer Verlag AG, 1944)

— *Der Erlöser - dreissig Predigten* (Basel: F. Reinhardt, 1961)

— *Der ich dich aus demn Sklavenhause geführt habe - Bibelarbeit und Predigt gehalten am deutschen evangelischen Kirchentag 1952 in Stuttgart* (Zürich: Evangelischer Verlag, 1952)

— *Du sollst mich preisen - 30 Predigten* (Bonn: Cohen, 1915)

— *Gerechtigkeit!* (Basel: Friedrich Reinhardt 1950)

— *Preaching, Confession, The Lord's Supper - Essays By Two Swiss Theologians* (trans. Francis J. Brooke; Richmond: John Knox Press, 1960)

— *Predigt Beicht Abendmah - Ein Wort an unsere Gemeinden* (Zollikon-Zürich: Evangelischer Verlag AG, 1957)

EDUARD THURNEYSEN: PRIMARY SOURCES
ESSAYS, ARTICLES, PAPERS AND REVIEWS

Thurneysen, Eduard, ' "A theology of pastoral care", by E. Thurneysen, and its relation to Barthian theology, reply to S. Hiltner and J.A. Worthington', *Pastoral Psychology* 13 (Fall 1962), pp. 59-60

— 'die Anfänge', in Eduard Thurneysen (ed.), *Antwort Festschrift zum 70. Geburtstag von Karl Barth* (Zollikon-Zürich: Evangelischer Verlag AG, 1956), pp. 831-864

— 'End of all Things: a Sermon' (trans. Donald G. Miller), *Interpretation* 12.4 (October 1958), pp. 407-411

— 'Offenbarung als Sprachereignis', *Theologische Zeitschrift* 20 (May-June 1964), pp. 192-206

— 'Predigt über Matthäus 16:13-16, 21-28, Gehalten in der deutsch-lutherischen Kirche zu Utrecht, Sonntag, 1 März 1936', *Evangelische Theologie* 3.4 (April 1936), pp. 127-135

— 'Predigt über Römer 8:11', *Evangelische Theologie* 2.1 (April 1935), pp. 1-8

— 'Rédaction et mémorisation de la prédication - étude homilétique', *Revue d'histoire et de philosophie religieuses* 36.3 (1956), pp. 202-207

— 'Seelsorge als Verkündigung', *Evangelische Theologie* 22.6 (1962), pp. 297-303

— 'Warum nicht Gollwitzer - Ein Wort zum Kampf um die Nachfolge Karl Barths in Basel', *Evangelische Theologie* 22.5 (1962), pp. 271-277

— 'Zum Prolog des John', *Zwischen den Zeiten* 3 (1925), pp. 12-37

EDUARD THURNEYSEN: SECONDARY SOURCES - BOOKS

Algner, Caren, *Kirchliche Dogmatik im Vollzug: Karl Barths Kampf um die Kirche im Spiegel von seiner und Charlotte von Kirschbaums Korrespondenz mit Eduard Thurneysen 1930-1935* (Neukirchen-Vluyn: Neukirchener, 2004)

Barth, Karl (ed.), *Gottesdienst-Menschendienst: Eduard Thurneysen zum 70 Geburtstag am 10 Juli 1958* (Zollikon-Zürich: Evangelischer Verlag AG, 1958)

Bohren, Rudolf and Max Geiger (eds.), *Wort und Gemeinde Problem und Aufgaben der praktischen Theologie: Edward Thurneysen zum 80 Geburtstag* (Zollikon-Zürich: Evangelischer Verlag AG, 1968)

Bohren, Rudolf, *Prophetie und Seelsorge - Eduard Thurneysen* (Neukirchen-Vluyn: Neukirchener Verlag, 1982)

Fürst, Walther (ed.), *Dialektische Theologie in Scheidung und Bewährung 1933-1936, Aufsätze, Gutachten und Erklärungen* (München: Christian Kaiser Verlag, 1966)

Jochheim, Martin, *Seelsorge und Psychotherapie - historisch-systematische Studien zur Lehre von der Seelsorge bei Oskar Pfister, Eduard Thurneysen und Walter Uhsadel* (Bochum: Winkler, 1998)

Köhler, Rudolf, *Kritik der Theologie der Krisis: eine Auseinandersetzung mit Karl Barth, Friedrich Gogarten, Emil Brunner und Eduard Thurneysen* (Berlin: Hutten, 1925)

Moltmann, Jürgen (ed.), *Anfänge der dialektischen Theologie* (München, Christian Kaiser Verlag, 1962)

Quervain, Paul Fredi de, *Psychoanalyse und dialektische Theologie: zum Freud-Verständnis bei K. Barth, E. Thurneysen und P. Ricoeur* (Bern: H. Huber, 1978)

Rim, Gol, *Gottes Wort, Verkündigung und Kirche: die systematisch-theologischen Grundlagen der Theologie Eduard Thurneysens* (Münster and London: Lit Verlag, 2000)

Selinger, Suzanne, *Charlotte von Kirschbaum and Karl Barth: a Study in Biography and the History of Theology* (Pennsylvania, PA: Pennsylvania State University Press, 1998)

Worthington, Jack Austin, 'Anxiety and Forgiveness in Pastoral Care a Critical and Constructive Study of the Adequacy of Eduard Thurneysen's Theology of Pastoral Care and Oskar Pfister's Pastoral Analysis for Facing the Parishioner's Anxiety' (PhD thesis; University of Chicago, 1961)

EDUARD THURNEYSEN: SECONDARY SOURCES - ESSAYS, ARTICLES, PAPERS AND REVIEWS

Bäumlin, Klaus, 'Gesamtausgabe, Karl Barth-Eduard Thurneysen Briefwechsel, VI 1913-1921', *Reformatio* 22 (December 1973), pp. 646-647

Bentley, James, 'Christoph Blumhardt - Preacher of Hope', *Theology* 78 (November, 1975), pp. 577-582

Bohren, Rudolf, 'Das Wort Gottes und die Kirche', *Evangelische Theologie* 36 (July-August 1976), pp. 312-324

— 'Werweisen über Gotthelf', *Reformatio* 31 (Fall 1982), pp. 69-80

Bryner, Erich, 'Die Bedeutung Dostojewskis für die Anfänge der dialektischen Theologie', *Theologische Zeitschrift* 38 (May-June 1982), pp. 147-167

Busch, Ebejardt, 'Prophetie und Seelsorge: Eduard Thurneysen', *Zwingliana* 16.4

(1984), pp. 374-377

Calian, Carnegie Samuel, 'Revolutionary Theology in the Making: Barth-Thurneysen Correspondence, 1914-1925', *Journal of Bible and Religion* 33 (April 1965), pp. 188-190

Campbell, Alastair V., 'Is practical theology possible', *Scottish Journal of Theology* (May 1972), pp. 217-227

— 'The nature of practical theology', in Duncan B. Forrester (editor), *Theology and Practice* (London: Epworth Press, 1990), pp. 10-20

Dunn, Ross D., 'The pastoral theology of Eduard Thurneysen: considered in its historical and contemporary contexts', *Austin Seminary Bulletin Faculty Edition* 81 (November 1965), pp. 26-40

Genest, Hartmut, 'Kerygmatische und therapeutische Seelsorge: Zur Konzeption der Seelsorge bei Eduard Thurneysen und Dietrich Stollberg', in D. Jeschke, *Das Wort, das in Erstaunen setzt, verpflichtet. Dankesgabe für Jürgen Fangmeier* (Wuppertal: R Brockhaus, 1994), pp. 251-261

Girardet, Giorgio, 'Metodi e prospettive della cura pastorale nella società contemporanea', *Protestantesimo* 41.1 (1986), pp. 1-21

Homrighausen, Elmer George, 'Pastoral counseling as proclamation', *Christian Century* 79.22 (1962), pp. 1008-1010

— 'The preaching of Karl Barth and Eduard Thurneysen', *Religion in Life* 3.2 (Spring 1934), pp. 231-244

Hunsinger, Deborah van Deusen, 'The Chalcedon pattern - critique of Thurneysen, critique of Edinger, critique of Tillich', in Deborah van Deusen Hunsinger, *Theology and Pastoral Counseling: a New Interdisciplinary Approach* (Grand Rapids, MI: Eerdmans, 1995)

Kantzenbach, Friedrich W., 'Das Ende von "Zwischen den Zeiten"', *Theologische Zeitschrift* 31, (May-June 1975), pp. 161-172

Koch, Gerhard, 'Tauferkündigung und Taufpraxis Eduard Thurneysen, den 10 Juli achtzig Jahre alt geworden ist', (polygraph, articles by G. Koch, G. Harder, H. Gollwitzer, M. Fischer, M. Barth, E. Volk, M. Mezger, H. Bernau, G. Bauer, K. Schmidt, J.D. Fischer, H. Falcke, E. Tischer, H. Tischer, H. Ruppell, and T. Mann), *Pastoral Theologie Wissenschaft u Praxis* 57 (1968), pp. 335-435

Landau, Rudolf, ' "Bruchlinien": Beobachtungen zum Aufbruch einer Theologie - Erinnerungen an die Theologie Eduard Thurneysens', *Evangelische Theologie* 45 (March-April 1985), pp. 139-158

— ' "Komm, Heiliger Geist, du Tröster wert": Gestaltungen des Heiligen Geistes', *Evangelische Theologie* 41, (May-June 1981), pp. 187-211

Marquard, Reiner, 'Dass es Gnade ist, so dran zu sein: über die Notgemeinschaft Karl Barth, Charlotte von Kirschbaum und Nelly Barth anhand des Briefwechsels zwischen Karl Barth und Eduard Thurneysen 1930-1935', *Theologische Literaturzeitung* 126.5 (May 2001), pp. 580-590

McLelland, Joseph C., 'Revolutionary Theology in the Making: Barth-Thurneysen Correspondence, 1914-1925', *Canadian Journal of Theology* 11 (January 1965), p. 71

Osborn, Robert T., 'Revolutionary Theology in the Making: Barth-Thurneysen Correspondence, 1914-1925', *Duke Divinity School Review* 29 (Autumn 1964), pp. 194-195

Panichas, George A., ' "A study in spiritual art" - *Dostoevsky* by E. Thurneysen', *Christian Scholar* 48 (Spring 1965), pp. 74-79

Reymond, Bernard, 'Lettres de Pierre Maury à Eduard Thurneysen', *Études théologiques et religieuses* 60.1 (1985), pp. 7-29

— 'Prophetie und Seelsorge: Eduard Thurneysen', *Études théologiques et religieuses* 59.1 (1984), pp. 126-127

Ritter, Hans Adam, 'Wort und Gemeinde: Probleme und Aufgaben der praktischen Theologie - Eduard Thurneysen zum 80 Geburtstag', *Theologische Zeitschrift* 26 (January-February 1970), pp. 69-70

Rohkrämer, Martin, 'Zur Erinnerung an Eduard Thurneysen, 1888-1974', *Evangelische Theologie* 34 (November-December 1974), pp. 515-518

Sasse, Hermann, 'Revolutionary Theology in the Making: Barth-Thurneysen Correspondence 1914-1925', *Reformed Theological Review* 23 (October 1964), pp. 88-89

Schjørring, Jens Holger and Peter Widmann, 'Karl Barth Gesamtausgabe', *Dansk teologisk tidsskrift* 40.3 (1977), pp. 181-201

Seim, J., 'Prophetie und Seelsorge - Eduard Thurneysen', *Evangelische Theologie* 43 (July-August 1983), pp. 383-392

Smart, James D., 'Eduard Thurneysen - pastor-theologian', *Theology Today* 16.1 (April 1959), pp. 74-89

— 'The Karl Barth-Eduard Thurneysen Letters - Karl Barth in Review', *Pittsburgh Theological Monograph Series* (1981), pp. 55-64

Smolík, J., 'Prophetie und Seelsorge: Eduard Thurneysen', *Communio viatorum* 26.4 (1983), pp. 259-262

Stauffer, R., 'Gottesdienst-Menschendienst: Eduard Thurneysen zum 70 Geburtstag am 10 Juli 1958', *Theologische Zeitschrift* 15 (July-August 1959), pp. 313-315

Stefan, Jan, 'Karl Barth-Eduard Thurneysen Briefwechsel 3, 1930-1935', *Teologická reflexe* 7.2 (2001), pp. 180-181

Winkler, Eberhard, 'Wort und Gemeinde: Probleme und Aufgaben der praktischen Theologie - Eduard Thurneysen zum 80 Geburtstag', *Theologische Literaturzeitung* 94 (Spring 1969), pp. 653-655

3. Karl Barth and Eduard Thurneysen: Joint Works

KARL BARTH AND EDUARD THURNEYSEN: PRIMARY SOURCES - BOOKS

Barth, Karl and Eduard Thurneysen, *Andachten für die Advents-, Weihnachts-, Passions- und Osterzeit* (Berlin: Furche Verlag, 1936)
— *Come Holy Spirit* (trans. George W. Richards, Elmer G. Homrighausen and Karl J. Ernst; New York, NY: Round Table Press, 1933)
— *Die Große Barmherzigkeit - Predigten* (München: Christian Kaiser Verlag, 1935)
— *Ein Briefwechsel aus der Frühzeit der dialektischen Theologie* (series, Siebenstern Taschenbuch 71; München and Hamburg: Siebenstern Taschenbuch Verlag, 1966)
— *God's Search for Man* (trans. George W. Richards, Elmer G. Homrighausen and Karl J. Ernst; New York, NY: Round Table Press, 1935)
— *Karl Barth-Eduard Thurneysen Briefwechsel Band I 1913-1921* (Gesamtausgabe Bearbeitet und herausgegeben von Eduard Thurneysen; Zürich: Theologischer Verlag Zürich, 1973)
— *Karl Barth-Eduard Thurneysen Briefwechsel Band II 1921-1930* (Gesamtausgabe Bearbeitet und herausgegeben von Eduard Thurneysen; Zürich: Theologischer Verlag Zürich, 1973)
— *Karl Barth-Eduard Thurneysen Briefwechsel Band III 1930-1935* (Gesamtausgabe Bearbeitet und herausgegeben von Eduard Thurneysen; Zürich: Theologischer Verlag Zürich, 1986)
— *Klärung und Wirkung: zur Vorgeschichte der (Kirchlichen Dogmatik) und zum Kirchenkampf* (ed. Walter Feurich; Berlin: Union Verlag, 1966)
— *Komm Schöpfer Geist! Predigten* (München: Christian Kaiser Verlag, 1924)
— *Revolutionary Theology in the Making Barth-Thurneysen Correspondence 1914-1925* (trans. James D. Smart; Richmond, VA: John Knox Press, 1967)
— *Suchet Gott, so werdet ihr Leben!* (Bern: G.A. Bäschlin, 1917)
— *Suchet Gott, so werdet ihr Leben!* (expanded second edition; München: Christian Kaiser Verlag, 1928)
— *Zur inneren Lage des Christentums: eine Buchanzeige und eine Predigt* (München: Christian Kaiser Verlag, 1920)
— *Zwei Johannespredigten* (Basel: H. Maser, 1937)

4. Fyodor Mikhailovich Dostoevsky: Works

FYODOR MIKHAILOVICH DOSTOEVSKY:
PRIMARY SOURCES - NOVELS AND SHORT STORIES

Dostoevsky, Fyodor Mikhailovich, *Crime and Punishment* (trans. Richard Pevear and Larissa Volokhonsky; London: Everyman's Library, 1993)
— *Demons* (trans. Richard Pevear and Larissa Volokhonsky; London: Everyman's Library, 1994)
— *Fyodor Mikhailovich Dostoevsky: Complete Letters* (trans. and ed. David A. Lowe, 5 vols; New York, NY: Ardis Publishers, 1989-91)
— *Memoirs from the House of the Dead* (trans. Jessie Coulson, Oxford World's Classics; Oxford: Oxford University Press, 2001)
— *Notes From Underground* and *The Gambler* (trans. Jane Kentish, Oxford World's Classics; Oxford: Oxford University Press, 1999)
— *The Brothers Karamazov* (trans. Richard Pevear and Larissa Volokhonsky; London: Everyman's Library, 1990)
— *The Diary of a Writer* (trans. and annotated Boris Brasol, 2 vols; New York, NY: Charles Scribner's Sons, 1949)
— *The Dream of a Ridiculous Man*, in Fyodor Mikhailovich Dostoevsky, *A Gentle Creature and Other Stories* (trans. Alan Myers, Oxford World's Classics; Oxford: Oxford University Press, 1995), pp. 107-128
— *The Gospel in Dostoevsky - Selections from his Works* (ed. The Bruderhof Community, illustrations Fritz Eichenberg; Robertsbridge, East Sussex: Plough Publishing, 1988)
— *The Grand Inquisitor with Related Chapters from The Brothers Karamazov* (trans. and intro. Charles B. Guignon; Chicago, IL: University of Chicago Press, 1968)
— *The Idiot* (trans. Richard Pevear and Larissa Volokhonsky; London: Everyman's Library, 1993)
— *The Notebooks for Crime and Punishment* (trans. Edward Wasiolek; Chicago, IL: University of Chicago Press, 1967)
— *The Notebooks for The Brothers Karamazov* (trans. Edward Wasiolek; Chicago, IL: University of Chicago Press, 1971)
— *The Notebooks for The Idiot* (trans. Edward Wasiolek; Chicago, IL: University of Chicago Press, 1967)
— *The Notebooks for The Possessed* (trans. Edward Wasiolek; Chicago, IL: University of Chicago Press, 1968)
— *Winter Notes on Summer Impressions* (trans. Kyril Fitzlyon; London: Quartet Books, 1985)
Dostojewski, Fjodor Michailowitsch, *Der Idiot* (trans. E. K. Rahsin, Nachwort Ilma Rakusa; München: R. Piper Verlag, 2002 [1909])
— *Die Brüder Karamasoff* (trans. Karl Nötzel; Leipzig: Insel, 1919)
— *Die Brüder Karamasoff* (trans. E. K. Rahsin; München: R. Piper Verlag, 1906)
— *Die Brüder Karamasow* (trans. Hans Ruolf und Richard Hoffmann, Nachwort Horst-Jürgen Gerik; München: Deutscher Taschenbuch Verlag, 2002)
— *Schuld und Sühne* (trans. Margit und Rolf Baüer; Berlin: Aufbau Taschenbuch Verlag, 1998)

FYODOR MIKHAILOVICH DOSTOEVSKY
PRIMARY SOURCES - ONLINE RESOURCES

1. The Christian Classics Ethereal Library a website located at and run by Calvin College, 3201 Burton SE, Grand Rapids, MI 49546: http://www.ccel.org. The original English translations by Constance Garnett from the late nineteenth- and early twentieth-centuries of Dostoevsky's novels were consulted:
   Братья Карамазовы (*The Brothers Karamazov*):
   http://www.ccel.org/d/dostoevsky/karamozov/htm/
   Преступление и наказание (*Crime and Punishment*):
   http://www.ccel.org/d/dostoevsky/crime/crime.htm
2. Christiaan Stange's Dostoevsky Research Station, run by an academic from Prague, the Czech Republic:
   Записки из подполья (*Notes from Underground*, unacknowledged translation):
   http://www.kiosek.com/dostoevsky/library/underground.txt
   Сон смешного человека (*The Dream of a Ridiculous Man*):
   http://www.kiosek.com/dostoevsky/library/ridiculousman.txt
3. The Literature Network, an American website:
   Идиот (*The Idiot*, unacknowledged translation):
   http://www.online-literature.com/dostoevsky/idiot/
4. Литературно-мемориальный музеи Ф.М. Достоевского (F.M. Dostoevsky Literary-Memorial Museum) a Russian website devoted to photographs, graphics, paintings and illustrations of Dostoevsky:
   http://www.md.spb.ru/nd/e-people-1.html
5. Official website of the International Dostoevsky Society founded 1971: http://www.dostoevsky.org
6. Site of the Dostoevsky Society in Germany:
   http://www.dostojewskij-gesellschaft.de

FYODOR MIKHAILOVICH DOSTOEVSKY:
SECONDARY SOURCES - BOOKS

Bozanov, Vasily, *Dostoevsky and the Legend of the Grand Inquisitor* (trans. Spencer E. Roberts; Ithaca, NY and London: Cornell University Press, 1972)
Carr, Edward Hallett, *Dostoevsky* (London: Unwin Books, 1962)
Chapple, Richard, *A Dostoevsky Dictionary* (Ann Arbor, MI: Ardis Publishers, 1983)
Condradi, Peter Fyodor, *Dostoevsky* (series, Macmillan Modern Novelists; Basingstoke: Macmillan, 1988)
Coulson, Jessie, *Dostoevsky: A Self-Portrait* (Oxford: Oxford University Press, 1962)
Davison, Ray, *Camus: the challenge of Dostoevsky* (Exeter: University of Exeter Press, 1997)
Dirscherl, Denis S.J., *Dostoevsky and the Catholic Church* (Chicago, IL: Loyola University Press, 1986)
Dostoevsky, Anna Grigorievna, *Dostoevsky Reminiscences* (trans. Beatrice Stillman; London: Wildwood House, 1975)
Fanger, Donald, *Dostoevsky and Romantic Realism: a Study of Dostoevsky in Relation to Balzac, Dickens, and Gogol* (Cambridge, MA: Harvard University Press, 1965)
Gibson, Alexander Boyce, *The Religion of Dostoevsky* (London: SCM Press, 1973)
Gorodetzky, Nadejda, *Saint Tikhon of Zadonsk: Inspirer of Dostoevsky* (London: SPCK, 1951)
Hesse, Hermann, *Blick ins Chaos - Drei Aufsätze* (Bern: Verlag Seldwyla, 1920)
Jones, John, *Dostoevsky* (Oxford: Clarendon Press, 1983)

Kaufmann, Walter (ed.), *Existentialism from Dostoevsky to Sartre* (New York, NY: New American Library, c1975)
Kjetsaa, Geir, *Dostoevsky - A Writer's Life* (Basingstoke: Macmillan, 1988)
— *Dostoevsky and his New Testament* (Oslo: Solum Forlag A.S., 1984)
Kroeker, P. Travis and Bruce K. Ward, *Remembering the End: Dostoevsky as a Prophet of Modernity* (Oxford: Westview Press Radical Traditions, 2001)
Leatherbarrow, William J., *Fyodor Dostoevsky: a Reference Guide* (Boston, MA: G.K. Hall and Co, 1990)
Murav, Harriet, *Holy Foolishness: Dostoevsky's Novels and the Poetics of Cultural Critique* (Stanford, CA: Stanford University Press, 1992)
Murray, John Middleton, *Fyodor Dostoevsky: A Critical Study* (London: M. Secker, 1916)
Nötzel, Karl, *Das Leben Dostojewskis*, (Osnabrück: Biblio Verlag, 1925)
— *Dostojewsky und wir: ein Deutungsversuch des voraussetzungslosen Menschens* (München: Musarion Verlag, 1920)
Panichas, George Andrew, *The Burden of Vision: Dostoevsky's Spiritual Art* (Chicago, IL: Gateway Editions, 1985)
Pattison, George and Diane Oenning Thompson, *Dostoevsky and the Christian Tradition* (Cambridge: Cambridge University Press, 2001)
Rozanov, Vasilii Vasilievich, *Dostoevsky and the Legend of the Grand Inquisitor* (trans. Spencer E. Roberts from *Legenda o velikom inkvizitorie*; London: Cornell University Press, 1972 [1906])
Sandoz, Ellis, *Political Apocalypse: A Study of Dostoevsky's Grand Inquisitor* (Baton Rouge, LA: Louisiana State University Press, 1971)
Simmons, Ernest Joseph, *Fyodor Dostoevsky* (Columbia Essays on Modern Writers, no. 40; New York, NY: Columbia University Press, 1969)
— *Introduction to Russian Realism: Pushkin, Gogol, Dostoevsky, Tolstoi, Chekhov, Sholokhov* (Bloomington, IN: Indiana University Press, 1965)
Snow, Charles Percy, *The Realists Portraits of Eight Novelists - Stendhal, Balzac, Dickens, Dostoevsky, Tolstoy, Galdós, Henry James, Proust* (London: Macmillan, 1978)
Steiner, George, *Tolstoy or Dostoevsky* (London, Harmondsworth: Penguin Books, 1967)
Terras, Victor, *A Karamazov Companion: Commentary on the Genesis, Language, and Style of Dostoevsky's Novel* (Madison, WI: University of Wisconsin Press, 1980)
Trace, Arthur, *Dostoevsky and the Brothers Karamazov* (Philadelphia, PA: Xlibris Publishing, 2000)
Troyat, Henri, *Firebrand: the Life of Dostoevsky* (trans. Norbert Güterman, woodcuts S. Mrozewski; London: Heinemann, 1946)
Wolynski, Akim Lwowitsch, *Das Buch vom grossen Zorn* (Frankfurt: Literarische Anstalt Rütten and Loening, 1905)
— *Das Reich der Karamosoff* (München: R. Piper Verlag, 1920)

FYODOR MIKHAILOVICH DOSTOEVSKY:
SECONDARY SOURCES - ESSAYS, ARTICLES, PAPERS AND REVIEWS

Bauckham, Richard, 'Theodicy from Ivan Karamazov to Moltmann', *Modern Theology* 4.1, (October 1987), pp. 83-97
Crowder, Colin, 'The Appropriation of Dostoevsky in the early twentieth century: cult, counter-cult and incarnation', in D. Jasper, *European Literature and Theology in the Twentieth Century* (New York, NY: St Martin's Press, 1990), pp. 15-33

Cunningham, David S., 'The Brothers Karamazov as Trinitarian Theology', in George Pattison and Diane Oenning Thompson, *Dostoevsky and the Christian Tradition* (Cambridge: Cambridge University Press, 2001), pp. 134-155

Delasanta, Rodney, 'Putting off the Old Man and putting on the New: Ephesians 4:22-24 in Chaucer, Shakespeare, Swift, and Dostoevsky', *Christianity and Literature* 51.3 (Spring 2002), pp. 339-362

Esaulov, Ivan, 'The Categories of Law and Grace in Dostoevsky's Poetics', in George Pattison and Diane Oenning Thompson, *Dostoevsky and the Christian Tradition* (Cambridge: Cambridge University Press, 2001), pp. 116-133

Florovsky, Georges, 'The Quest for Religion in 19th Century Russian Literature: Three Masters: Gogol, Dostoevsky, Tolstoy', *Epiphany* 10 (Summer 1990), pp. 43-58

Frank, Joseph, 'Introduction', in Fyodor Mikhailovich Dostoevsky, *Crime and Punishment* (trans Richard Pevear and Larissa Volokhonsky; London: Everyman's Library, 1994), pp. xi-xxxi

— 'Introduction', in Fyodor Mikhailovich Dostoevsky, *Demons* (trans. Richard Pevear and Larissa Volokhonsky; London: Everyman's Library, 1994), pp. xi-xxxi

Friedman, Maurice S., 'Modern Job: on Melville, Dostoevsky, and Kafka', *Judaism* 12 (Autumn 1963), pp. 436-455

Fuller, Michael, 'The Brothers Karamazov as Christian Apologetic', *Theology* 98 (September-October 1995), pp. 344-350

Gustafson, Scott W., 'From Theodicy to Discipleship: Dostoevsky's Contribution to the Pastoral Task in The Brothers Karamazov', *Scottish Journal of Theology* 45.2 (1992), pp. 209-222

Hamilton, William, 'Banished from the land of unity: a study of Dostoevsky's religious vision through the eyes of Ivan and Alyosha Karamazov', *Journal of Religion* 39 (1959), pp. 245-262

Hegedus, Lorant, 'Jesus and Dostoevsky', *European Journal of Theology* 1.1 (1992), pp. 49-62

Hesse, Hermann, 'Die Brüder Karamasow oder Der Untergang Europas', in Hermann Hesse, *Blick ins Chaos - Drei Aufsätze* (Bern: Verlag Seldwyla, 1920). ET: Hesse, Hermann (trans. Stephen Hudson), 'The Brothers Karamazov or the Downfall of Europe', *The Dial Magazine*, New York, NY, 72.6, (June 1922), pp.607-618

— 'Gedanken über Dostojewskis Idiot', in Hermann Hesse, *Blick ins Chaos - Drei Aufsätze* (Bern: Verlag Seldwyla, 1920). ET: Hesse, Hermann (trans. Stephen Hudson), 'Thoughts on Dostoevsky's *The Idiot*', *The Dial Magazine*, New York, NY, 73.2, (August 1922), pp.199-204

Hollander, Robert, 'The Apocalyptic Framework of Dostoevsky's *The Idiot*', *Mosaic* 6 (1974), pp. 123-139

Idinopulos, Thomas A., 'Mystery of suffering in the art of Dostoevsky, Camus, Wiesel, and Grünewald', *Journal of the American Academy of Religion* 43 (March 1975), pp. 51-61

Jasper, David, 'The limits of formalism and the theology of hope: Ricoeur, Moltmann and Dostoevsky', *Literature and Theology* 1.1, (March 1987), pp. 1-10

Johae, Anthony, 'Expressive Symbols in Dostoevsky's *Crime and Punishment*', *Scottish Slavonic Review* 20 (1993), pp. 17-22

— 'Towards an Iconography of Crime and Punishment', in George Pattison and Diane Oenning Thompson, *Dostoevsky and the Christian Tradition* (Cambridge: Cambridge University Press, 2001), pp. 173-188

Jones, Malcolm V., 'Introduction', in Fyodor Mikhailovich Dostoevsky, *The Brothers Karamazov*, (trans. Richard Pevear and Larissa Volokhonsky; London: Everyman's Library, 1990), pp. ix-xxv

Kantor, Vladimir, 'Pavel Smerdyakov and Ivan Karamazov: the Problem of Temptation', in George Pattison and Diane Oenning Thompson, *Dostoevsky and the*

Christian Tradition (Cambridge: Cambridge University Press, 2001), pp. 173-188
Kesich, Veselin, 'The Grand Inquisitor', *St Vladimir's Seminary Quarterly* 2.3 (Spring 1954), pp. 29-32
King-Farlow, John and Niall Shanks, 'Theodicy: Two Moral Extremes', *Scottish Journal of Theology* 41.2 (1988), pp. 153-176
Kirillova, Irina, 'Dostoevsky's Markings in the Gospel According to St. John', in George Pattison and Diane Oenning Thompson, *Dostoevsky and the Christian Tradition* (Cambridge: Cambridge University Press, 2001), pp. 41-50
Kraeger, Linda L. and Joe Barnhart, 'The God-Nature Relationship in Dostoevsky's Personalism', *Scottish Journal of Religious Studies* 14.2, (Autumn 1993), pp. 71-88
Leatherbarrow, William J., 'Apocalyptic Imagery in Dostoevsky's *The Idiot* and *The Devils*', *Dostoevsky Studies* 3 (1982), pp. 43-51
— 'Introduction', in Fyodor Mikhailovich Dostoevsky, *Crime and Punishment* (trans. Richard Pevear and Larissa Volokhonsky; London: Everyman's Library, 1993), pp. vii-xxii
— 'Introduction', in Fyodor Mikhailovich Dostoevsky, *The Idiot* (trans. Richard Pevear and Larissa Volokhonsky; London: Everyman's Library, 1993), pp. xi-xxvi
Moltmann, Jürgen, 'Dostoevsky and the theology of hope', in Joseph Armenti, *Papin Festschrif: Essays in Honour of Joseph Papin, vol. 2* (Villanova, PA: Villanova University Press, 1976), pp. 399-407
Onasch, Konrad, 'Gleichzeitigkeit und Geschichte: Randbemerkungen zum Vergleich Dostojevskijs mit Kierkegaard', *Zeitschrift für Religions- und Geistesgeschichte* 25.1 (1973), pp. 46-57
Padfield, Deborah, 'Christianity: a religion of protest?', *Theology* 90 (May 1987), pp. 186-193
Panichas, George Andrew, 'Dostoevsky and Satanism', *Journal of Religion* 45.1 (1965), pp. 12-29
— 'F.M. Dostoevsky and D.H. Lawrence: their visions of evil', in George Andrew Panichas, *The Reverent Discipline: Essays in Literary Criticism and Culture* (Knoxville, TN: University of Tennessee Press, 1974)
— 'Freedom's Dangerous Dialogue: Reading Dostoevsky and Kierkegaard Together', in George Pattison and Diane Oenning Thompson, *Dostoevsky and the Christian Tradition* (Cambridge: Cambridge University Press, 2001), pp. 237-256)
— 'Fyodor Dostoevsky and Roman Catholicism', *Greek Orthodox Theological Review* 4 (Summer 1958), pp. 16-34
— 'In Sight of the Logos: Dostoevsky's *Crime and Punishment* as Spiritual Art', *St Vladimir's Theological Quarterly* 15.3 (1971), pp. 130-150
— 'Pater Seraphicus: Dostoevsky's Metaphysics of a New Saintliness', in George Andrew Panichas, *The Reverent Discipline: Essays in Literary Criticism and Culture* (Knoxville, TN: University of Tennessee Press, (1974)
Peace, Richard, 'Introduction', in Fyodor Mikhailovich Dostoevsky, *Crime and Punishment*, (trans. Jessie Coulson; Oxford: Oxford University Press, 1995), pp. vii-xxiii
Pevear, Richard, 'The Mystery of Man in Dostoevsky', *Sourozh* 66 (December 1996), pp. 31-35
Polka, Brayton, 'Psychology and Theology in The Brothers Karamazov: Everything is Permitted and the Two Fictions of Contradiction and Paradox', *Literature and Theology* 5 (Summer 1991), pp. 253-276
Purinton, Carl Everett, 'The Christ Image in the Novels of Dostoevsky', *Religion in Life* 16.1 (Winter 1946-1947), pp. 42-54
Ramsey, Paul, 'No Morality Without Immortality: Dostoevsky and the Meaning of Atheism', *Journal of Religion* 36 (1956), pp. 90-108
Rochelle, Jay C., 'The Gospel in Dostoevsky', *Currents in Theology and Mission* 17

(August 1990), pp. 306-307

Rosenshield, Gary, 'Mystery and Commandment in The Brothers Karamazov: Leo Baeck and Fedor Dostoevsky', *Journal of the American Academy of Religion* 62 (Summer 1994), pp. 483-508

Rother, Siegfried 'Die Brüder Karamasow - Dostojewskijs Analyse menschlicher Existenz', *Internationale katholische Zeitschrift Communio* 18.6 (1989), pp. 597-609

Russell, Henry M. W., 'Beyond the Will: Humiliation as Christian Necessity in Crime and Punishment', in George Pattison and Diane Oenning Thompson, *Dostoevsky and the Christian Tradition* (Cambridge: Cambridge University Press, 2001), pp. 226-236

Schroeder, C Paul, 'Suffering Towards Personhood: John Zizioulas and Fyodor Dostoevsky in Conversation on Freedom and the Human Person', *St Vladimir's Theological Quarterly* 45.3 (2001), pp. 243-264

Sherry, Patrick, 'Novels of redemption', *Literature and Theology* 14.3 (Summer 2000), pp. 249-260

Stoeber, Michael, 'Dostoevsky's Devil: the Will to Power', *Journal of Religion* 74.1 (January 1994), pp. 26-44

Sykes, John, 'Literature and Religion: Pascal, Gryphius, Lessing, Hölderlin, Novalis, Kierkegaard, Dostoevsky, Kafka', *Christian Century* 108, (October 16 1991), pp. 945-946

Thompson, Dianne Oenning, 'Problems of the Biblical Word in Dostoevsky's Poetics', in George Pattison and Diane Oenning Thompson, *Dostoevsky and the Christian Tradition* (Cambridge: Cambridge University Press, 2001) (pp. 69-102)

Walsh, David, 'Dostoevsky's Discovery of the Christian Foundation of Politics', *Religion and Literature* 19.2 (Summer 1987) pp. 49-72

Ward, Bruce K., 'Christianity and the Modern Eclipse of Nature: Two Perspectives (Camus and Dostoevsky)', *Journal of the American Academy of Religion* 63 (Winter 1995), pp. 823-843

— 'Dostoevsky and the Hermeneutics of Suspicion', *Literature and Theology* 11 (Summer 1997), pp. 270-283

Webster, Alexander F.C., 'The Exemplary Kenotic Holiness of Prince Myshkin in Dostoevsky's The Idiot', *St Vladimir's Theological Quarterly* 28.3 (1984), pp. 189-216

Westphal, Merold, 'The Phenomenology of Guilt and the Theology of Forgiveness', in Ronald Bruzina (ed.), *Crosscurrents in Phenomenology* (The Hague, Netherlands: Martinus Nijhoff, 1978), pp. 231-261

Wienhorst, Sue E., 'Vision and Structure in The Possessed', *Religion in Life* 45 (Winter 1976), pp. 490-498

Wikström, Owe, 'Soul Recovery through Remystification: Dostoevsky as a Challenger of Modern Psychology', *On Losing The Soul* (Albany, NY: State University of New York Press, 1995), pp. 119-136

Wood, Ralph C., 'Dostoevsky on Evil as a Perversion of Personhood: A Reading of Ivan Karamazov and the Grand Inquisitor', *Perspectives in Religious Studies* 26.3 (Fall 1999), pp. 331-348

Zabolotsky, Nikolai A., 'Fyodor Mikhailovich, Dostoevsky Today', *Scottish Journal of Theology* 37.1 (1984), pp. 41-57

Ziolkowski, Margaret, 'Dostoevsky and the Kenotic Tradition', in George Pattison and Diane Oenning Thompson, *Dostoevsky and the Christian Tradition* (Cambridge University Press, 2001), pp. 31-40

5. General Sources

GENERAL SOURCES: BOOKS

Augustine, *Sancti Aurelii Augustini Retractationum Libri II* (ed. Almut Mutzenbecher; Turnholti: Brepols, 1984)
Barth, Heinrich, 'Descartes Begründung der Erkenntnis' (PhD thesis, University of Bern, 1913)
— *Das Problem des Ursprungs in der platonischen Philosophie* (Munich: Christian Kaiser Verlag, 1921)
Bartos, Emil, *Deification in Eastern Orthodox Theology* (foreword Kallistos Ware, Paternoster Theological Monographs; Milton Keynes: Paternoster, 1999)
Bolshakoff, Sergius, *Russian Mystics* (series, Cistercian Studies 26; Kalamazoo, MN: Cistercian Publications, 1977)
Bradshaw, David, *Aristotle East and West: Metaphysics and the Division of Christendom* (Cambridge: Cambridge University Press, 2004)
Calvin, John, *Institutes of the Christian Religion* (ed. John T. McNeill, The Library of Christian Classics; Louisville, KY: Westminster John Knox Press, 2006 [1960])
Creeger, George R. (ed.) *George Eliot: A Collection of Critical Essays* (Englewood Cliffs, NJ: Prentice-Hall, 1970)
Cross, F.L. and Livingstone, E.A., *The Oxford Dictionary of the Christian Church* (Oxford: Oxford University Press, 1997)
Edie, James M.; James P. Scanlan and Mary-Barbara Zeldin (eds), *Russian Philosophy vol. I: The Slavophiles, The Westerners* (Chicago, IL: Quadrangle, 1965)
— *Russian Philosophy vol. II: The Nihilists, the Populists, Critics of Religion and Culture* (Chicago, IL: Quadrangle, 1965)
— *Russian Philosophy vol. III: Pre-Revolutionary Philosophy and Theology, Philosophers in Exile and Marxists and Communists* (Chicago, IL: Quadrangle, 1965)
Fedotov, G.P. (ed.), *A Treasury of Russian Spirituality* (New York, NY: Harper Touchstone, 1965)
Feuerbach, Ludwig, *The Essence of Christianity* (ed. W. Schuffenhauer, Gesammelte Werke, vol. 5; Berlin: Akademie Verlag, 1973)
Fisher, Simon, *Revelatory Positivism? Barth's Earliest Theology and the Marburg School* (Oxford: Oxford University Press, 1988)
Florovsky, Archpriest Georges, *Bible, Church, Tradition: An Eastern Orthodox View, Collected works of Georges Florovsky, vol. 1* (Belmont, MA: Nordland, 1972)
Forsyth, P.T., *The Charter of the Church* (London: Alexander and Shepheard, 1896)
Geffre, Claude and Jossua, Jean P., *Nietzsche and Christianity* (New York, NY: Seabury Press, 1981)
Gotthelf, Jeremias, *Bilder und Sagen aus der Schweiz* (Bern: Solothurner Verlag Jent und Gassmann, 1842-6)
— *Der Oberamtmann und der Amtsrichter* (Leben: Proehle H. Deutsches, 1853)
— *Die Schwarze Spinne* (Stuttgart: Philipp Reclam jun. Verlag, 1986 [1842])
Happé, Peter (ed.), *English Mystery Plays* (London, Harmondsworth: Penguin Books, 1975)
Hegel, Georg Wilhelm Friedrich, *Phenomenology of Spirit* (trans. A.V. Miller, foreword J.N. Findlay; Oxford: Oxford University Press, 1979)
Hermann Kutter, *Sie Müssen - ein offenes Wort an die christliche Gesellschaft* (Berlin: H. Walther Verlagsbuchhandlung, 1904)
— *The Communion of the Christian with God* (Philadelphia, PA: Fortress Press, 1971)

Hesse, Herman, *Das Glasperlenspiel* (Zürich: Fretz and Wasmuth Verlag, 1943)
Jenson, Robert, *Systematic Theology vol. 1: The Triune God* (Oxford: Oxford University Press, 1997)
Johnson, Howard Albert and Niels Thulstrup (eds), *A Kierkegaard critique - An international selection of essays interpreting Kierkegaard* (New York, NY: Harper and Bros., 1962)
Kant, Immanel, *Critique of Practical Reason* (ed. Mary J. Gregor, Cambridge Texts in the History of Philosophy; Cambridge: Cambridge University Press, 1990)
— *Critique of Pure Reason* (eds. Paul Guyer and Allen W. Wood, The Cambridge Edition of the Works of Immanuel Kant in Translation; Cambridge: Cambridge University Press, 1999)
— *Critique of the Power of Judgment* (ed. Paul Guyer, The Cambridge Edition of the Works of Immanuel Kant in Translation; Cambridge: Cambridge University Press, 2000)
Kierkegaard, Søren, *Concluding Unscientific Postscript to Philosophical Fragments* (ed. and trans. Howard V. Hong and Edna H. Kong; New York, NY: Princeton University Press, 1992)
— *Einübung in Christentum* (Erste Fassung; Halle: Fricke, 1878)
— *Einübung in Christentum* (Zweite Fassung; Jena: Eugen Diederichs, 1924)
— *Philosophical Fragments: Johannes Climacus* (ed. and trans. Howard V. Hong and Edna H. Kong; New York, NY: Princeton University Press, 1985)
— *Purity of Heart is to Will One Thing* (New York, NY: Harper and Row, 1938)
— *The Sickness Unto Death* (trans. Alistair Hannay; London, Harmondsworth: Penguin, 1989)
— *Training in Christianity* (trans. Walter Lowrie; Oxford: Oxford University Press, 1941)
Kutter, Hermann, *Gerechtigeit, ein altes Wort an die moderne Christenheit*, (Jena: Diederichs, 1905)
— *Wir Pfarrer* (Leipzig: H. Haessel, 1907)
Lindberg, Carter, *The European Reformations Sourcebook* (Oxford: Blackwell Publishers, 1999)
Lindt, Andreas, *Leonhardt Ragaz: Eine Studie zur Geschichte und Theologie des Religiösen Sozialismus* (Zollikon-Zürich: Evangelischer Verlag AG, 1957)
Lossky, Vladimir, *The Mystical Theology of the Eastern Church* (Cambridge: James Clarke, 1957)
McGrath, Alister, *Christian Theology* (Oxford: Blackwell Publishers, 1994)
— *Iustitia Dei- a History of the Christian Doctrine of Justification. vol. 2 from 1500 to the Present Day* (Cambridge: Cambridge University Press, 1986)
Nietzsche, Friedrich, *Twilight of the Idols* (trans. Walter Kaufmann and R.J. Hollingdale; London, Harmondsworth: Penguin Books, 1985)
Niewyk, Donald L., *Jews in Weimar Germany* (Manchester: Manchester University Press, 1981)
Overbeck, Franz, *Christianity and Culture: Thoughts and Observations on Modern Theology* (ed. Carl Albrecht Bernoulli; Basel: Benno Schwabe, 1919)
Pannenberg, Wolfhart, *Systematic Theology vol. 1 (Edinburgh: T&T Clark, 1991)*
Przywara, Erich, *Das Geheimnis Kierkegaards* (München: R. Oldenbourg, 1929)
— *Gespräch zwischen den Kirchen* (zusammen mit Hermann Sauer), (Nürnberg: Glock und Lutz, 1956)
— *Religionsbegründung Max Scheler - J.H. Newman* (Freiburg: Herder, 1923)
Ragaz, Leonhard, *Du Sollst - Grundzüge einer sittlichen Weltanschaung* (Leipzig: Waetzel, 1904)
Rzhevsky, Nicholas (ed.), *An Anthology of Russian Literature from Earliest Writings to Modern Fiction: Introduction to a Culture* (Armonk, NY: M.E. Sharpe, 1997)

Smart, Ninian, John Clayton, Patrick Sherry and Steven T. Katz (eds.), *Nineteenth Century Religious Thought in the West* (3 vols; Cambridge: Cambridge University Press, 1985)
Solzhenitsyn, Aleksandr, *One Day in the Life of Ivan Denisovich* (trans. Ralph Parker; London, Harmondsworth: Penguin Books, 2000)
Stapel, Wilhelm, *Antisemitismus und Antigermanismus. Über das seelischer Problem der Symbiose des deutschen und jüdischen Volkes* (Hamburg: Hanseatische Verlagsanstalt, 1928)
— *Der christliche Staatsmann - eine Theologie des National-sozialismus* (Hamburg: Hanseatische Verlag, 1932)
— *Die drei Stände Versuch einer Morphologie des deutschen Volkes* (Hamburg: Hanseatische Verlag, 1941)
— *The Heiland* (München: Hanser, 1953 [1932])
Wingren, Gustaf, *Theology in Conflict* (Philadelphia, PA: Muhlenberg Press, 1958)
Zweig, Stefan, *Drei Meistes* (Leipzig: Insel Verlag, 1920)

GENERAL SOURCES: ESSAYS, ARTICLES, PAPERS AND REVIEWS

Arbaugh, George E., 'Kierkegaard and Feuerbach', *Kierkegaardiana* 11, (1980), pp. 7-10
Evans, C.S., 'Is Kierkegaard an Irrationalist? Reason, Paradox and Faith', *Religious Studies* 25 (September 1989), pp.347-62
Fabro, Cornelio, 'Faith and Reason in Kierkegaard's Dialectic', in H. A. Johnson and Neils Thulstrup (eds.), *A Kierkegaard Critique*, (New York, NY: Harper and Brothers, 1962)
Gerrish, Brian A. 'Feuerbach's Religious Illusion', *Christian Century* 114 (April 1997), pp. 362-365 and 367
Harvey, Van A., 'Ludwig Feuerbach and Karl Marx', in Ninian Smart, John Clayton, Patrick Sherry and Steven T. Katz (eds.), *Nineteenth Century Religious Thought in the West vol. 2* (Cambridge: Cambridge University Press, 1985), pp. 291-328
Hill, Susan E. 'Translating Feuerbach, Constructing Morality: The Theological and Literary Significance of Translation for George Eliot', *Journal of the American Academy of Religion* 65 (Fall 1997), pp. 635-653
Kline, George L., 'Russian religious thought', in Ninian Smart, John Clayton, Patrick Sherry and Steven T. Katz (eds.), *Nineteenth Century Religious Thought in the West vol. 2* (Cambridge: Cambridge University Press, 1985), pp.179-229
Knoepflmacher U.C., 'George Eliot, Feuerbach, and the question of criticism', in George R. Creeger (ed.) *George Eliot: a Collection of Critical Essays* (Englewood Cliffs, NJ: Prentice-Hall, 1970), pp. 79-85
McKinnon, Alastair, 'Kierkegaard's Attack on Christendom - Its Lexical History', *Toronto Journal of Theology* 9.1 (1993), pp. 95-106
Paris, B.J., 'George Eliot's Religion of Humanity', in George R. Creeger, (ed.) *George Eliot: a Collection of Critical Essays* (Englewood Cliffs, NJ: Prentice-Hall, 1970)
Stenger, Mary Ann, 'Crisis in our Speaking about God: Derrida and Barth's Epistle to the Romans', in Isle N. Bulhof and Laurens ten Kate, *Flight of the Gods - Philosophical Perspectives on Negative Theology* (New York, NY: Fordham University Press, 2000)
Traupé, A. 'Saint Augustine', in Quasten, Johannes and Angelo Di Berardino (eds.) *Patrology: The Golden Age of Latin Patristic Literature vol. 4* (Westminster, MD: Christian Classics, 1986)

Index

1. **Index of Names**   233
2. **Index of Subjects**   236
    GENERAL SUBJECT INDEX   236
    KARL BARTH: INDEX   242
    EDUARD THURNEYSEN: INDEX   243
    FYODOR MIKHAILOVICH DOSTOEVSKY: INDEX   244

1. Index of Names

Aarau, 13, 47, 145
Aarauer Studentenkonferenz, 92, 96, 107, 142, 144, 145
Aargau, 7, 11, 12, 75, 92, 124
Aberdeen, University of, 93, 205
Adam, Karl (1876-1966), 69, 149, 177
Anselm of Canterbury (1033-1109), 67, 199
Anzinger, Herbert, 19, 20, 150, 152
Aquinas, Thomas (1225-1274), 67
Augustine of Hippo, 14, 67, 173, 174
Austro-Hungarian Empire, 10, 119
Bad Boll, 18, 92, 117, 177, 204
Balthasar, Hans Urs von (1905-1988), 2, 76, 87, 124, 125, 149, 151, 154, 155, 159, 204
Barashkov, Nastasya Filippovna (*The Idiot*), 38, 121, 158, 198
Barth
    Heinrich Barth (brother) (1890-1965), 20, 23, 28, 88, 125, 149, 153, 159, 164, 169, 170
    Karl Barth, see subject index
Basel, 19, 60, 61, 91, 92, 97, 99, 148, 160
    Reformed Cathedral in, 93, 94, 99
    University of, 93, 98
Becks, Johann Tobias (1804-1878), 91
Beintker, Michael, 111, 150, 152, 160, 164

Belinsky, Vissarion Grigorievich (1811-1848), 44, 81, 82
Berne, 28, 95, 108, 118, 121, 206
Blumhardts, the, 11, 58, 79, 86, 88, 92, 165, 172, 204
    Christoph Friedrich Blumhardt (1842-1919), 11, 18, 92, 93, 96, 102, 103, 117, 118, 124, 156, 204, 206
    Johann Christoph Blumhardt (1805-1880), 11, 92, 204
Bolshevik, 141, 145, 150, 195
Bonaparte, Napoleon (1769-1821), 31, 39, 43
Bonn, 1, 98
Britain, 7, 14, 74
Bruggen, 92
Brunner, Emil (1889-1966), 93, 96
Bultmann, Rudolf (1874-1976), 16, 96
Buonarroti Simoni, Michelangelo di Lodovico (1475-1564), 172, 173
Busch, Eberhard, 1, 3, 7, 8, 10, 17, 67, 68, 80, 93, 97, 98, 99, 149, 172, 202, 205, 206
Calvin, John (1509-1564), 27, 62, 64, 69, 75, 76, 86, 87, 104, 117, 141, 149, 172, 173, 174, 177, 182, 205, 207
Comte, Auguste (1798-1857), 81
Crystal Palace, the, 53, 54, 55

CVJM (Der Christlicher Verein von jungem Mann), 92
Dostoevsky
  Anna Dostoevsky, (née Anna Grigorievna Snitkina) (1846-1918), 60, 61, 83
  Fyodor Mikhailovich Dostoevsky, see subject index
  Mikhail Mikhaylovich Dostoevsky (1820-1864), 42
Dresden, 1
Dusseldorf, 65
England, 53, 56, 99
Erasmus, Desiderius Roterodamus (1466?-1536), 172, 173
Europe, 10, 48, 49, 52, 54, 58, 81, 91, 93, 113, 118, 119, 122, 192
  European, 4, 7, 10, 35, 42, 51, 52, 54, 59, 62, 74, 119, 121, 127, 128, 160, 182
Feuerbach, Ludwig (1804-1872), 35, 45, 82, 133, 134, 135, 172, 173, 174, 194
Forsyth, Peter Taylor (1848-1921), 196
Fourier, Jean Baptiste Joseph (1768-1830), 81
France, 53, 74
Francis of Assisi (1182-1226), 173, 174
Geneva, 3, 9, 10, 60, 206, 207
Germany, 1, 10, 13, 16, 18, 25, 43, 53, 55, 56, 61, 74, 97, 118, 119, 120, 122, 123, 125, 132, 144, 172, 178
Goethe, Johann Wolfgang von (1749-1832), 119, 156
Gogarten, Friedrich (1887-1967), 22, 93, 96, 97
Gotthelf, Jeremias (1797-1854), 103, 119, 121, 122, 142, 143
Göttingen, 8, 9, 73, 93, 94, 117, 121, 146, 148, 149, 171, 178, 183, 197, 199, 205, 206
Grand Inquisitor, the Legend of the (*The Brothers Karamazov*)
  Grand Inquisitor, 48, 54, 56, 69, 71, 72, 84, 104, 105, 112, 113, 114, 141, 145, 146, 148, 165, 167, 174, 175, 179, 184, 187, 188, 189, 190, 191, 192, 193, 194, 195, 196, 199, 202, 206
  Großinquisitor, 71, 72, 196
Grünewald, Matthias (1475-1528), 172, 173, 176
Grushenka, see Svetlova
Hardy, Thomas (1840-1928), 121
Harnack, Adolf von (1851-1930), 3, 4, 18

Hegel, Georg Wilhelm Friedrich (1770-1831), 8, 66, 68, 81, 97, 133, 150, 151, 170
Heppe, Heinrich (1820-1879), 74
Herrmann, Wilhelm (1846-1922), 3, 4, 8, 9, 12, 18, 26, 73, 92, 103, 206
Hesse, Hermann (1877-1962), 108, 118, 119, 122, 192
Hitler, Adolf (1889-1945), 97, 98
Holbein, Hans, the Younger (1497-1543), 60, 61
Hoskins, Edwyn (1884-1937), 3, 195
Ivanova
  Alena Ivanova (*Crime and Punishment*), 31, 104
  Lizaveta Ivanova (*Crime and Punishment*), 31, 40, 188, 201
Jenson, Robert, 134, 135
Jesus of Nazareth, Jesus Christ
  Christ, 11, 18, 20, 22, 23, 24, 33, 34, 35, 36, 39, 40, 42, 52, 60, 61, 62, 63, 72, 82, 83, 84, 85, 86, 92, 99, 101, 102, 113, 114, 115, 127, 128, 129, 135, 136, 138, 141, 143, 145, 147, 149, 150, 152, 153, 154, 155, 157, 158, 161, 164, 167, 168, 169, 170, 175, 183, 185, 187, 189, 190, 191, 193, 194, 195, 196, 197, 198, 199, 200, 201, 202, 207, 208
  Jesus, 8, 9, 11, 16, 18, 20, 22, 27, 36, 37, 60, 86, 99, 101, 102, 135, 147, 153, 154, 167, 170, 183, 187, 190, 194, 197, 207, 208
John the Baptist, 49, 50
Kant, Immanuel (1724-1804), 3, 8, 28, 67, 79, 133, 148, 156, 159, 160, 161, 165, 170, 172, 173, 174, 199
Karamazov
  Alexei Fyodorovich Karamazov - Alyosha (*The Brothers Karamazov*), 113, 121, 188, 189, 190, 192, 199, 201
  Dmitri Fyodorovich Karamazov - Mitya (*The Brothers Karamazov*), 108, 109, 188, 189, 192, 200
  Fyodor Pavlovich Karamazov (*The Brothers Karamazov*), 109, 188, 189
  Ivan Fyodorovich Karamazov (*The Brothers Karamazov*), 35, 41, 43, 108, 112, 113, 129, 145, 146, 165, 167, 168, 174, 175, 176, 179, 188, 189, 190, 191, 192, 193, 194, 195, 199, 200, 201, 202
  See, Smerdyakov

Index 235

Kierkegaard, Søren (1813-1855), 2, 15, 23, 27, 28, 67, 71, 75, 76, 77, 87, 88, 107, 123, 134, 143, 154, 156, 158, 159, 160, 161, 162, 163, 164, 165, 166, 167, 168, 169, 170, 172, 173, 174, 176, 177, 183, 202, 203, 204, 207
Kirillova, Irina, 82, 83
Kutter, Hermann (1863-1931), 11, 16, 17, 21, 26, 37, 75, 79, 80, 81, 86, 88, 92, 94, 103, 124, 139, 142, 145, 148, 153, 156, 172, 173, 176, 184, 204, 206, 207
Lazarus (St John's Gospel), 32
Leutwil, 7, 16, 75, 79, 84, 92
London, 1, 2, 4, 10, 24, 27, 33, 36, 42, 48, 54, 55, 59, 61, 65, 74, 83, 107, 127, 159, 162, 196
Luther, Martin (1483-1546), 27, 62, 63, 64, 69, 75, 76, 77, 86, 87, 117, 148, 149, 165, 172, 173, 174, 175, 176, 177, 178, 181, 182, 184, 193, 205, 207
Luzhin, Pyotr Petrovich (*Crime and Punishment*), 166
Marburg, 3, 7, 8, 9, 18, 73, 87, 92, 114, 148
Marie (*The Idiot*), 34, 199, 200, 201
Marmeladov
   Polina Mikhailovna Marmeladova - Polenka (*Crime and Punishment*), 61, 201
   Semyon Zakharovich Marmeladov (*Crime and Punishment*), 85, 175
   Sofya Semyonovna Marmeladova - Sonya or sometimes Sonechka (*Crime and Punishment*), 31, 32, 35, 39, 40, 58, 60, 61, 62, 63, 65, 76, 85, 87, 103, 104, 109, 110, 129, 136, 157, 163, 166, 176, 184, 201
Marx, Karl (1818-1883), 45, 134
McCormack, Bruce, 3, 9, 13, 14, 19, 21, 25, 26, 59, 60, 103, 111, 149, 150, 151, 152, 154, 155, 156, 159, 160, 161, 162, 164
McGrath, Alister, 133
Moscow, 42, 43, 60, 81, 188
Münster, 16, 66, 67, 68, 73, 93, 94
Myshkin, Prince Lev Nikolayevich (*The Idiot*), 33, 34, 35, 38, 108, 110, 119, 136, 137, 138, 157, 166, 167, 198, 199, 200, 201, 202
Nastasya Filippovna, see Barashkov
Neue Werk, 142
Nietzsche, 38, 41, 42, 43, 45, 48, 97, 119, 120, 142, 143, 154, 156, 158, 172, 173, 174, 176, 185, 194, 198, 204

Nötzel, Karl, (1870-1945), 118, 119, 120, 121, 122
Omsk, Siberia, 82, 125, 128, 135
Origen (c.185-c.254), 76, 149
Overbeck, Franz (1837-1905), 15, 28, 76, 123, 148, 154, 159, 160, 161, 166, 170, 172, 173, 174, 176, 177, 188, 194, 204, 207
Paris, 10, 43, 54, 107, 134
Paul, the Apostle, 9, 24, 27, 77, 79, 80, 81, 87, 93, 149, 151, 152, 154, 159, 178, 182, 185, 205
Petrashevskii, Mikhail Butashevich (1821-66), 44, 81, 133, 134
Plato (427-347BC), 125, 126, 149, 154, 156, 159, 160, 161, 165, 172, 173, 176
Polenka, see Marmeladov
Porfiry, Pyotr Petrovich (*Crime and Punishment*), 35, 104
Przywara, Erich (1889-1972), 67, 68, 69, 177
Ragaz, Leonhard (1868-1945), 11, 16, 17, 26, 80, 86, 92, 124, 204
Raskolnikov
   Avdotya Romanovna Raskolnikova - Dunya or Dunechka (*Crime and Punishment*), 166
   Pulcheria Alexandrovna Raskolnikova (*Crime and Punishment*), 166
   Rodion Romanovich Raskolnikov (*Crime and Punishment*), 31, 32, 33, 35, 36, 39, 40, 41, 43, 48, 49, 51, 54, 55, 56, 58, 59, 60, 61, 62, 63, 65, 76, 85, 87, 102, 104, 108, 109, 110, 113, 129, 136, 151, 157, 163, 164, 165, 166, 175, 176, 183, 185, 193, 200, 201
Razumikhin, Dmitri Prokofich (*Crime and Punishment*), 54
ridiculous man, the (*The Dream of a Ridiculous Man*), 44, 117, 130, 131, 132, 135, 136, 149, 151, 163, 181
Ritschl, Albrecht (1822-1889), 3, 8, 10, 28, 65, 69, 73, 147, 199
Rogozhin, Parfon Semyonovich (*The Idiot*), 33, 34, 121, 158, 199
Rousseau, Jean-Jacques (1712-1778), 172, 173
Russia, 10, 38, 39, 54, 56, 81, 114, 123, 141, 145, 150, 182, 195
Safenwil, 7, 10, 11, 14, 15, 16, 25, 28, 73, 178, 205, 206, 207
Safenwil Workers' Association, 11

Schiller, Johann Christoph Friedrich von (1759-1805), 172, 173
Schleiermacher, Friedrich (1768-1834), 3, 8, 13, 18, 36, 65, 66, 68, 69, 73, 133, 150, 172, 173, 199
Schweitzer, Albert (1875-1965), 160
Scotland, 99
Seville, 190
Smerdyakov, Pavel Fyodorovich (*The Brothers Karamazov*), 43, 109, 176, 188, 189, 192
Social Democratic Party, 11, 79
Socrates (470-399BC), 156, 172, 173
Soviet, 1, 123, 132
Spieckermann, Ingrid, 19, 160
St Gall, 92
St Petersburg, 31, 32, 35, 39, 47, 48, 59, 60, 81, 121, 124, 131, 132, 133, 138, 166, 188, 191, 199
Stapel, Wilhelm (1882-1954), 97
Stepanovich, see Verkhovensky
Stavrogin, Nicolas Vsevolodovich (*The Demons*), 38, 39, 43, 113
Strauss, David Friedrich (1808-1874), 134, 172, 173
Svetlova, Agrafena Alexandrovna - Grushenka (*The Brothers Karamazov*), 109, 188, 189
Svidrigailov, Arkady Ivanovich (*Crime and Punishment*), 43, 176, 201
Swiss Religious Socialism, 11, 16, 92, 204, 207
Switzerland, 7, 9, 19, 25, 34, 38, 60, 64, 91, 93, 94, 98, 99, 122, 125
Tambach, 92, 117, 155, 156, 158, 171, 176, 184, 197, 198
Tolstoy, Count Lev Nikolayevich (1828-1910), 114, 156, 157, 158, 172, 173, 175, 177, 178, 184, 197, 198
Tröltsch, Ernst (1865-1923), 15, 69, 92, 103, 124, 172, 173
Verkhovensky, Pyotr Stepanovich (The Demons), 54
Voltaire (pen-name of Arouet, François-Marie 1694-1778), 53
Walker, James Silas, 150, 153, 154
Webb, Stephen, 59, 60, 62
Wilhelm II, Kaiser (1859-1941), 10, 13
Wolynski, Akim Lwowitsch (1863-1926), 118, 119, 121, 122
Yepanchin
   General Ivan Fyodorovich Yepanchin (*The Idiot*), 166
   Elizaveta Prokofyevna Yepanchina *(The Idiot)*, 166, 167
Zossima, Father, the elder (*The Brothers Karamazov*), 41, 113, 114, 121, 136, 188, 189, 191, 198, 201
Zürich, 3, 4, 7, 16, 22, 26, 31, 56, 66, 73, 92, 94, 100, 107, 118, 130, 143, 178, 202
Zweig, Stefan (1881-1942), 118, 119, 120, 122, 144
Zwingli, Ulrich (1484-1531), 172, 173
Zwischen den Zeiten, 67, 68, 70, 92, 93, 96, 97, 148

2. Index of Subjects

GENERAL SUBJECT INDEX

apophatic, 9, 26, 27, 150, 166, 201, 208
   affirmation, resulting from, 89, 108, 113, 201, 208
deus absconditus, 15, 20, 177
incomprehensible, 109
mystery, 12, 24, 28, 53, 110, 190, 199
mysticism, 8, 206
negation, 20, 21, 23, 24, 25, 72, 110, 137, 166, 169, 191, 201
negations, 24, 89, 108, 113, 137, 201
negative, 12, 22, 23, 24, 25, 26, 27, 38, 68, 114, 154, 162, 172, 199, 201, 208
negativity, 27, 112, 114, 201
paradox, paradoxical, 4, 12, 21, 23, 24, 25, 28, 35, 36, 37, 38, 40, 43, 71, 85, 110, 113, 114, 126, 137, 138, 153, 157, 161, 169, 170, 174, 179, 189, 191, 197, 198, 201
unknowability, 24
unknowingly, 24

Index

unwissentlich, 24
Verneinungenswort, 24
Verneinungsfall, 24
atheist, 4, 16, 33, 35, 45, 81, 127, 160, 172, 174, 188, 189, 190, 199
  atheism, 4, 23, 24, 33, 35, 41, 42, 55, 56, 59, 71, 112, 113, 125, 136, 160, 168, 191, 192, 194, 201
  atheistic, 35, 45, 103, 129, 134, 154, 188, 191, 199
atonement, 32, 62, 73, 102, 103, 125, 129, 135, 143
Augustinianism, 206
Bible, 13, 16, 37, 40, 48, 52, 56, 76, 79, 80, 81, 82, 84, 86, 88, 91, 94, 99, 103, 110, 125, 127, 129, 130, 201, 204, 205, 206
  1 Corinthians, 24, 114, 200, 201
  biblical, 48, 49, 73, 74, 79, 82, 83, 86, 92, 102, 103, 119, 123, 125, 128, 130, 149, 154, 206
  Exodus, 70
  Genesis, 48, 49, 50, 56, 151, 176, 184
  Gospel, 10, 17, 23, 25, 26, 27, 32, 33, 36, 37, 38, 40, 41, 52, 61, 62, 67, 68, 74, 81, 82, 83, 86, 97, 100, 101, 102, 103, 109, 113, 115, 124, 125, 128, 130, 134, 136, 138, 142, 147, 150, 156, 157, 165, 166, 167, 168, 169, 170, 187, 188, 191, 198, 207, 208
  Hebrews, 183
  holy scripture, 101
  John the Baptist, 49, 50
  John, Epistles of, 82, 83, 124
  John, Gospel of, 32, 36, 37, 61, 81, 82, 83, 97, 109, 113, 115, 128
  John, Revelation to, 82
  Luke, 82, 167
  Mark, 38, 82
  Matthew, 24, 35, 49, 85, 184
  New Testament, 12, 24, 36, 37, 40, 66, 74, 75, 79, 81, 82, 83, 84, 88, 94, 96, 97, 103, 119, 123, 125, 126, 127, 159, 160, 164, 165, 167, 169, 201
  parable, 33, 34, 35, 51, 87, 104, 130, 132, 135, 156, 167, 198
  Paul, epistles of, 9, 27, 76, 79, 81, 149, 152, 154, 159, 178, 185
  Paul, the apostle, 9, 24, 27, 77, 79, 80, 81, 84, 87, 149, 151, 152, 154, 159, 178, 185, 205
  Pauline, 81, 84, 159, 205
  Romans, Epistle to the, 3, 9, 19, 21, 22, 63, 72, 75, 76, 77, 79, 80, 81, 84, 96, 139, 146, 149, 150, 151, 152, 153, 154, 155, 156, 159, 161, 163, 164, 176, 178, 182, 183, 184, 185, 192, 194, 195, 196, 205
  sacred scripture, 36, 37, 83
  scripture, 4, 9, 36, 37, 83, 85, 95, 96, 99, 101, 134, 182
Calvinism, 72
Calvinistic, 72, 73
Christ, 11, 18, 20, 22, 23, 24, 33, 34, 35, 36, 39, 40, 42, 52, 60, 61, 62, 63, 72, 82, 83, 85, 86, 92, 99, 101, 102, 113, 114, 115, 127, 128, 129, 135, 136, 138, 141, 143, 145, 147, 149, 150, 152, 153, 154, 155, 157, 158, 161, 164, 167, 168, 169, 170, 175, 183, 185, 187, 189, 190, 191, 193, 194, 195, 196, 197, 198, 199, 200, 201, 202, 207, 208
  apostles of, 8
  Christendom, 74, 123, 124
  Christian, 1, 3, 4, 9, 11, 14, 15, 16, 19, 22, 24, 26, 27, 32, 33, 35, 41, 42, 43, 45, 52, 59, 60, 62, 71, 76, 80, 82, 87, 92, 94, 96, 97, 99, 101, 102, 104, 107, 111, 125, 127, 133, 134, 135, 136, 142, 149, 153, 155, 157, 158, 160, 163, 167, 172, 174, 178, 182, 189, 200, 201, 202, 204, 207
  Christianity, 12, 23, 27, 34, 41, 42, 47, 52, 82, 85, 127, 133, 160, 161, 162, 166, 167, 168, 170, 202
  Christlikeness, 38, 110, 119, 130, 136, 157, 167, 174, 179, 197, 198, 199, 200
  Christology, 8, 66, 160
  Jesus, 8, 9, 11, 16, 18, 20, 22, 27, 36, 37, 60, 86, 99, 101, 102, 135, 147, 153, 154, 167, 170, 183, 187, 190, 194, 197, 207, 208
  kiss of Christ, the, 175, 190, 194, 195, 199, 202
  virginal conception, 8
Church, the, 1, 3, 7, 8, 9, 11, 16, 17, 24, 25, 26, 27, 28, 33, 34, 37, 47, 48, 55, 56, 62, 63, 65, 66, 67, 68, 69, 70, 71, 72, 73, 74, 79, 80, 82, 83, 84, 85, 86, 91, 93, 94, 95, 96, 99, 100, 101, 102, 103, 104, 112, 113, 114, 122, 123, 124, 125, 126, 127, 128, 129, 144, 150, 154, 155, 160, 163, 166, 167, 169, 172, 173, 174, 183, 184, 185, 187, 188, 190, 191, 192, 193, 194, 196, 203, 206, 207
  ecclesial, 25, 26, 33, 71, 82, 124, 125, 171, 172

ecclesiological, 66, 70
papacy, 191
Patristic, 14, 72, 74, 79, 102, 123, 125, 126, 174
Peter's rock, 70, 190
conscience, 31, 47, 49, 50, 51, 52, 59, 60, 62, 63, 111, 129, 177
culture, 14, 23, 38, 43, 68, 107, 128, 167, 191
death, 2, 31, 38, 40, 44, 58, 61, 82, 84, 120, 129, 135, 137, 151, 155, 166, 176, 185, 188, 189, 194
dialectic, 9, 24, 25, 28, 34, 36, 38, 58, 61, 84, 111, 135, 150, 152, 153, 162, 164, 166, 167, 168, 169, 170, 184, 191
  antinomy, 35, 58, 84, 108, 111, 126, 153, 168, 189
  dialectically, 12, 21, 27, 79, 136, 149, 152, 200
  Dialektik, 24, 111, 150, 152, 160, 164
  dialektische Theologie, 8, 61, 92, 93, 94, 96, 97, 111, 160
  disjuncture, 35, 36
  paradox, paradoxical, 4, 12, 21, 23, 24, 25, 28, 35, 36, 37, 38, 40, 43, 71, 85, 110, 113, 114, 126, 137, 138, 153, 157, 161, 169, 170, 174, 179, 189, 191, 197, 198, 201
  Paradoxon, 24
doctrine of God, 12, 14, 19, 20, 23, 36, 40, 111, 126
  absoluteness, 12
  aseity, 12, 19, 20, 21, 23, 73, 163, 164, 204
  critical realism, 58
  critically realistic, 19, 58, 59, 112, 147, 169
  deus absconditus, 15, 20, 177
  deus dixit, 15, 20, 22, 147, 201, 208
  domestication of God, 27
  God is, 12, 15, 17, 18, 19, 20, 21, 22, 23, 31, 34, 36, 37, 38, 40, 47, 48, 49, 52, 58, 59, 69, 72, 74, 86, 87, 102, 111, 113, 126, 133, 135, 136, 137, 138, 149, 151, 152, 163, 189, 198
  God is God, 15, 17, 20, 74, 111, 126, 137, 138, 152
  God's righteousness, 47, 49, 51, 132, 168, 184
  God-man, the, 36, 61, 84, 162, 190
  Kingdom of God, 9, 12, 17, 20, 79, 88, 92, 150, 152, 165, 204
  love of God, 35, 53, 62

personal God, 12
transcendence, 12, 28, 35, 36, 37, 81, 136, 204
Word of God, 27, 35, 47, 70, 84, 100, 101, 102, 130, 155, 178
epistemology, 36, 86, 150, 179, 198, 199
  epistemic, 12, 21, 169
  epistemological, 36, 113, 117
eritis sicut deus, 39, 40, 43, 47, 48, 50, 51, 55, 56, 58, 62, 87, 112, 132, 138, 150, 163, 183, 188, 191, 195, 196, 207
eschatology, 9, 76, 86, 92, 149, 150, 155, 156, 157, 188, 204
  eschatological, 12, 58, 60, 79, 92, 111, 142, 153, 160
  eschaton, 58, 153, 196
Euclidean, 112
existential, 2, 31, 37, 38, 43, 58, 60, 62, 76, 95, 103, 129, 130, 131, 134, 135, 136, 138, 142, 147, 157, 169, 170, 207
  decision, 31, 36, 37, 43, 63, 81, 95, 129, 131, 170
  existence, 32, 34, 35, 37, 40, 58, 68, 70, 95, 101, 114, 129, 130, 132, 137, 162, 165, 178, 189, 190
  existentialism, 121, 122, 129, 147, 165, 204, 208
  life, 10, 16, 18, 20, 24, 25, 26, 28, 34, 35, 36, 37, 38, 39, 40, 41, 42, 43, 48, 49, 50, 51, 58, 61, 63, 70, 72, 74, 83, 84, 92, 93, 103, 109, 110, 111, 112, 113, 114, 115, 120, 121, 122, 124, 127, 129, 130, 132, 136, 137, 142, 149, 153, 156, 157, 163, 165, 169, 177, 178, 185, 188, 189, 191, 194, 197, 198, 199, 200, 202
  predicament, 44, 182
Expressionism, 61, 111
First World War, the,, 7, 9, 13, 14, 19, 32, 51, 55, 58, 81, 107, 119, 123, 148, 149, 155, 168
French Revolution, the,, 55, 81, 132
grace (and sin), 2, 31, 37, 39, 48, 58, 60, 61, 63, 64, 65, 66, 67, 68, 69, 70, 71, 72, 73, 74, 75, 79, 85, 86, 87, 88, 93, 94, 95, 101, 103, 104, 123, 136, 142, 143, 149, 159, 166, 174, 175, 176, 177, 178, 181, 182, 183, 184, 185, 187, 189, 203, 204, 205, 206, 207, 208
  altrusitic, 200
  appropriation, 67, 68, 71, 83
  faith, 9, 34, 35, 42, 47, 52, 53, 54, 60, 61, 62, 71, 82, 83, 84, 86, 95, 102, 109,

110, 113, 123, 124, 125, 127, 128, 129, 131, 134, 135, 149, 153, 163, 167, 168, 169, 170, 175, 176, 188, 189, 191, 193, 194, 203, 206, 207, 208
faithfulness, 49
forensic, 62, 64, 66, 70, 72, 73, 74, 75, 87, 88, 104, 125, 185, 189
forgiveness, 33, 34, 40, 58, 66, 69, 70, 71, 72, 74, 85, 86, 87, 101, 102, 103, 104, 110, 112, 113, 123, 125, 136, 142, 164, 167, 182, 185, 187, 189, 195, 199, 200, 202
freedom, 58, 67, 70, 72, 95, 163, 175, 176, 178, 185, 187, 190, 191, 194, 195, 196
holiness, 34, 50, 61, 166, 188, 200
imputation, 71, 104
judgement, 26, 47, 58, 65, 66, 70, 72, 101, 112, 177, 178, 185, 195, 196, 205
justification, 27, 101, 103, 123, 151, 206
legalistic, 62, 66, 72, 185
love, 16, 20, 24, 27, 31, 34, 35, 39, 40, 41, 52, 58, 60, 62, 81, 83, 85, 89, 92, 108, 114, 123, 124, 128, 129, 131, 136, 144, 164, 166, 167, 191, 195, 198, 200, 201, 202
merciful, 35, 40, 83, 84, 135, 189
mercy, 27, 40, 58, 84, 189, 194
pardon, 65, 66, 70, 72, 86, 104, 205
reparation, 32, 87
repentance, 38, 60, 101, 124, 129, 167, 177, 189, 206
repentant, 38, 125
sanctification, 34, 61, 63, 66, 72, 101, 104, 108, 125, 185, 200, 206

Hegelian, 19, 21, 38, 48, 133, 150, 152, 153, 167
Holy Spirit, 36, 37, 60, 63, 96, 101, 129, 149, 187, 207
Idealism, 150, 157, 165
Kierkegaard, Søren (1813-1855), 2, 15, 23, 27, 28, 67, 71, 75, 76, 77, 87, 88, 107, 123, 134, 143, 154, 156, 158, 159, 160, 161, 162, 163, 164, 165, 166, 167, 168, 169, 170, 172, 173, 174, 176, 177, 183, 202, 203, 204, 207
Concluding Unscientific Postscript, 168
dialectic in, 162, 163, 164, 166, 167, 169
dialectic of antinomies, 162, 169, 199
infinite qualitative distinction, 161, 162, 163, 164, 170
innere dialektik der Sache, 162

Kierkegaard or Dostoevsky, 161, 164, 168
Kierkegaardian, 71, 164, 170
problem of contemporaneity with Christ, 161, 169
the incarnation as the divine incognito, 161, 170, 202
The Instant, 161
The Philosophical Fragments, 143, 168
Training in Christianity, 161, 168
Unterschied, 162, 163, 164
writings of, 2, 15, 23, 27, 28, 71, 75, 87, 134, 143, 159, 160, 161, 163, 164, 168, 173
Krisis, 2, 8, 13, 60, 62, 72, 96, 149, 159, 164, 177, 178
law, 31, 32, 47, 51, 97, 101, 196
Lutheran, 25, 26, 28, 69, 144, 145
ministry, 3, 7, 9, 10, 16, 17, 18, 25, 26, 79, 88, 91, 92, 94, 95, 118, 121, 204, 206
Napoleonic delusion, 41, 55, 58, 108, 109
Nazis, 1, 97, 132
Blood and Soil religion, 97, 132
National Socialists, 97
nineteenth-century liberal neo-Protestant, 1, 14, 160, 206
Herrmannian, 9, 10, 14, 38, 48
humanism, 17, 41, 59, 67, 68, 69, 73, 114, 135, 147
humanist, 40, 53, 55, 70, 81, 134, 190
liberal, 3, 4, 7, 10, 11, 12, 17, 18, 19, 35, 41, 53, 54, 55, 59, 60, 64, 68, 69, 70, 73, 74, 80, 86, 87, 102, 124, 125, 127, 128, 133, 134, 135, 147, 150, 156, 170, 174, 190, 205
liberalism, 3, 4, 8, 9, 11, 14, 26, 38, 48, 67, 70, 71, 72, 124, 125, 127, 150
Ritschlian, 8, 19
pastoral theology, 92, 93, 100
pastoral care, 80, 91, 92, 93, 100, 101, 102, 103, 105
pastoral counsellor, 102, 104, 105
psychological, 41, 43, 103, 111, 124, 143, 193, 200
psychologist, 42, 114
psychology, 101, 111, 114, 151, 164
psychotherapy, 94, 101, 102
Seelsorge, 92, 99, 100, 101, 102, 103, 104, 105, 123
Platonism, 126, 152, 156, 172
Diesseit, 126, 152
Eastern Platonism, 123, 125, 127
ganz andere, 14, 22, 80, 126

jenseits, 111, 126, 152
Neoplatonism, 124
Platonic, 15, 76, 87, 125, 126, 157
unbekannten, 126
politics, 11, 38, 73, 145, 155, 196, 198
  Bolshevik, 10, 141, 145, 150, 196
  communism, 174, 175, 195
  empire, 10, 74, 119, 123
  feudal, 10
  government, 10, 195, 196
  Marxism, 56, 132
  Marxist, 7, 26
  National Socialism, 97, 132
  pacifist, 38
  religious socialism, 11, 16, 79, 92, 93, 150, 155, 156, 158, 195, 196, 204, 206, 207
  revolution, 7, 10, 11, 60, 91, 97, 141, 145, 150, 196
  revolutionary, 38, 53, 55, 60, 81, 132, 195, 196
  revolutions, 8, 10
  serfs, 114, 127
  Slavophile, 123
  socialist, 8, 10, 11, 16, 17, 25, 26, 28, 53, 54, 55, 56, 66, 79, 81, 92, 93, 135, 141, 155, 156, 158, 174, 175, 176, 184, 187, 190, 195, 196, 204, 207
socio-political, 4, 81
poverty, 7, 10, 12, 25, 35, 54, 55, 122, 166
Protestant, 1, 3, 4, 8, 14, 25, 28, 53, 59, 66, 67, 68, 69, 70, 73, 86, 96, 114, 124, 125, 174, 177
rational, 31, 32, 35, 53, 77, 124, 128, 132, 151
redemption, 18, 33, 61, 62, 79, 86, 87, 88, 104, 113
Reformed, 7, 8, 9, 13, 25, 31, 34, 48, 56, 64, 68, 73, 74, 91, 93, 94, 121, 122, 125, 145, 171, 178, 203, 205, 207
  Reformation, 68, 69, 71, 76, 77, 87, 125, 172, 205, 206
  Reformed Confessions, 73, 74, 171
  Reformers, the, 27, 29, 63, 65, 66, 70, 72, 73, 74, 86, 87, 96, 104, 148, 154, 204, 205, 206, 208
religion, 5, 11, 17, 18, 21, 23, 25, 27, 28, 33, 34, 35, 38, 43, 47, 50, 51, 52, 55, 59, 62, 66, 67, 68, 72, 80, 84, 97, 112, 113, 127, 128, 130, 131, 132, 133, 134, 135, 136, 149, 150, 154, 155, 157, 160, 165, 166, 167, 168, 170, 172, 174, 176, 177, 184,
187, 191, 193, 194, 195, 196, 200, 201, 204, 207
  moralistic, 102, 114, 188, 197, 198
  pietistic, 18, 26, 60, 62, 124, 130, 158, 198, 200
  religious, 8, 9, 10, 11, 12, 16, 17, 18, 19, 23, 25, 26, 27, 28, 31, 34, 37, 38, 47, 52, 55, 60, 63, 68, 83, 93, 95, 97, 103, 112, 121, 125, 127, 129, 130, 132, 133, 135, 141, 144, 150, 155, 156, 157, 158, 172, 173, 176, 177, 178, 184, 185, 188, 190, 191, 194, 195, 196, 198, 201
  secular, 17, 37, 54, 156, 157, 171, 172, 173, 176, 184, 207
Resurrection, 8, 23, 32, 38, 61, 63, 74, 82, 83, 108, 109, 111, 114, 129, 145, 153, 157
revelation, 18, 20, 22, 23, 66, 70, 83, 95, 99, 135, 147, 168, 183, 208
  self-revelation, God's, 20, 22, 23, 25, 67, 99, 135, 147, 183, 208
Roman Catholic, 55, 66, 67, 68, 102, 104, 113, 190, 195, 207
  Catholicism, 55, 65, 68, 187
  Rome, 25, 56, 66, 67, 68, 69, 70, 71, 72, 101, 107, 190, 191
Russian, 1, 2, 4, 8, 29, 31, 32, 36, 37, 39, 42, 48, 60, 65, 66, 70, 72, 73, 75, 81, 82, 83, 87, 103, 113, 114, 118, 120, 121, 122, 123, 124, 125, 126, 128, 130, 134, 141, 145, 149, 157, 161, 167, 176, 179, 184, 188, 191, 198, 199, 200, 203, 205
Russian Orthodoxy, 36, 125, 127
  Eastern concept of identity, 76
  Eastern Orthodox theology, 76, 83, 87, 123, 124, 125, 126, 127
  iurodivyi, 199, 200, 201
  iurodstvo, 200
  pravda, 128
  Raskolniki, 33
  Russian Christ, 114, 127
  Russian Orthodox Church, 33, 82, 114, 123, 124, 125, 128
  Russian Orthodox Theology, 72, 124
  smirenie, 200
  sobornost, 127, 131
salvation, 32, 37, 66, 73, 74, 95, 102, 153, 190, 195, 197, 208
sin (and grace), 2, 13, 16, 26, 31, 32, 33, 35, 37, 39, 43, 48, 54, 60, 61, 63, 64, 65, 67, 68, 69, 70, 71, 72, 73, 74, 75, 76, 77, 79, 86, 87, 88, 94, 102, 103, 104, 110, 119,

129, 131, 135, 143, 149, 150, 151, 159, 163, 165, 166, 174, 181, 182, 183, 185, 187, 189, 193, 194, 198, 203, 204, 205, 206, 207, 208
caprice, 49
corrupt, 42, 47, 49, 50, 52, 54, 55, 56, 59, 63, 73, 74, 104, 136, 181, 182, 195
crime, 31, 32, 33, 36, 37, 38, 39, 40, 41, 42, 43, 44, 47, 48, 50, 54, 55, 56, 58, 60, 61, 62, 64, 70, 73, 74, 75, 76, 79, 83, 85, 86, 87, 102, 103, 104, 108, 109, 111, 117, 124, 125, 141, 143, 147, 149, 150, 157, 164, 165, 166, 175, 176, 181, 182, 184, 190, 201
depravity, 31, 32, 39, 48, 49, 55, 61, 70, 71, 72, 86, 108, 134, 181, 182, 192
disorder, 54
egocentric, 189
evil, 24, 39, 44, 49, 55, 61, 67, 83, 102, 113, 135, 151, 169, 177, 178, 182, 189, 191, 194, 195, 196, 201
Fall, the 33, 36, 37, 61, 104, 111, 130, 136, 151, 182, 183, 189, 202, 207
fallen will, 11, 20, 31, 36, 47, 48, 50, 51, 61, 63, 70, 73, 131, 136, 149, 153, 155, 163, 169, 178, 181, 201
fiendishness, 49
guilt, 26, 32, 60, 64, 86, 87, 88, 129, 132, 188, 196
human achievement, 51, 81
human condition, 44, 103, 104, 108, 119, 182, 183, 185, 190
human righteousness, 47, 50, 52, 96
individualistic, 26, 56, 127, 131, 135
murder, 31, 32, 33, 38, 40, 60, 104, 109, 110, 131, 136, 158, 163, 188, 189, 194, 198
nihilism, 31, 32, 35, 41, 42, 45, 52, 62, 76, 131, 136, 166, 192
perversity, 53
pretensions, 33, 156, 190
pride, 14, 34, 37, 38, 40, 51, 52, 53, 55, 132, 142, 191
Promethean rebellion, 138, 163
prostitution, 32, 39, 40, 52, 61, 85, 103, 166, 167
punishment, 31, 32, 33, 36, 37, 38, 39, 40, 41, 42, 43, 44, 47, 48, 50, 54, 55, 56, 58, 60, 61, 62, 64, 73, 74, 75, 76, 79, 83, 85, 86, 87, 102, 103, 108, 109, 111, 117, 118, 124, 125, 141, 143, 147, 149, 150, 164, 165, 166, 175, 176, 181, 182, 184, 201

rebellious, 60, 112, 151, 189, 199, 201
satanic, 33, 191, 192, 194
Schächergnade, 70
schism, 32, 33
schismatic, 32, 33, 56
sedition, 60, 82
self-righteous, 34, 102, 167, 200
self-seeking, 47, 49
sinfulness, 70
sordidness, 108
storm heaven, to, 43, 49
subjectivity, 3, 59, 62, 150
sublapsarian, 41, 47, 131, 135
Sündenbabel, 54
surd-like, 35, 76, 77, 136, 159
Tower of Babel, 47, 48, 49, 50, 51, 52, 53, 54, 55, 56, 57, 58, 59, 62, 87, 112, 153, 191, 195
unrepentant, 27
wilfulness, 41, 43, 47, 61
see, *eritis sicut deus*
society, 14, 27, 40, 42, 43, 53, 81, 85, 95, 107, 114, 118, 122, 132, 136, 155, 157, 158, 176, 191, 197, 198
theology, 1, 2, 3, 4, 5, 7, 8, 9, 11, 13, 14, 15, 16, 18, 19, 20, 21, 22, 23, 24, 25, 27, 28, 31, 36, 37, 48, 49, 59, 63, 65, 67, 70, 71, 72, 73, 74, 79, 80, 81, 82, 83, 84, 86, 87, 91, 92, 93, 94, 95, 96, 97, 100, 103, 107, 118, 121, 123, 124, 133, 135, 145, 147, 150, 152, 155, 163, 165, 166, 167, 168, 169, 174, 177, 178, 189, 199, 203, 204, 205, 206, 208
theological, 1, 2, 3, 4, 7, 8, 9, 10, 11, 12, 13, 14, 15, 16, 17, 18, 19, 22, 23, 24, 26, 27, 32, 33, 36, 39, 44, 47, 48, 51, 56, 58, 62, 63, 66, 69, 70, 72, 73, 74, 75, 80, 81, 82, 84, 86, 87, 88, 91, 92, 93, 94, 95, 97, 99, 101, 103, 107, 108, 109, 110, 113, 114, 117, 118, 119, 123, 124, 125, 126, 129, 130, 135, 138, 142, 144, 147, 149, 150, 154, 156, 159, 160, 163, 164, 165, 167, 168, 170, 171, 172, 174, 176, 178, 179, 181, 182, 183, 184, 188, 189, 192, 194, 197, 198, 199, 200, 203, 204, 205, 206, 207, 208
theological anthropology, 1, 2, 39, 44, 47, 48, 70, 73, 87, 101, 108, 109, 110, 117, 118, 130, 163, 164, 174, 176, 178, 179, 181, 182, 183, 184
Trinity, 36, 37, 66, 134

truth, 23, 27, 29, 36, 37, 58, 62, 63, 65, 66, 67, 70, 71, 73, 80, 110, 111, 125, 126, 128, 131, 135, 136, 137, 150, 151, 157, 164, 167, 183, 191, 195, 198, 199, 205

Wendung und Retraktation, 7, 14, 15, 19, 21, 74, 75, 81, 86, 91, 124, 171, 172, 174, 177, 204, 206, 208

Western civilization, 33, 74

Zwischen den Zeiten, 67, 68, 70, 92, 93, 96, 97, 148

KARL BARTH: INDEX

Barth, Karl (1886-1968)
'Abschied', 97
'Autobiographische Skizzen Karl Barths aus den Fakultätsalben der Evangelical Theologie Fakultät in Münster (1927)', 16, 74, 80
'Das Wort Gottes als Aufgabe der Theologie', 27
'Der Christ in der Gesellschaft', 92, 117, 155, 156, 157, 158, 171, 176, 184, 197, 198
'Der Glaube an den persönlichen Gott', 12, 13, 28
'Der Glaube und die Geschichte', 9
'Der römische Katholizismus als Frage an die protestantische Kirche', 65, 66, 68, 69, 70, 71, 74, 86, 123, 149, 171, 194, 205, 206
'Die Gerechtigkeit Gottes', 40, 47, 48, 49, 50, 51, 52, 53, 56, 57, 58, 59, 60, 62, 74, 75, 87, 109, 111, 112, 152
'Die Menschlichkeit Gottes', 13, 14, 15, 165, 171
'Die neue Welt in der Bibel', 84, 85
'Die Theologie und der heutige Mensch', 67, 70, 71
'Die Theologie und der moderne Mensch', 67, 70
'Evangelische Theologie im 19 Jahrhundert', 13
'Geleitwort', 94, 95
'Jesus Christus und die soziale Bewegung', 11
'Kriegszeit und Gottesreich', 19, 20, 21, 28, 58, 75, 87, 119, 126, 162
'Lebendige Vergangenheit', 7, 8, 75, 81, 87
'Moderne Theologie und Reichgottesarbeit', 9
'Nachwort', 13, 14, 17, 75, 79, 80, 88
'Unerledigte Anfragen an die heitige Theologie', 160

analogia fidei, 13, 169
and religious socialism, 11, 16, 25, 26, 28, 79, 92, 93, 141, 150, 155, 156, 195, 204, 207
and socialism, 10, 11, 16, 17, 25, 26, 28, 55, 56, 66, 79, 92, 93, 97, 132, 141, 150, 155, 156, 174, 187, 190, 191, 195, 204, 206, 207
Andachten für die Advents-, Weihnachts-, Passions- und Osterzeit, 99
as theological student, 8, 9, 14, 124
Barthian, 2, 59, 75, 76, 125, 162, 164, 168, 197
Church Dogmatics, The, 24, 25, 96, 99, 100, 129, 169, 203, 207
correspondence, 2, 7, 15, 75, 117, 123, 127, 130, 141, 142, 143, 144, 145, 146, 147, 148, 154, 161, 171, 179, 202, 205
critical preaching, 26, 56
Der Römerbrief, 3, 24, 25, 43, 75, 87, 141, 154, 158, 159, 161, 165, 168, 169, 171, 173, 206
Barth on Romans, 3, 9, 75, 76, 77, 79, 80, 81, 84, 141, 145, 149, 151, 154, 159, 163, 171, 173, 181, 187, 197
Römerbrief 1, 9, 20, 21, 22, 23, 25, 63, 76, 80, 81, 86, 95, 96, 117, 141, 144, 149, 150, 151, 152, 153, 154, 156, 162, 168, 170, 172, 181
Römerbrief 2, 3, 9, 10, 23, 24, 28, 43, 63, 72, 75, 76, 86, 87, 88, 91, 96, 117, 122, 143, 144, 145, 146, 150, 154, 155, 156, 157, 158, 159, 160, 161, 162, 163, 164, 165, 166, 168, 169, 170, 171, 172, 174, 176, 177, 178, 181, 182, 183, 184, 185, 187, 189, 192, 193, 194, 195, 196, 197, 198, 201, 207
Die Grosse Barmherzigkeit, 99
Die Theoligie und die Kirche, 65, 67, 160

Dogmatik im Grundriß, 1
expelled by the Nazis, 1, 98
friendship with Thurneysen, 7, 8, 10, 14,
  16, 17, 24, 31, 32, 37, 38, 40, 45, 48,
  56, 61, 68, 69, 79, 87, 92, 95, 97, 98,
  99, 117, 130, 141, 142, 144, 145, 148,
  205
God's Search for Man, 99
impact of *eritis sicut deus*, 47, 48, 49, 50,
  51, 56, 58, 62, 87, 112, 132, 150, 163,
  183, 191, 195, 196, 207
influence of Hermann Kutter, 11, 16, 17,
  21, 26, 37, 75, 79, 80, 81, 86, 88, 139,
  142, 145, 148, 153, 156, 172, 173,
  176, 184, 204, 206, 207
installed at Safenwil, 7, 10, 11
Komm Schöpfer Geist!, 96
on conscience, 47, 48, 49, 50, 51, 52, 53,
  57, 58, 59, 60
on the influence of Dostoevsky, 65, 73,
  86, 203
on the influence of Kierkegaard, 159,
  160, 161, 203
Overbeck, 15, 28, 76, 123, 148, 154, 159,
  160, 166, 170, 172, 173, 174, 176,
  177, 188, 194, 204, 207
primary influence of Dostoevsky, 31, 65,
  86
reading of *Crime and Punishment*, 31, 40,
  48, 56, 143, 182
relations with Rome, 65, 66, 69
return to Basel, 98, 99
seminars at Göttingen, 178, 179
starting point, year of the new 19, 20, 21,
  22, 65, 75, 84, 86, 88, 92, 123, 125,
  206
Suchet Gott, so werdet ihr leben!, 95, 144
the marginalizing of Dostoevsky, 203
the secret conversation with Thurneysen,
  144
theological anthropology, 1, 2, 39, 44, 47,
  48, 70, 73, 87, 101, 108, 109, 110,
  117, 118, 130, 163, 164, 174, 176,
  178, 181, 183, 184
theological development, 8, 14, 18, 204
this Russian, 1, 31, 65, 75, 82, 87, 122,
  123, 141, 149, 203
Tower of Babel, the, 47, 48, 50, 51, 52,
  53, 54, 55, 56, 57, 58, 59, 62, 87, 112,
  153, 191, 195
travels to Bad Boll with Thurneysen, 18,
  92, 117
travels to Britain with Thurneysen, 99
via dialectica, 169, 170
Welt bleibt Welt ... Daß Gott Gott ist, 20,
  23, 28, 88, 126, 162

EDUARD THURNEYSEN: INDEX

Thurneysen, Eduard (1888-1974)
  'die Anfänge', 130, 148
  'Zum Prolog des John', 97
  *Andachten für die Advents-, Weihnachts-,
    Passions- und Osterzeit*, 99
  apophatic concepts, 10, 24, 25
  appointment Basler Münstergemeinde, 93
  appointment lecturer, 93
  as theological student, 8, 92
  at Bruggen, 92, 93
  background, 7, 8, 9, 14, 91, 92, 94
  Christoph Blumhardt, with, 11, 18, 93,
    96, 102, 103, 156, 206
  correspondence, 2, 7, 15, 75, 117, 118,
    123, 130, 141, 143, 144, 147, 154, 179
  Das Wort Gottes und die Kirche, 94, 97
  Der Brief des Paulus an die Philipper, 97
  Die Grosse Barmherzigkeit, 99
  Die Kraft der Geringen. Drei Predigten,
    97
  Die Lehre von der Seelsorge, 99, 100,
    101, 102, 103, 104, 105, 123
  Dostojewski, 24, 31, 36, 37, 38, 48, 51,
    57, 74, 96, 107, 108, 109, 110, 111,
    112, 113, 114, 117, 118, 119, 120,
    121, 122, 123, 126, 127, 130, 136,
    137, 138, 143, 144, 145, 146, 147,
    148, 150, 152, 153, 159, 178, 192,
    193, 194, 197, 198, 200, 201, 202,
    205, 206
  family, 91, 92
  God's Search for Man, 99
  influence on Barth, 7, 8, 14, 16, 17, 18,
    24, 25, 32, 37, 40, 41, 45, 48, 50, 56,
    57, 58, 61, 68, 69, 74, 79, 81, 82, 86,
    92, 93, 95, 97, 99, 102, 103, 104, 109,
    110, 111, 117, 119, 120, 121, 123,

124, 126, 127, 141, 142, 145, 149,
152, 161, 167, 168, 171, 174, 176,
181, 184, 185, 189, 195, 200, 201,
203, 205, 207, 208
influences on Thurneysen, 91, 92, 93, 94,
98, 99, 102
installed at Leutwil, 7, 16, 75, 92
Johannine disposition, for Barth, 81, 84,
95, 96, 124, 205
Komm Schöpfer Geist!, 96
ministerial works, 94
parish work, 7, 92, 93
pastoral theology, 92, 93, 94, 99, 100,
103
relationship with and influence of
Blumhardts, 11, 58, 79, 86, 88, 92,
165, 172, 204

Seelsorge, 92, 100, 104
Suchet Gott, so werdet ihr Leben, 95, 97,
144
theological development, 7, 16, 17, 31,
51, 57, 79, 86, 91, 92, 93, 103
theological works, 95
understanding of Dostoevsky, 31, 32, 35,
36, 37, 38, 39, 40, 41, 45, 48, 50, 51,
56, 57, 58, 61, 68, 69, 74, 75, 86, 87,
88, 89, 96, 102, 107, 108, 109, 110,
112, 113, 114, 117, 118, 122, 123,
130, 132, 134, 136, 138, 157, 159,
197, 198, 199, 200, 201, 202, 203,
205, 207, 208

FYODOR MIKHAILOVICH DOSTOEVSKY: INDEX

Dostoevsky, Fyodor Mikhailovich (1821-
1881)
'The Idea', 35, 40, 41, 43, 45, 53, 56, 76,
134, 192
ant heap, the, 53, 56
antinomy/dialectic in, 35, 36, 38, 39, 40,
53, 86, 108, 111, 113, 126, 135, 166,
167, 168, 170, 174, 184, 189, 191,
193, 200, 202
Baal/Babylon, 54, 55, 59, 62
conviction for sedition, 44, 60, 82, 120
correspondence, 127
Crime and Punishment, 31, 32, 33, 36,
37, 38, 39, 40, 41, 42, 43, 44, 47, 48,
50, 54, 55, 56, 58, 60, 61, 62, 73, 74,
75, 76, 79, 83, 85, 86, 87, 102, 103,
108, 109, 111, 117, 124, 125, 141,
143, 147, 149, 150, 164, 165, 166,
175, 176, 181, 182, 184, 201
critique of London, 54, 55
Crystal Palace, the, 53, 54, 55, 56
eritis sicut deus, 39, 40, 43, 47, 48, 50,
51, 55, 56, 58, 62, 87, 112, 132, 138,
150, 163, 183, 188, 191, 195, 196, 207
European tour, 54, 55, 60
humanity, 1, 2, 32, 33, 35, 36, 37, 38, 39,
40, 41, 44, 50, 52, 53, 55, 61, 62, 66,
70, 74, 80, 86, 101, 103, 104, 107,
108, 109, 110, 111, 112, 114, 115,
129, 130, 131, 132, 133, 134, 135,
136, 137, 138, 144, 149, 152, 153,
163, 166, 175, 182, 183, 184, 185,
189, 190, 191, 192, 194, 199
hunger for eternity, 115, 176, 177, 184
imprisonment, 41, 82
influence on Barth, 1, 3, 31, 41, 42, 43,
45, 49, 53, 57, 65, 68, 71, 73, 74, 75,
76, 77, 79, 86, 87, 88, 117, 122, 123,
126, 128, 129, 143, 145, 146, 149,
154, 159, 161, 166, 168, 171, 172,
173, 174, 175, 182, 189, 193, 195,
197, 199, 203, 206, 207
Notes from the House of the Dead, 39, 44
Notes From Underground, 39, 41, 42
Poor Folk, 39, 44
religion for, 33, 34, 35, 36, 38, 43, 55, 59,
72, 73, 99, 112, 113, 127, 128, 130,
131, 132, 133, 134, 135, 136, 149,
166, 167, 168, 174, 176, 177, 184,
187, 188, 191, 192, 193, 194, 195,
200, 201, 204, 207
resurrection in, 32, 38, 61, 74, 82, 83,
108, 109, 111, 114, 129, 145, 153, 157
Russian New Testament, 36, 37, 81, 82,
123, 125, 126, 167
sentenced to death, 82, 120
student days, 35, 39, 124, 134, 135
The Brothers Karamazov, 35, 38, 40, 41,
42, 43, 44, 48, 56, 71, 72, 84, 104,
105, 108, 109, 111, 112, 113, 117,

Index 245

118, 119, 120, 136, 143, 165, 174, 175, 176, 179, 181, 182, 188, 191, 192, 193, 198, 200, 201
The Demons, 38, 43, 44, 54, 56, 113, 117, 142
The Double, 39, 44
The Dream of the Ridiculous Man, 44, 117, 130, 131, 132, 134, 135, 136, 149, 151, 163, 181
The Idiot, 33, 34, 38, 39, 44, 73, 76, 86, 108, 109, 117, 118, 119, 138, 157, 158, 165, 166, 167, 175, 176, 185, 198, 199, 200, 201, 202
the question for, 33, 34, 36, 38, 40, 52, 110, 113, 119, 130, 136, 137, 141, 199

theological anthropology, 1, 2, 39, 44, 48, 73, 101, 108, 109, 110, 117, 118, 130, 163, 164, 174, 175, 178, 179, 181, 182, 183, 184
theological beliefs of, 2, 3, 36, 82, 87, 124, 125, 174, 188, 205
titanism, 114
Tower of Babel, 47, 48, 49, 50, 51, 52, 53, 54, 55, 56, 57, 58, 59, 62, 87, 112, 153, 191, 195
White Nights, 39, 44
See, Name Index for characters from novels

Paternoster Biblical Monographs

(All titles uniform with this volume)
Dates in bold are of projected publication

Joseph Abraham
Eve: Accused or Acquitted?
A Reconsideration of Feminist Readings of the Creation Narrative Texts in Genesis 1–3

Two contrary views dominate contemporary feminist biblical scholarship. One finds in the Bible an unequivocal equality between the sexes from the very creation of humanity, whilst the other sees the biblical text as irredeemably patriarchal and androcentric. Dr Abraham enters into dialogue with both camps as well as introducing his own method of approach. An invaluable tool for any one who is interested in this contemporary debate.

2002 / 0-85364-971-5 / xxiv + 272pp

Octavian D. Baban
Mimesis and Luke's on the Road Encounters in Luke-Acts
Luke's Theology of the Way and its Literary Representation

The book argues on theological and literary (mimetic) grounds that Luke's on-the-road encounters, especially those belonging to the post-Easter period, are part of his complex theology of the Way. Jesus' teaching and that of the apostles is presented by Luke as a challenging answer to the Hellenistic reader's thirst for adventure, good literature, and existential paradigms.

2005 / 1-84227-253-5 / approx. 374pp

Paul Barker
The Triumph of Grace in Deuteronomy

This book is a textual and theological analysis of the interaction between the sin and faithlessness of Israel and the grace of Yahweh in response, looking especially at Deuteronomy chapters 1–3, 8–10 and 29–30. The author argues that the grace of Yahweh is determinative for the ongoing relationship between Yahweh and Israel and that Deuteronomy anticipates and fully expects Israel to be faithless.

2004 / 1-84227-226-8 / xxii + 270pp

Jonathan F. Bayes
The Weakness of the Law
God's Law and the Christian in New Testament Perspective

A study of the four New Testament books which refer to the law as weak (Acts, Romans, Galatians, Hebrews) leads to a defence of the third use in the Reformed debate about the law in the life of the believer.

2000 / 0-85364-957-X / xii + 244pp

Mark Bonnington
The Antioch Episode of Galatians 2:11-14 in Historical and Cultural Context

The Galatians 2 'incident' in Antioch over table-fellowship suggests significant disagreement between the leading apostles. This book analyses the background to the disagreement by locating the incident within the dynamics of social interaction between Jews and Gentiles. It proposes a new way of understanding the relationship between the individuals and issues involved.

2005 / 1-84227-050-8 / approx. 350pp

David Bostock
A Portrayal of Trust
The Theme of Faith in the Hezekiah Narratives

This study provides detailed and sensitive readings of the Hezekiah narratives (2 Kings 18–20 and Isaiah 36–39) from a theological perspective. It concentrates on the theme of faith, using narrative criticism as its methodology. Attention is paid especially to setting, plot, point of view and characterization within the narratives. A largely positive portrayal of Hezekiah emerges that underlines the importance and relevance of scripture.

2005 / 1-84227-314-0 / approx. 300pp

Mark Bredin
Jesus, Revolutionary of Peace
A Non-violent Christology in the Book of Revelation

This book aims to demonstrate that the figure of Jesus in the Book of Revelation can best be understood as an active non-violent revolutionary.

2003 / 1-84227-153-9 / xviii + 262pp

Robinson Butarbutar
Paul and Conflict Resolution
An Exegetical Study of Paul's Apostolic Paradigm in 1 Corinthians 9

The author sees the apostolic paradigm in 1 Corinthians 9 as part of Paul's unified arguments in 1 Corinthians 8–10 in which he seeks to mediate in the dispute over the issue of food offered to idols. The book also sees its relevance for dispute-resolution today, taking the conflict within the author's church as an example.

2006 / 1-84227-315-9 / approx. 280pp

Daniel J-S Chae
Paul as Apostle to the Gentiles
His Apostolic Self-awareness and its Influence on the Soteriological Argument in Romans

Opposing 'the post-Holocaust interpretation of Romans', Daniel Chae competently demonstrates that Paul argues for the equality of Jew and Gentile in Romans. Chae's fresh exegetical interpretation is academically outstanding and spiritually encouraging.

1997 / 0-85364-829-8 / xiv + 378pp

Luke L. Cheung
The Genre, Composition and Hermeneutics of the Epistle of James

The present work examines the employment of the wisdom genre with a certain compositional structure and the interpretation of the law through the Jesus tradition of the double love command by the author of the Epistle of James to serve his purpose in promoting perfection and warning against doubleness among the eschatologically renewed people of God in the Diaspora.

2003 / 1-84227-062-1 / xvi + 372pp

Youngmo Cho
Spirit and Kingdom in the Writings of Luke and Paul

The relationship between Spirit and Kingdom is a relatively unexplored area in Lukan and Pauline studies. This book offers a fresh perspective of two biblical writers on the subject. It explores the difference between Luke's and Paul's understanding of the Spirit by examining the specific question of the relationship of the concept of the Spirit to the concept of the Kingdom of God in each writer.

2005 / 1-84227-316-7 / approx. 270pp

Andrew C. Clark
Parallel Lives
The Relation of Paul to the Apostles in the Lucan Perspective

This study of the Peter-Paul parallels in Acts argues that their purpose was to emphasize the themes of continuity in salvation history and the unity of the Jewish and Gentile missions. New light is shed on Luke's literary techniques, partly through a comparison with Plutarch.

2001 / 1-84227-035-4 / xviii + 386pp

Andrew D. Clarke
Secular and Christian Leadership in Corinth
A Socio-Historical and Exegetical Study of 1 Corinthians 1–6
This volume is an investigation into the leadership structures and dynamics of first-century Roman Corinth. These are compared with the practice of leadership in the Corinthian Christian community which are reflected in 1 Corinthians 1–6, and contrasted with Paul's own principles of Christian leadership.
2005 / 1-84227-229-2 / 200pp

Stephen Finamore
God, Order and Chaos
René Girard and the Apocalypse
Readers are often disturbed by the images of destruction in the book of Revelation and unsure why they are unleashed after the exaltation of Jesus. This book examines past approaches to these texts and uses René Girard's theories to revive some old ideas and propose some new ones.
2005 / 1-84227-197-0 / approx. 344pp

David G. Firth
Surrendering Retribution in the Psalms
Responses to Violence in the Individual Complaints
In *Surrendering Retribution in the Psalms*, David Firth examines the ways in which the book of Psalms inculcates a model response to violence through the repetition of standard patterns of prayer. Rather than seeking justification for retributive violence, Psalms encourages not only a surrender of the right of retribution to Yahweh, but also sets limits on the retribution that can be sought in imprecations. Arising initially from the author's experience in South Africa, the possibilities of this model to a particular context of violence is then briefly explored.
2005 / 1-84227-337-X / xviii + 154pp

Scott J. Hafemann
Suffering and Ministry in the Spirit
Paul's Defence of His Ministry in II Corinthians 2:14–3:3
Shedding new light on the way Paul defended his apostleship, the author offers a careful, detailed study of 2 Corinthians 2:14–3:3 linked with other key passages throughout 1 and 2 Corinthians. Demonstrating the unity and coherence of Paul's argument in this passage, the author shows that Paul's suffering served as the vehicle for revealing God's power and glory through the Spirit.
2000 / 0-85364-967-7 / xiv + 262pp

Scott J. Hafemann
Paul, Moses and the History of Israel
The Letter/Spirit Contrast and the Argument from Scripture in 2 Corinthians 3
An exegetical study of the call of Moses, the second giving of the Law (Exodus 32–34), the new covenant, and the prophetic understanding of the history of Israel in 2 Corinthians 3. Hafemann's work demonstrates Paul's contextual use of the Old Testament and the essential unity between the Law and the Gospel within the context of the distinctive ministries of Moses and Paul.
2005 / 1-84227-317-5 / xii + 498pp

Douglas S. McComiskey
Lukan Theology in the Light of the Gospel's Literary Structure
Luke's Gospel was purposefully written with theology embedded in its patterned literary structure. A critical analysis of this cyclical structure provides new windows into Luke's interpretation of the individual pericopes comprising the Gospel and illuminates several of his theological interests.
2004 / 1-84227-148-2 / xviii + 388pp

Stephen Motyer
Your Father the Devil?
A New Approach to John and 'The Jews'
Who are 'the Jews' in John's Gospel? Defending John against the charge of antisemitism, Motyer argues that, far from demonising the Jews, the Gospel seeks to present Jesus as 'Good News for Jews' in a late first century setting.
1997 / 0-85364-832-8 / xiv + 260pp

Esther Ng
Reconstructing Christian Origins?
The Feminist Theology of Elizabeth Schüssler Fiorenza: An Evaluation
In a detailed evaluation, the author challenges Elizabeth Schüssler Fiorenza's reconstruction of early Christian origins and her underlying presuppositions. The author also presents her own views on women's roles both then and now.
2002 / 1-84227-055-9 / xxiv + 468pp

Robin Parry
Old Testament Story and Christian Ethics
The Rape of Dinah as a Case Study

What is the role of story in ethics and, more particularly, what is the role of Old Testament story in Christian ethics? This book, drawing on the work of contemporary philosophers, argues that narrative is crucial in the ethical shaping of people and, drawing on the work of contemporary Old Testament scholars, that story plays a key role in Old Testament ethics. Parry then argues that when situated in canonical context Old Testament stories can be reappropriated by Christian readers in their own ethical formation. The shocking story of the rape of Dinah and the massacre of the Shechemites provides a fascinating case study for exploring the parameters within which Christian ethical appropriations of Old Testament stories can live.

2004 / 1-84227-210-1 / xx + 350pp

Ian Paul
Power to See the World Anew
The Value of Paul Ricoeur's Hermeneutic of Metaphor in Interpreting the Symbolism of Revelation 12 and 13

This book is a study of the hermeneutics of metaphor of Paul Ricoeur, one of the most important writers on hermeneutics and metaphor of the last century. It sets out the key points of his theory, important criticisms of his work, and how his approach, modified in the light of these criticisms, offers a methodological framework for reading apocalyptic texts.

2006 / 1-84227-056-7 / approx. 350pp

Robert L. Plummer
Paul's Understanding of the Church's Mission
Did the Apostle Paul Expect the Early Christian Communities to Evangelize?

This book engages in a careful study of Paul's letters to determine if the apostle expected the communities to which he wrote to engage in missionary activity. It helpfully summarizes the discussion on this debated issue, judiciously handling contested texts, and provides a way forward in addressing this critical question. While admitting that Paul rarely explicitly commands the communities he founded to evangelize, Plummer amasses significant incidental data to provide a convincing case that Paul did indeed expect his churches to engage in mission activity. Throughout the study, Plummer progressively builds a theological basis for the church's mission that is both distinctively Pauline and compelling.

2006 / 1-84227-333-7 / approx. 324pp

David Powys
'Hell': A Hard Look at a Hard Question
The Fate of the Unrighteous in New Testament Thought
This comprehensive treatment seeks to unlock the original meaning of terms and phrases long thought to support the traditional doctrine of hell. It concludes that there is an alternative—one which is more biblical, and which can positively revive the rationale for Christian mission.

1997 / 0-85364-831-X / xxii + 478pp

Sorin Sabou
Between Horror and Hope
Paul's Metaphorical Language of Death in Romans 6.1-11
This book argues that Paul's metaphorical language of death in Romans 6.1-11 conveys two aspects: horror and hope. The 'horror' aspect is conveyed by the 'crucifixion' language, and the 'hope' aspect by 'burial' language. The life of the Christian believer is understood, as relationship with sin is concerned ('death to sin'), between these two realities: horror and hope.

2005 / 1-84227-322-1 / approx. 224pp

Rosalind Selby
The Comical Doctrine
The Epistemology of New Testament Hermeneutics
This book argues that the gospel breaks through postmodernity's critique of truth and the referential possibilities of textuality with its gift of grace. With a rigorous, philosophical challenge to modernist and postmodernist assumptions, Selby offers an alternative epistemology to all who would still read with faith *and* with academic credibility.

2005 / 1-84227-212-8 / approx. 350pp

Kiwoong Son
Zion Symbolism in Hebrews
Hebrews 12.18-24 as a Hermeneutical Key to the Epistle
This book challenges the general tendency of understanding the Epistle to the Hebrews against a Hellenistic background and suggests that the Epistle should be understood in the light of the Jewish apocalyptic tradition. The author especially argues for the importance of the theological symbolism of Sinai and Zion (Heb. 12:18-24) as it provides the Epistle's theological background as well as the rhetorical basis of the superiority motif of Jesus throughout the Epistle.

2005 / 1-84227-368-X / approx. 280pp

Kevin Walton
Thou Traveller Unknown
The Presence and Absence of God in the Jacob Narrative
The author offers a fresh reading of the story of Jacob in the book of Genesis through the paradox of divine presence and absence. The work also seeks to make a contribution to Pentateuchal studies by bringing together a close reading of the final text with historical critical insights, doing justice to the text's historical depth, final form and canonical status.
2003 / 1-84227-059-1 / xvi + 238pp

George M. Wieland
The Significance of Salvation
A Study of Salvation Language in the Pastoral Epistles
The language and ideas of salvation pervade the three Pastoral Epistles. This study offers a close examination of their soteriological statements. In all three letters the idea of salvation is found to play a vital paraenetic role, but each also exhibits distinctive soteriological emphases. The results challenge common assumptions about the Pastoral Epistles as a corpus.
2005 / 1-84227-257-8 / approx. 324pp

Alistair Wilson
When Will These Things Happen?
A Study of Jesus as Judge in Matthew 21–25
This study seeks to allow Matthew's carefully constructed presentation of Jesus to be given full weight in the modern evaluation of Jesus' eschatology. Careful analysis of the text of Matthew 21–25 reveals Jesus to be standing firmly in the Jewish prophetic and wisdom traditions as he proclaims and enacts imminent judgement on the Jewish authorities then boldly claims the central role in the final and universal judgement.
2004 / 1-84227-146-6 / xxii + 272pp

Lindsay Wilson
Joseph Wise and Otherwise
The Intersection of Covenant and Wisdom in Genesis 37–50
This book offers a careful literary reading of Genesis 37–50 that argues that the Joseph story contains both strong covenant themes and many wisdom-like elements. The connections between the two helps to explore how covenant and wisdom might intersect in an integrated biblical theology.
2004 / 1-84227-140-7 / xvi + 340pp

Stephen I. Wright
The Voice of Jesus
Studies in the Interpretation of Six Gospel Parables
This literary study considers how the 'voice' of Jesus has been heard in different periods of parable interpretation, and how the categories of figure and trope may help us towards a sensitive reading of the parables today.
2000 / 0-85364-975-8 / xiv + 280pp

Paternoster
9 Holdom Avenue,
Bletchley,
Milton Keynes MK1 1QR,
United Kingdom
Web: www.authenticmedia.co.uk/paternoster

July 2005

Paternoster Theological Monographs
(All titles uniform with this volume)
Dates in bold are of projected publication

Emil Bartos
Deification in Eastern Orthodox Theology
An Evaluation and Critique of the Theology of Dumitru Staniloae

Bartos studies a fundamental yet neglected aspect of Orthodox theology: deification. By examining the doctrines of anthropology, christology, soteriology and ecclesiology as they relate to deification, he provides an important contribution to contemporary dialogue between Eastern and Western theologians.

1999 / 0-85364-956-1 / xii + 370pp

Graham Buxton
The Trinity, Creation and Pastoral Ministry
Imaging the Perichoretic God

In this book the author proposes a three-way conversation between theology, science and pastoral ministry. His approach draws on a Trinitarian understanding of God as a relational being of love, whose life 'spills over' into all created reality, human and non-human. By locating human meaning and purpose within God's 'creation-community' this book offers the possibility of a transforming engagement between those in pastoral ministry and the scientific community.

2005 / 1-84227-369-8 / approx. 380 pp

Iain D. Campbell
Fixing the Indemnity
The Life and Work of George Adam Smith

When Old Testament scholar George Adam Smith (1856–1942) delivered the Lyman Beecher lectures at Yale University in 1899, he confidently declared that 'modern criticism has won its war against traditional theories. It only remains to fix the amount of the indemnity.' In this biography, Iain D. Campbell assesses Smith's critical approach to the Old Testament and evaluates its consequences, showing that Smith's life and work still raises questions about the relationship between biblical scholarship and evangelical faith.

2004 / 1-84227-228-4 / xx + 256pp

Tim Chester
Mission and the Coming of God
Eschatology, the Trinity and Mission in the Theology of Jürgen Moltmann
This book explores the theology and missiology of the influential contemporary theologian, Jürgen Moltmann. It highlights the important contribution Moltmann has made while offering a critique of his thought from an evangelical perspective. In so doing, it touches on pertinent issues for evangelical missiology. The conclusion takes Calvin as a starting point, proposing 'an eschatology of the cross' which offers a critique of the over-realised eschatologies in liberation theology and certain forms of evangelicalism.
2006 / 1-84227-320-5 / approx. 224pp

Sylvia Wilkey Collinson
Making Disciples
The Significance of Jesus' Educational Strategy for Today's Church
This study examines the biblical practice of discipling, formulates a definition, and makes comparisons with modern models of education. A recommendation is made for greater attention to its practice today.
2004 / 1-84227-116-4 / xiv + 278pp

Darrell Cosden
A Theology of Work
Work and the New Creation
Through dialogue with Moltmann, Pope John Paul II and others, this book develops a genitive 'theology of work', presenting a theological definition of work and a model for a theological ethics of work that shows work's nature, value and meaning now and eschatologically. Work is shown to be a transformative activity consisting of three dynamically inter-related dimensions: the instrumental, relational and ontological.
2005 / 1-84227-332-9 / xvi + 208pp

Stephen M. Dunning
The Crisis and the Quest
A Kierkegaardian Reading of Charles Williams
Employing Kierkegaardian categories and analysis, this study investigates both the central crisis in Charles Williams's authorship between hermetism and Christianity (Kierkegaard's Religions A and B), and the quest to resolve this crisis, a quest that ultimately presses the bounds of orthodoxy.
2000 / 0-85364-985-5 / xxiv + 254pp

Keith Ferdinando
The Triumph of Christ in African Perspective
A Study of Demonology and Redemption in the African Context
The book explores the implications of the gospel for traditional African fears of occult aggression. It analyses such traditional approaches to suffering and biblical responses to fears of demonic evil, concluding with an evaluation of African beliefs from the perspective of the gospel.
1999 / 0-85364-830-1 / xviii + 450pp

Andrew Goddard
Living the Word, Resisting the World
The Life and Thought of Jacques Ellul
This work offers a definitive study of both the life and thought of the French Reformed thinker Jacques Ellul (1912-1994). It will prove an indispensable resource for those interested in this influential theologian and sociologist and for Christian ethics and political thought generally.
2002 / 1-84227-053-2 / xxiv + 378pp

David Hilborn
The Words of our Lips
Language-Use in Free Church Worship
Studies of liturgical language have tended to focus on the written canons of Roman Catholic and Anglican communities. By contrast, David Hilborn analyses the more extemporary approach of English Nonconformity. Drawing on recent developments in linguistic pragmatics, he explores similarities and differences between 'fixed' and 'free' worship, and argues for the interdependence of each.
2006 / 0-85364-977-4 / approx. 350pp

Roger Hitching
The Church and Deaf People
A Study of Identity, Communication and Relationships with Special Reference to the Ecclesiology of Jürgen Moltmann
In *The Church and Deaf People* Roger Hitching sensitively examines the history and present experience of deaf people and finds similarities between aspects of sign language and Moltmann's theological method that 'open up' new ways of understanding theological concepts.
2003 / 1-84227-222-5 / xxii + 236pp

John G. Kelly
One God, One People
The Differentiated Unity of the People of God in the Theology of Jürgen Moltmann
The author expounds and critiques Moltmann's doctrine of God and highlights the systematic connections between it and Moltmann's influential discussion of Israel. He then proposes a fresh approach to Jewish–Christian relations building on Moltmann's work using insights from Habermas and Rawls.
2005 / 0-85346-969-3 / approx. 350pp

Mark F.W. Lovatt
Confronting the Will-to-Power
A Reconsideration of the Theology of Reinhold Niebuhr
Confronting the Will-to-Power is an analysis of the theology of Reinhold Niebuhr, arguing that his work is an attempt to identify, and provide a practical theological answer to, the existence and nature of human evil.
2001 / 1-84227-054-0 / xviii + 216pp

Neil B. MacDonald
Karl Barth and the Strange New World within the Bible
Barth, Wittgenstein, and the Metadilemmas of the Enlightenment
Barth's discovery of the strange new world within the Bible is examined in the context of Kant, Hume, Overbeck, and, most importantly, Wittgenstein. MacDonald covers some fundamental issues in theology today: epistemology, the final form of the text and biblical truth-claims.
2000 / 0-85364-970-7 / xxvi + 374pp

Keith A. Mascord
Alvin Plantinga and Christian Apologetics
This book draws together the contributions of the philosopher Alvin Plantinga to the major contemporary challenges to Christian belief, highlighting in particular his ground-breaking work in epistemology and the problem of evil. Plantinga's theory that both theistic and Christian belief is warrantedly basic is explored and critiqued, and an assessment offered as to the significance of his work for apologetic theory and practice.
2005 / 1-84227-256-X / approx. 304pp

Gillian McCulloch
The Deconstruction of Dualism in Theology
With Reference to Ecofeminist Theology and New Age Spirituality
This book challenges eco-theological anti-dualism in Christian theology, arguing that dualism has a twofold function in Christian religious discourse. Firstly, it enables us to express the discontinuities and divisions that are part of the process of reality. Secondly, dualistic language allows us to express the mysteries of divine transcendence/immanence and the survival of the soul without collapsing into monism and materialism, both of which are problematic for Christian epistemology.
2002 / 1-84227-044-3 / xii + 282pp

Leslie McCurdy
Attributes and Atonement
The Holy Love of God in the Theology of P.T. Forsyth
Attributes and Atonement is an intriguing full-length study of P.T. Forsyth's doctrine of the cross as it relates particularly to God's holy love. It includes an unparalleled bibliography of both primary and secondary material relating to Forsyth.
1999 / 0-85364-833-6 / xiv + 328pp

Nozomu Miyahira
Towards a Theology of the Concord of God
A Japanese Perspective on the Trinity
This book introduces a new Japanese theology and a unique Trinitarian formula based on the Japanese intellectual climate: three betweennesses and one concord. It also presents a new interpretation of the Trinity, a co-subordinationism, which is in line with orthodox Trinitarianism; each single person of the Trinity is eternally and equally subordinate (or serviceable) to the other persons, so that they retain the mutual dynamic equality.
2000 / 0-85364-863-8 / xiv + 256pp

Eddy José Muskus
The Origins and Early Development of Liberation Theology in Latin America
With Particular Reference to Gustavo Gutiérrez
This work challenges the fundamental premise of Liberation Theology, 'opting for the poor', and its claim that Christ is found in them. It also argues that Liberation Theology emerged as a direct result of the failure of the Roman Catholic Church in Latin America.
2002 / 0-85364-974-X / xiv + 296pp

Jim Purves
The Triune God and the Charismatic Movement
A Critical Appraisal from a Scottish Perspective

All emotion and no theology? Or a fundamental challenge to reappraise and realign our trinitarian theology in the light of Christian experience? This study of charismatic renewal as it found expression within Scotland at the end of the twentieth century evaluates the use of Patristic, Reformed and contemporary models of the Trinity in explaining the workings of the Holy Spirit.

2004 / 1-84227-321-3 / xxiv + 246pp

Anna Robbins
Methods in the Madness
Diversity in Twentieth-Century Christian Social Ethics

The author compares the ethical methods of Walter Rauschenbusch, Reinhold Niebuhr and others. She argues that unless Christians are clear about the ways that theology and philosophy are expressed practically they may lose the ability to discuss social ethics across contexts, let alone reach effective agreements.

2004 / 1-84227-211-X / xx + 294pp

Ed Rybarczyk
Beyond Salvation
Eastern Orthodoxy and Classical Pentecostalism on Becoming Like Christ

At first glance eastern Orthodoxy and classical Pentecostalism seem quite distinct. This ground-breaking study shows they share much in common, especially as it concerns the experiential elements of following Christ. Both traditions assert that authentic Christianity transcends the wooden categories of modernism.

2004 / 1-84227-144-X / xii + 356pp

Signe Sandsmark
Is World View Neutral Education Possible and Desirable?
A Christian Response to Liberal Arguments
(Published jointly with The Stapleford Centre)

This book discusses reasons for belief in world view neutrality, and argues that 'neutral' education will have a hidden, but strong world view influence. It discusses the place for Christian education in the common school.

2000 / 0-85364-973-1 / xiv + 182pp

Hazel Sherman
Reading Zechariah
The Allegorical Tradition of Biblical Interpretation through the Commentary of Didymus the Blind and Theodore of Mopsuestia

A close reading of the commentary on Zechariah by Didymus the Blind alongside that of Theodore of Mopsuestia suggests that popular categorising of Antiochene and Alexandrian biblical exegesis as 'historical' or 'allegorical' is inadequate and misleading.

2005 / 1-84227-213-6 / approx. 280pp

Andrew Sloane
On Being a Christian in the Academy
Nicholas Wolterstorff and the Practice of Christian Scholarship

An exposition and critical appraisal of Nicholas Wolterstorff's epistemology in the light of the philosophy of science, and an application of his thought to the practice of Christian scholarship.

2003 / 1-84227-058-3 / xvi + 274pp

Damon W.K. So
Jesus' Revelation of His Father
A Narrative-Conceptual Study of the Trinity with Special Reference to Karl Barth

This book explores the trinitarian dynamics in the context of Jesus' revelation of his Father in his earthly ministry with references to key passages in Matthew's Gospel. It develops from the exegeses of these passages a non-linear concept of revelation which links Jesus' communion with his Father to his revelatory words and actions through a nuanced understanding of the Holy Spirit, with references to K. Barth, G.W.H. Lampe, J.D.G. Dunn and E. Irving.

2005 / 1-84227-323-X / approx. 380pp

Daniel Strange
The Possibility of Salvation Among the Unevangelised
An Analysis of Inclusivism in Recent Evangelical Theology

For evangelical theologians the 'fate of the unevangelised' impinges upon fundamental tenets of evangelical identity. The position known as 'inclusivism', defined by the belief that the unevangelised can be ontologically saved by Christ whilst being epistemologically unaware of him, has been defended most vigorously by the Canadian evangelical Clark H. Pinnock. Through a detailed analysis and critique of Pinnock's work, this book examines a cluster of issues surrounding the unevangelised and its implications for christology, soteriology and the doctrine of revelation.

2002 / 1-84227-047-8 / xviii + 362pp

Scott Swain
God According to the Gospel
Biblical Narrative and the Identity of God in the Theology of Robert W. Jenson
Robert W. Jenson is one of the leading voices in contemporary Trinitarian theology. His boldest contribution in this area concerns his use of biblical narrative both to ground and explicate the Christian doctrine of God. *God According to the Gospel* critically examines Jenson's proposal and suggests an alternative way of reading the biblical portrayal of the triune God.
2006 / 1-84227-258-6 / approx. 180pp

Justyn Terry
The Justifying Judgement of God
A Reassessment of the Place of Judgement in the Saving Work of Christ
The argument of this book is that judgement, understood as the whole process of bringing justice, is the primary metaphor of atonement, with others, such as victory, redemption and sacrifice, subordinate to it. Judgement also provides the proper context for understanding penal substitution and the call to repentance, baptism, eucharist and holiness.
2005 / 1-84227-370-1 / approx. 274 pp

Graham Tomlin
The Power of the Cross
Theology and the Death of Christ in Paul, Luther and Pascal
This book explores the theology of the cross in St Paul, Luther and Pascal. It offers new perspectives on the theology of each, and some implications for the nature of power, apologetics, theology and church life in a postmodern context.
1999 / 0-85364-984-7 / xiv + 344pp

Adonis Vidu
Postliberal Theological Method
A Critical Study
The postliberal theology of Hans Frei, George Lindbeck, Ronald Thiemann, John Milbank and others is one of the more influential contemporary options. This book focuses on several aspects pertaining to its theological method, specifically its understanding of background, hermeneutics, epistemic justification, ontology, the nature of doctrine and, finally, Christological method.
2005 / 1-84227-395-7 / approx. 324pp

Graham J. Watts
Revelation and the Spirit
A Comparative Study of the Relationship between the Doctrine of Revelation and Pneumatology in the Theology of Eberhard Jüngel and of Wolfhart Pannenberg

The relationship between revelation and pneumatology is relatively unexplored. This approach offers a fresh angle on two important twentieth century theologians and raises pneumatological questions which are theologically crucial and relevant to mission in a postmodern culture.

2005 / 1-84227-104-0 / xxii + 232pp

Nigel G. Wright
Disavowing Constantine
Mission, Church and the Social Order in the Theologies of John Howard Yoder and Jürgen Moltmann

This book is a timely restatement of a radical theology of church and state in the Anabaptist and Baptist tradition. Dr Wright constructs his argument in dialogue and debate with Yoder and Moltmann, major contributors to a free church perspective.

2000 / 0-85364-978-2 / xvi + 252pp

Paternoster
9 Holdom Avenue,
Bletchley,
Milton Keynes MK1 1QR,
United Kingdom
Web: www.authenticmedia.co.uk/paternoster

www.ingramcontent.com/pod-product-compliance
Lightning Source LLC
Chambersburg PA
CBHW071240230426
43668CB00011B/1519